Camping
Oregon

Rhonda and George Ostertag

FALCON®

HELENA, MONTANA

A FALCON GUIDE ®

Falcon® Publishing is continually expanding its list of recreation guidebooks. All books include detailed descriptions, accurate maps, and all the information necessary for enjoyable trips. You can order extra copies of this book and get information and prices for other Falcon® guidebooks by writing Falcon, P.O. Box 1718, Helena, MT 59624, or by calling toll-free 1-800-582-2665. Also, please ask for a free copy of our current catalog. Visit our website at www.FalconOutdoors.com or contact us by e-mail at falcon@falcon.com.

1 2 3 4 5 6 7 8 9 0 MG 04 03 02 01 00 99

All photos by George Ostertag.

Library of Congress Cataloging-in-Publication Data

Ostertag, Rhonda, 1957–
    Camping Oregon / Rhonda and George Ostertag ; [all photos by the authors unless otherwise noted].
        p.   cm. — (A Falcon guide)
    Includes index.
    ISBN 1-56044-707-9 (pbk.)
    1. Camping—Oregon Guidebooks. 2. Camp sites, facilities, etc.— Oregon Directories. 3. Oregon Guidebooks. I. Ostertag, George, 1957– . II. Title. III. Series.
GV191.42.07084 1999   99-29579
647.9795'09'025—dc21   CIP

CAUTION

Outdoor recreational activities are by their very nature potentially hazardous. All participants in such activities must assume the responsibility for their own actions and safety. The information contained in this guidebook cannot replace sound judgment and good decision-making skills, which help reduce risk exposure, nor does the scope of this book allow for disclosure of all the potential hazards and risks involved in such activities.

Learn as much as possible about the outdoor recreational activities in which you participate, prepare for the unexpected, and be cautious. The reward will be a safer and more enjoyable experience.

♻ Text pages printed on recycled paper.

Contents

Acknowledgments

We would like to thank the staffs of the local chambers of commerce and visitor bureaus, the city and county parks departments, the state parks and forest departments, the state and federal fish and wildlife offices, Crater Lake National Park, and the district offices of the USDA Forest Service and Bureau of Land Management for the help they provided us in compiling this book. We also would like to thank the people we met along the way, who shared their enthusiasm for camping in Oregon.

—*Rhonda and George Ostertag*

Introduction

Oregon is one of the most naturally diverse states in the union, with elevations ranging from sea level to 11,000 feet. Along the Pacific Coast, you may encounter quiet coves, uninterrupted sandy beaches, and the exciting collision of wave and headland. As you move east toward the Cascades, you pass through temperate rain forests, chiseled coastal mountains, and the fertile Willamette Valley—destination of early emigrants on the Oregon Trail. The Cascade Range will captivate you with its chain of conical volcanic peaks, extensive fir forests, and high-mountain lakes, including its crown jewel, Crater Lake.

In the shadow of the Cascades, shaping the central part of the state, are plateaus, lava fields, desert plains, and, to the south, a sweeping expanse of playa, lakes, and wildlife habitat. Farther to the east are the signature peaks and meadows of the Blue Mountains. Then the northeastern corner of the state presents a stirring juxtaposition: the glacial high country of the Wallowa Mountains and the arid steppes of Hells Canyon National Recreation Area. Secreted in the southeastern corner are colorful canyons, rocky rims, and lonesome sagebrush flats.

This amazingly varied terrain has combined with distinctive climatic differences to produce ideal habitat for a menagerie of wildlife. A number of public and private wildlife preserves harbor native and migrant species: Antelope congregate on the Hart Mountain National Antelope Refuge, Kiger wild horses gallop at Steens Mountain, great gray owls nest in the Blue Mountains, elk gather in the winter at feeding stations in Union and Baker Counties, and gray whales migrate along the Oregon coast each spring and fall. Each of these events suggests a potential vacation theme.

Campsite raider.

Other seasonal changes and natural attractions may serve as the impetus for a camping trip: the blaze of fall foliage, the bloom of rhododendrons, the harvest season, the ripening of huckleberries, and the Perseid meteor showers, to name a few. At the annual mosquito festival in Paisley—"if you can't beat 'em, celebrate 'em"—there is even a tongue-in-cheek crowning of Oregon's very own "Miss-Quito." (By the way, the birding in the area is fabulous.)

Oregon's many spectacular rivers—which served as highways for early American Indians, explorers, and settlers—now guide contemporary explorers through the best the state has to offer. Among the contiguous United States, Oregon leads the way in protecting its waterways. As a result, the recreational opportunities are superb. You can indulge in summer swimming; salmon, steelhead, sturgeon, and trout fishing; whitewater rafting, canoeing, and kayaking; drift boating; mailboat rides; and sternwheeler tours. There is also an impressive collection of waterfalls and hot springs. You will be surprised by what Oregon can do with a raindrop!

While Oregon's natural bounty is unparalleled, the state also caters to more cultured tastes, with fine museums, concerts, wineries, art galleries, aquariums, zoos, and shops. The Ashland Shakespeare Festival has an excellent national reputation, and a host of other festivals, Saturday markets, community theaters, and art fairs add to the allure of Oregon's towns and cities. If you are in the mood to "let 'er rip," the Pendleton Rodeo is an ideal venue, or you may choose to try your luck at one of a growing number of Indian-owned casinos.

Best of all, Oregon has fine public campgrounds from which to explore its exciting attractions. This book includes not only detailed information about those campgrounds, but also information about a myriad of nearby activities, ranging from urban excursions to outdoor adventures to driving tours.

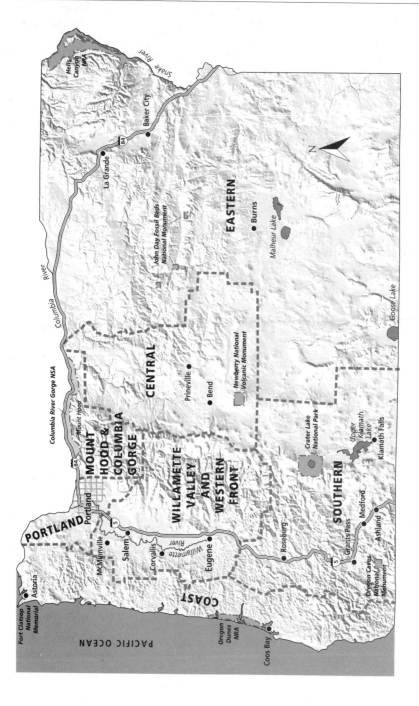

How to Use This Book

This book focuses on public campgrounds and parks that are readily accessible by car, motor home, and recreational vehicle (RV). While the list is not exhaustive, it is comprehensive. Some public campgrounds were excluded because they were unreasonably isolated, were in disrepair, or had rough access roads, too few sites, or no facilities. Group campgrounds and strictly walk-in facilities were also omitted.

To keep this book as useful and up to date as possible, we invite readers to alert us to new campgrounds, those that have improved or deteriorated, and those that have closed. Send suggestions to Rhonda and George Ostertag, c/o Falcon Publishing, P.O. Box 1718, Helena, MT 59624.

CHOOSING A CAMPGROUND

To help you locate and select a campground, we have organized the book using the seven travel regions established by the Oregon Department of Tourism: the Coast, the Portland area, the Willamette Valley and Western Front, Mount Hood and the Columbia River Gorge, Southern Oregon, Central Oregon, and Eastern Oregon (see map).Within each of these regions, we have assembled the campgrounds based on their proximity to key towns or landmarks. Within each of these subsections, campgrounds are listed alphabetically.

Each campground description includes key information on location, the number of sites, availability of facilities and services, contact information, price, and what you can expect to see and do once you are at the campground. The numbers assigned to the campgrounds coincide with those on the regional maps. By consulting the appropriate regional map and scanning the descriptions, you should be able to select a campground that will appeal to your interests and that is most convenient for your travel plans.

INFORMATION INCLUDED IN THE "AT-A-GLANCE" SECTIONS

The specific categories in these sections are Location, Sites, Maximum length, Facilities, Fee per night, Management, Contact, and Finding the campground. Following are explanations of some of the information provided within these categories.

Sites. The sites are labeled as hookup, basic, RV, tent, or walk-in tent. Throughout this book, RV refers to a broad class of recreational vehicles, including trailers, campers, motor homes, tent trailers, and vans. Basic sites are those suitable for either tent or RV camping but without hookups.

Under the heading of "sites," we have also indicated whether any cabins, tepees, or yurts are available for rent. Yurts are domed canvas structures with wooden floors, heating, electricity, lock-secured doors, and bunks. Yurt users bring their own bedding or sleeping bags and have access to a campground's restroom and shower facilities.

Fee per night. Because prices change from year to year, we have opted to use the following price-range code, based on 1998 prices:

$ – for campsites costing from $1 to $9

$$ – for campsites costing from $10 to $19

$$$ – for campsites costing from $20 to $29

$$$$ – for campsites costing from $30 to $39

The price refers to campsites only. Expect cabins, yurts, and tepees to cost more. Many camps charge for additional vehicles, pets, or large parties, so these could increase your costs.

Some campground fees hovered near the upper end of a price range in 1998 and may have spilled over into the next range by the time you use this book. Accordingly, the primary usefulness of these symbols is for comparative purposes and for gaining a relative idea of out-of-pocket expenses.

Season. Many campgrounds remain open during fair weather, closing when frost, ice, and snow threaten plumbing and safety, or when rain makes the ground and roads unsuitable for camping. Wherever possible we have listed the typical operating seasons for the camps.

For some of the USDA Forest Service and Bureau of Land Management campgrounds, the more remote and primitive offerings can remain open year-round but go without service after the summer visitor season (June through September 1). When frequenting these camps after the peak camping season, bring your own toilet tissue, water, and other comforts, and pack out all garbage—never leave unburned garbage in a fire ring or grill. Snow can prevent access.

Generally, the state and county parks have specified their operating times for this book, but a few go unlisted. In some cases, winter camping may be restricted to self-contained RVs only or offer limited sites, reduced services, or dry camping

Reserving a campsite is a good idea.

only. For general information on the state parks, including their operating seasons, you can always call the Oregon Department of Parks and Recreation information number: 800-551-6949.

If an entry in the book does not indicate the operating season, we advise telephoning the managing agency for up-to-the-minute information before making an off-season visit. Keep in mind, too, that even the listed operating times are subject to change. Weather, budget cuts, ongoing events, a change-over in the concessionaire, and vandalism can all influence opening and closing policies. The price of a phone call is small relative to the cost of a misspent trip.

Within the camp descriptions, the mentioned nearby attractions may also have seasonal schedules. If the success of your trip depends on seeing a particular museum or attraction, you may wish to call ahead.

Reservations. Making reservations is a good idea, especially during peak summer travel months, weekends, holidays, fish runs, or when your travel plans hinge on getting a campsite and there are no alternative camping options in the area. If you want a site on a beach or lake or in other prized locations, reservations are the only way to go. The state park system has a contract with a fee reservation service to handle the booking of state park campsites (800-452-5687). Although most Forest Service campgrounds are available on a first-come, first-served basis, the agency does have a reservation line for a few of its larger, more popular campgrounds; this, too, is a fee service (800-280-CAMP). A recent trend in Oregon is for Forest Service campgrounds to be managed by concessionaires, who set pricing and reservation rules that can vary depending on the operator.

Water. We have tried to list the campgrounds that offer developed drinking water systems. But because these systems can pass water quality tests one week and fail the next, you should always carry an emergency supply of safe drinking water and be prepared to treat campground water by boiling. This becomes especially important as you travel farther from safe city water sources.

Pets. Unless specified otherwise in the campground descriptions, pets restrained on leashes are generally allowed.

GETTING TO THE CAMPGROUND

The best way to reach your intended campsite is to use the individual campground description in conjunction with a detailed state map or the appropriate Forest Service or Bureau of Land Management map. The maps in this book are meant only as general locator tools.

MAP LEGEND

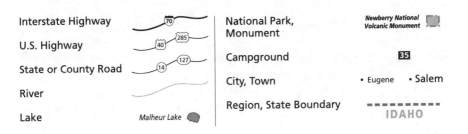

Interstate Highway	National Park, Monument — Newberry National Volcanic Monument
U.S. Highway	Campground — 35
State or County Road	City, Town — • Eugene • Salem
River	Region, State Boundary — IDAHO
Lake — Malheur Lake	

Outdoor and Camping Refresher Course

Responsible use of the outdoors and of campground and trail facilities is the best way to protect and preserve the privilege of a quality outdoor experience. It is also the best way to control campground costs.

PREPARATION

The drive. Traveling to campgrounds and RV parks along major highways poses little problem. The roads are well maintained, a town or passing vehicle is never far away, and the reception of your cellular phone seems just fine.

But backcountry roads present a challenge. For this type of travel, it is mandatory that you keep your tires and engine in good repair. Top the gas tank at the last point of civilization and carry emergency vehicle gear: jack, spare tire, tire pump, jumper cables, spare belts, and, if the weather is foul, tire chains.

Basic survival gear. This includes water, blankets, food, matches, a first-aid kit, and a flashlight. A downed tree, road washout, or rock slide need not spoil a trip if you carry supplies for an unintended stop and maps for plotting an alternative destination and route. Before making any long journey from home, it is advisable to phone the appropriate agency about facility openings and road conditions.

Notification safeguard. Because being stranded or injured in the wild poses a greater danger than at home or in town, it is critical before any outdoor adventure to notify a responsible party of your intended destination and time of return. Contacting that individual upon your return completes the safety procedure. This also works in reverse: If an emergency occurs on the home front while you are gone, someone will be able to alert you or help authorities locate you.

CAMPING

Low-impact camping should be the goal of everyone, even at developed campgrounds. Do not rearrange the site, pound nails, remove ground cover, or dig drainage channels. If you build a campfire, keep it small and inside the provided container. If grills or fire rings are not provided, do not build a campfire. Heed all regulations regarding fires, smoking, and wood gathering.

Setting up. Exercise courtesy when you select your site and keep the area neat. Avoid blocking roads and spilling out of your assigned space into your neighbor's site.

Storing food. Food should be stored in closed containers. At night, be sure all foods and coolers are stowed in your vehicle. In some areas, you will also want to cover the coolers, because some bears have learned that coolers hold food and have ripped open car doors just to reach them.

Garbage. Dispose of litter properly and often. If no facility is provided, pack it out. Use sturdy garbage bags to collect the garbage at your site and store the bags where they are handy for use but not an eyesore to fellow campers. At night, you should stash the garbage bags in a vehicle to avoid raids by raccoons or bears. Never put garbage down toilets, leave it in the outhouse, or abandon it in the fire pit. If you did not burn your flammable garbage during your stay, pack it out.

Sanitation. Dispose of waste water in the provided sites. Bathing or washing dishes should be done well away from natural bodies of water, such as lakes or streams, and away from campground supplies of drinking water.

Smoking. Where fires present extreme danger or where habitats are particularly vulnerable, smoking may be prohibited; heed posted regulations. Where and when smoking is allowed, stop to have your smoke; never smoke while hiking. Use an ashtray at camp. In the wild, clear an area to the mineral soil, smoke the cigarette, and then crush it out in the dirt. Pack out the cigarette butts.

Pets. In campgrounds that allow pets, keep your animal(s) at your site, restrained and quiet. If your pet is not comfortable around strangers, it does not belong in a public campground. On trails, pets must be leashed at all times to protect habitat and wildlife.

Courtesy. Keep your noise down and your site neat, ration your use of showers, and clean up after yourself and your youngsters in the restrooms. There is no maid service here!

Stay limits. Public campgrounds typically have stay limits ranging from a few days up to two weeks, although a few facilities will accommodate campers on a monthly basis. Be sure to limit your stay accordingly.

GEARING UP FOR THE OUTDOORS

Clothing. Layering is the way to go. Wool is the fabric for cold, wet, or changeable weather conditions. It retains heat even when wet. Cotton is the fabric of warm summer days. In Oregon, a clothing necessity is a good suit of rain gear—jacket and pants (or chaps).

Footgear. Sneakers are appropriate for town walks or nature trails, but for longer hikes, boots provide both comfort and protection.

Equipment. The quantity and variety of equipment you carry will depend on where you are going and how long you will be away from your vehicle. Day packs with padded straps or fanny packs provide convenient storage while keeping your hands free. Water, snacks, a sweater, money, keys, tissues, sunglasses, a camera, and binoculars are fine for short hops. The greater the adventure, the greater the quantity of required gear, including safety and first-aid supplies.

Atlases, maps, and brochures. Maps are important tools. They provide an orientation to the area, suggest alternative routes, present new areas to explore, and aid in planning and preparation. Be sure to have the correct maps for your trip. The farther your travels take you from the beaten path, the more important specific area maps become. County, Forest Service, BLM, and topographic maps all generally show greater detail than the standard state road map.

Fees and permits. Trail park passes, wilderness permits, and day-use permits may be required to travel the trails in the area where you are camping. While you may be able to pick up or purchase some of these at the site, you may need to secure others from a ranger station in advance.

ACTIVITIES

Beachcombing. Learn the rules for tidepooling and collecting; these are generally posted at the beach. Before taking a long stroll on the beach, find out when the tide is highest and lowest to avoid becoming stranded. Make sure there will be adequate time to complete your hike or reach safety before the incoming tide. Irregular "sneaker" waves occur along the Oregon coast and can arrive suddenly, sweeping you off your feet. Drift logs do not provide a safe haven from incoming waves because the logs can roll in the surf, unseating and striking would-be riders.

Fishing. A current fishing license from the state of Oregon is a must, and for a few places along the Deschutes River, you will also need to purchase a separate fishing license from the Warm Springs Indian Reservation. It is essential that you possess and study a copy of the most current *Oregon Sport Fishing Regulations.* They outline in detail which waterways are open to anglers, what types of bait or fishing are allowed, catch limits, and size restrictions. You may pick up a copy of the regulations where you purchase your fishing license or at bait and tackle stores, outdoor stores, and nearly everywhere gear is sold. A state map will help you sort out your options and ensure compliance with the rules, which can vary depending on your location along a river or stream.

Since the initiation of the Oregon Salmon Recovery Plan in 1997, and as the federal listing of threatened and endangered fish evolves, the fishing rules change continuously, so do not trust memory or hearsay. What was acceptable in the past may no longer be permissible. Use only barbless hooks in catch-and-release waters and always wet your hands before handling fish. Minimize contact if the fish is to be returned to the wild.

Swimming. Swimming areas mentioned in this book are typically unguarded, so you swim at your own risk. You should never swim alone; always supervise children; survey the area for hazards beforehand; and use common sense with regard to water levels, flow, and temperature. Chilly temperatures and undercurrents can disable even the strongest swimmer. Horseplay, drinking alcohol, and diving are inappropriate and dangerous.

Hiking with children. When hiking with young children, choose simple routes and do not insist on reaching any particular destination. Allow for differences in attention span, interests, and energy level. Encourage children's natural curiosity, but come prepared for sun, mosquitoes, wasps, and poison oak. Do not become so focused on what you want to share with your children that you dismiss their discoveries. Get down on your hands and knees, peer into that puddle, admire that ugly rock. For safety's sake, discuss what to do if you become separated; even small ones should carry some essential items, such as a sweater, a water bottle, and food.

Hiking shared-use trails. Unless otherwise posted, mountain bikers are expected to yield the right of way to hikers and horseback riders, while hikers, in turn, should yield to equestrians. Because horses may spook and put their riders at risk, yielding means that all members of a group should come to a complete halt and step to the same side of the trail. Avoid any sudden movements, but feel free to speak in normal tones. Voices reassure horses that you are indeed human and not some alien creature; backpacks, tripods, and walking sticks can confuse or alarm the animals.

Hiking with pets. Owners should strictly adhere to posted rules for pets. Controlling your animal on a leash is not just a courtesy reserved for times when other campers and hikers are present; it is an ongoing requirement to protect wildlife and groundcover. Know that dogs represent a threat to horses and may create problems with bears. Clean up after your pet, keeping trails free of debris.

SAFETY

While this book attempts to alert you to safe methods and warn of potential dangers, it can only accomplish so much. Nature is unpredictable, and humans are fallible. Good judgment and common sense remain your best allies. When you travel the backcountry, you assume some risks, but you also reap the rewards.

Water. To avoid dehydration, carry ample drinking water with you. When using outdoor sources, be sure to treat the water by using an approved filter or by boiling it for ten minutes. Even if you plan to use trailside sources, you should carry an emergency supply in case those sources have dried up or become fouled. Even on short nature walks and city outings, water is a good companion. If you are thirsty, you cannot enjoy yourself.

Getting lost. Before venturing on any hike, leave word with someone about where you are going and when you plan to return. Keep to your plan and notify the informed party upon your return. Do not hike alone. If you get lost, sit down and try to think calmly. You are in no immediate danger as long as you have packed properly and followed the notification procedure. If you are hiking with a group, do not wander off on your own. If you do get separated, try signaling to others in the area by shouting or whistling in sets of three, which is a universally recognized distress call. If it is getting late, use whatever light remains to prepare for the night; conserve your energy.

Hypothermia. Hypothermia is a dramatic cooling of the body. Cold, wet, and windy weather demand respect. Eating properly, avoiding fatigue, and being alert to the symptoms (sluggishness, clumsiness, and incoherence) remain the best protection. Should someone in your hiking party display these symptoms, stop and get that person dry and warm. Hot fluids can help restore body heat.

Heat exhaustion. Overwhelming your body's own cooling system is also a danger in warm weather. To protect yourself from overheating, wear a hat, drink plenty of water, eat properly, and take rests as needed.

Poison oak and ivy. To avoid the irritating oils of these plants, learn what the plants look like and in what environments they grow. Scientists have developed creams and lotions to apply both before and after contact to reduce the risk of developing a rash, but avoidance is still the best tactic.

Poison oak

Poison ivy

Stings and bites. The best protection against stings and bites is knowledge. It is important to be aware of any allergies or sensitivities that you may have and to learn about the habits and habitats of snakes, bees, ticks, and other potentially threatening creatures. In the case of a tick bite, carefully remove the tick and then watch for signs of redness and swelling, which could be early indications of Lyme disease. Consult a physician if bites or wounds show any sign of infection.

Bears. Bears have a supersensitive sense of smell and tend to be curious. So avoid any strong smells that may intrigue them. In particular, be careful how and where you store food at camp and never store food in a tent. (See "Storing food," above, for correct procedures.) If you are tent camping, avoid sleeping in clothes that may have picked up cooking odors. Also avoid sweet-smelling lotions, cosmetics, and perfumes, which may attract bears. While hiking, make ample noise and try not to come between a sow and her cubs. If you see a bear, do not try to get closer for a better look. For more information about hiking and camping in bear country, see *Bear Aware,* by Bill Schneider (Falcon, 1996).

OUTDOOR AWARENESS

There is risk associated with any trip into the backcountry. Changes occur all the time, in nature and in the maintenance of roads, campgrounds, and trails. Just because a campground or trip is represented within these pages does not mean that it will be safe when you get there. Common sense and good judgment, paired with careful preparation and a realistic assessment of your skills and abilities, are the best means for ensuring a safe, fun, fulfilling outing.

The Campgrounds

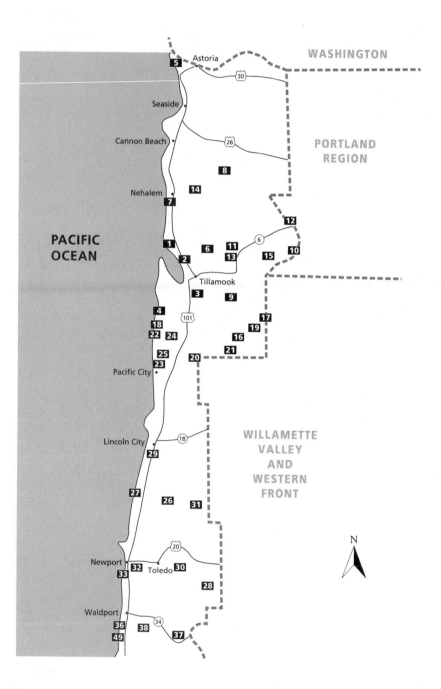

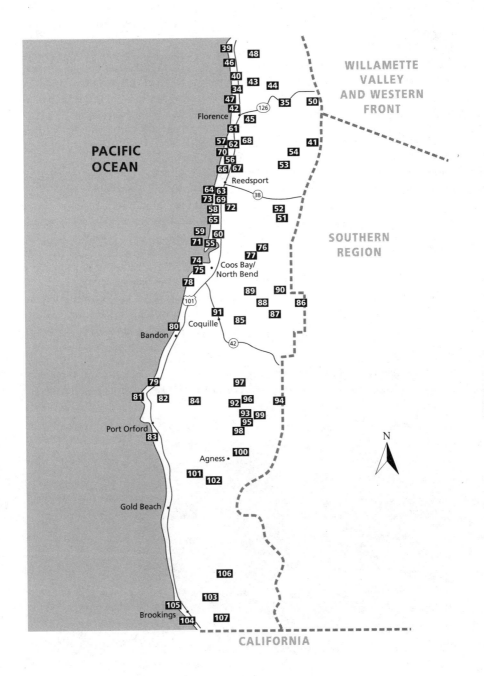

PACIFIC OCEAN

WILLAMETTE VALLEY AND WESTERN FRONT

SOUTHERN REGION

Florence

Reedsport

Coos Bay/ North Bend

Coquille

Bandon

Port Orford

Agness

Gold Beach

Brookings

CALIFORNIA

N

Coast

Next to thick carpets of trees and, of course, rain, Oregon is probably best known for its coastline. In the shadow of the Coast Range and Siskiyou Mountains, rumpled dunes, sandy strands, natural spits, rugged headlands, sea lion rookeries, sea stacks, and verdant coastal valleys combine to create one incredible welcome mat. The explorers who first visited the coast—James Cook, Robert Gray, Lewis and Clark, and Don Bruno de Heceta—live on in the place names. Gold rushes and Indian encounters pepper coastal tales of Oregon, while lighthouses and shipwrecks supply the romance. To preserve this 350-mile-long treasure, the state has elected to keep its beaches open to the public. Nearly 100 state parks and waysides help to do just that, providing residents and visitors with unmatched coastal access.

The coastal mountains and the rivers that drain them add to the bounty, with elk herds, waterfalls, hidden lakes, record-size trees, pockets of old growth, natural meadows, and Oregon's lone redwood forest. Historically, the rivers hosted sizable salmon and steelhead runs, but modern-day pressures leave the fishing in question. Today's anglers must keep current with sport-fishing regulations and restrictions.

Nonetheless, outdoor activities abound. Hiking, kite flying, beachcombing and tidepooling, whale watching, birding, surf and freshwater fishing, crabbing and clamming, dune play, all-terrain-vehicle driving, and horseback riding will get you started. Shops, museums, and aquariums allow you to dodge the rain when necessary. Festivals crowd the beach calendar, with kites, sandcastles, storms, azaleas, rhododendrons, and cranberries all providing reasons to celebrate.

Coastal recreation is year-round. In winter, storm fronts laden with rain pass over the coast, interspersed with bold bursts of sunshine. In summer, soaring temperatures in the Willamette Valley create an inversion that cloaks the coast in morning fog and summons sea-cooled afternoon winds. (Do not pack those jackets at the bottom of your suitcase.) Spring and fall promise clear skies, mild temperatures, and less wind. In the coastal mountains, you will find a vibrant, temperate rain forest in winter and sun-drenched peaks and shady canyons in summer.

Whalehead Rocks, one of many coastal attractions.

ASTORIA-TILLAMOOK AREA

	Hookup sites	Total sites	Max. RV length	Hookups	Toilets	Showers	Drinking water	Dump station	Recreation	Fee	Can reserve
1 Barview Jetty County Park	60	250	40	WES	F	•	•	•	HSF	$$	•
2 Bay City Park	4	11	small	WS	F		•			$-$$	
3 Blimp Base RV Park		65	50		F					$	
4 Cape Lookout State Park	46	228	60	WES	F	•	•	•	HSF	$$-$$$	•
5 Fort Stevens State Park	341	594	50	WES	F	•	•	•	HSFBRC	$$-$$$	•
6 Kilchis River County Park		34	40		F		•	•	SFBL	$$	•
7 Nehalem Bay State Park	284	301	60	WE	F	•	•	•	HSFRC	$$	•
8 Spruce Run County Park		40	35		F		•		FB	$	
9 Trask County Park		60	40		NF		•	•	HSFBL	$$	•

Hookups: W = Water E = Electric S = Sewer **Total sites:** T = Tent-only campground **Maximum trailer/RV length** given in feet.
Toilets: F = Flush NF = No Flush **Recreation:** H = Hiking S = Swimming F = Fishing B = Boating L = Boat Launch
O = Off-Highway Driving R = Horseback Riding C = Cycling
Fee: $ = $1-9 $$ = $10-19 $$$ = $20-29 $$$$ = $30-39. If no entry under **Fee,** camping is free.

1 Barview Jetty County Park

Location: In Barview, about 12 miles north of Tillamook.
Sites: 60 hookup sites, 190 basic sites; water, electric, and sewer hookups.
Maximum length: 40 feet.
Facilities: Tables, flush toilets, drinking water, showers, dump station, telephone.
Fee per night: $$.
Management: Tillamook County.
Contact: 503-322-3522.
Finding the campground: From U.S. Highway 101 in Barview, turn west onto Cedar Street and follow it 0.2 mile to its end at the campground and beach.

About the campground: A tall dune rises to the east of this campground, which is situated on a large coastal flat; to its west stretches a wild beach scattered with drift logs. Sites are roomy and private in a natural setting of low, twisted shore-pine and salal. Fishing from North Jetty is popular. Youngsters will enjoy romping, sliding, and exploring the dune. The campground is open year-round.

2 Bay City Park

Location: In Bay City, about 5 miles north of Tillamook.
Sites: 4 hookup sites, 7 tent sites; water and sewer hookups.
Maximum length: Small RV units.
Facilities: Tables, grills, flush toilets, drinking water, playground, sports courts.
Fee per night: $ to $$.

Management: Bay City.
Contact: 503-377-2288.
Finding the campground: In Bay City, turn east off U.S. Highway 101 onto Hayes Oyster Drive and then take the first left onto 4th Street. Follow it to the park at the corner of 4th and Trade Streets.

About the campground: This campground is located in a city park in a quiet residential area removed from the highway. Alders shade its grassy sites. A bridge spans a small creek that threads through the park and links the camp to a playground. The coastal-maritime diversions are just a skip away. The campground is open from May through September.

3 Blimp Base RV Park

Location: South end of Tillamook.
Sites: 53 basic sites, 12 tent sites; no hookups.
Maximum length: 50 feet.
Facilities: Tables, flush toilets. No drinking water.
Fee per night: $.
Management: Port of Tillamook Bay.
Contact: 503-842-2413.
Finding the campground: From the junction of U.S. Highway 101 and Oregon 6 in Tillamook, go 2.8 miles south on US 101 and turn east onto Blimp Boulevard. Drive 0.2 mile to reach the campground.

About the campground: Located near the Tillamook County Airport and the Air Museum, this large campground sits on an open, grassy plain with views of the coastal foothills. Sites have ample room for setting out chairs or raising tents. Shade sources can make a stay more pleasant. The attractions of Tillamook and the Tillamook–Three Capes coast await. On occasion, heavy, continuous rains can flood some sites. The campground is open from February through November.

4 Cape Lookout State Park

Location: About 12 miles southwest of Tillamook.
Sites: 46 hookup sites, 182 basic, 4 yurts; water, electric, and sewer hookups.
Maximum length: 60 feet.
Facilities: Tables, grills, flush toilets, drinking water, showers, dump station, telephone.
Fee per night: $$ to $$$.
Management: Oregon State Parks and Recreation Department.
Contact: 503-842-4981; 1-800-452-5687 for reservations.
Finding the campground: From U.S. Highway 101 in Tillamook, head west and then southwest on Netarts Highway/Three Capes Scenic Loop for 12 miles. The park entrance is west off the scenic loop.

About the campground: This large coastal campground with closely spaced forested sites that sit just inland from the beach provides campers with convenient access to an ocean spit with 5 miles of uninterrupted beach, dunes, and bay shoreline. A haul-out for harbor seals is at its tip. A forested headland and cedar swamp are also worth exploring. The park's location along Three Capes Scenic Loop allows easy access to Cape Meares State Park to the north, with its lighthouse and octopus-shaped spruce, and Cape Kiwanda State Park to the south, with its hang gliders and dory fleet. Along this coast, scenic offshore rocks delight photographers and provide seabird nesting. The campground is open year-round.

5 Fort Stevens State Park

Location: About 5 miles west of Astoria, near Hammond.
Sites: 341 sites with full or partial hookups, 253 basic sites, 9 yurts; water, sewer, and electric hookups.
Maximum length: 50 feet.
Facilities: Tables, grills, flush toilets, drinking water, showers, dump station, playground, nearby boat docks and launch.
Fee per night: $$ to $$$.
Management: Oregon State Parks and Recreation Department.
Contact: 503-861-1671; 1-800-452-5687 for reservations.
Finding the campground: From the junction of U.S. Highways 30 and 101 in Astoria, go 2.7 miles south on US 101, turn right onto East Harbor Drive, and travel 4.4 miles to Hammond. From there, go south 1 mile on Lake Drive.

About the campground: This large campground is essentially a miniature town. Sites are closely spaced, but you are not likely to spend much time in camp because you can hike, bicycle, explore historic military bunkers, fish Coffenbury Lake, and walk the beach along the ocean or at the mouth of the Columbia River, all without ever leaving the state park. From mid-December to mid-May, you will want to take along your binoculars, because bald eagles congregate along the river mouth to feed on migrating shorebirds weakened by their journey south. The Columbia River Maritime Museum in Astoria and Fort Clatsop National Memorial southeast of Warrenton are worth a visit. The campground is open year-round.

6 Kilchis River County Park

Location: About 7 miles northeast of Tillamook.
Sites: 34 basic sites; no hookups.
Maximum length: 40 feet.
Facilities: Tables, fire rings, flush toilets, drinking water, dump station, telephone, playground, horseshoe pits, primitive boat launch.
Fee per night: $$.
Management: Tillamook County.
Contact: 503-842-6694.
Finding the campground: From U.S. Highway 101, 1.5 miles north of Tillamook, turn east onto Alderbrook Road and drive 1 mile. At the fork, bear right on Kilchis River Road and drive north for 4 miles to reach the park.

About the campground: This family campground sits along the Kilchis River. The paved loop road through camp circles a playing field; sites are grassy and shaded by alders and statuesque Sitka spruce. The Kilchis is a beautiful coastal river coursing through a scenic, forested canyon. Drift boating, fishing, and bird watching help guests while away the day. The campground is open from May through late September.

7 Nehalem Bay State Park

Location: About 24 miles north of Tillamook.
Sites: 284 hookup sites, 17 horse campsites, 9 yurts; water and electric hookups.
Maximum length: 60 feet.
Facilities: Tables, grills, flush toilets, drinking water, showers, dump station, corrals at horse sites.
Fee per night: $$.
Management: Oregon State Parks and Recreation Department.
Contact: 503-368-5154; 1-800-452-5687 for reservations.
Finding the campground: It is 1.5 miles west off U.S. Highway 101, 21 miles south of the US 101–US 26 junction, 3 miles south of Manzanita.

About the campground: Sheltered by a coastal dune, this bayside campground offers convenient access to the old-growth Sitka spruce forests at Oswald West State Park and Cape Falcon and to the summit views at Neahkahnie Mountain. Nehalem Bay State Park features a 2-mile-long spit and 6 miles of coastal beach;

Cannon Beach sand castle contest.

bring binoculars to watch birds, whales, and harbor seals. However, boating and fishing top the list of things to do in the area. Tent campers may prefer the picturesque, walk-in sites in the deep old-growth woods at Oswald West State Park, a few miles to the north. The campground is open year-round.

8 Spruce Run County Park

Location: About 32 miles southeast of Seaside.
Sites: 40 basic sites; no hookups.
Maximum length: 35 feet.
Facilities: Tables, grills, flush and vault toilets, drinking water.
Fee per night: $.
Management: Clatsop County.
Contact: 503-325-9306.
Finding the campground: From U.S. Highway 26, east of Elsie and west of Jewell Junction, turn south at a sign for the county park on Lower Nehalem River Road and proceed 7 miles to the camp.

About the campground: In the Nehalem River Valley, this 128-acre, rustic camp claims a tree-shaded flat parted by Spruce Run Creek. The lower river is open to canoeing for a short time in early spring, and river sightseeing is always inviting. A possible excursion is to see the elk herd at Jewell Meadows Wildlife Area. You can sometimes see wild turkeys in the same vicinity. The campground is open from May 15 to September 15.

9 Trask County Park

Location: About 14 miles east of Tillamook.
Sites: 60 basic sites; no hookups.
Maximum length: 40 feet.
Facilities: Tables, grills, vault toilets, drinking water, dump station, telephone, horseshoe pits; boat launch 4 miles downstream at Peninsula Day Use.
Fee per night: $$.
Management: Tillamook County.
Contact: 503-842-4559.
Finding the campground: From U.S. Highway 101 in Tillamook, go east on Oregon 6 for 2.5 miles and turn right (south) onto Trask River Road. Drive 1.8 miles and bear left to remain on Trask River Road. Continue east another 10 miles to the park.

About the campground: Situated along the Trask River and its North Fork is this rustic campground and day-use area. The campground is woodsy, with earthen roads and parking spots. Some sites are more level than others. The day-use area is a grassy flat above the river. When adequately high, the Trask River is popular with rafters; it features fast channels interspersed with quiet flow. A trail allows exploration along the river at Peninsula boat take-out and launch, 4 miles downstream. The campground is open from May through late September.

TILLAMOOK STATE FOREST

		Hookup sites	Total sites	Max. RV length	Hookups	Toilets	Showers	Drinking water	Dump station	Recreation	Fee	Can reserve
10	Browns OHV Campground		29	40		NF		•		HO	$$	
11	Diamond Mill		20	40		NF				O		
12	Gales Creek		23	25		NF		•		HFR	$–$$	
13	Jones Creek		37	40		NF		•		HSF	$–$$	
14	Nehalem Falls		19	30		NF		•		SFB	$$	
15	Stagecoach Horse Camp		10	25		NF				HR	$	

Hookups: W = Water E = Electric S = Sewer **Total sites:** T = Tent-only campground **Maximum trailer/RV length** given in feet.
Toilets: F = Flush NF = No Flush **Recreation:** H = Hiking S = Swimming F = Fishing B = Boating L = Boat Launch
O = Off-Highway Driving R = Horseback Riding C = Cycling
Fee: $ = $1-9 $$ = $10-19 $$$ = $20-29 $$$$ = $30-39. If no entry under **Fee,** camping is free.

10 Browns Off-Highway Vehicle Campground

Location: About 21 miles northwest of Forest Grove.
Sites: 29 basic sites; no hookups.
Maximum length: 40 feet.
Facilities: Tables, grills, vault toilets, drinking water, OHV loading ramps and staging area.
Fee per night: $$.
Management: Tillamook State Forest.
Contact: 503-357-2191.
Finding the campground: From the summit of Oregon 6, 19 miles west of Forest Grove, turn south at a sign for Browns Camp and quickly bear right to follow a single-lane dirt road marred by potholes. At 0.8 mile, bear right again, go another 0.4 mile, and bear left. Drive 0.2 mile to a T intersection, turn left, and proceed 0.3 mile. Bear right and proceed another 0.4 mile to the campground on Scoggins Creek Road. A few temporary signs may help guide you.

About the campground: This campground for the off-highway-vehicle enthusiast is generally open year round. At the edge of a forest of alders and evergreens, it is laid out as a three-leaf clover, with three separate camping loops nudging a central revegetated area. Boulders shape the campground's graveled sites and roads, and Scoggins Creek threads past the camp. Trails and roads for off-highway vehicles are the primary draw, and you can expect a noisy neighborhood. Elsewhere in historic Tillamook State Forest, you can enjoy quieter pursuits, such as horseback riding, hiking, fishing, and sightseeing.

11 Diamond Mill

Location: About 24 miles east of Tillamook.
Sites: 20 basic sites; no hookups.
Maximum length: 40 feet.
Facilities: Tables, pit toilets. No drinking water.
Fee per night: None.
Management: Tillamook State Forest.
Contact: 503-842-2545.
Finding the campground: From Oregon 6, 23 miles east of Tillamook and 29 miles west of Forest Grove, turn north onto gravel North Fork Road and go 0.3 mile. Bear right at the fork and drive another 1.3 miles to the camp.

About the campground: Tables mark off the campsites, which border a central, gravel, off-highway-vehicle (OHV) staging area. A forest of firs and alders shapes the camp perimeter. The camp is often noisy and bustling but attracts a like-minded group interested in the sport of OHV driving.

12 Gales Creek

Location: About 17 miles northwest of Forest Grove.
Sites: 19 basic sites, 4 walk-in tent sites; no hookups.
Maximum length: 25 feet.
Facilities: Tables, grills, vault toilets, drinking water.
Fee per night: $ to $$.
Management: Tillamook State Forest.
Contact: 503-357-2191.
Finding the campground: The campground is 0.7 mile north off Oregon 6, 17 miles northwest of Forest Grove and 33.6 miles east of Tillamook.

About the campground: Situated in historic Tillamook State Forest, this campground offers family campsites in a second-growth forest of alders and firs along Gales Creek. A series of fires that burned the forest in the 1930s is considered one of the worst disasters to strike the Pacific Northwest; the reforestation is one of the region's great success stories. From camp, hikers may access the historic Gales Creek Trail, which in turn leads to University Falls Loop. Additional trails in the state forest serve hikers, equestrians, and off-highway-vehicle users. Fishing, sightseeing, and relaxing are also popular activities. Tent campers might prefer the Elk Creek Campground, 7 miles farther west on OR 6. It has 15 walk-in sites in the forest along Elk Creek and a bend of the Wilson River and offers similar services. Elk Mountain Trail leaves from that camp, and the newly flagged Wilson River Trail provides a link between the Elk Mountain Trail and the Kings Mountain Trail. Both campgrounds are open from Memorial Day to October 31.

13 Jones Creek

Location: About 22 miles east of Tillamook.
Sites: 28 basic sites, 9 walk-in tent sites; no hookups.
Maximum length: 40 feet.
Facilities: Tables, grills, vault toilets, drinking water, horseshoe pit.
Fee per night: $ to $$.
Management: Tillamook State Forest.
Contact: 503-842-2545.
Finding the campground: From U.S. Highway 101 in Tillamook, go east on Oregon 6 for 21.5 miles and then turn left at the sign for the camp. Drive 0.3 mile, crossing the bridge over the Wilson River, to enter the camp.

About the campground: Located in historic Tillamook State Forest, this campground offers beautiful sites in a mature Douglas-fir forest riddled with alders. The campsites are aesthetically inviting and spacious, with long gravel parking pads. A few sites are situated close to the Wilson River. The park offers convenient access to the varied recreation of the forest: off-highway-vehicle driving, horseback riding, hiking, fishing, and sightseeing. Swimming and kayaking are also possible here, and the River Trail offers a short walk to a picturesque rock ledge. The campground is open from Memorial Day to October 31.

14 Nehalem Falls

Location: About 11 miles northeast of Nehalem.
Sites: 15 basic sites, 4 walk-in tent sites; no hookups.
Maximum length: 30 feet.
Facilities: Tables, grills, vault toilets, drinking water.
Fee per night: $$.
Management: Tillamook State Forest.
Contact: 503-842-2545.
Finding the campground: From U.S. Highway 101, 8.5 miles north of Rockaway Beach and 1.5 miles south of Nehalem, turn east onto Oregon 53 toward Mohler and Portland. Go 1.4 miles and turn right toward Nehalem River and Foley Creek, and in another 0.9 mile, turn left onto Foss Road. Follow it 7 miles to the campground entrance on the left.

About the campground: This pleasant family campground sits in an alder, bigleaf maple, and mixed evergreen forest within earshot of the Nehalem River. The walk-in sites rest in an old-growth stand. Elsewhere, a few old stumps rise amid the thimbleberry, ferns, and elderberry. The river features dark, deep pools alternating with riffles. A path leads to the falls, which is contained in an outcrop gorge. A fish ladder bypasses the falls. The campground is open from Memorial Day through Labor Day.

15 Stagecoach Horse Camp

Location: About 24 miles west of Forest Grove.
Sites: 10 basic sites; no hookups.
Maximum length: 25 feet.
Facilities: Tables, grills, vault toilets, shelter, corrals, water only for horses. No drinking water.
Fee per night: $.
Management: Tillamook State Forest.
Contact: 503-357-2191.
Finding the campground: At the summit of Oregon 6, 19 miles west of Forest Grove and 31.3 miles east of Tillamook, turn south at the sign for Browns Camp and quickly bear right to follow a single-lane, pot-holed gravel road. Continue to bear right at the junctions at 0.8 mile, 1.2 miles, 2.7 miles, and 4.4 miles, staying on the primary gravel road. At 4.7 miles, turn left onto Rutherford Road for a steep, 0.3-mile descent into the camp. Temporary signs may help to guide you to the horse camp. A state forest map is also helpful.

About the campground: Equestrians will appreciate this relaxing camp, snuggled in a second-growth fir forest with a lush understory. An information board in camp shows the locations of trailheads. The historic trails in this forest (all signed) are open to hikers and equestrians only and, for the most part, keep animals safely away from off-highway vehicles. Still, when riding the trails, remain attentive at intersections. The campground is open from May 1 to September 15.

PACIFIC CITY–NESTUCCA RIVER AREA

		Hookup sites	Total sites	Max. RV length	Hookups	Toilets	Showers	Drinking water	Dump station	Recreation	Fee	Can reserve
16	Alder Glen Recreation Site		11	40		NF		•		F	$	
17	Dovre Recreation Site		10	30		NF		•		F	$	
18	East Dunes, West Winds		140	40		F		•		HSFO	$	
19	Fan Creek Recreation Site		11	24		NF		•		F	$	
20	Hebo Lake		15	18		NF		•		HFB	$	
21	Rocky Bend		6	30		NF				F		
22	Sandbeach		101	30		F		•	•	HFO	$$	•
23	Webb County Park		30	30		F		•	•	HSF	$$	
24	Whalin Island County Park		26	25		F		•	•	F	$$	•
25	Woods County Park	5	7	40	WES	F		•		FBL	$$	

Hookups: W = Water E = Electric S = Sewer **Total sites:** T = Tent-only campground **Maximum trailer/RV length** given in feet.
Toilets: F = Flush NF = No Flush **Recreation:** H = Hiking S = Swimming F = Fishing B = Boating L = Boat Launch
O = Off-Highway Driving R = Horseback Riding C = Cycling
Fee: $ = $1-9 $$ = $10-19 $$$ = $20-29 $$$$ = $30-39. If no entry under **Fee,** camping is free.

16 Alder Glen Recreation Site

Location: About 16 miles northeast of Beaver, 28 miles northeast of Pacific City.
Sites: 11 basic sites; no hookups.
Maximum length: 40 feet.
Facilities: Tables, grills, vault toilets, drinking water, fishing dock.
Fee per night: $.
Management: Bureau of Land Management.
Contact: 503-815-1100.
Finding the campground: From U.S. Highway 101 at Beaver, turn east onto Nestucca River Road, a BLM Back Country Byway, and go 16.4 miles to the campground.

About the campground: Situated along the Nestucca River in a moss-draped, alder and maple forest, this welcoming campground sits on the opposite bank from an attractive, lacy, pyramid-shaped falls. Sites have paved parking spaces, and a paved path leads to a fishing dock. The relaxing sound of the water erases tension. The campground is open from April 1 to November 30.

17 Dovre Recreation Site

Location: About 25 miles northeast of Beaver, 37 miles northeast of Pacific City.
Sites: 10 basic sites; no hookups.
Maximum length: 30 feet.
Facilities: Tables, grills, vault toilets, drinking water, covered picnic shelter.

Fee per night: $.
Management: Bureau of Land Management.
Contact: 503-815-1100.
Finding the campground: From U.S. Highway 101 at Beaver, turn east onto Nestucca River Road and go 25 miles to the campground.

About the campground: The sites of this campground on the Nestucca River sit on a terraced slope shaded by tall hemlocks and Douglas-firs. A large side creek lends its voice to the river's music. Most sites have paved parking pads, although a few have graveled off-shoulder parking. From the lower reaches of camp, there is direct access to the river. Here, riffles alternate with glassy pools, and the slope across from camp is strewn with mossy rocks and cascading ferns. If quiet is your goal, you will find it at this camp. It is open from April 1 to November 30.

18 East Dunes, West Winds

Location: About 12 miles north of Pacific City.
Sites: 100 basic sites at East Dunes, 40 basic sites at West Winds; no hookups.
Facilities: Flush and pit toilets, drinking water, playground.
Fee per night: $.
Management: Forest Service.
Contact: 503-392-3161.
Finding the campgrounds: From the junction of U.S. Highway 101 and Oregon 6 in Tillamook, go south on US 101 for 10.7 miles. Turn west onto Sand Lake Road and proceed another 4.3 miles. Turn left to remain on Sand Lake Road for another 0.9 mile. Then turn right onto Galloway, go 2.3 miles, and keep right at the junction. The campgrounds are just ahead, with West Winds at road's end.

About the campgrounds: This pair of campgrounds caters exclusively to off-highway-vehicle enthusiasts. Large, open, paved parking areas serve RVers and truck campers pulling OHV trailers. The sites are side by side; a few individuals manage to set up tents where the pavement meets the dunes. The roar of engines may be heard 24 hours a day. The campground is open year-round.

19 Fan Creek Recreation Site

Location: About 22 miles northeast of Beaver, 34 miles northeast of Pacific City.
Sites: 11 basic sites; no hookups.
Maximum length: 24 feet.
Facilities: Tables, grills, vault toilets, drinking water.
Fee per night: $.
Management: Bureau of Land Management.
Contact: 503-815-1100.
Finding the campground: From U.S. Highway 101 in Beaver, turn east onto Nestucca River Road and go 22.4 miles to the campground.

About the campground: This campground sits along the shores of the Nestucca River and Fan Creek in a forest of hemlocks, firs, and alders. Thorny salmonberry abounds in the understory, helping to assure site privacy. All sites have paved parking, with some more level than others. The waterways are the primary attraction of this camp. Tent campers may prefer the five walk-in sites at Elk Bend, 3.5 miles to the west. That no-fee camp features a canopy of bigleaf maples, as well as river access and similar amenities. Fan Creek Campground is open from April 1 to November 30.

20 Hebo Lake

Location: About 5 miles east of Hebo, 15 miles northeast of Pacific City.
Sites: 15 basic sites; no hookups.
Maximum length: 18 feet.
Facilities: Tables, grills, vault toilets, drinking water, rustic picnic shelter, barrier-free fishing docks.
Fee per night: $.
Management: Forest Service.
Contact: 503-392-3161.
Finding the campground: From Oregon 22 in Hebo, turn east onto Forest Road 14 just north of the Hebo Ranger District office and drive 4.5 miles to reach the campground on the right.

About the campground: Sites radiate around Hebo Lake, a small coastal mountain lake stocked with pan-sized trout and said to contain some big catfish. Rafts and small rowboats may ply the water, but three is definitely a crowd. A rich coastal woods enfolds the lake and camp, and a barrier-free trail travels two-thirds of the way around the lake. Lily pads, alder reflections, and newts bubbling the water's surface add to the lake's charm. From camp, the 7-mile Pioneer-Indian Trail leads hikers over Mount Hebo and past vegetated North Lake to the larger, more isolated South Lake, which also offers fishing. En route to camp, you pass the Hebo Plantation Trail, a half-mile interpretive walk that tells the mountain's history of fire and reforestation. The campground is open year-round.

21 Rocky Bend

Location: About 14 miles northeast of Beaver, 26 miles northeast of Pacific City.
Sites: 6 basic sites; no hookups.
Maximum length: 30 feet.
Facilities: Tables, grills, pit toilets. No drinking water.
Fee per night: None.
Management: Forest Service and Bureau of Land Management.
Contact: 503-392-3161.
Finding the campground: From U.S. Highway 101 in Beaver, turn east onto Nestucca River Road and go 13.8 miles to the campground.

About the campground: Jointly operated by the Bureau of Land Management and Hebo Ranger District, this tiny, primitive camp rests amid alders on the bank of the Nestucca River. Sites have gravel parking. The campground is open year-round.

22 Sandbeach

Location: About 12 miles north of Pacific City.
Sites: 101 basic sites; no hookups.
Maximum length: 30 feet.
Facilities: Tables, grills, flush toilets, drinking water, dump station.
Fee per night: $$.
Management: Forest Service.
Contact: 503-392-3161; 1-800-280-CAMP for reservations.
Finding the campground: From the junction of U.S. Highway 101 and Oregon 6 in Tillamook, go south on US 101 for 10.7 miles, then turn right (west) onto Sand Lake Road. Go 4.3 miles and turn left to remain on Sand Lake Road for another 0.9 mile. Turn right onto Galloway, go 2.3 miles, and turn left at the junction for Sandbeach Campground.

About the campground: Although off-highway vehicles are prohibited from driving through the camp, the roar of engines still carries over the dunes 24 hours a day. Campers with OHVs can use a designated side route to reach the dunes. If you prefer quieter pursuits, the beach is closed to OHVs between the campground and Fisherman's Parking; this stretch of beach is 0.1 mile away via Sand Lake Estuary. Sand Lake is a big, shallow tidal lake that becomes a sand flat at low tide. It contains flounder and perch, which dig into the wet sand or congregate in remaining pools at low tide, making easy pickings for eagles and other birds. The camp sits in a weather gap between coastal capes and often gets sun when the rest of the coast is cloaked in fog. The camp is open from mid-April to October 1.

23 Webb County Park

Location: In Pacific City.
Sites: 30 basic sites; no hookups.
Maximum length: 30 feet.
Facilities: Tables, grills, flush toilets, drinking water, dump station.
Fee per night: $$.
Management: Tillamook County.
Contact: 503-965-5001.
Finding the campground: From Cape Kiwanda Drive 1.1 miles northwest of Pacific City center, turn right onto Webb Park Road to enter the park. The turnoff for the campground is opposite the parking lot for Cape Kiwanda State Natural Area.

About the campground: Inland from Haystack Rock, this pleasant campground is an easy walk away from a state beach where dories (flat-bottomed fishing boats) are launched into the surf and where hang gliders soar from the Cape Kiwanda headland. This county park claims an out-of-the-way, shorepine-shaded coastal property. Other activities to pursue from the camp are driving the Three Capes Scenic Loop, hiking the ocean spit at Robert W. Straub State Park, and fishing the Nestucca River and tiny Hebo Lake.

24 Whalin Island County Park

Location: About 7 miles north of Pacific City.
Sites: 26 basic sites; no hookups.
Maximum length: 25 feet.
Facilities: Tables, fire rings, flush toilets, drinking water, dump station.
Fee per night: $$.
Management: Tillamook County.
Contact: 503-965-5001 or 503-322-3477.
Finding the campground: From the junction of U.S. Highway 101 and Oregon 6 in Tillamook, go south on US 101 for 10.7 miles, turn west onto Sand Lake Road, and proceed 4.3 miles. Turn left to remain on Sand Lake Road for another 3.3 miles. Turn right and cross a Sand Lake levee road to enter the camp in 0.2 mile.

About the campground: Most of the informal sites of this campground stretch across a grassy flat overlooking the Sand Lake estuary, but a few are set back on a rise at the edge of the trees. Bald eagles, shorebirds, and frogs contribute to the campground's attractions. Fishing, crabbing, exploring the Three Capes Coast, and romping at the area dunes will keep you busy. This camp offers a quiet alternative to the area's off-highway-vehicle campgrounds. The campground is open year-round.

25 Woods County Park

Location: Less than a mile east of Pacific City.
Sites: 5 hookup sites, 2 tent sites; water, electric, and sewer hookups.
Maximum length: 40 feet.
Facilities: Tables at tent sites and a shelter with tables and fireplace, flush toilets, drinking water. There is a public boat launch and fishing access area 0.4 mile west of camp.
Fee per night: $$.
Management: Tillamook County.
Contact: 503-322-3477.
Finding the campground: From the center of Pacific City, go 0.8 mile east on Brooten Road to find the campground on the corner at Woods Bridge.

About the campground: In a rural-residential setting, this small campground occupies a corner green at Woods Bridge above the Nestucca River. The camp's small, sandy river access often holds the tracks of the previous night's wildlife visitors, and the river here shows a tidal influence. Meadowlarks in the open field across from the park may serenade you. The campsites occupy an open lawn, but trees grow closer to the riverbank. RVers should avoid camping here when conditions are wet, because the soft, grassy sites turn to mud under the weight of a heavy vehicle. The campground is open year-round.

LINCOLN CITY–NEWPORT AREA

	Hookup sites	Total sites	Max. RV length	Hookups	Toilets	Showers	Drinking water	Dump station	Recreation	Fee	Can reserve
26 A. W. "Jack" Morgan County Park		6	small		NF				FBL		
27 Beverly Beach State Park	129	265	65	WES	F	•	•	•	HSF	$$-$$$	•
28 Big Elk		10	small		NF	•			F	$	
29 Devils Lake State Recreation Area	32	100	62	WES	F	•	•		SFBL	$$-$$$	•
30 Elk City Park		11	40		F		•		FBL	$$	
31 Moonshine County Park		35	40		F		•		FBL	$$	
32 Newport Marina RV Park	130	130	60	WES	F	•	•	•	FBL	$$$	•
33 South Beach State Park	244	244	60	WE	F	•	•	•	HSF	$$-$$$	•

Hookups: W = Water E = Electric S = Sewer **Total sites:** T = Tent-only campground **Maximum trailer/RV length** given in feet.
Toilets: F = Flush NF = No Flush **Recreation:** H = Hiking S = Swimming F = Fishing B = Boating L = Boat Launch
O = Off-Highway Driving R = Horseback Riding C = Cycling
Fee: $ = $1-9 $$ = $10-19 $$$ = $20-29 $$$$ = $30-39. If no entry under **Fee,** camping is free.

26 A. W. "Jack" Morgan County Park

Location: About 20 miles southeast of Lincoln City.
Sites: 6 basic sites; no hookups.
Maximum length: Small units only.
Facilities: Tables, grills, pit toilets, drift/car-top boat launch (across road from camp). No drinking water.
Fee per night: None.
Management: Lincoln County.
Contact: 541-265-5747.
Finding the campground: From the junction of U.S. Highway 101 and Oregon 229, a few miles south of Lincoln City, go east on OR 229 for 17 miles to the campground. It is 6 miles northwest of Siletz.

About the campground: This tiny, rustic park sits in a beautiful old-growth stand of western hemlock and spruce, across a quiet highway from the Siletz River. Oxalis and ferns dress the feet of the towering trees. The camp has dirt roads and parking. The coastal river may draw you away for fishing or drift boating, but the rich forest eventually will call you back. The campground is open from May 1 to October 31.

27 Beverly Beach State Park

Location: About 7 miles north of Newport.
Sites: 129 full or partial hookup sites, 136 basic sites, 14 yurts; water and electric hookups, with some sites offering sewer and cable.
Maximum length: 65 feet.

Facilities: Tables, grills, flush toilets, drinking water, showers, dump station, telephone, playground, visitor center.
Fee per night: $$ to $$$.
Management: Oregon State Parks and Recreation Department.
Contact: 541-265-9278; 1-800-452-5687 for reservations.
Finding the campground: From Newport, go about 7 miles north on U.S. Highway 101. The campground is on the right (east) side of the highway.

About the campground: Spencer Creek threads through this campground, which occupies a coastal forest of Sitka spruce, wax myrtles, and rhododendrons. It features beach access and a short nature trail and is within easy reach of Yaquina Head Outstanding Resource Natural Area, with its visitor center, historic lighthouse, and manmade tidepool. At Yaquina Head, you can train your binoculars on gray whales migrating along the coast, sea birds nesting on the cliffs, and harbor seals sunning on the offshore rocks. South of the park is Newport, with its city, port, and beach attractions. The campground is open year-round.

28 Big Elk

Location: About 40 miles east of Newport.
Sites: 10 basic sites; no hookups.
Maximum length: Best suited for small vehicles due to winding roads.
Facilities: Tables, grills, vault toilets, drinking water.
Fee per night: $.
Management: Lincoln County.
Contact: 541-265-5747.
Finding the campground: From U.S. Highway 20 at Burnt Woods, 16 miles west of Philomath and 31 miles east of Newport, turn south onto Harlan-Burnt Woods Road (County Road 547). Go 7.5 miles to Harlan, turn right onto gravel Harlan Road (CR 538), and continue for 1.5 miles, following Big Elk Creek downstream to the campground on the left. It is a winding route the entire way.

About the campground: Situated on a pleasant creek flat in a rural valley, this quiet, out-of-the-way campground offers mostly shaded, well-spaced sites beneath bigleaf maples, alders, and firs. Ferns claim the perimeters of the sites, and Big Elk Creek provides a soothing backdrop. Although site pads can accommodate units up to 40 feet long, the twisting route to camp makes it more suitable for tents and small rigs. Fishing and kicking back are the best forms of entertainment here. The campground is open year-round.

29 Devils Lake State Recreation Area

Location: In Lincoln City.
Sites: 32 hookup sites, 68 basic sites; water, electric, and sewer hookups.
Maximum length: 62 feet.
Facilities: Tables, grills, flush toilets, drinking water, showers, telephone, launch, dock, moorage slips.

Fee per night: $$ to $$$.
Management: Oregon State Parks and Recreation Department.
Contact: 541-994-2002; 1-800-452-5687 for reservations.
Finding the campground: From U.S. Highway 101 in Lincoln City, go east on 6th Street for 0.1 mile to the campground.

About the campground: Attractive shorepines shade and seclude these campsites, which are not far from the shore of Devils Lake. The individual sites are level and have paved parking pads. Lake access is available at the dock and at the park's day-use area off 1st Street. Besides fishing and boating at the lake, you can spend your time prowling the coastal beaches, attending spring and fall kite festivals, or trying your luck at the Chinook Winds Indian Casino. It is an easy walk to the shops, diners, and motels of Lincoln City. The campground is open year-round.

30 Elk City Park

Location: About 10 miles southeast of Toledo, 20 miles southeast of Newport.
Sites: 11 basic sites; no hookups.
Maximum length: 40 feet.
Facilities: Tables, grills, flush toilets, drinking water, drift/car-top boat launch.
Fee per night: $$.
Management: Lincoln County.
Contact: 541-265-5747.
Finding the campground: From the junction of Main Street and Butler Bridge Road in Toledo, follow Butler Bridge Road for 0.8 mile as it curves south past the Georgia-Pacific Paper Mill and crosses the Yaquina River. Bear left at the next fork onto Elk City Road and follow it 8.7 miles upstream to the park, which is at the intersection of Elk City and Harlan Roads.

About the campground: Located at the confluence of Big Elk Creek and the Yaquina River, this campground occupies a large, open meadow with a handful of shade trees. It mainly attracts anglers and boaters. Vultures commonly ride the thermals overhead. In 1866, the first stage line between the Willamette Valley and the coast stopped here; coast-bound travelers then proceeded by boat on the Yaquina River. The campground is open from April 1 to October 31.

31 Moonshine County Park

Location: About 12 miles northeast of Siletz.
Sites: 10 RV sites, 25 tent sites; no hookups.
Maximum length: 40 feet.
Facilities: Tables, grills, flush toilets, drinking water, drift/car-top boat launch, horseshoe pits. Running water available from May 1 to October 31 only; dry camping allowed in winter.
Fee per night: $$.
Management: Lincoln County.
Contact: 541-265-5747.

Finding the campground: From Oregon 229 at Siletz, 23 miles southeast of Lincoln City and 7 miles north of Toledo, go east on East Logsden Road, which becomes Upper Siletz Road. Drive 7.5 miles to Logsden, turn left (north) at the sign for the park, and continue another 4 miles to the camp.

About the campground: This park serves up Siletz River hospitality in an attractive valley location. Campsites occupy a large, open lawn above the river, with pines, spruces, and cedars distributing some shade to each site. Paved pads serve RVs; the tent sites rim the lawn and sit above the tree-lined riverbank. Across from the campground, a waterfall spills into this large coastal river, which sustains a salmon and steelhead fishery. The campground is open year-round.

32 Newport Marina RV Park

Location: In Newport.
Sites: 130 hookup sites; water, electric, sewer, and cable hookups.
Maximum length: 40 feet at marina sites, 60 feet at south RV area.
Facilities: Flush toilets, drinking water, showers, laundry, dump station, telephone, camp store, café, pier, charters, dock, boat rental, fish-cleaning station.
Fee per night: $$$.
Management: Port of Newport.
Contact: 541-867-3321.
Finding the campground: From Yaquina Bay Bridge in Newport, take Southeast Pacific Way and follow the signs for the Oregon Coast Aquarium to reach the marina in 0.6 mile. The park is on the east side of the bridge.

About the campground: RVers may choose between two camp areas: the paved lot of the marina for waterfront camping or the inland coastal flat of the south RV area, which has grass and a few shorepines. The marina offers everything that nautical and fishing enthusiasts might want, and its campsites are only a hat's throw from a microbrewery, the Oregon Coast Aquarium, and the Mark O. Hatfield Marine Science Center. Seasonal attractions include jigging for herring, crabbing on the pier, clamming in the bay, or watching the larceny of the sea lions or the diving of loons. Newport and the coastal beaches may lure you away from camp. The campground is open year-round.

33 South Beach State Park

Location: 1.5 miles south of Newport.
Sites: 244 hookup sites, 10 yurts; water and electric hookups.
Maximum length: 60 feet.
Facilities: Tables, grills, flush toilets, drinking water, showers, dump station, telephone, playground, volleyball and basketball courts.
Fee per night: $$ to $$$.
Management: Oregon State Parks and Recreation Department.
Contact: 541-867-4715; 1-800-452-5687 for reservations.

Finding the campground: From the Yaquina Bay Bridge in Newport, drive 1.5 miles south on U.S. Highway 101 and turn west into the campground.

About the campground: This jumbo, year-round campground occupies a broad coastal plain behind the swale and low dunes of a prized beach. Shorepines isolate and lend shade to the campsites, which are nicely spaced for privacy and comfort. The paths to the beach range between a quarter and a half a mile in length. If you hike north along the beach, you reach a coastal jetty from which you may fish, watch seals in the bay, or just explore. The state park offers convenient access to Newport's tourist shops and Old Town attractions, coastal features, Oregon Coast Aquarium, and Mark O. Hatfield Marine Science Center. The campground is open year-round.

WALDPORT-FLORENCE AREA

		Hookup sites	Total sites	Max. RV length	Hookups	Toilets	Showers	Drinking water	Dump station	Recreation	Fee	Can reserve
34	Alder Dune		39	30		F		•		HSF	$$	
35	Archie Knowles		9	18		F		•			$$	
36	Beachside State Recreation Area	32	82	30	WE	F	•	•		HSF	$$–$$$	•
37	Blackberry		33	40		F		•		FBL	$	
38	Canal Creek		11	22		NF		•		F	$	
39	Cape Perpetua		38	32		F		•	•	HF	$$	
40	Carl G. Washburne Memorial St. Park	58	66	45	WES	F	•	•	•	HSF	$$–$$$	•
41	Clay Creek Recreation Site		21	32		NF		•		HSBFL	$	
42	Harbor Vista	32	38	40	WE	F	•	•	•		$$	
43	Horse Creek		10	60		NF				HR	donation	
44	North Fork Siuslaw		7	T		NF				HF	$	
45	Port of Siuslaw RV Park	85	85	40	WES	F	•	•	•	FBL	$$	•
46	Rock Creek		16	22		F		•		HF	$$	
47	Sutton		80	30		F		•		HFBL	$$	
48	Tenmile Creek		10	T		NF				F		
49	Tillicum Beach		60	40		F		•		HSF	$$	
50	Whittaker Creek Recreation Site		31	32		NF		•		HFBL	$	

Hookups: W = Water E = Electric S = Sewer **Total sites:** T = Tent-only campground **Maximum trailer/RV length** given in feet.
Toilets: F = Flush NF = No Flush   **Recreation:** H = Hiking S = Swimming F = Fishing B = Boating L = Boat Launch
O = Off-Highway Driving R = Horseback Riding C = Cycling
Fee: $ = $1-9 $$ = $10-19 $$$ = $20-29 $$$$ = $30-39. If no entry under **Fee,** camping is free.

34 Alder Dune

Location: About 6 miles north of Florence.
Sites: 39 basic sites; no hookups.
Maximum length: 30 feet.
Facilities: Tables, grills, flush toilets, drinking water.
Fee per night: $$.
Management: Forest Service.
Contact: 541-902-6940.
Finding the campground: From the junction of U.S. Highway 101 and Oregon 126 in Florence, drive 6.4 miles north on US 101. The campground is on the (left) west side of the highway.

About the campground: This campground, with paved sites and roads, is situated amid alders and mixed conifers along Alder and Dune Lakes. Dune Lake is scenic and green, with an irregular shoreline; Alder Lake has a marshy side arm and grassy spits, but its main body is larger and deeper than Dune Lake. Fishing, swimming, and canoeing are possible in both lakes. Hiking trails cross dunes and coastal forest to link up with Sutton Creek Recreation Area to the south.

East of US 101, 1.6 miles south of camp, is Darlingtonia State Wayside; its nature trail visits a bog of cobra lilies (or pitcher plants), carnivores in the plant world that flower in May and June. Sutton Lake, slightly farther south, has a ramp for boating. Alder Dune Campground is open from mid-May to September.

35 Archie Knowles

Location: About 3 miles east of Mapleton, 18 miles east of Florence.
Sites: 9 basic sites; no hookups.
Maximum length: 18 feet.
Facilities: Tables, grills, flush toilets, drinking water.
Fee per night: $$.
Management: Forest Service.
Contact: 541-902-6940.
Finding the campground: It is south off Oregon 126, 3 miles east of Mapleton and 42 miles west of Eugene.

About the campground: Because this charming campground is just off OR 126, vehicle noise can be intrusive. The sites have gravel pads and are well spaced across a grassy flat above Knowles Creek. Big alders, hemlocks, and firs lend shade. This is an ideal campground for kicking back, opening a newspaper, and reading it from cover to cover. From camp, you may go 9 miles east to reach the Siuslaw River or 18 miles west to the coastal attractions around Florence. The campground is open from May through September.

36 Beachside State Recreation Area

Location: About 3 miles south of Waldport.
Sites: 32 hookup sites, 50 basic sites; water and electric hookups.
Maximum length: 30 feet.
Facilities: Tables, grills, flush toilets, drinking water, showers, telephone.
Fee per night: $$ to $$$.
Management: Oregon State Parks and Recreation Department.
Contact: 541-563-3220; 1-800-452-5687 for reservations.
Finding the campground: From the junction of Oregon 34 and U.S. Highway 101 in Waldport, go 3.4 miles south on US 101. The campground is on the right (west) side of the highway.

About the campground: This year-round beach campground features private, well-shaded sites in a forest of coastal pines and Sitka spruces. Salal and wax myrtle contribute to the privacy of the sites. The camp affords easy access to miles of broad, sandy beach and beautiful ocean. Traffic noise from US 101 carries to the sites that sit closer to the highway. The sites with electric hookups typically have longer parking spurs. In addition to beachcombing, beach strolling, sunning, and playing in the surf, you can pursue clams and crabs in Alsea Bay or fish for steelhead or salmon on the Alsea River, both just north of the park. For trout fishing, try the Yachats River, to the south. The campground is open year-round.

37 Blackberry

Location: About 17 miles east of Waldport.
Sites: 33 basic sites; no hookups.
Maximum length: 40 feet.
Facilities: Tables, grills, flush toilets, drinking water, telephone, drift/car-top boat launch.
Fee per night: $.
Management: Forest Service.
Contact: 541-563-3211.
Finding the campground: It is south off Oregon 34, 17.1 miles east of Waldport.

About the campground: Overnighters will enjoy this beautiful campground on the Alsea River. It offers paved parking pads and lots of open grass, tall hemlocks, Sitka spruces, Douglas-firs, and cedars. Bigleaf maples lean out over the river. Some sites directly overlook the river and all lie within easy access of it. Fishing and relaxing are the primary draws to this campground, and the coast is only minutes away. The campground is open year-round.

38 Canal Creek

Location: About 11 miles southeast of Waldport.
Sites: 11 basic sites; no hookups.
Maximum length: 22 feet.
Facilities: Tables, grills, vault toilets, drinking water.
Fee per night: $.
Management: Forest Service.
Contact: 541-563-3211.
Finding the campground: From U.S. Highway 101 in Waldport, go 6.7 miles east on Oregon 34 and turn south onto Canal Creek Road. Drive another 3.8 miles to the campground. The road is narrow, paved, and winding, with turnouts for passing.

About the campground: This scenic, out-of-the-way campground in a forest of alders and firs along Canal Creek suggests a quiet getaway. The creek is open to catch-and-release fishing only, but thickets of prickly salmonberry may keep you away from the creek altogether. In camp, the salmonberry thickets form ideal privacy borders between sites. Attractive mosses coat the tree trunks and site posts. The campground is open year-round.

39 Cape Perpetua

Location: About 3 miles south of Yachats, 11 miles south of Waldport.
Sites: 38 basic sites; no hookups.
Maximum length: 32 feet.
Facilities: Tables, grills, flush toilets, drinking water, dump station, telephone at interpretive center.
Fee per night: $$.

Management: Forest Service.
Contact: 541-563-3211.
Finding the campground: It is east off U.S. Highway 101, 3.3 miles south of Yachats.

About the campground: This serene campground in the Cape Creek Valley charms guests with its grassy sites and wooded hillside. Footbridges span the creek and link the campground to a nature trail, which leads to a 500-year-old Sitka spruce and an interpretive center. An underpass allows for safe passage beneath US 101 to a trail system along a jagged seashore punctuated by blowholes, crashing waves, chasms, and tidepools. A scenic drive or foot trail leads to the top of the headland for whale watching; longer trails explore ridge and creek canyon. Captain James Cook named this headland Cape Perpetua when he explored the area in 1778. The campground is open from Memorial Day into October.

40 Carl G. Washburne Memorial State Park

Location: About 14 miles north of Florence.
Sites: 58 hookup sites, 2 basic sites, 6 walk-in tent sites; water, electric, and sewer hookups.
Maximum length: 45 feet.
Facilities: Tables, grills, flush toilets, drinking water, showers, telephone, dump station across U.S. Highway 101.
Fee per night: $$ to $$$.
Management: Oregon State Parks and Recreation Department.
Contact: 541-997-3641.
Finding the campground: From Florence, drive 13.9 miles north on US 101. The campground is on the right (east) side of the highway. The beach and day-use area are on the west side.

About the campground: Snuggled in coastal forest with a lush understory that includes blooming rhododendrons in early summer, this spacious campground offers a pleasing retreat at which to relax. China and Blowout Creeks thread through the park. Elk and tidepools are possible nature discoveries. A trail from camp passes under US 101 for safe, convenient access to the beach, while another trail links the park to Heceta Head Lighthouse. You can also drive the 2.1 miles south to this photogenic lighthouse. Sea Lion Caves, a popular private attraction featuring a Steller's sea lion rookery, is 3.2 miles south of the park. The campground is open year-round.

41 Clay Creek Recreation Site

Location: About 28 miles southeast of Mapleton.
Sites: 21 basic sites; no hookups.
Maximum length: 32 feet.
Facilities: Tables, grills, vault toilets, drinking water, playground, ball field, horseshoe pits, drift/car-top boat launch.
Fee per night: $.

Management: Bureau of Land Management.
Contact: 541-683-6600.
Finding the campground: From Oregon 126, 12 miles east of Mapleton and 33 miles west of Eugene, turn south onto Siuslaw River Road, go 9.7 miles, and bear left on Siuslaw River Access Road. Proceed another 6 miles and turn right to reach the entrance to the recreation site.

About the campground: Spacious sites with paved parking pads, mossy vine maple tangles, and tall straight firs make up this camp along Clay Creek and the Siuslaw River. The river flows broad, cloudy, and green and calls to anglers; check current fishing regulations. A small swimming area invites you to cool off. The 1-mile Clay Creek Trail ascends a ridge above camp to visit a remnant old-growth stand: From camp, cross the concrete bridge on Clay Creek Road and ford or rock-hop across Clay Creek to begin the hike. The camp is open from May through October.

42 Harbor Vista

Location: In Florence.
Sites: 32 hookup sites, 6 tent sites; water and electric hookups.
Maximum length: 40 feet.
Facilities: Tables, grills, flush and chemical toilets, drinking water, showers, dump station, telephone, playground, vista shelter.
Fee per night: $$.
Management: Lane County.
Contact: 541-341-6940.
Finding the campground: In Florence, turn west off U.S. Highway 101 onto Heceta Beach Road, go 1.8 miles, and turn left onto Rhododendron Drive. Proceed another 1.2 miles, turn right onto Jetty Road North, and go another 0.1 mile to the campground on the left. Or, turn west off US 101 onto 35th Street, go 0.9 mile, and turn right onto Rhododendron Drive. Proceed another 1.3 miles, turn left onto Jetty Road North, and go 0.1 mile to reach the campground.

About the campground: This campground offers a quiet, clean, comfortable base from which to explore the area. Sites rest among shorepines, salal, rhododendrons, and wax myrtles; some of the sites are sunnier and more exposed than others. From the vista shelter, you can see North Jetty and the mouth of the Siuslaw River. By venturing away from camp, you can explore the beach, dunes, coastal lakes, jetty, and Old Town Florence. The campground is open year-round.

43 Horse Creek

Location: About 14 miles northeast of Florence.
Sites: 10 basic sites; no hookups.
Maximum length: 60 feet.
Facilities: Tables, grills, vault toilets, corrals, hitching posts, horse loading ramp. No drinking water.
Fee per night: Donation.

Management: Forest Service.
Contact: 541-902-6940.
Finding the campground: From U.S. Highway 101, 10.3 miles north of Florence and 0.5 mile south of Sea Lion Caves, turn east onto Forest Road 5800 (Horse Creek Road), which is paved to begin with but becomes single-lane gravel with turnouts. Follow it 3.2 miles to the campground.

About the campground: In a dense forest of tall Sitka spruce, this pleasant, out-of-the-way campground serves a burgeoning hiking/horse trail system that already includes 14 miles of path through the coastal mountains. The camp is functional, clean, and comfortable, and the sites are well spaced for campers with horses. The campground is open year-round.

44 North Fork Siuslaw

Location: About 17 miles northeast of Florence.
Sites: 7 basic sites; no hookups.
Maximum length: Small units; primarily a tent area.
Facilities: Tables, grills, pit toilet (in disrepair). No drinking water.
Fee per night: $.
Management: Forest Service.
Contact: 541-902-6940.
Finding the campground: From Florence, go 2 miles east on Oregon 126, turn north onto North Fork Siuslaw Road, and drive 15 miles to the camp.

About the campground: This primitive campground is on the site of an old homestead above the North Fork Siuslaw River. Tall firs and a grassy flat comprise the camp setting. Within a short drive of the camp is the Pawn Old Growth Trail, which loops for 1 mile through an exceptional pocket of 500-year-old trees: From the camp, drive another 2.3 miles north, turn right, and cross a bridge to reach the trailhead on the right side of Forest Road 2553.

45 Port of Siuslaw RV Park

Location: On the bay in Florence.
Sites: 85 full and partial hookup sites; all hookups but telephone.
Maximum length: 40 feet.
Facilities: Tables, flush toilets, drinking water, showers, laundry, dump station, telephone, boat launch, sports marina.
Fee per night: $$.
Management: Port of Suislaw.
Contact: 541-997-3040.
Finding the campground: In Florence, take the Old Town Loop off U.S. Highway 101 to 1st Street and drive less than a quarter mile to find the campground at the corner of 1st and Harbor Streets.

About the campground: At the Port of Siuslaw, in the heart of Old Town Florence, you have a choice between pleasant, shorepine-shaded lawn sites or open, graveled sites that overlook the bay. This is an ideal base from which to explore the area. It is an easy walk to the marina and to the shops and eateries of Florence. The beach and dunes are just a short drive away. Boating, sport fishing, crabbing from the dock, and clamming in the mudflats are popular pursuits. Plans call for a new restroom and laundry facility that should make a stay here all the more appealing. The campground is open year-round.

46 Rock Creek

Location: About 16 miles north of Florence.
Sites: 16 basic sites; no hookups.
Maximum length: 22 feet.
Facilities: Tables, grills, flush toilets, drinking water.
Fee per night: $$.
Management: Forest Service.
Contact: 541-563-3211.
Finding the campground: From U.S. Highway 101, 9.7 miles south of Yachats and 15.6 miles north of Florence, turn east to enter the campground.

About the campground: At the gateway to Rock Creek Wilderness, this small campground overlooks the point where Rock Creek empties into the ocean and the valley broadens into scenic meadows. Rock Creek is a beautiful, sparkling coastal waterway that flows through a forested canyon. A path heading upstream from the camp is the only entryway to the wilderness, but check current fishing regulations before fishing the creek. The path passes through old homestead meadows that are now frequented by elk. It is an easy jaunt from the campground to Cape Perpetua, Old Town Florence, and the northern reaches of Oregon Dunes National Recreation Area. The campground is open from Memorial Day through September.

47 Sutton

Location: About 5 miles north of Florence.
Sites: 80 basic sites; no hookups.
Maximum length: 30 feet.
Facilities: Tables, grills, flush toilets, drinking water, playground, boat launch (at Sutton Lake to the north).
Fee per night: $$.
Management: Forest Service.
Contact: 541-902-6940.
Finding the campground: From the junction of Oregon 126 and U.S. Highway 101 in Florence, drive 4.5 miles north on US 101. Turn west and follow the entrance road into Sutton Creek Recreation Area to reach the camp.

About the campground: This charming coastal campground is nestled among cedars, shorepines, hemlocks, and spruces along Sutton Creek. Sites offer plenty of privacy and ample space. Parking spurs are paved. Trails lead from the camp to ocean, dune, estuary, and lake attractions. In the camp, a nature trail journeys through the boggy habitat of the rare, carnivorous *Darlingtonia* (or pitcher plant). This unusual plant is also featured at Darlingtonia State Wayside, 0.1 mile north on US 101. Sutton Lake draws boaters and anglers, and Florence and the Oregon Dunes National Recreation Area are but a short drive south. Sea Lion Caves are 9 miles north on US 101. The campground is open year-round.

48 Tenmile Creek

Location: About 24 miles northeast of Florence.
Sites: 10 tent sites; no hookups.
Maximum length: Tent units only.
Facilities: Tables, grills, pit toilet. No drinking water.
Fee per night: None.
Management: Forest Service.
Contact: 541-563-3211.
Finding the campground: At the north end of the Tenmile Creek bridge on U.S. Highway 101, about 7 miles south of Yachats and 18 miles north of Florence, turn east onto Tenmile Creek Road. Follow this eroding, single-lane, gravel road with turnouts for 5.6 miles to reach the campground on the right.

About the campground: This rustic campground on Tenmile Creek sits amid a beautiful, mossy, old-growth forest. Bigleaf maples grow near the creek. Tenmile Creek could pass for a river during times of high water. It is generally large and courses swiftly over a rocky bed. Currently, catch-and-release fishing is permitted, but check fishing regulations for the most up-to-date restrictions. The campground is open year-round.

49 Tillicum Beach

Location: About 5 miles south of Waldport.
Sites: 60 basic sites; no hookups.
Maximum length: 40 feet.
Facilities: Tables, grills, flush toilets, drinking water.
Fee per night: $$.
Management: Forest Service.
Contact: 541-563-3211.
Finding the campground: From the junction of Oregon 34 and U.S. Highway 101 in Waldport, go 4.5 miles south on US 101 and turn west to enter the campground.

About the campground: On a low bluff above the beach, this campground sits in a dense growth of low shorepine, salal, evergreen huckleberry, and wax myrtle. The sites closer to shore tend to be more exposed to sun and weather. Silvered snags and wind-sculpted spruces add their striking silhouettes to the sunset views and photographs. Beach pursuits and visits to Cape Perpetua or Waldport will keep you occupied. The campground is open year-round.

50 Whittaker Creek Recreation Site

Location: About 14 miles southeast of Mapleton.
Sites: 31 basic sites; no hookups.
Maximum length: 32 feet.
Facilities: Tables, grills, vault and pit toilets, drinking water, playground, drift/car-top boat launch.
Fee per night: $.
Management: Bureau of Land Management.
Contact: 541-683-6600.
Finding the campground: From Oregon 126, 12 miles east of Mapleton and 33 miles west of Eugene, turn south onto Siuslaw River Road, go 1.5 miles, and turn right onto Whittaker Creek Road. Go another 0.2 mile to reach the entrance to the recreation site on the right.

About the campground: This campground is bisected by Whittaker Creek, which contains an experimental fish trap and is closed to fishing. The spacious sites are set amid either alder woodland or fir forest. Close by, the Siuslaw River suggests drift boating or fishing, but check current fishing regulations. This large coastal river flows broad, cloudy, and green. The interpretive Old Growth Ridge National Recreation Trail begins in camp and climbs 1.4 miles to a river overlook and an old-growth grove. Look for the trailhead opposite campsites 23 and 24. The campground is open from May through October.

REEDSPORT AREA

	Hookup sites	Total sites	Max. RV length	Hookups	Toilets	Showers	Drinking water	Dump station	Recreation	Fee	Can reserve
51 East Shore Recreation Site		6	40		NF				SFB	$	
52 Loon Lake Recreation Site		61	40		F	•	•	•	SFBL	$$	
53 Smith River Falls Recreation Site		10	small		NF				SF		
54 Vincent Creek Recreation Site		6	small		NF						

Hookups: W = Water E = Electric S = Sewer **Total sites:** T = Tent-only campground **Maximum trailer/RV length** given in feet.
Toilets: F = Flush NF = No Flush **Recreation:** H = Hiking S = Swimming F = Fishing B = Boating L = Boat Launch
O = Off-Highway Driving R = Horseback Riding C = Cycling
Fee: $ = $1-9 $$ = $10-19 $$$ = $20-29 $$$$ = $30-39. If no entry under **Fee,** camping is free.

51 East Shore Recreation Site

Location: About 22 miles southeast of Reedsport.
Sites: 6 basic sites; no hookups.
Maximum length: 40 feet.
Facilities: Tables, grills, vault toilets, boat dock. No drinking water.
Fee per night: $.
Management: Bureau of Land Management.
Contact: 541-756-0100.
Finding the campground: From Oregon 38, 22.5 miles west of Elkton and 13 miles east of Reedsport, head south on winding Loon Lake Road for 7.5 miles.

About the campground: This small campground occupies a forested slope above Loon Lake; there is a separate day-use area across the road on the lakeshore. Fishing, boating, jet skiing, and swimming are among the popular lake pastimes. A boat launch is located at Loon Lake Recreation Site (see below). East Shore Recreation Site is open from Memorial Day weekend through September.

52 Loon Lake Recreation Site

Location: About 20 miles southeast of Reedsport.
Sites: 53 basic sites, 8 tent sites; no hookups.
Maximum length: 40 feet.
Facilities: Tables, flush toilets, drinking water, showers, dump station, telephone, playground, boat launch, fish-cleaning station.
Fee per night: $$.
Management: Bureau of Land Management.
Contact: 541-756-0100.
Finding the campground: From Oregon 38, 22.5 miles west of Elkton and 13 miles east of Reedsport, head south on winding Loon Lake Road for 6.6 miles.

About the campground: Situated in a stately Douglas-fir forest interspersed with bigleaf maples and coastal shrubs is this fully accommodating BLM campground on Loon Lake. Although the campground is on a mild slope, parking spaces are level and paved. Guests have access to boating, fishing, swimming, and waterskiing on lovely Loon Lake. During the first week in August, an annual fishing derby provides fun for the whole family. The campground is open from Memorial Day weekend through September.

53 Smith River Falls Recreation Site

Location: About 26 miles northeast of Reedsport.
Sites: 10 basic sites; no hookups.
Maximum length: Small units only.
Facilities: Tables, grills, vault toilets. No drinking water.
Fee per night: None.
Management: Bureau of Land Management.
Contact: 541-756-0100.
Finding the campground: From U.S. Highway 101, 0.3 mile north of the Umpqua River bridge on the northern outskirts of Reedsport, turn east onto County Road 48 (Smith River Road) and go 25.3 miles to reach the recreation site on the right.

About the campground: Located 0.2 mile upstream from Smith River Falls, this small, rustic campground is arrayed across a terraced slope. Alders grow near the river, and firs, hemlocks, and cedars shade the campsites. A few glorious old-growth trees tower above the camp. Because of the short, uneven gravel or earthen parking pads and the sometimes awkward approach to them, this campground is better suited for tents and pickup campers. At Smith River Falls, rounded rock ledges part and fold the river, creating tiers of rushing water. Near the falls, flat-topped rocks attract sunbathers; elsewhere, potholes lend interest to the river rock. You may spy a fish enhancement project near the falls. The campground is open from May through October.

54 Vincent Creek Recreation Site

Location: About 29 miles northeast of Reedsport.
Sites: 6 basic sites; no hookups.
Maximum length: Small units only.
Facilities: Tables, grills, vault and pit toilets. No drinking water.
Fee per night: None.
Management: Bureau of Land Management.
Contact: 541-756-0100.
Finding the campground: From U.S. Highway 101, 0.3 mile north of the Umpqua River bridge on the northern outskirts of Reedsport, turn east onto County Road 48 (Smith River Road). Drive 28.7 miles to reach the recreation site on the right. The entry road passes a guard station on its way into the camp.

About the campground: This small, no-frills campground sits near the confluence of Vincent Creek and the Smith River. Alders and firs shade the river bench. The sites lack established parking pads, and you should be aware that rain-soaked ground can cause trouble for heavier vehicles. The campground is open from May through October.

OREGON DUNES NATIONAL RECREATION AREA

	Hookup sites	Total sites	Max. RV length	Hookups	Toilets	Showers	Drinking water	Dump station	Recreation	Fee	Can reserve
55 Bluebill		18	30		F		•		HF	$$	
56 Carter Lake		24	35		F		•		HFBL	$$	
57 Driftwood II		70	40		F		•		FO	$$	•
58 Eel Creek		52	30		F		•		H	$$	
59 Horsfall Beach		34	50		F		•		HSFOR	$$	
60 Horsfall		69	50		F	•	•		O	$$	•
61 Jessie M. Honeyman Memorial St. Pk.	141	378	60	WES	F	•	•	•	HSFBLO	$$–$$$	•
62 Lagoon		40	35		F		•		HF	$$	
63 Salmon Harbor Marina RV Park		300	40		F	•	•	•	FBL	$	
64 Salmon Harbor Marina RV Resort	57	57	40	WES	F	•	•	•	FBLC	$$	•
65 Spinreel		36	40		F		•		O	$$	
66 Tahkenitch		36	30		F		•		HFBL	$$	
67 Tahkenitch Landing		26	30		NF				FBL	$$	
68 Tyee		14	22		NF		•		FBL	$$	
69 Umpqua Lighthouse State Park	22	64	45	WES	F	•	•		HSF	$$–$$$	•
70 Waxmyrtle		55	35		F		•		HFO	$$	
71 Wild Mare Horse Camp		12	50		NF		•		HR	$$	•
72 William M. Tugman State Park	115	115	50	WE	F	•	•	•	FBL	$$	•
73 Windy Cove	69	98	30	WES	F	•	•		FBL	$$	

Hookups: W = Water E = Electric S = Sewer **Total sites:** T = Tent-only campground **Maximum trailer/RV length** given in feet.
Toilets: F = Flush NF = No Flush **Recreation:** H = Hiking S = Swimming F = Fishing B = Boating L = Boat Launch
O = Off-Highway Driving R = Horseback Riding C = Cycling
Fee: $ = $1-9 $$ = $10-19 $$$ = $20-29 $$$$ = $30-39. If no entry under **Fee**, camping is free.

55 Bluebill

Location: About 4 miles north of North Bend/Coos Bay.
Sites: 18 basic sites; no hookups.
Maximum length: 30 feet.
Facilities: Tables, grills, flush toilets, drinking water.
Fee per night: $$.
Management: Forest Service.
Contact: 541-271-3611.
Finding the campground: From U.S. Highway 101, 0.6 mile north of the Coos Bay Bridge, turn west toward Horsfall Dune and Beach. Go 1 mile, turn right onto Horsfall Beach Road, and drive another 1.7 miles to the campground.

About the campground: This family campground near Bluebill Lake and seasonal ponds and lagoons has paved parking and is at least partially shaded by shorepines and myrtles. Pussy willows and Indian plum grow in the wetlands. The Bluebill Lake Trail begins near camp and offers an easy walk to and around the lake. A nearby off-highway-vehicle area offers a more boisterous dune experience. The campground is open from May 1 to November 1.

56 Carter Lake

Location: About 8 miles south of Florence.
Sites: 24 basic sites; no hookups.
Maximum length: 35 feet.
Facilities: Tables, grills, flush toilets, drinking water, boat launch (0.4 mile south of campground).
Fee per night: $$.
Management: Forest Service.
Contact: 541-271-3611.
Finding the campground: From the Siuslaw River Bridge in Florence, drive 7.4 miles south on U.S. Highway 101 and turn west into the camp. The Taylor Dunes Trailhead is located here.

About the campground: Located next to an undisturbed dune field and mile-long Carter Lake, this campground particularly appeals to the naturalist. A tall coastal forest intermingled with rhododendrons enfolds the camp. Some highway noise carries across the lake. A half-mile, wheelchair-accessible trail travels through the dunes to Taylor Lake, while cedar posts guide hikers along a 1.5-mile route that leads west across the open sand to the beach. With off-highway vehicles prohibited on the dunes, hikers can study animal tracks and wind patterns in the sand. The mirror-black water of Carter Lake calls to anglers and welcomes small boats and rafts. The camp is closed in winter.

57 Driftwood II

Location: About 8 miles south of Florence.
Sites: 70 basic sites; no hookups.
Maximum length: 40 feet.
Facilities: Flush toilets, drinking water, sand access point for OHVs.
Fee per night: $$.
Management: Forest Service.
Contact: 541-271-3611; 1-800-280-CAMP for reservations.
Finding the campground: From the Siuslaw River Bridge in Florence, drive 6.8 miles south on U.S. Highway 101, turn west toward Siltcoos Recreation Area, and go 1.2 miles to the campground.

About the campground: Used almost exclusively by off-highway-vehicle enthusiasts, this campground is more practical than scenic. It consists of a large, paved parking area for vehicle camping, with a few areas amid the shorepines that are suitable for tents. Islands of shorepine also divide the blocks of paved sites, lending modest shade and a sense of landscaping. One side of the OHV camp abuts the dunes—the primary draw for camp guests. Hiking, lake and ocean fishing, and beachcombing may also appeal to visitors. The campground is open year-round.

58 Eel Creek

Location: About 10 miles south of Reedsport.
Sites: 52 basic sites; no hookups.
Maximum length: 30 feet.
Facilities: Tables, grills, flush toilets, drinking water.
Fee per night: $$.
Management: Forest Service.
Contact: 541-271-3611.
Finding the campground: From Reedsport, drive about 10 miles south on U.S. Highway 101. The campground is on the right (west) side of the road.

About the campground: This family campground is situated in a reclaimed dune forest and rich coastal thicket at the back side of an exciting dune field. Sites have paved parking and basic amenities; tree frogs and hummingbirds provide seasonal entertainment. Adjacent to the camp and closed to motorized vehicles, Umpqua Scenic Dunes invite carefree wandering and nature study, with cedar posts to guide you across the dunes and through the deflation plain to the beach. Some dunes are as high as 400 feet. Eel Lake at William M. Tugman State Park, 1 mile to the north, offers fishing and boating (10 miles per hour maximum). To the south, Tenmile Lake offers bass fishing, speed boating, and waterskiing.

59 Horsfall Beach

Location: About 5 miles north of North Bend/Coos Bay.
Sites: 34 basic sites; no hookups.
Maximum length: 50 feet.
Facilities: Flush toilets, drinking water, telephone.
Fee per night: $$.
Management: Forest Service.
Contact: 541-271-3611.
Finding the campground: From U.S. Highway 101, 0.6 mile north of the Coos Bay Bridge, turn west toward Horsfall Dune and Beach, and go 1 mile. Turn right onto Horsfall Beach Road to reach the campground at road's end in 2.3 miles.

About the campground: Primarily for off-highway-vehicle enthusiasts, this campground consists of a large, open paved area, with numbered sites. The campground rests behind the foredune to the beach, with paths crossing to the ocean shore for surf play or fishing. Horse trails are to the south. The campground is open year-round.

60 Horsfall

Location: About 3 miles north of North Bend/Coos Bay.
Sites: 69 basic sites; no hookups.
Maximum length: 50 feet.
Facilities: Some tables and fire rings, flush toilets, drinking water, showers, telephone.
Fee per night: $$.
Management: Forest Service.
Contact: 541-271-3611; 1-800-280-CAMP for reservations (available from May 15 to September 15).
Finding the campground: From U.S. Highway 101, 0.6 mile north of the Coos Bay Bridge, turn west toward Horsfall Dune and Beach. Go 1 mile, turn right onto Horsfall Beach Road, and drive another 0.5 mile to the campground.

About the campground: This campground features clusters of paved sites rimmed by shorepines and coastal scrub and separated by meridians of native vegetation. The camp provides a pleasant stay for off-highway-vehicle enthusiasts; there is direct dune access from the camp. The campground is open year-round.

61 Jessie M. Honeyman Memorial State Park

Location: About 3 miles south of Florence.
Sites: 141 full and partial hookup sites, 237 basic sites, 4 yurts; water, electric, and sewer hookups.
Maximum length: 60 feet.
Facilities: Tables, grills, flush toilets, drinking water, showers, dump station, telephone, boat launches, boat rentals, swimming beaches, playground, food concession.
Fee per night: $$ to $$$.
Management: Oregon State Parks and Recreation Department.
Contact: 541-997-3641; 1-800-452-5687 for reservations.
Finding the campground: It is west off U.S. Highway 101, 2.5 miles south of the Siuslaw River bridge at the south end of Florence.

About the campground: This bustling campground receives some noise from the off-highway vehicles on the neighboring dunes, but mostly it offers a pleasant stay for active families. Sites are spacious and private. Those without hookups are in a beautiful, tall forest of hemlocks, spruces, and towering rhododendrons, while those with hookups are on a shorepine plain. Campers have direct access to two freshwater, coastal lakes: Cleawox (closest to camp) and Woahink (the larger of the two, across US 101). Only nonmotorized boating is allowed on Cleawox Lake; Woahink Lake serves larger, motorized boats. Both welcome swimmers. Dune play and OHV driving are also popular pastimes. OHVs have direct access to the dunes from loop L at the south end of the camp. Dunes in the area are up to 500 feet high. The campground is open year-round.

62 Lagoon

Location: About 8 miles south of Florence.
Sites: 40 basic sites; no hookups.
Maximum length: 35 feet.
Facilities: Tables, grills, flush toilets, drinking water, telephone.
Fee per night: $$.
Management: Forest Service.
Contact: 541-271-3611.
Finding the campground: From the Siuslaw River bridge in Florence, drive 6.8 miles south on U.S. Highway 101 and turn right (west) at the turnoff for Siltcoos Recreation Area. The campground is on the right in 0.8 mile.

About the campground: Adjacent to a scenic, black lagoon, this family campground occupies a semi-open shorepine forest and is the farthest removed of the Siltcoos Recreation Area camps from the off-highway-vehicle activity. The operation of OHVs is prohibited in camp. Hiking trails skirt the lagoon and Siltcoos River, and a foot trail to Siltcoos Lake begins on the opposite side of US 101. Another area to take a walk is a section of beach near the river mouth that is off-limits to OHVs. The campground is open year-round.

63 Salmon Harbor Marina RV Park

Location: About 4 miles south of Reedsport, in Winchester Bay.
Sites: 300 RV sites, no tent sites; no hookups.
Maximum length: 40 feet.
Facilities: Small gazebo, flush toilets, drinking water, showers (in restroom 6), dump station, telephone, playground (at adjacent county park at far end of camp area), 2 boat launches, 850 slips, fish-cleaning station, boat wash, designated fishing and crabbing docks.
Fee per night: $.
Management: Salmon Harbor.
Contact: 541-271-3407.
Finding the campground: In Winchester Bay, 4 miles south of Reedsport, turn west off U.S. Highway 101 onto Salmon Harbor Drive and go 0.2 mile to the marina complex.

About the campground: Located 1 mile upstream from where the Umpqua River empties into the ocean is this 5-acre, open, paved camping area, which suits both through-travelers and those looking for a base from which to explore the coast. Sea birds and Canada geese share the bay location. The docks and boat moorings add atmosphere, and sidewalks encourage morning and evening strolls along the marina. You may view recreational and working boats, along with a sternwheeler. Attractions in the area include fishing charters, a commercial cannery, the dunes, Umpqua River Lighthouse, a tour of the vessel *Hero* at Reedsport, and Dean Creek Elk Viewing Site (east of Reedsport on Oregon 38). The campground is open year-round.

64 Salmon Harbor Marina RV Resort

Location: About 4 miles south of Reedsport, in Winchester Bay.
Sites: 57 hookup sites, no tent sites; full hookups.
Maximum length: 40 feet.
Facilities: Flush toilets, drinking water, showers, dump station (at marina complex), laundry, telephone. Convenient access to 2 boat launches, 850 slips, fish-cleaning station, and designated fishing and crabbing docks (at marina complex).
Fee per night: $$.
Management: Salmon Harbor.
Contact: 541-271-0287 or 541-271-3407; reservations currently accepted for holidays only.
Finding the campground: In Winchester Bay, 4 miles south of Reedsport, turn west off U.S. Highway 101 onto Salmon Harbor Drive and go 0.25 mile to the resort, which is on the right.

About the campground: This new, landscaped RV resort sits just upstream from where the Umpqua River meets the ocean and is surrounded on three sides by water. Lawn, shrubs, and native shorepines dress the grounds, and a mile-long, paved, pedestrian/bicycle trail circles the resort. Campers enjoy a wide range of amenities as well as convenient access to the marina and to the attractions of Reedsport and Winchester Bay. Plans call for additional sites and facilities. The campground is open year-round.

65 Spinreel

Location: About 14 miles south of Reedsport.
Sites: 36 basic sites; no hookups.
Maximum length: 40 feet.
Facilities: Tables, grills, flush toilets, drinking water.
Fee per night: $$.
Management: Forest Service.
Contact: 541-271-3611.
Finding the campground: From the junction of U.S. Highway 101 and Oregon 38 in Reedsport, go 13.4 miles south on US 101 and turn right (west) onto Wildwood Drive. Go 0.3 mile to reach the campground on the left.

About the campground: This campground provides off-highway-vehicle access to the dunes and is located near a dune vehicle rental for the curious who wish to sample the sport. Sites are wide, paved, and suitable for OHVs. A backdrop of shrubs and trees adds to the camp's ambiance. The campground is open year-round.

66 Tahkenitch

Location: About 12 miles south of Florence.
Sites: 36 basic sites; no hookups.
Maximum length: 30 feet.

Facilities: Tables, grills, flush toilets, drinking water (sometimes smells of sulphur and tastes bad), boat launch (on Tahkenitch Lake at Tahkenitch Landing 0.2 mile north). Recommend you bring drinking water.
Fee per night: $$.
Management: Forest Service.
Contact: 541-271-3611.
Finding the campground: From the Siuslaw River bridge in Florence, drive 12 miles south on U.S. Highway 101. The campground is on the right (west) side of the highway.

About the campground: At the base of a forested dune, this campground is set amid spruces, hemlocks, alders, and cedars. Its proximity to US 101 does mean traffic noise, but traffic generally quiets by nightfall. Sites are more closely spaced than at other public coastal campgrounds. From camp, you may explore dunes that are off-limits to off-highway vehicles, making them ideal for a carefree romp or roam, nature study, and photography. From camp, the Tahkenitch Dunes Trail travels 2.75 miles through coastal woods, over dunes, and along the beach, passing Threemile Lake along the way. Anglers may try their luck there, at Tahkenitch Lake, or in the ocean surf. The campground is open year-round.

67 Tahkenitch Landing

Location: About 12 miles south of Florence.
Sites: 26 basic sites; no hookups.
Maximum length: 30 feet.
Facilities: Tables, grills, vault toilets, barrier-free dock, boat launch. No drinking water.
Fee per night: $$.
Management: Forest Service.
Contact: 541-271-3611.
Finding the campground: From the Siuslaw River bridge in Florence, drive 11.8 miles south on U.S. Highway 101. The campground is on the east side of the road.

About the campground: This attractive campground offers prized sites overlooking Tahkenitch Lake, a large, coastal lake with mostly undeveloped, wooded shores and uncut forest framing its basin. At the day-use area just below the camp, you will find a rustic dock and boat ramp. The western arm of the lake is capped with lily pads. Ospreys soar over the lake and dive for their dinner, while geese plod along shore in search of handouts. Although sites are numbered, there are no developed parking pads. On the west side of US 101, the Tahkenitch Dunes Trail travels 2.75 miles through woods, over dunes, and along the beach, passing Threemile Lake along the way. (See Tahkenitch Campground above.) The campground is open year-round.

68 Tyee

Location: About 6 miles south of Florence.
Sites: 14 basic sites; no hookups.
Maximum length: 22 feet.
Facilities: Tables, grills, vault toilets, drinking water, boat launch.
Fee per night: $$.
Management: Forest Service.
Contact: 541-271-3611.
Finding the campground: From the Siuslaw River bridge in Florence, drive 5.5 miles south on U.S. Highway 101 and turn east onto Pacific Avenue. You will reach the campground soon after taking the turn.

About the campground: This campground sits along the Siltcoos River, many of its sites shaded by tall spruce, fir, and cedar trees. Other sites edge an open lawn overlooking the glassy river. An attractive rockwork border can be found toward the river. Boating and fishing are the chief activities, with large, adjacent Siltcoos Lake hosting much of the fun. Vying for visitors' time are dune recreation and the hiking trails that lead to Siltcoos Lake and along the lagoon and beach in Siltcoos Recreation Area to the south. The campground is open from late April through September.

69 Umpqua Lighthouse State Park

Location: About 6 miles south of Reedsport.
Sites: 22 hookup sites, 42 basic sites; water, electric, and sewer hookups.
Maximum length: 45 feet.
Facilities: Tables, grills, flush toilets, drinking water, showers, telephone.
Fee per night: $$ to $$$.
Management: Oregon State Parks and Recreation Department.
Contact: 541-271-4118; 1-800-452-5687 for reservations.
Finding the campground: From the junction of U.S. Highway 101 and Oregon 38 in Reedsport, go south on US 101 for 5 miles and turn right (west) onto Umpqua Lighthouse Road. Go 0.2 mile, turn right, and go another 0.3 mile to the campground.

About the campground: This campground occupies a wooded slope above Lake Marie, a scenic coastal lake rimmed by forest and possessing dark, still reflections. The camp is also adjacent to the Umpqua River Lighthouse, built in 1894. Shrubs separate the sites, which are situated in coastal forest. The parking is paved. Although hiking trails and fishing at Lake Marie may keep you busy in the park, the Oregon Dunes, Reedsport, and Deans Creek Elk Viewing Site make worthwhile outings. The campground is open year-round.

70 Waxmyrtle

Location: About 8 miles south of Florence.
Sites: 55 basic sites; no hookups.
Maximum length: 35 feet.
Facilities: Tables, grills, flush toilets, drinking water.
Fee per night: $$.
Management: Forest Service.
Contact: 541-271-3611.
Finding the campground: From the Siuslaw River bridge in Florence, drive 6.8 miles south on U.S. Highway 101 and turn right (west) to enter Siltcoos Recreation Area. The campground is on the left in 0.9 mile, opposite a black lagoon.

About the campground: Located along the Siltcoos River, this family campground features sites amid tall shorepines, with black huckleberry and wax myrtle creating effective privacy borders. The operation of off-highway vehicles is prohibited in camp, but OHV enthusiasts do have access to their "field of dreams" via a path that passes the camp. Hiking trails along the river and lagoon, a section of beach near the river mouth that is off-limits to OHVs, and a trail to Siltcoos Lake appeal to the foot-powered crowd. The campground is closed in winter.

71 Wild Mare Horse Camp

Location: About 4 miles north of North Bend/Coos Bay.
Sites: 12 basic sites; no hookups.
Maximum length: 50 feet.
Facilities: Tables, grills, vault toilets, drinking water, rustic horse corrals.
Fee per night: $$.
Management: Forest Service.
Contact: 541-271-3611; 1-800-280-CAMP for reservations (available from May 15 to September 15).
Finding the campground: From U.S. Highway 101, 0.6 mile north of the Coos Bay Bridge, turn west toward Horsfall Dune and Beach. Go 1 mile, turn right onto Horsfall Beach Road, and go 1.8 miles to the campground.

About the campground: Closed to off-highway vehicles, this campground exclusively serves equestrians, who can explore the dunes and coastal scrub habitat via a network of horse trails that begin nearby. The sites are widely spaced and substantial for ease of parking. Shorepines and coastal scrub surround and divide them. The North Bend/Coos Bay area suggests outings for services, coastal recreation, and perhaps even an evening at a casino. The campground is open year-round.

72 William M. Tugman State Park

Location: About 9 miles south of Reedsport.
Sites: 115 hookup sites; water and electric hookups.
Maximum length: 50 feet.
Facilities: Tables, grills, flush toilets, drinking water, showers, dump station, fishing docks for the disabled, boat launch.
Fee per night: $$.
Management: Oregon State Parks and Recreation Department.
Contact: 541-888-4902; 1-800-452-5687 for reservations.
Finding the campground: It is east off U.S. Highway 101, about 9 miles south of Reedsport.

About the campground: This landscaped campground and adjoining day-use area provide convenient boating and fishing access to scenic Eel Lake. They also offer access to nearby Tenmile Lake, which allows faster boat speeds and is noted for its bass fishery; Umpqua Scenic Dunes, for quiet exploration; and the coastal and inland attractions of the Reedsport area. The campground is open year-round.

73 Windy Cove

Location: About 4 miles south of Reedsport, in Winchester Bay.
Sites: 69 hookup sites, 29 tent sites; all hookups except telephone.
Maximum length: 30 feet.
Facilities: Tables, flush toilets, drinking water, showers, telephone, boat docks and launch (across road from park at Salmon Harbor Marina).
Fee per night: $$.
Management: Douglas County.
Contact: 541-271-4138 or 541-271-5634.
Finding the campground: In Winchester Bay, 4 miles south of Reedsport, turn west off U.S. Highway 101 onto Salmon Harbor Drive and go 0.2 mile to reach this park on the left, across from Salmon Harbor Marina.

About the campground: At the foot of a forested hill and across the road from Salmon Harbor sits this 10-acre park with its two camp areas of groomed lawns and shade trees. Tent and RV sites are separated. From the camp, you can easily access the harbor for fishing, boating, and sightseeing; explore Oregon Dunes National Recreation Area on foot or via a bouncing dune vehicle; visit Umpqua River Lighthouse; tour the *Hero* at Reedsport; or aim a spotting scope at a bull elk at Deans Creek Elk Viewing Site (4 miles east of Reedsport along Oregon 38). The campground is open year-round.

NORTH BEND–COOS BAY AREA

		Hookup sites	Total sites	Max. RV length	Hookups	Toilets	Showers	Drinking water	Dump station	Recreation	Fee	Can reserve
74	Bastendorff Beach County Park	56	81	50	WE	F	•	•	•	HSF	$$	•
75	Charleston Marina RV Park	110	118	35	WES	F	•	•	•	FBL	$$	
76	Nesika County Park		20	small		NF					F	$	
77	Rooke-Higgins County Park		26	small		NF					FBL	$	
78	Sunset Bay State Park	63	135	45	WES	F	•	•		HSF	$$–$$$	•

Hookups: W = Water E = Electric S = Sewer **Total sites:** T = Tent-only campground **Maximum trailer/RV length** given in feet.
Toilets: F = Flush NF = No Flush **Recreation:** H = Hiking S = Swimming F = Fishing B = Boating L = Boat Launch O = Off-Highway Driving R = Horseback Riding C = Cycling
Fee: $ = $1-9 $$ = $10-19 $$$ = $20-29 $$$$ = $30-39. If no entry under **Fee,** camping is free.

74 Bastendorff Beach County Park

Location: About 10 miles west of North Bend/Coos Bay, outside Charleston.
Sites: 56 hookup sites, 25 tent sites; water and electric hookups.
Maximum length: 50 feet.
Facilities: Tables, grills, flush toilets, drinking water, showers, dump station, telephone, playground, horseshoe pits, basketball court, fish-cleaning sink.
Fee per night: $$.
Management: Coos County.
Contact: 541-888-5353.
Finding the campground: From Charleston, 8 miles west of North Bend/Coos Bay, travel 1.6 miles west on Cape Arago Highway and turn right at the sign for the county park. Drive another 0.2 mile to reach the campground.

About the campground: This quiet county park stretches across 91 acres of beach and woods. Attractive thickets form privacy borders between the campsites, which are all wooded and which all have paved parking. Some sites require more leveling than others. Other public parks along the Cape Arago coast offer stirring views of cliffs, coves, and offshore rocks where seals and sea lions gather. South Slough National Estuarine Reserve, with its visitor center and hiking and canoe trails, is another alternative. The campground is open year-round.

75 Charleston Marina RV Park

Location: In Charleston, 8 miles west of Coos Bay.
Sites: 110 hookup sites, 8 tent sites; water, electric, sewer, and cable hookups.
Maximum length: 35 feet.
Facilities: Tables, flush toilets, drinking water, showers, dump station, laundry, telephone, playground, boat launch, crab cooking area.
Fee per night: $$.

Management: Port of Coos Bay.
Contact: 541-888-9512.
Finding the campground: From Cape Arago Highway in Charleston, take Boat Basin Drive north for 0.2 mile and turn right onto Kingfisher Drive to reach this park.

About the campground: This port campground has numbered, paved sites paired with gravel meridians and tables and a separate, grassy tent camping area. Raucous gulls contribute to the seaside ambiance. Campers enjoy direct access to the bay and marina, where they can go boating, sport fishing, crabbing, etc. Restaurants lie within walking distance, and the Cape Arago coast is worth a sightseeing drive. The campground is open year-round.

76 Nesika County Park

Location: About 18 miles northeast of North Bend/Coos Bay.
Sites: 20 basic sites; no hookups.
Maximum length: Best suited for small units.
Facilities: Tables, fire rings, vault toilets. No drinking water.
Fee per night: $.
Management: Coos County.
Contact: 541-396-3121, ext. 354.
Finding the campground: From Coos River Junction at the south end of Coos Bay, turn east off U.S. Highway 101 onto 6th Avenue and follow the signs for Allegany. You zigzag through the outskirts of town and soon come out onto Coos River Road. Remain on it all the way to Allegany (13.5 miles from US 101). From there, follow the signs for Golden and Silver Falls State Park, continuing 4.2 miles east on East Fork Millicoma Road. You will reach the campground on the right, 0.2 mile beyond the park's day-use area. The route is winding and narrow.

About the campground: This attractive, rustic, linear campground occupies a low terrace along the East Fork Millicoma River and offers relatively spacious, private sites nestled in a forest of Douglas-firs and myrtles. Thimbleberry and salmonberry abound in the understory. Most sites have gravel parking; a few are grassy. A stairway descends to the shallow Millicoma River, which courses over bedrock and is punctuated by low cascades. A 0.2-mile foot trail links the camp and day-use areas. Golden and Silver Falls State Park is 6 miles east past the county park off Glenn Creek Road. It features short trails to a pair of picturesque, 200-foot waterfalls.

77 Rooke-Higgins County Park

Location: About 9 miles east of Coos Bay.
Sites: 26 basic sites; no hookups.
Maximum length: Best suited for small units.
Facilities: Tables, fire rings, vault toilets, boat launch (0.2 mile east). No drinking water.

Fee per night: $.
Management: Coos County.
Contact: 541-396-3121, ext. 354.
Finding the campground: From Coos River Junction at the south end of Coos Bay, turn east off U.S. Highway 101 onto 6th Avenue and follow the signs for Allegany. You zigzag through the outskirts of town and soon come out on Coos River Road. Remain on it all the way to the park campground, which is on the left, 9.3 miles from US 101.

About the campground: This county campground spreads across a wooded flat at the foot of a forested slope and across the road from the tidewater-influenced Millicoma River. It offers a quiet, rustic camping experience. Fishing and drift boating or canoeing the sleepy Millicoma are common diversions. If you continue driving upstream past Allegany, you can visit Golden and Silver Falls State Park, with its pair of cool, shady waterfall glens. The campground is open year-round.

78 Sunset Bay State Park

Location: About 12 miles southwest of North Bend/Coos Bay.
Sites: 63 full and partial hookup sites, 72 basic sites, 4 yurts; water, electric, and sewer hookups.
Maximum length: 45 feet.
Facilities: Tables, grills, flush toilets, drinking water, showers, telephone, playground.
Fee per night: $$ to $$$.
Management: Oregon State Parks and Recreation Department.
Contact: 541-888-4902; 1-800-452-5687 for reservations.
Finding the campground: From U.S. Highway 101 in North Bend/Coos Bay, go 12 miles southwest on Cape Arago Highway, following the signs for Charleston and the state park. The campground is on the left.

About the campground: Across the road from Sunset Bay—a quiet ocean cove that reflects the setting sun—this campground offers closely spaced, landscaped sites. Surf fishing and swimming are popular, and a segment of the Oregon Coast Trail follows the shoreline through the park to visit eroding cliffs, the sculptured gardens of Shore Acres State Park, and an overlook of an offshore reef where sea lions—and in recent years elephant seals—haul out. Shore Acres State Park and Simpson Reef Viewpoint may also be accessed via Cape Arago Highway. Other attractions in the area include South Slough National Estuarine Reserve and The Mill Casino in Coos Bay.

BANDON–PORT ORFORD AREA

	Hookup sites	Total sites	Max. RV length	Hookups	Toilets	Showers	Drinking water	Dump station	Recreation	Fee	Can reserve
79 Boice-Cope County Park		32	40		F	•	•	•	HFBL	$	
80 Bullards Beach State Park	191	199	55	WES	F	•	•	•	HSFBLR	$$-$$$	•
81 Cape Blanco State Park	58	64	65	WE	F	•	•	•	HSFR	$$	•
82 Edson Creek Recreation Site		15	40		NF				F	$	
83 Humbug Mountain State Park	30	108	55	WE	F	•	•	•	HSFC	$$	•
84 Sixes River Recreation Site		22	small		NF				F	$	

Hookups: W = Water E = Electric S = Sewer   **Total sites:** T = Tent-only campground   **Maximum trailer/RV length** given in feet.
Toilets: F = Flush NF = No Flush   **Recreation:** H = Hiking S = Swimming F = Fishing B = Boating L = Boat Launch O = Off-Highway Driving R = Horseback Riding C = Cycling
Fee: $ = $1-9 $$ = $10-19 $$$ = $20-29 $$$$ = $30-39. If no entry under **Fee,** camping is free.

79 Boice-Cope County Park

Location: About 17 miles south of Bandon.
Sites: 17 hookup sites, 15 tent sites; no hookups.
Maximum length: 40 feet.
Facilities: Tables, grills and barbecues, flush toilets, drinking water, showers, dump station, telephone, boat launch.
Fee per night: $.
Management: Currie County.
Contact: 541-247-7011.
Finding the campground: From downtown Bandon, go 14.2 miles south on U.S. Highway 101 and turn right (west) onto Floras Lake Loop Road. Proceed 1.1 miles and turn right onto County Road 136, following signs for the boat ramp. In another 1.3 miles bear left, go 0.1 mile, and turn right onto Boice-Cope Road. The campground is 0.3 mile ahead on the left; the boat ramp is just beyond it, at road's end. Campground is open year-round.

About the campground: Rimmed by Sitka spruces and shorepines, this crisp, clean campground occupies a level, groomed lawn above Floras Lake. Dunes and seashore are a short walk beyond the lake, which attracts sailboarders, anglers, and migrating birds. A footbridge at the outlet leads to the dunes and the long, wild beach. Hikers must heed protective closures for the snowy plover. Information about when and which areas are closed is posted at the bridge. The campground is open year-round.

80 Bullards Beach State Park

Location: 2 miles north of Bandon.
Sites: 191 full and partial hookup sites, 8 horse sites, 6 yurts; water, electric, and sewer hookups.
Maximum length: 55 feet.
Facilities: Tables, grills, flush toilets, drinking water, showers, dump station, telephone, playground, boat ramp, corrals at horse camp.
Fee per night: $$ to $$$.
Management: Oregon State Parks and Recreation Department.
Contact: 541-347-2209; 1-800-452-5687 for reservations.
Finding the campground: It is west off U.S. Highway 101, 2 miles north of Bandon.

About the campground: On the coast at the mouth of the Coquille River, in a protected area behind the beach foredune, sits this large campground with paved sites. Campers have access to hiking and horse trails, a long stretch of wild beach, jetty fishing, and the photogenic Coquille River Lighthouse, built in 1896. The adjoining Bandon Marsh Wildlife Refuge brings a bounty of birds to your doorstep. The waterfront, shops, and cheese factory of Old Town Bandon invite investigation. The campground is open year-round.

Coquille River Lighthouse.

81 Cape Blanco State Park

Location: About 9 miles north of Port Orford.
Sites: 58 hookup sites, 6 horse sites; water and electric hookups.
Maximum length: 65 feet.
Facilities: Tables, grills, flush toilets, drinking water, showers, dump station, telephone, corrals at horse camp.
Fee per night: $$.
Management: Oregon State Parks and Recreation Department.
Contact: 541-332-6774; 1-800-452-5687 for reservations.
Finding the campground: From Port Orford, go 4 miles north on U.S. Highway 101, turn west onto Cape Blanco Road, and follow it 5 miles to the park.

About the campground: You will find this comfortable family campground inland from a bluff in a protective stand of trees. The horse camp occupies a grassland below. At this exciting, wild strip of Oregon coast, you can photograph the 1870 Cape Blanco Lighthouse, which braves wind and storms from atop the bluff, or tour the 1898 Hughes House, which sits above the floodplain of the Sixes River. At the beach, agate hunters scour the black sand and gravel for prized, naturally polished stones, many of them golden in hue. Anglers fish for salmon on the Sixes River, and the Elk River is just a short drive away. The Oregon Coast Trail and the beach invite hikers, while equestrians can enjoy 7 miles of horse trail and 150 acres of open riding range. The campground is open year-round.

82 Edson Creek Recreation Site

Location: About 9 miles northeast of Port Orford.
Sites: 15 basic sites; no hookups.
Maximum length: 40 feet.
Facilities: Tables, grills, vault toilets. No drinking water.
Fee per night: $.
Management: Bureau of Land Management.
Contact: 541-756-0100.
Finding the campground: From U.S. Highway 101, 5 miles north of Port Orford, turn east onto Sixes River Road and go 4.1 miles to reach the campground on the left.

About the campground: Below a forested slope, these campsites dot the grassy bench along Edson Creek, just above its confluence with the Sixes River. Myrtles and alders flourish along the creek bank and in camp. You have a choice here between sunny or shady locations. RVers should avoid the area during rainy weather because the parking areas are grassy rather than paved. River fishing and coastal attractions lie within convenient reach. The campground is open year-round.

83 Humbug Mountain State Park

Location: 6 miles south of Port Orford.
Sites: 30 hookup sites, 78 basic sites; water and electric hookups.
Maximum length: 55 feet.
Facilities: Tables, grills, flush toilets, drinking water, showers, dump station, telephone.
Fee per night: $$.
Management: Oregon State Parks and Recreation Department.
Contact: 541-332-6774; 1-800-452-5687 for reservations.
Finding the campground: It is east off U.S. Highway 101 near milepost 307, 6 miles south of Port Orford.

About the campground: This campground occupies a scenic lawn and shore-pine flat at the base of a forested ridge, in the shadow of Humbug Mountain. Brush Creek threads through camp and drains into the ocean at a sandy cove on the north side of the mountain. Underpasses allow you to safely access both the beach and the 3-mile trail to the top of Humbug. Along the foot of the camp's eastern ridge, an abandoned section of Old Highway 101 is ideal for walking or jogging. You may also choose to search for agates on the beach, fish the nearby Elk and Sixes Rivers, or visit the harbor at Port Orford. The campground is open year-round.

84 Sixes River Recreation Site

Location: About 16 miles northeast of Port Orford.
Sites: 22 basic sites; no hookups.
Maximum length: Small units only.
Facilities: Tables, grills, vault toilets. No drinking water.
Fee per night: $.
Management: Bureau of Land Management.
Contact: 541-756-0100.
Finding the campground: From U.S. Highway 101, 5 miles north of Port Orford, turn east onto Sixes River Road and go 10.7 miles to reach the campground on the right. The access road narrows and becomes dirt for the final half mile. Be careful making the descent into camp.

About the campground: This restful campground occupies a slope above the beautiful Sixes River. Myrtle, alders, maples, and a few firs frame and shade the sites. Recreational gold panning (study posted restrictions) and fishing are popular river pursuits. Because of the narrow, dirt access road, the camp is better suited to tents and small rigs. The campground is open year-round.

COQUILLE–MYRTLE POINT AREA

	Hookup sites	Total sites	Max. RV length	Hookups	Toilets	Showers	Drinking water	Dump station	Recreation	Fee	Can reserve
85 Bennet County Park		10	T		NF					$	
86 Burnt Mountain Recreation Site		6	small		NF						
87 Frona County Park		17	small		NF					$	
88 Ham Bunch–Cherry Creek County Park		6	T		NF					$	
89 Laverne County Park	42	76	40	WE	F	•	•	•	SF	$–$$	•
90 Park Creek Recreation Site		16	small		NF		•				
91 Sturdivant City Park		9	25		F		•		FBL	$	

Hookups: W = Water E = Electric S = Sewer **Total sites:** T = Tent-only campground **Maximum trailer/RV length** given in feet.
Toilets: F = Flush NF = No Flush **Recreation:** H = Hiking S = Swimming F = Fishing B = Boating L = Boat Launch
O = Off-Highway Driving R = Horseback Riding C = Cycling
Fee: $ = $1-9 $$ = $10-19 $$$ = $20-29 $$$$ = $30-39. If no entry under **Fee,** camping is free.

85 Bennet County Park

Location: About 8 miles northeast of Myrtle Point.
Sites: 10 tent sites; no hookups.
Maximum length: Suitable for tents only.
Facilities: Some tables and grills, pit toilet. No drinking water.
Fee per night: $.
Management: Coos County.
Contact: 541-396-3121, ext. 354.
Finding the campground: From Myrtle Point, turn north off Oregon 42 onto 8th Street, which becomes Myrtle Point–Sitkum Road, and head toward Dora. Go 7.7 miles, crossing the bridge at Gravelford, and turn left onto the gravel road indicated for the park. Go another 0.5 mile to the campground, on the left.

About the campground: Myrtle and bigleaf maple trees punctuate this quiet, primitive campground. Woodland flora carpet the ground beneath the trees, and a gravel access road leads to individual sites.

86 Burnt Mountain Recreation Site

Location: About 39 miles northeast of Myrtle Point.
Sites: 6 basic sites; no hookups.
Maximum length: Small units.
Facilities: Tables, grills, pit toilets. No drinking water.
Fee per night: None.
Management: Bureau of Land Management.
Contact: 541-756-0100.

Finding the campground: At the west end of Myrtle Point, turn north off Oregon 42 at the sign for Sitkum, Dora, and Gravelford and follow Myrtle Point–Sitkum Road for 25.7 miles to Sitkum. Turn left (north) onto Brummit Creek Road, which begins as dirt but becomes paved, and follow it 6.4 miles to a T intersection. Turn right at the intersection onto paved Burnt Mountain Access Road, go 0.7 mile, and turn right again to remain on this road. You are now following part of the Growing Forest Driving Tour. Go 5.5 miles and proceed straight on Bureau of Land Management 27-11-12.0 (which is still Burnt Mountain Access Road) to reach the campground another 0.6 mile farther.

About the campground: This small campground lies 8.5 miles west of the key stop on the BLM's Growing Forest Driving Tour. That stop (#5) is the trailhead for the Doerner Fir Trail, which weaves 0.6 mile through an enchanting old-growth grove to reach a coastal Douglas-fir estimated to be between 700 and 900 years old. The Doerner fir shoots 329 feet skyward and boasts a diameter of 11.5 feet, making it the world's largest Douglas-fir. The trees in the campground are much younger, but they are still tall second-growth firs. Salal, rhododendron, and Oregon grape add to the understory. An old logging road leads 0.2 mile from camp to a lovely thicket of rhododendrons. Any winter access to the camp depends on the snow level.

87 Frona County Park

Location: About 17 miles northeast of Myrtle Point.
Sites: 17 basic sites; no hookups.
Maximum length: Best suited for small units.
Facilities: Tables, fire rings, pit toilet. No drinking water.
Fee per night: $.
Management: Coos County.
Contact: 541-396-3121, ext. 354.
Finding the campground: From Myrtle Point, turn north off Oregon 42 onto 8th Street, which becomes Myrtle Point–Sitkum Road, heading for Dora. Go 17.1 miles to reach the campground on the left.

About the campground: This rustic campground is graced by tall Douglas-firs and attractive myrtle trees and carpeted in grass and wildflowers. It offers campers an off-the-beaten-track retreat for relaxing and forgetting the workaday world. The campground is open year-round, weather permitting.

88 Ham Bunch–Cherry Creek County Park

Location: About 15 miles east of Coquille.
Sites: 6 tent sites; no hookups.
Maximum length: Suitable for tents only.
Facilities: Pit toilet. No drinking water.
Fee per night: $.
Management: Coos County.

Contact: 541-396-3121, ext. 354.

Finding the campground: From Coquille, take Coquille-Fairview Road 9 miles northeast to Fairview. Turn south at the signs for Dora, go 5.4 miles, and bear left. Drive another mile, still heading toward Dora, to reach the park. From Myrtle Point, turn north off Oregon 42 onto 8th Street, which becomes Myrtle Point–Sitkum Road, heading for Dora. Go 16.6 miles and turn left to reach the campground on the left in 1.6 miles.

About the campground: This small, primitive campground is nestled in a fragrant myrtle grove above shallow Cherry Creek, which sings a gentle lullaby. The campground is within 5.6 miles of the Bureau of Land Management's Big Tree Recreation Area and Trail: Head north on Cherry Creek Road opposite the park and follow the signs. The campground is open year-round, weather permitting.

89 Laverne County Park

Location: About 14 miles northeast of Coquille.
Sites: 42 hookup sites, 34 basic sites; water and electric hookups.
Maximum length: 40 feet.
Facilities: Tables, grills, flush and vault toilets, drinking water, showers, dump station, telephone, playground.
Fee per night: $ to $$.
Management: Coos County.
Contact: 541-396-2344.
Finding the campground: From Oregon 42 (Main Street) in Coquille, turn north onto North Central Boulevard and go 0.7 mile to Coquille-Fairview Road. Turn right and continue 13 miles to reach the camp on the right.

About the campground: This family campground sits on a 350-acre, wooded flat above the North Fork Coquille River. Sites offer gravel parking, tables, and fire rings. Tall fir and myrtle trees and mossy stumps contribute to the cool, relaxing atmosphere. The camp's out-of-the-way location helps ensure quiet. Fishing and swimming in the river are popular. The campground is open year-round, weather permitting.

90 Park Creek Recreation Site

Location: About 23 miles northeast of Coquille.
Sites: 16 basic sites; no hookups.
Maximum length: Small units only.
Facilities: Tables, grills and/or barbecues, vault toilets, drinking water.
Fee per night: None.
Management: Bureau of Land Management.
Contact: 541-756-0100.
Finding the campground: From Coquille, take the Coquille-Fairview Road 9 miles northeast to Fairview. Turn south onto Fairview–Middle Creek Road, go 3.8 miles, and turn left onto Middle Creek Road. Go 7.8 miles and bear right at

the fork to remain on Middle Creek Road. Continue 2.4 miles, turn right toward the recreation site, and follow the single-lane, paved entry road 0.2 mile into the camp.

About the campground: For the long, out-of-the-way drive to this campground, you will be rewarded with an attractive, remote, forest retreat. Park Creek flows through camp, and big mossy maple and myrtle trees cloak the area above the Middle Creek confluence. If you do not require a lot of diversions to be content, this is the camp for you. Bring a soft pillow and a good book. The campground is open year-round, weather permitting.

91 Sturdivant City Park

Location: In Coquille.
Sites: 9 basic sites; no hookups.
Maximum length: 25 feet.
Facilities: Tables, fire rings, flush and chemical toilets, drinking water, telephone, playground, ball field, horseshoe pits, boat launch and dock.
Fee per night: $.
Management: City of Coquille.
Contact: 541-396-2613.
Finding the campground: In Coquille, turn south off Oregon 42 onto OR 42S, the Coquille-Bandon Highway. Cross the railroad tracks and drive 0.1 mile to the park entrance on the right.

About the campground: Campsites dot a grassy bench at one edge of this park on the Coquille River. Besides tables and fire rings, a few young trees may be found in the camping area. The river here flows broad and slow. While in Coquille, you might check out the old-fashioned melodramas playing at the Sawdust Theater on summer Saturday nights.

POWERS AREA

		Hookup sites	Total sites	Max. RV length	Hookups	Toilets	Showers	Drinking water	Dump station	Recreation	Fee	Can reserve
92	China Flat Recreation Area		6	40		NF				S		
93	Daphne Grove		14	35		NF		•		S	$	
94	Eden Valley		8	30		NF				C		
95	Island		5	30		NF						
96	Myrtle Grove		5	T		NF				S		
97	Powers County Park	30	50	40	WE	F	•	•	•	F	$–$$	
98	Rock Creek		7	small		NF		•		HF	$–$$	
99	Squaw Lake		6	small		NF		•		F		

Hookups: W = Water E = Electric S = Sewer **Total sites:** T = Tent-only campground **Maximum trailer/RV length** given in feet.
Toilets: F = Flush NF = No Flush **Recreation:** H = Hiking S = Swimming F = Fishing B = Boating L = Boat Launch
O = Off-Highway Driving R = Horseback Riding C = Cycling
Fee: $ = $1-9 $$ = $10-19 $$$ = $20-29 $$$$ = $30-39. If no entry under **Fee,** camping is free.

92 China Flat Recreation Area

Location: About 11 miles south of Powers.
Sites: 6 basic sites and open camping; no hookups.
Maximum length: 40 feet.
Facilities: A few scattered tables and fire rings, pit toilets. No drinking water.
Fee per night: None.
Management: Forest Service.
Contact: 541-439-3011.
Finding the campground: From Powers, go 10.7 miles south toward Agness on Powers Road South/Forest Road 33. Turn right (west) onto FR 3353 to find this campground, which straddles FR 3353 at the intersection.

About the campground: This primitive camp is courtesy of the Georgia-Pacific Company. It has two parts: The lower camp occupies a plateau of trees and grass above the South Fork Coquille River; the upper camp covers a meadow and forested area within easy walking distance of the river. Rough dirt roads connect the informal sites. River relaxation and recreation engage campers. Access is controlled by weather.

93 Daphne Grove

Location: 14 miles south of Powers.
Sites: 14 basic sites; no hookups.
Maximum length: 35 feet.
Facilities: Tables, fire rings, vault toilets, drinking water (June through October), covered day-use shelter.

Fee per night: $ when water provided; otherwise free.
Management: Forest Service.
Contact: 541-439-3011.
Finding the campground: From Powers, go south 14 miles on Powers Road South/Forest Road 33 toward Agness. The campground is on the right.

About the campground: This campground occupies a semi-open flat above the South Fork Coquille River. Live oak, maple, myrtle, tanoak, and conifer trees provide shade. The roads and parking pads are paved. Although this stretch of the South Fork is closed to angling, the river still provides a soothing backdrop for relaxation, as well as a place to cool your ankles. The campground is open year-round, weather permitting.

94 Eden Valley

Location: About 30 miles southeast of Powers.
Sites: 8 basic sites; no hookups.
Maximum length: 30 feet.
Facilities: Tables, grills, vault toilets. No drinking water.
Fee per night: None.
Management: Forest Service.
Contact: 541-439-3011.
Finding the campground: From Powers, go south 16.1 miles on Powers Road South/Forest Road 33 toward Agness. Turn left (east) onto FR 3348 and continue for another 13.6 miles to reach the campground. It is on the right off FR 280.

About the campground: This recreation area east of Foggy Creek claims both sides of FR 3348; the campground is on the south side. It has gravel roads and parking, and the surrounding forest of Douglas-firs contributes to a relaxing stay. The campground is conveniently located along the Glendale to Powers Bicycle Recreation Area route. Access is controlled by weather.

95 Island

Location: About 16 miles south of Powers.
Sites: 5 basic sites; no hookups.
Maximum length: 30 feet.
Facilities: Tables, fire rings and grills, vault toilets. No drinking water.
Fee per night: None.
Management: Forest Service.
Contact: 541-439-3011.
Finding the campground: From Powers, go 15.3 miles south on Powers Road South/Forest Road 33 toward Agness. Turn right (west) onto FR 3300.490 to enter the camp. Be sure to watch for this numbered side road, because there is no campground sign.

About the campground: This small, developed campground affords a pleasant stay along the South Fork Coquille River. It has gravel roads and parking, an attractive woods setting, and a dense understory adorned with rhododendrons. Sites are partially shaded most of the day. Check regulations before fishing. The campground is open year-round, weather permitting.

96 Myrtle Grove

Location: About 8 miles south of Powers.
Sites: 5 tent sites; no hookups.
Maximum length: Suitable for tents only.
Facilities: Tables, fire rings, vault toilets. No drinking water.
Fee per night: None.
Management: Forest Service.
Contact: 541-439-3011.
Finding the campground: From Powers, go south 8.4 miles on Powers Road South/Forest Road 33 toward Agness. The campground is on the right.

About the campground: Myrtles, maples, and a few firs shade this small, attractive campground on a slope along the South Fork Coquille River. Big boulders add to the character of the river, which is closed to fishing. Swimming and relaxing are the favored pastimes here. Elk Creek Falls (its trailhead is 3 miles north of camp off FR 33) is worth the short drive and hike to see. The campground is open year-round, weather permitting.

97 Powers County Park

Location: About 19 miles southeast of Myrtle Point, at the north end of Powers.
Sites: 30 hookup sites, 20 tent sites; water and electric hookups.
Maximum length: 40 feet.
Facilities: Tables, grills, flush toilets, drinking water, showers, dump station, telephone, playground, fish-cleaning station, horseshoe pits, sports courts and fields.
Fee per night: $ to $$.
Management: Coos County.
Contact: 541-439-2791.
Finding the campground: From the Powers Junction on Oregon 42, 2.5 miles east of Myrtle Point, go 16.7 miles south to the park on the northern outskirts of Powers.

About the campground: Restful, spotlessly clean, and landscaped with native vegetation, this campground serves family campers well. Wake up to birdsongs and study the stars at night. A 30-acre pond is stocked with trout and occasionally with surplus steelhead. There is ample room to roam or just settle back and relax. The campground is open year-round.

98 Rock Creek

Location: About 18 miles south of Powers.
Sites: 7 basic sites; no hookups.
Maximum length: Best for small units.
Facilities: Tables, grills, vault toilets, drinking water.
Fee per night: $.
Management: Forest Service.
Contact: 541-439-3011.
Finding the campground: From Powers, go 16.5 miles south on Powers Road South/Forest Road 33 toward Agness and turn southwest onto FR 3347. Drive 1 mile to find the camp.

About the campground: This campground is located beside Rock Creek in an isolated stand of old-growth firs intermingled with myrtle and tanoak trees. Rock Creek rushes over rounded stones, collecting in a few deep, clear pools. Upstream from camp is the trailhead for the 1.2-mile trail to 2-acre Azalea Lake, which is stocked with trout and decorated in July with azalea blooms. By backtracking north to the junction of FR 33 and FR 3348 and then following FR 3348 east for 1.6 miles, you will find the trail to Coquille River Falls, an exciting destination at the end of a short, steep hike.

99 Squaw Lake

Location: About 21 miles southeast of Powers.
Sites: 6 basic sites; no hookups.
Maximum length: Small units only.
Facilities: Tables, grills, vault toilets, drinking water (June through October).
Fee per night: None.
Management: Forest Service.
Contact: 541-439-3011.
Finding the campground: From Powers, go south 16.1 miles on Powers Road South/Forest Road 33 toward Agness. Turn left (east) onto FR 3348 and continue for 4 miles to FR 080. There turn right and proceed another 0.8 mile to the campground entrance on the left.

About the campground: These six well-spaced sites occupy the basin of Squaw Lake, which is fringed by a remnant stand of old-growth trees and alders and willows closer to camp. You can choose a site in full or partial shade. Without developed parking pads, these sites are better suited to tent camping. You can try your luck at catching lake trout for the evening meal. The campground is open year-round, weather permitting.

GOLD BEACH–AGNESS AREA

		Hookup sites	Total sites	Max. RV length	Hookups	Toilets	Showers	Drinking water	Dump station	Recreation	Fee	Can reserve
100	Illahe		14	22		F		•		HFBL	$	
101	Lobster Creek		7	20		F		•		FBL	$	
102	Quosatana		43	30		F		•	•	SFBL	$	

Hookups: W = Water E = Electric S = Sewer **Total sites:** T = Tent-only campground **Maximum trailer/RV length** given in feet.
Toilets: F = Flush NF = No Flush **Recreation:** H = Hiking S = Swimming F = Fishing B = Boating L = Boat Launch
O = Off-Highway Driving R = Horseback Riding C = Cycling
Fee: $ = $1-9 $$ = $10-19 $$$ = $20-29 $$$$ = $30-39. If no entry under **Fee,** camping is free.

100 Illahe

Location: 5 miles north of Agness.
Sites: 14 basic sites; no hookups.
Maximum length: 22 feet, but with road better suited to small units.
Facilities: Tables, fire rings, vault and flush toilets, drinking water, boat launch (1 mile farther north at Foster Bar).
Fee per night: $.
Management: Forest Service.
Contact: 541-247-3600.
Finding the campground: From Agness, go 5 miles north on County Road 375.

About the campground: This Rogue River campground has gravel roads and parking, nicely spaced sites amid second-growth forest, and a river-access trail. You can fish right from camp or put in with a raft or boat upstream at Foster Bar. From Foster Bar Trailhead on Forest Road 3700.300 (near the boating access), you can hike the superb 40-mile Rogue River Trail, which follows the Rogue National Wild and Scenic River. The campground is open from mid-May to mid-October.

101 Lobster Creek

Location: About 9 miles northeast of Gold Beach.
Sites: 7 basic sites, with open camping on the gravel river bar; no hookups.
Maximum length: 20 feet (for basic sites).
Facilities: Tables, grills, flush toilets, drinking water, telephone, boat launch. No facilities on gravel bar.
Fee per night: $.
Management: Forest Service.
Contact: 541-247-3600.
Finding the campground: In Gold Beach, turn east off U.S. Highway 101 onto Jerry's Flat Road/ Forest Road 33 and proceed 9.3 miles to the campground entrance on the left.

About the campground: Tucked away in a forest of myrtles, maples, and alders with a luxurious understory is this small campground primarily for tent campers. There are a few sites suitable for RVs, but most RVers choose to set up along the gravel bar for direct access to the lower Rogue River. Fishing and boating are key draws, but there are trails in the area to explore as well. The campground is closed in winter.

102 Quosatana

Location: About 14 miles northeast of Gold Beach.
Sites: 43 basic sites; no hookups.
Maximum length: 30 feet.
Facilities: Tables, grills, flush toilets, drinking water, dump station, telephone, boat launch.
Fee per night: $.
Management: Forest Service.
Contact: 541-247-3600.
Finding the campground: In Gold Beach, turn east off U.S. Highway 101 onto Jerry's Flat Road/Forest Road 33 and proceed 13.9 miles to the campground.

About the campground: This beautiful, sprawling campground claims a prized flat on the lower Rogue River, with sites both at the edge of a meadow and within a tranquil myrtle grove. The mature myrtle trees seasonally scent the air with a eucalyptus-like aroma and draw the attention of photographers with their mossy, multiple trunks. There is access to the river for fishing, boating, and swimming and an open, mowed field for sports. The campground is closed in winter.

BROOKINGS AREA

	Hookup sites	Total sites	Max. RV length	Hookups	Toilets	Showers	Drinking water	Dump station	Recreation	Fee	Can reserve
103 Alfred A. Loeb State Park	53	53	50	WE	F	•	•		HSFBL	$$	
104 Beachfront RV Park	138	153	40	WES	F	•	•	•	FBL	$$–$$$	•
105 Harris Beach State Park	86	152	50	WES	F	•	•	•	HSF	$$–$$$	•
106 Little Redwood		12	25		NF		•		SFBL	$	
107 Winchuck		15	40		NF		•		HSF	$	

Hookups: W = Water E = Electric S = Sewer **Total sites:** T = Tent-only campground **Maximum trailer/RV length** given in feet.
Toilets: F = Flush NF = No Flush **Recreation:** H = Hiking S = Swimming F = Fishing B = Boating L = Boat Launch
O = Off-Highway Driving R = Horseback Riding C = Cycling
Fee: $ = $1-9 $$ = $10-19 $$$ = $20-29 $$$$ = $30-39. If no entry under **Fee,** camping is free.

103 Alfred A. Loeb State Park

Location: 8 miles northeast of Brookings.
Sites: 53 hookup sites; water and electric hookups.
Maximum length: 50 feet.
Facilities: Tables, grills, flush toilets, drinking water, showers, telephone, boat ramp.
Fee per night: $$.
Management: Oregon State Parks and Recreation.
Contact: 541-469-2021.
Finding the campground: From the junction of U.S. Highway 101 and North Bank Chetco River Road in Brookings, go 8 miles northeast on North Bank Chetco River Road to reach the park on the right.

About the campground: This quiet campground sits in a scenic, old-growth myrtle and evergreen grove along the north bank of the pristine Chetco River. The park's Riverside Trail journeys upstream along the steep riverbank to link up with the Forest Service's Redwood Nature Trail, which tours the nation's northernmost redwood grove; a crosswalk links the two trails for a 2.5-mile round-trip hike. The big attraction, though, is fishing the Chetco River, and for sheer relaxation, how can you miss with such an inviting camp setting? The campground is open year-round.

104 Beachfront RV Park

Location: In Brookings.
Sites: 138 hookup sites, 15 tent sites; full hookups.
Maximum length: 40 feet.
Facilities: Flush toilets, drinking water, showers, laundry, dump station, telephone, restaurant, tables, barbecues in tent area, boat launch.
Fee per night: $$ to $$$.

Management: Port of Brookings.
Contact: 541-469-5867; 1-800-441-0856 for reservations.
Finding the campground: From U.S. Highway 101 in Brookings, turn west onto Lower Harbor Road, drive 0.1 mile to a junction, and bear left. Proceed another 0.8 mile, turn right onto Boat Basin Road, and drive 0.1 mile to the park entrance.

About the campground: This RV park offers campsites on a gravel flat overlooking the ocean; the harbor is at its back. The park is clean, orderly, and convenient, and it has easy parking but no shade. Only at the tent area will you find lawn and a few low shorepines. Views of the ocean, the sound of the surf, and the tang of sea air grace your stay. Beach-going and jetty fishing for perch and fall salmon are among the popular pastimes. Along the harbor, you will find fresh-fish counters, seafood eateries, and fishing charters. The campground is open year-round.

105 Harris Beach State Park

Location: In Brookings.
Sites: 86 full and partial hookup sites, 66 basic sites, 4 yurts; water, electric, sewer, and cable hookups.
Maximum length: 50 feet.
Facilities: Tables, grills, flush toilets, drinking water, showers, dump station, telephone, playground.
Fee per night: $$ to $$$.
Management: Oregon State Parks and Recreation Department.
Contact: 541-469-2021; 1-800-452-5687 for reservations.
Finding the campground: It is west off U.S. Highway 101 at the north end of Brookings.

About the campground: Occupying a prized coastal location, this developed campground has sites set back from the ocean in dense vegetation. A wildlife refuge on Goat Island, weathered cliffs, sea stacks, and a sandy beach are among its attractions. The Viewpoint Trail leads from the camp to an overlook of a natural bridge. Sea and shorebirds add to the coastal ambiance. You may want to extend your stay to shop and dine in Brookings, fish in the Chetco River, or visit Samuel H. Boardman State Park (to the north), which offers hiking, picnicking, scenic vistas, and quiet beaches. The campground is open year-round.

106 Little Redwood

Location: About 13 miles northeast of Brookings.
Sites: 12 basic sites; no hookups.
Maximum length: 25 feet.
Facilities: Tables, grills, vault toilets, drinking water, drift/car-top boat launch (0.1 mile upstream at Redwood Bar).
Fee per night: $.
Management: Forest Service.
Contact: 541-469-2196.

Finding the campground: From U.S. Highway 101 in Brookings, turn east onto North Bank Chetco River Road and continue 12.6 miles to this campground on the south bank of the river. It is on the left 4 miles after you cross the bridge.

About the campground: This attractive, forested campground stretched along the Chetco River offers nicely spaced sites, paved roads, and parking. Here, big Douglas-firs, tanoaks, vine maples, and huckleberry bushes thrive, and the river is just an easy walk away for admiring or angling. For additional but more primitive camping or for boat access, you will find Redwood Bar 0.1 mile upstream. It is just an open, no-frills gravel bar for recreational use; a camp fee is charged. Little Redwood Campground is open from May 15 into October.

107 Winchuck

Location: About 12 miles southeast of Brookings.
Sites: 15 basic sites; no hookups.
Maximum length: 40 feet.
Facilities: Tables, grills, vault toilets, drinking water, wheelchair access to river.
Fee per night: $.
Management: Forest Service.
Contact: 541-469-2196.
Finding the campground: From the Chetco River bridge in Brookings, go south on U.S. Highway 101 for 4.1 miles and turn left (east) onto Winchuck Road. Go 8 miles, bear right, and drive 0.1 mile to the campground, which straddles the road.

Southern Oregon coastline.

About the campground: The two halves of this relaxing forest campground are wrapped in a bend of the sparkling green Winchuck River, another prized coastal waterway of incredible clarity. Crosswalks link the camp areas, and short trails allow you to explore along the river. Myrtles, tanoaks, alders, and mossy boulders and outcrops contribute to the soothing spell of the river. Fishing and a gravel-bar beach and swimming hole upstream keep campers happy. The campground is open from May 15 into October.

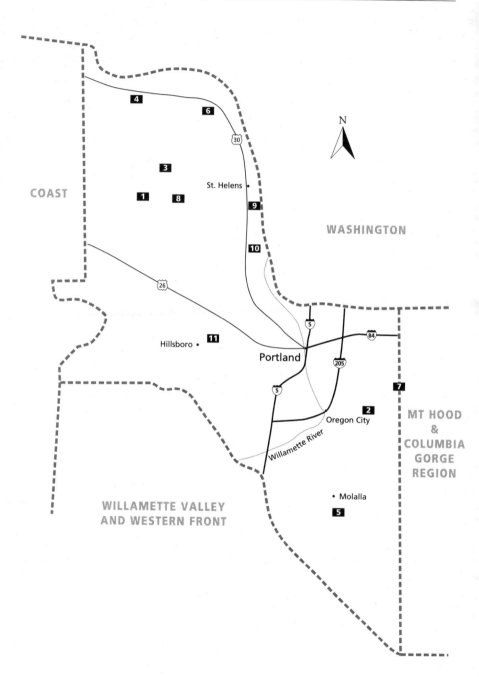

COAST

WASHINGTON

St. Helens

Hillsboro

Portland

Oregon City

Willamette River

Molalla

MT HOOD
&
COLUMBIA
GORGE
REGION

WILLAMETTE VALLEY
AND WESTERN FRONT

N

Portland Area

Portland, the "City of Roses," sits at the confluence of the Willamette and Columbia Rivers and is the heart of Oregon. A city of bridges and beauty, it succeeds in blending culture, progress, industry, and nature into a very livable metropolis. Its downtown district is vibrant and pedestrian friendly, and if the recently instituted "free ride" program succeeds, Portland will also be a good place to bicycle. Under this program, yellow bicycles have been distributed throughout the city and are available for anyone to borrow temporarily.

Portland boasts a fine ensemble of museums, theaters, concert halls, and gardens, as well as a Saturday Market, where artisans sell their creations; the acclaimed Oregon Zoo; and the popular Oregon Museum of Science and Industry (OMSI). Forest Park is an unrivaled wilderness island within a city of this size, and the trails that explore it are first-rate. Elsewhere, wetlands and estuarine lakes attract wildlife and naturalists.

Special events include the Rose Festival, with its Grand Floral Parade, Dragon Boat Races, Festival Fleet, and other associated events; The Bite, an annual waterfront event at which local eateries serve up their specialties; the Brewer's Festival; and the sailing of the Christmas Ships. Restaurants treat patrons to an array of ethnic tastes, street concerts enliven Pioneer Courthouse Square, the Trail Blazers bring basketball fans to their feet at the Rose Garden, and the waterfront invites sunset-gazing and romancing.

Nature study in Forest Park, Portland.

Outside the metropolitan center, you will find that the pace slows and tranquil images of farms, Coast Range foothills, and the Columbia River drainage replace the bright city lights. "U-Pick" signs and produce stands tempt you to stop and collect farm-fresh goodies for the dinner table. Hot-air balloons may grace the sky, and abandoned railroad grades may suggest a hike or bicycle ride through the rural countryside.

Portland and its outlying areas typically share in the year-round mild weather of the Willamette Valley. Wind funnels through the Columbia River Gorge. Summers are warm and inviting; spring and fall feature a mix of showers and clear skies; and winter brings rain interspersed with crisp, cool, clear days. You can also expect snow and ice for a day or two each winter—the perfect time to purchase a latte and curl up with a good book: With more bookstores per capita than any other U.S. city, Portland is known as the "reading capital of the nation" and it pioneered the specialty-coffee fad.

PORTLAND AREA

	Hookup sites	Total sites	Max. RV length	Hookups	Toilets	Showers	Drinking water	Dump station	Recreation	Fee	Can reserve
1 Anderson Park	20	50	40	WES	F		•	•	HFC	$	•
2 Barton County Park	45	57	40	WE	F	•	•	•	SFBL	$$	•
3 Big Eddy	19	29	40	WE	F		•	•	FBL	$$	•
4 Clatskanie City Park	4	4	40	WES	F	•	•		SFBL	$–$$	
5 Feyrer Memorial County Park	20	20	40	WE	F	•	•	•	F	$$	•
6 Hudson/Parcher County Park	15	36	40	WES	F	•	•	•		$$	•
7 Oxbow County Park		45	35		NF		•		HSFBL	$$	
8 Scaponia County Park		7	small		NF		•			$	
9 Scappoose Bay Marine Park		open	40		F		•		HFBL	$$	
10 Scappoose RV Park	7	7	40	WES	F	•	•	•		$$	
11 Washington County FairPlex RV	14	14	30	WE	F	•	•			$$	

Hookups: W = Water E = Electric S = Sewer **Total sites:** T = Tent-only campground **Maximum trailer/RV length** given in feet.
Toilets: F = Flush NF = No Flush **Recreation:** H = Hiking S = Swimming F = Fishing B = Boating L = Boat Launch
O = Off-Highway Driving R = Horseback Riding C = Cycling
Fee: $ = $1-9 $$ = $10-19 $$$ = $20-29 $$$$ = $30-39. If no entry under **Fee**, camping is free.

1 Anderson Park

Location: In Vernonia, about 35 miles northwest of Portland.
Sites: 20 hookup sites, up to 30 tent sites; water, electric, and sewer hookups.
Maximum length: 40 feet.
Facilities: Flush toilets, drinking water, dump station, playground.
Fee per night: $.
Management: City of Vernonia.
Contact: 503-429-5291.
Finding the campground: From Oregon 47 in Vernonia, turn southeast onto Jefferson Avenue at the sign for Anderson Park. Proceed 0.2 mile to the park.

About the campground: This peaceful park and campground are on the north bank of the upper Nehalem River near its confluence with Rock Creek. A scattering of big conifers shades the open camp. Fishing is possible in the river, and bass are ready for the taking at nearby Vernonia Lake. The northern terminus of the 21-mile Banks-Vernonia Rails-to-Trails Linear State Park is located in camp. The first 7 miles are paved for family bike rides, hikes, and strolls. The park is busiest during the first weekend in August, when Vernonia Days is held. Events celebrate logging skills, and there is a small-town parade. The campground is open year-round.

2 Barton County Park

Location: About 10 miles east of Oregon City, near Barton.
Sites: 45 hookup sites, 12 basic sites; water and electric hookups.
Maximum length: 40 feet.
Facilities: Tables, grills, flush toilets, drinking water, showers, dump station, telephone, playground, horseshoe pits, sports fields, boat ramp (drift boat or raft).
Fee per night: $$.
Management: Clackamas County.
Contact: 503-655-8521; 503-650-3484 for reservations.
Finding the campground: From Oregon 224 at Barton, 9 miles northwest of Estacada or 9.5 miles southeast of Exit 12, Interstate 205 north of Oregon City, go southwest at the sign for the park on Bakers Ferry Road, drive 0.2 mile, and bear left to enter the park.

About the campground: At this park on the Clackamas River, campsites are secluded in the trees or lined up at the edge of the woods ringing a central lawn above the river. Big cottonwood, ash, and cedar trees contribute shade. The park is a popular river take-out point for rafters who start their float at Milo McIver State Park (northwest of Estacada, off OR 224). Fishing and swimming are also popular, and there is a large, riverside day-use area. The campground is open from May 1 to September 30.

3 Big Eddy

Location: About 8 miles north of Vernonia.
Sites: 19 hookup sites, 10 tent sites; water and electric hookups.
Maximum length: 40 feet.
Facilities: Tables, grills, flush toilets, drinking water, dump station, telephone, playground, horseshoe pits, primitive boat launch.
Fee per night: $$.
Management: Columbia County.
Contact: 503-429-6982.
Finding the campground: Drive 7.8 miles north of Vernonia on Oregon 47. The park is on the left (west) side of the highway.

About the campground: Situated on a bend of the Nehalem River where an eddy occurs is this large, mostly shaded family campground with gravel site parking. Ample lawn and tall firs and cedars contribute to the camp atmosphere, and alders and bigleaf maples line the riverbank. The river is open to drift boats and canoes, and fishing is popular. You may want to make the trip to Vernonia to see the Banks-Vernonia Rail Trail, Vernonia Days (in August), and the Columbia County Historical Museum. The campground is open year-round.

4 Clatskanie City Park

Location: In Clatskanie, about 60 miles northwest of Portland.
Sites: 4 hookup sites, open areas for dry camping and tent camping; water, electric, and sewer hookups.
Maximum length: 40 feet.
Facilities: Flush toilets, drinking water, showers (at city pool during summer months), playground, horseshoe pits, volleyball, ball fields, tennis and basketball courts, swimming pool, boat launch, picnic shelters.
Fee per night: $ to $$.
Management: City of Clatskanie.
Contact: 503-728-2038.
Finding the campground: From U.S. Highway 30 in Clatskanie, 1 block east of the traffic signal at Nehalem Street, turn north onto Conyers Street, go 1 block, and turn right onto Park Street to enter this city park/campground.

About the campground: This city park welcomes overnighters with four gravel hookup sites, dry camping in the parking area, and tent camping anywhere on the grounds except the picnic area. The park is an attractive, groomed recreational facility, bordered by the tide-influenced Clatskanie River on two sides. If you are traveling through town on US 30, keep this camp in mind. The campground is open year-round.

5 Feyrer Memorial County Park

Location: About 2 miles southeast of Molalla and 40 miles south of Portland.
Sites: 20 hookup sites; water and electric hookups.
Maximum length: 40 feet.
Facilities: Tables, grills, flush toilets, drinking water, showers, dump station, telephone, playground, horseshoes, sports fields, raft/drift boat ramp.
Fee per night: $$.
Management: Clackamas County.
Contact: 503-655-8521.
Finding the campground: From Oregon 211 on the east side of Molalla, turn south onto South Mathias Road and go 0.3 mile. Bear left (east) on Feyrer Park Road and drive 1.5 miles to reach the campground on the left. The boat ramp is on the right.

About the campground: This park along the Molalla River offers both camping and day use. Campsites have paved parking and are set back from the day-use area at the edge of a mature forest of cedar, maple, and Douglas-fir, with an effusive green understory. Family recreation, fishing, and wading engage campers. The shallow Molalla River flows over a rocky bed with cobble bars and a forested far shore. The campground is open from May 1 to September 30.

6 Hudson/Parcher County Park

Location: About 4 miles west of Rainier.
Sites: 15 hookup sites, 21 basic sites; water, electric, and sewer hookups.
Maximum length: 40 feet.
Facilities: Tables, fire pits, flush toilets, drinking water, showers, dump station, telephone, playground, ball field.
Fee per night: $$.
Management: Columbia County.
Contact: 503-556-9050. Reservations recommended.
Finding the campground: From Rainier, which is 48 miles northwest of Portland, go west on U.S. Highway 30 for 3.1 miles and turn left (south) onto Larson Road. Drive another 0.8 mile to reach the park.

About the campground: This family park is located on a grassy flat with mature fir, spruce, cedar, maple, and alder trees providing shade. Preacher Creek, which threads through the park, supports a population of native trout but is closed to fishing. The campground offers quiet, relaxation, and a convenient stopover for US 30 travelers passing between Portland and the coast. It also lies within easy reach of the Columbia River, where you can indulge in boating, windsurfing, and fishing. The camp is closed in December. In winter, call regarding water.

7 Oxbow County Park

Location: About 8 miles east of Gresham.
Sites: 45 basic sites; no hookups.
Maximum length: 35 feet.
Facilities: Tables, pit toilets, drinking water, telephone, playground, horseshoe pits, boat ramp. No pets allowed.
Fee per night: $$.
Management: Metro Regional Parks and Greenspaces.
Contact: 503-797-1850.
Finding the campground: From Interstate 205 in Portland, go east on Division Street and Oxbow Parkway, following signs 13 miles to the park.

About the campground: This park, wrapped in a horseshoe bend of the Sandy Wild and Scenic River, encompasses 1,000 wooded acres to explore. You can also fish, swim, canoe, raft, or go drift boating in the Sandy River. The campsites rest mainly in second-growth forest within an easy walk of the river. Areas of old-growth also remain in the park, contributing to the diversity of birds and other wildlife. Interwoven footpaths travel Alder Ridge, the bend of the river, and the river flat. A popular 10-mile float trip begins at the park and ends at Lewis and Clark State Park, which is south off I-84 east of Troutdale. Fall visitors sometimes are treated to the spectacle of spawning Chinook salmon. The campground is open year-round except when the river is high; the gates are locked at sunset.

8 Scaponia County Park

Location: About 10 miles northeast of Vernonia.
Sites: 7 basic sites; no hookups.
Maximum length: Best for tents and small units.
Facilities: Tables, grills, pit toilets, drinking water.
Fee per night: $.
Management: Columbia County.
Contact: 503-397-2353.
Finding the campground: From Vernonia, travel 5 miles north on Oregon 47 and turn right (east) onto Scappoose-Vernonia Road. Drive another 5.2 miles to reach the park, which is on the right. It is 15 miles west of Scappoose.

About the campground: This small, rustic, wayside campground rests in a second-growth forest along the slow, creek-sized East Fork Nehalem River. Although the quiet is occasionally broken by the sound of traffic, the park encourages relaxation. It has informal parking at shady lawn sites. In fall, hunters use the camp as a base.

9 Scappoose Bay Marine Park

Location: About 2 miles southwest of St. Helens.
Sites: Self-contained RV camping; no hookups.
Maximum length: 40 feet.
Facilities: Flush toilets, drinking water, pump-out station, telephone, three-lane boat launch, marina, moorage, store, deli, picnic shelter.
Fee per night: $$.
Management: Port of St. Helens.
Contact: 503-397-6924 or 503-397-2888.
Finding the campground: From U.S. Highway 30, 5 miles northwest of Scappoose and 1.5 miles southeast of St. Helens city center, turn east onto Millard Road, go 0.3 mile, and turn right onto Old Portland Road. Follow it 0.4 mile to this park on the left.

About the campground: This 23-acre facility on the Columbia River features a well-kept marina and allows self-contained, dry camping in the parking area. An RV park is planned. Some large oaks dot the grassy perimeter of the "camp." Primarily, this is a boater's access on Scappoose Bay that feeds into Multnomah Channel on the Columbia River. Nature trails allow you to stretch your legs. The campground is open year-round.

10 Scappoose RV Park

Location: About 2 miles north of Scappoose.
Sites: 7 RV sites; water, electric, and sewer hookups.
Maximum length: 40 feet.
Facilities: Tables, grills, toilets, drinking water, showers, dump station, playground.
Fee per night: $$.
Management: Columbia County.
Contact: 503-397-2353.
Finding the campground: From Scappoose, which is 20 miles northwest of Portland, go 1.5 miles north on U.S. Highway 30 and turn east onto West Lane Road at the sign for the park. Continue 0.6 mile and turn left onto North Honeyman Road. Drive 0.1 mile to reach the park on the right.

About the campground: This small, well-kept park is located near the rural airport and surrounded by open fields. It gets some noise from a nearby gravel operation, but sites are pleasant, with lawn and full shade from the park's mature firs and bigleaf maples. Scappoose celebrates Airport Appreciation Day in June and holds a Sauerkraut Festival in October. The campground is open year-round.

11 Washington County FairPlex RV

Location: In Hillsboro.
Sites: 14 RV sites, no tent sites; water and electric hookups.
Maximum length: 30 feet.
Facilities: Toilets, drinking water, showers, telephone (at fairgrounds).
Fee per night: $$.
Management: Washington County.
Contact: 503-648-1416. (Call ahead; sometimes closed for seasonal events.)
Finding the campground: The Fairplex entrance is on Cornell Road south of the Portland Hillsboro Airport, in Hillsboro.

About the campground: This small overnight facility is an extension of the main fairgrounds parking lot. The side-by-side sites are numbered; all are back-ins toward a mesh fence. The camping area overlooks a lawn and conifers. The campground is open year-round.

Mount Hood and Columbia Gorge

Two striking geographic features are the centerpieces of this region. The first is Mount Hood, the tallest, most famous, and most-climbed peak in the Cascades, Oregon's chain of dormant volcanoes. From a height of 11,235 feet, it reigns over a prized wilderness area, sweeping forests, high mountain lakes, and wild and scenic waterways. The second focal attraction is the spectacular gorge of the Columbia River, recognized as a national scenic area. More than a dozen major waterfalls streak its steep basalt walls. Sailboarders bounce across the choppy river that separates Oregon and Washington, propelled by winds funneled through the gorge.

Uniting the dynamic duo is the Mount Hood–Columbia Gorge Scenic Loop. This sightseeing drive follows Interstate 84 and the Historic Columbia River Highway east from Troutdale to the city of Hood River. From there, the tour continues south on Oregon 35 and then west on OR 26, rounding the mountain and entering Gresham. Finally, from Gresham, the tour follows 242nd Avenue north back to I-84 and Troutdale.

Historically, the Columbia River gave rise to Indian fishing camps, carried Lewis and Clark and the Corps of Discovery west, and tested the mettle of the Oregon Trail pioneers in the years before Barlow Road provided an overland route around Mount Hood and into the Willamette Valley. Mount Hood has long been an explorer's landmark, adventurer's challenge, and artist's inspiration.

Columbia River Gorge.

MOUNT HOOD AND COLUMBIA GORGE

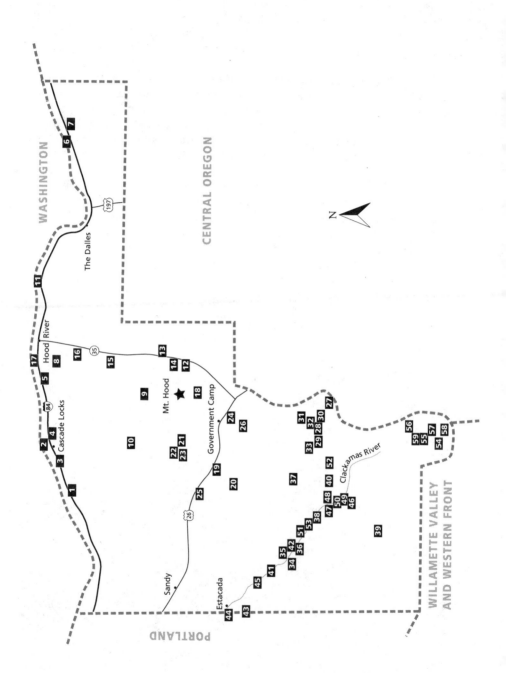

Spectacular scenery and outstanding outdoor recreation are common to both areas. The Gorge offers more attractions and pursuits for sightseers, while Mount Hood tends to draw an active crowd, including downhill and cross-country skiers, snowboarders, snowmobilers, anglers, hikers, climbers, golfers, and huckleberry pickers. Mount Hood is one of the few areas in the country to offer summer downhill skiing.

There are plenty of active pursuits available in the Gorge, too, including hiking, sturgeon fishing, windsurfing, and boating, but there are also museums, visitor centers, historic walking tours, Bonneville Dam and fish hatchery, cherry and apple orchards, and sternwheeler and historic train rides. Both areas feature historic lodges, wonderful campgrounds, and superb vistas, and although both are popular playgrounds for the Portland metropolitan area, they still embrace unspoiled places for quiet reflection.

Visitors to this region enjoy four distinct seasons. At the higher elevations, you will find cool summer temperatures and winter snow. At the lower elevations, the weather generally remains mild most of the year, although the drier, eastern end of the Gorge can heat up in summer. West winds typically funnel through the Gorge in summer. In winter, winds penetrating the Gorge may be icy, making travel treacherous and turning the waterfalls into frozen works of art. Rain is more common in winter, both in the Gorge and on the lower slopes of the mountain.

CASCADE LOCKS–MULTNOMAH FALLS AREA

		Hookup sites	Total sites	Max. RV length	Hookups	Toilets	Showers	Drinking water	Dump station	Recreation	Fee	Can reserve
1	Ainsworth State Park	45	45	60	WES	F	•	•	•	H	$$	
2	Cascade Locks Marine Park		30	35		F	•	•	•	FBL	$$	
3	Eagle Creek		19	20		F		•		H	$$	
4	Herman Creek Horse Camp		7	24		NF		•		HR	$	
5	Wyeth		17	32		F		•		H	$	

Hookups: W = Water E = Electric S = Sewer **Total sites:** T = Tent-only campground **Maximum trailer/RV length** given in feet.
Toilets: F = Flush NF = No Flush **Recreation:** H = Hiking S = Swimming F = Fishing B = Boating L = Boat Launch
O = Off-Highway Driving R = Horseback Riding C = Cycling
Fee: $ = $1-9 $$ = $10-19 $$$ = $20-29 $$$$ = $30-39. If no entry under **Fee**, camping is free.

1 Ainsworth State Park

Location: About 9 miles west of Cascade Locks.
Sites: 45 hookup sites; water, electric, and sewer hookups.
Maximum length: 60 feet.
Facilities: Tables, grills, flush toilets, drinking water, showers, dump station.
Fee per night: $$.
Management: Oregon State Parks and Recreation Department.
Contact: 503-695-2301.
Finding the campground: Take Exit 35 off Interstate 84, 35 miles east of Portland and 9 miles west of Cascade Locks. On the south side of the freeway, follow the historic highway 0.6 mile west to the park entrance on the left.

About the campground: The developed campsites rest in close proximity to one another, with non-native landscaping between them, but they serve visitors well as a base for exploring the area. The Gorge holds a wealth of scenery, trails, and historic sites that you can discover by driving west on the historic Columbia River Highway. You can hike the nearby Gorge Trail to Ponytail, Horsetail, or Triple Falls or up narrow, green Oneonta Gorge. Autumn visitors to Multnomah Falls can spy spawning salmon in the creek below the falls. At 620 feet, Multnomah Falls is the fourth tallest falls in the nation; the historic lodge—with its visitor center, gift shop, and restaurant—is a popular stop. The campground is closed in winter.

2 Cascade Locks Marine Park

Location: In Cascade Locks.
Sites: 30 basic sites; no hookups.
Maximum length: 35 feet.
Facilities: Tables, flush toilets, drinking water, showers, dump station, telephone, playground, gift shop, boat ramp, small marina.
Fee per night: $$.

Management: Port of Cascade Locks.

Contact: 503-374-8619.

Finding the campground: From Interstate 84 Eastbound, take Exit 44 for Cascade Locks and go east about 0.5 mile on Wanapa Street before turning north at the sign for the marine park. Westbound travelers take Wanapa Street west from Exit 44 to the signed entry.

About the campground: A convenient place for an overnight stop, this campground sits on a groomed lawn atop a bluff overlooking the Columbia River; its central location is ideal if you want to explore the Gorge. The marine park is on the riverfront, where you can fish for salmon and sturgeon, visit the Cascade Locks Historical Museum, or book a tour on a sternwheeler. The campground is open from April 1 to late November.

3 Eagle Creek

Location: About 3 miles west of Cascade Locks.

Sites: 19 basic sites; no hookups.

Maximum length: 20 feet.

Facilities: Tables, grills, flush toilets, drinking water.

Fee per night: $$.

Management: Forest Service.

Contact: 503-386-2333.

Finding the campground: From Interstate 84, eastbound, 3 miles west of Cascade Locks, take Exit 41 to reach the campground. If you are westbound on I-84 from Cascade Locks, follow I-84 west 4 miles to the Bonneville Dam exit to get onto I-84 headed east, and then proceed 1 mile to Exit 41 and then on to the camp.

About the campground: This small, family campground is tucked away on a wooded hillside above Eagle Creek. Trails lead up the creek, past picturesque waterfalls, and into the Mark O. Hatfield Wilderness. Others trace the southern wall of the Gorge or climb the hills. In the fall, salmon migrate up the gravelly bed of Eagle Creek, sometimes drawing bald eagles to the canyon. Next door to the campground is the Cascade Salmon Fish Hatchery, but it does not encourage visitors. However, Bonneville Dam, to the west, has a visitor center with fish-viewing windows as well as a fish hatchery that can spark the imaginations of anglers. The campground is open from May 1 to October 1.

4 Herman Creek Horse Camp

Location: About 2 miles east of Cascade Locks.

Sites: 7 basic sites; no hookups.

Maximum length: 24 feet.

Facilities: Tables, grills, vault toilets, drinking water.

Fee per night: $.

Management: Forest Service.

Contact: 503-386-2333.

Finding the campground: From the east end of Cascade Locks, follow Forest Lane east for 1.7 miles, quickly crossing to the south side of Interstate 84. Past the Herman Creek Work Center, turn right into the campground.

About the campground: Located east of Herman Creek in a low-elevation forest is this small, basic camp facility, which can accommodate stock. The trail up Herman Creek into the Mark O. Hatfield Wilderness begins on the west side of the camp and ascends to Wahtum Lake, the Pacific Crest National Scenic Trail (PCT), and a host of other possible trail connections. Individuals with horses can transport them across the Bridge of the Gods into Washington to follow the PCT north; there is parking at the end of the bridge. This camp is also a potential base from which to fish or participate in the other activities at Cascade Locks. The campground is open from mid-May to October.

5 Wyeth

Location: About 8 miles east of Cascade Locks.
Sites: 17 basic sites; no hookups.
Maximum length: 32 feet.
Facilities: Tables, grills, flush toilets, drinking water.
Fee per night: $.
Management: Forest Service.
Contact: 503-386-2333.
Finding the campground: From Cascade Locks, drive 7 miles east on Interstate 84 to Exit 51. Take the exit and follow the county road 0.5 mile east along the south side of the freeway to the campground.

About the campground: This mostly forested campground along Gorton Creek has paved roads and sites, with ample spacing between the sites. Small firs and bigleaf maples offer shade. The Columbia River Gorge here is beginning to make the transition from the dense forests of its west end to the grassland steppes of its east end. You can access the Gorge and Wyeth Trails from the camp. Small cascades and falls are among Gorton Creek's attractions. The campground is open from May 15 to October.

THE DALLES–HOOD RIVER AREA

		Hookup sites	Total sites	Max. RV length	Hookups	Toilets	Showers	Drinking water	Dump station	Recreation	Fee	Can reserve
6	Celilo Park		open	40		F		•		SFBL		
7	Deschutes River State Recreation Area		89	30		F		•		HFBLRC	$$	
8	Kingsley County Park		20	small		NF				FBL		
9	Kinnikinnick		20	16		NF				HFBL	$$	
10	Lost Lake		117	40		NF	•	•	•	HFBLR	$$–$$$	•
11	Memaloose State Park	43	110	60	WES	F	•	•	•		$$	•
12	Robinhood		24	18		NF		•		HF	$$	
13	Routson County Park		10	T		NF		•		HF	$	
14	Sherwood		14	16		NF				HF	$$	
15	Toll Bridge County Park	65	81	40	WES	F	•	•	•	F	$$	•
16	Tucker County Park	13	79	30	WE	F	•	•		HF	$$	
17	Viento State Park	58	75	30	WE	F	•	•		H	$$	

Hookups: W = Water E = Electric S = Sewer **Total sites:** T = Tent-only campground **Maximum trailer/RV length** given in feet.
Toilets: F = Flush NF = No Flush **Recreation:** H = Hiking S = Swimming F = Fishing B = Boating L = Boat Launch
O = Off-Highway Driving R = Horseback Riding C = Cycling
Fee: $ = $1-9 $$ = $10-19 $$$ = $20-29 $$$$ = $30-39. If no entry under **Fee,** camping is free.

6 Celilo Park

Location: About 15 miles east of The Dalles.
Sites: Open camping; no hookups.
Maximum length: 40 feet.
Facilities: Flush toilets, drinking water, playground, boat launch.
Fee per night: None.
Management: U.S. Army Corps of Engineers.
Contact: 541-296-1181.
Finding the campground: From The Dalles, take Interstate 84 east 15 miles to Exit 97. The park is off this exit on the north side of the freeway.

About the campground: Formerly a day-use area, this Columbia River park now doubles as a campground, with RVs set up in the parking area and tents pitched on the lawns. Boating, fishing, and windsurfing are the preferred river activities. The cliffs and grassy hills of Washington make for attractive views across the river. Mature shade trees offer escape from the sun. The campground is open year-round.

7 | Deschutes River State Recreation Area

Location: About 18 miles east of The Dalles.
Sites: 89 basic sites; no hookups.
Maximum length: 30 feet.
Facilities: Tables, grills, flush toilets, drinking water, telephone, boat launch (on opposite shore of river), Oregon Trail exhibit.
Fee per night: $$.
Management: Oregon State Parks and Recreation Department.
Contact: 541-739-2322.
Finding the campground: From The Dalles, follow Interstate 84 east for 15 miles to Exit 97, take the exit, and head east along the south side of the freeway for 3 miles to the park entrance on the right.

About the campground: This highly appealing, grassy, and shady campground fronts the Deschutes Wild and Scenic River just upstream from its confluence with the Columbia River. The camp rests on a flat in an arid canyon of sagebrush and basalt hills. There is direct access to the riverbank at the camp, as well as footpaths that trace both shores. A bike trail explores the canyon. The world-class fishing on the Deschutes attracts fly fishers from all over, and the river is popular as well with boaters and floaters. A public boat launch is located across the way at Heritage Landing, a day-use area. Come with binoculars, because the river corridor attracts its share of birds. The campground is open year-round.

8 | Kingsley County Park

Location: About 12 miles southwest of Hood River, on Upper Green Point Reservoir.
Sites: Up to 20 open campsites; no hookups.
Maximum length: Small units.
Facilities: A few tables, fire rings, vault toilet, boat launch and dock near the dam. No drinking water.
Fee per night: None.
Management: Hood River County.
Contact: 541-387-6888.
Finding the campground: From U.S. Highway 30 in Hood River, go south on 13th Street for 0.4 mile. There, merge into 12th Street, which later becomes Tucker Road; go another 3.4 miles, taking several right angle turns to remain on Tucker. Turn right (west) onto Portland Drive and drive 2 miles to the community of Oak Grove. Bear right on Binns Hill Road, follow it 0.3 mile to Kingsley Road, turn left, and continue 5.9 miles to the park. All but the last 0.8 mile is paved.

About the campground: This park offers open, primitive camping along the east shore of Upper Green Point Reservoir. The sites are scattered through the select-cut forest of fir. Parking is what you can make of it, but the sites are generally well shaded. This moderate-sized reservoir welcomes boating (maximum 5 miles per hour) and fishing; Mount Defiance, topped by a radio tower, rises across the reservoir. The campground is open when free of snow.

9 Kinnikinnick

Location: About 24 miles southwest of Hood River, on Laurance Lake.
Sites: 20 basic sites; no hookups.
Maximum length: 16 feet.
Facilities: Tables, grills, vault toilets, small boat ramp (non-motorized boating). No drinking water.
Fee per night: $$.
Management: Forest Service.
Contact: 541-352-6002.
Finding the campground: From Hood River, go south on Oregon 35 for 14 miles and bear right (west) on Cooper Spur Road at Mount Hood Corner. Proceed 4.6 miles and turn right onto Forest Road 2840 (Evans Creek Road), which bears signs for Laurance Lake. Continue another 5 miles to the lake and campground.

About the campground: This camp along Laurance Lake, a reservoir on the Clear Branch of the Middle Fork Hood River, sits at the northern foot of Mount Hood, but the only views of the landmark peak are those gained while rowing and fishing the lake or hiking area trails. The sites occupy a dry, conifer forest, and a cliff forms one side of the lake basin. Although the area near the dam is open, brush adds to the character of the lake elsewhere. Jumbles of rocks provide habitat for pikas; look for the big-eared rodents with the high-pitched squeak. From the camp, you can head south along Cooper Spur Road through the Cloud Cap-Tilly Jane Historic Area, an old mining district. If you continue on, you come to the Cloud Cap Inn, built in 1889, from which you will have a superb view of Mount Hood and access to the Timberline Trail. Clark's nutcrackers favor the alpine trees at Cloud Cap. The campground is open from mid-May to October.

10 Lost Lake

Location: About 25 miles southwest of Hood River, on Lost Lake.
Sites: 80 basic sites, 31 walk-in tent sites, 6 horse sites, some cabins; no hookups.
Maximum length: 40 feet.
Facilities: Tables, grills, vault toilets, drinking water, showers, dump station, boat rental, boat ramp (non-motorized boating), fish-cleaning stations, barrier-free trails, corrals.
Fee per night: $$ to $$$.
Management: Forest Service.
Contact: 541-352-6002; 541-386-6366 for reservations.
Finding the campground: From U.S. Highway 30 (Oak Street) in Hood River, go south on 13th Street, following the signs for Odell and Parkdale. As the route weaves out of town, it becomes Tucker Road/Hood River Highway. After 3 miles the route turns left; after another 2 miles bear right, bypassing Tucker Park. Drive another 2.2 miles to a small village, where you turn right toward Dee and Lost Lake. Continue 4 miles, bear right at the Parkdale-Dee Junction for 0.2 mile, and then keep left to follow Lost Lake Road the remaining 13.4 miles to the campground.

About the campground: While it takes a bit of navigating to get there, Lost Lake and its neighborhood more than satisfy. The 290-acre, triangular lake offers quiet boating, fine fishing, and some of the best clear-day views of Mount Hood to be had anywhere. Old-growth forest and rhododendrons shape glorious realms to explore or savor at camp. Set back from shore on a wooded slope, the camp is highly attractive and orderly, with paved roads and parking. The camp concession operator assigns sites based on party size and the number of vehicles. Some sites are split-level, with the tables and grills on a different terrace than the parking. An ample day-use area provides lake access for all. Trails explore the lakeshore, an old-growth grove, Lost Lake Butte, and the Old Skyline route. Horse groups have access to the Old Skyline Trail. The Old-Growth Trail and the eastern part of the Lakeshore Trail are barrier free, with long stretches of boardwalk. The campground is open from May to mid-October.

Mount Hood from Lost Lake.

11 Memaloose State Park

Location: 11 miles west of The Dalles.
Sites: 43 hookup sites; 67 basic sites; water, electric, and sewer hookups.
Maximum length: 60 feet.
Facilities: Tables, grills, flush toilets, drinking water, showers, dump station, telephone.
Fee per night: $$.

Management: Oregon State Parks and Recreation Department.
Contact: 541-478-3008; 1-800-452-5687 for reservations.
Finding the campground: From The Dalles, drive 11 miles west on Interstate 84. The campground is on the north side of the interstate. Westbound access only.

About the campground: This park takes the name of an island in the Columbia River that was used by Indians as a sacred burial ground and was flooded by the damming of the river. The landscaped camp rests above the river and below the freeway; planted shade trees bring added comfort to a stay. Because there is no river access from the park, visitors must seek entertainment away from the camp. The Columbia Gorge welcomes fishing, hiking, boating, windsurfing, and sightseeing. Historic The Dalles and the Columbia Gorge Discover Center at the outskirts of town warrant a look. The campground is open from mid-April to late October.

12 Robinhood

Location: 28 miles south of Hood River.
Sites: 24 basic sites; no hookups.
Maximum length: 18 feet.
Facilities: Tables, grills, vault toilets, drinking water.
Fee per night: $$.
Management: Forest Service.
Contact: 541-352-6002.
Finding the campground: It is west off Oregon 35, 28 miles south of Hood River and 10 miles north of the OR 35-U.S. Highway 26 junction.

About the campground: This family campground is situated in the fir-hemlock forest along the East Fork Hood River, a milky waterway that pours off Mount Hood. The rocky streambed further contributes to the river's turbulence. Trails explore the riverbank and climb to Badger Creek Wilderness. Special fishing regulations apply on this river. The campground is open from late May to mid-October.

13 Routson County Park

Location: About 21 miles south of Hood River.
Sites: 10 tent sites; no hookups.
Maximum length: Suitable for tents only.
Facilities: Some tables and grills, flush toilets, drinking water.
Fee per night: $.
Management: Hood River County.
Contact: 541-387-6888.
Finding the campground: From Hood River, drive 20.7 miles south on Oregon 35. The camp is on the east side of the highway at the end of a short, narrow gravel road overhung with trees.

About the campground: While this park offers running water and toilets, the sites are primitive and scattered somewhat randomly. They occupy a stand of tall firs set slightly back from the East Fork Hood River, a racing stream of glacial runoff from Mount Hood. Special fishing regulations apply. While small RV units can park on the earthen flat of the camp, the blind access road with its overhanging limbs and the tight turnaround in the camp make this park more suitable for tent campers. An impressive cliff claims the opposite bank of the East Fork. The campground is open from April through October.

14 Sherwood

Location: About 25 miles south of Hood River.
Sites: 14 basic sites; no hookups.
Maximum length: 16 feet.
Facilities: Tables, grills, vault toilets. No drinking water.
Fee per night: $$.
Management: Forest Service.
Contact: 541-352-6002.
Finding the campground: From Hood River, drive 24.6 miles south on Oregon 35. The campground is on the west side of the highway.

About the campground: This campground on the East Fork Hood River is pleasantly forested and has access to fishing and hiking, but its proximity to OR 35 brings with it some traffic noise. Trails follow the river upstream and along Cold Spring Creek, which flows into the river north of camp. Tamanawas Falls—an elegant, broad falls with lacy streamers tumbling 100 feet over a basalt cliff—puts an exclamation mark on the journey up Cold Spring Creek. Special fishing regulations are in effect for both the river and creek to protect salmon and steelhead. The campground is open from late May to mid-October.

15 Toll Bridge County Park

Location: About 15 miles south of Hood River.
Sites: 65 full and partial hookup sites, 16 tent sites; water, electric, and sewer hookups.
Maximum length: 40 feet.
Facilities: Tables, grills, flush toilets, drinking water, showers, dump station, telephone.
Fee per night: $$.
Management: Hood River County.
Contact: 541-352-5522 for information and reservations.
Finding the campground: From Hood River, go 15 miles south on Oregon 35, turn right (west) onto Toll Bridge Road, and continue 0.3 mile to this campground on the right.

About the campground: This campground and its large, adjacent day-use area sit along the East Fork Hood River, a turbulent, cloudy, glacial-fed waterway racing down off Mount Hood. The full hookup sites occupy a more park-like setting, with lawn shaded by pines and firs. Elsewhere, the campsites are tucked into a semi-open, mixed woodland, with riparian vegetation and tree species common to both eastern and western Oregon. Fishing and touring the orchard country of Hood River County may provide amusement. In Parkdale, you may want to visit the Hutson Museum to view its Native American, pioneer, and gemstone collections. The campground is open from April through September.

16 Tucker County Park

Location: About 5 miles south of Hood River.
Sites: 13 hookup sites, 66 basic sites; water and electric hookups.
Maximum length: 30 feet.
Facilities: Tables, grills, flush toilets, drinking water, showers, telephone, playground, horseshoe pits.
Fee per night: $$.
Management: Hood River County.
Contact: 541-387-6888.
Finding the campground: From U.S. Highway 30 in Hood River, go south on 13th Street for 0.4 mile. There, merge into 12th Street, which later becomes Tucker Road; go another 4.3 miles, taking several right angle turns to remain on Tucker. Bear right on Hood River Highway toward Dee and drive 0.4 mile to the park entrance on the right.

About the campground: This family campground sits in an open, mostly natural forest setting of ponderosa pine and oak above the Hood River. Noisy and turbulent, the river courses past the camp, frequented occasionally by wood ducks. A short nature and river-access trail leads to viewpoints. The camp lies within convenient reach of the Columbia River Gorge to the north, and you can get to Lost Lake by traveling southwest on Hood River Highway and Forest Road 13. The campground is open from April 1 to October 31.

17 Viento State Park

Location: 8 miles west of Hood River.
Sites: 58 hookup sites, 17 basic sites; water and electric hookups.
Maximum length: 30 feet.
Facilities: Tables, grills, flush toilets, drinking water, showers, telephone.
Fee per night: $$.
Management: Oregon State Parks and Recreation Department.
Contact: 541-374-8811.
Finding the campground: From Hood River, drive 8 miles west on Interstate 84. The main campground is just north of the freeway, while the tent sites are on the south side.

About the campground: Among the maples and oaks with areas of lawn, this campground just off the interstate is convenient for both through-travelers and visitors to the Columbia River Gorge National Scenic Area. The separate tent area occupies a more natural woodland setting. The Columbia River is a 0.2-mile walk from camp. The park can also serve as a base for visits to Bonneville Dam, Cascade Locks, and Washington State; waterfall-sightseeing along the Old Scenic Highway; and windsurfing at Koberg Beach in Hood River. For hiking, head to Starvation Creek State Park (2 miles west), where trails lead to Mount Defiance and the heights of the gorge. A number of other first-rate trails lead from the Old Scenic Highway, and the old road between camp and Starvation Creek Falls makes a good walking path. The campground is open from mid-April to late October.

ZIGZAG–GOVERNMENT CAMP AREA

		Hookup sites	Total sites	Max. RV length	Hookups	Toilets	Showers	Drinking water	Dump station	Recreation	Fee	Can reserve
18	Alpine		16	T		NF		•		H	$	
19	Camp Creek		25	30		NF		•		HFR	$$	•
20	Green Canyon		15	22		NF		•		HSF	$$	
21	Lost Creek		15	22		NF		•		HF	$$	•
22	McNeil		34	22		NF				H	$	
23	Riley Horse Camp		14	16		NF		•		HR	$$	•
24	Still Creek		27	25		NF		•		H	$$	
25	Tollgate		15	16		NF		•		HFR	$$	•
26	Trillium Lake		57	40		NF		•		HSFBL	$$	•

Hookups: W = Water E = Electric S = Sewer **Total sites:** T = Tent-only campground **Maximum trailer/RV length** given in feet.
Toilets: F = Flush NF = No Flush **Recreation:** H = Hiking S = Swimming F = Fishing B = Boating L = Boat Launch
O = Off-Highway Driving R = Horseback Riding C = Cycling
Fee: $ = $1-9 $$ = $10-19 $$$ = $20-29 $$$$ = $30-39. If no entry under **Fee,** camping is free.

18 Alpine

Location: About 4 miles north of Government Camp.
Sites: 16 tent sites; no hookups.
Maximum length: Suitable for tents only.
Facilities: Tables, grills, vault toilets, drinking water.
Fee per night: $.
Management: Forest Service.
Contact: 503-622-7674.
Finding the campground: From U.S. Highway 26 east of Government Camp, drive 4.2 miles north on Timberline Road.

About the campground: This lofty camp is in an alpine meadow just below timberline on the slopes of majestic Mount Hood. The mountain offers year-round skiing and snowboarding, is one of the most climbed peaks in the country, is ringed by the superb Timberline Trail, and is the site of the historic Timberline Lodge, with its fine stone and wood craftsmanship. This lovely, small camp is best suited to tents, although some small RV units do venture to this spot. The camp tends to be a little more lively than others, appealing to snowboarders. The campground is open from July through September.

19 Camp Creek

Location: About 5 miles east of Zigzag.
Sites: 25 basic sites; no hookups.
Maximum length: 30 feet.
Facilities: Tables, grills, vault toilets, drinking water.

Old-growth forest.

Fee per night: $$.
Management: Forest Service.
Contact: 503-622-7674; 1-800-280-CAMP for reservations.
Finding the campground: It is south off U.S. Highway 26, 19.2 miles east of Sandy and 2.6 miles east of Rhododendron.

About the campground: In a deep, old-growth forest alongside sparkling Camp Creek sits this inviting campground, which makes an ideal base for exploring the Mount Hood area. The camp oozes charm with its many big trees and rich greenery. A small tributary through the camp supports bountiful skunk cabbage, pungent in spring. The sites have defined, surfaced parking and are well spaced for comfort. Creek fishing, hiking, and sightseeing may pull you away from the camp. The Pioneer Bridle Trail parallels US 26 at the north side of the campground, following the route of the Oregon Trail. Zigzag Falls and Flag Mountain Trails are also not far from camp; a visit to the Mount Hood Visitor Information Center in Zigzag (south off US 26 west of camp) will help you with trip planning. The campground is open from late May to late September.

20 Green Canyon

Location: About 5 miles south of Zigzag.
Sites: 15 basic sites; no hookups.
Maximum length: 22 feet.
Facilities: Tables, grills, vault toilets, drinking water.
Fee per night: $$.
Management: Forest Service.
Contact: 503-622-7674.
Finding the campground: From U.S. Highway 26 at Zigzag, go south on Forest Road 2618 (Salmon River Road) for 4.5 miles to reach the campground entrance on the right.

About the campground: On a flat covered in old-growth forest along the Salmon Wild and Scenic River, you will find this quiet retreat from the flurry of activity around Mount Hood. It can also serve as a base from which to join that flurry. The Mount Hood area boasts fishing, quiet boating, hiking, berry picking, sightseeing, history tracking, and summer skiing; a stop at the Mount Hood Visitor Center in Zigzag can help you plot your itinerary. Near camp, trails parallel the Salmon River; one leads upstream into the Salmon-Huckleberry Wilderness. The more challenging Green Canyon Way Trail begins across the road from camp and strikes straight uphill into the wilderness. The Salmon River is open to catch-and-release fishing only. The campground is open from late May to late September.

21 Lost Creek

Location: About 7 miles northeast of Zigzag.
Sites: 10 wheelchair-accessible sites, 5 pack-in/roll-in (wheelchair) sites; no hookups.
Maximum length: 22 feet.
Facilities: Tables, grills, vault toilets, drinking water; entire camp is wheelchair accessible.
Fee per night: $$.
Management: Forest Service.
Contact: 503-622-7674;1-800-280-CAMP for reservations.
Finding the campground: From U.S. Highway 26 at Zigzag, drive 4.2 miles north on Forest Road 18 (Lolo Pass Road). Turn right onto FR 1825 and follow it for another 2.7 miles to the campground entrance on the right.

About the campground: In a forest dominated by mountain hemlocks sits this picturesque campground with its level, paved sites. Lost Creek provides a soothing backdrop, and rhododendrons seasonally color the scene. A fine interpretive trail begins at camp and explores the immediate area. Fishing also entertains campers. The camp is open from May to October.

22 McNeil

Location: About 5 miles northeast of Zigzag.
Sites: 34 basic sites; no hookups.
Maximum length: 22 feet.
Facilities: Tables, grills, vault toilets. No drinking water.
Fee per night: $.
Management: Forest Service.
Contact: 503-622-7674.
Finding the campground: From U.S. Highway 26 at Zigzag, head north 4.2 miles on Forest Road 18 (Lolo Pass Road). Turn right onto FR 1825 and go 0.8 mile to enter this camp on the left.

About the campground: This camp above the Sandy River rests in an open forest of lodgepole pines on Old Maid Flat, a *lahar* (a volcanic flow of mud and debris) from Mount Hood's active days. Sites are mostly sunny and dry. Access to the river is difficult. The camp is within reach of trails in the Mount Hood Wilderness Area and lies just off the 70-mile Mount Hood Loop Drive. This loop travels Lolo Pass Road (paved and gravel) to the north side of the mountain, passes through Parkdale and Dee, and then follows Oregon 35 south and US 26 west to complete the cinch around Mount Hood. The campground is open from late May to late September.

23 Riley Horse Camp

Location: About 5 miles northeast of Zigzag.
Sites: 14 basic sites; no hookups.
Maximum length: 16 feet.
Facilities: Tables, grills, vault toilets, drinking water, tie stalls.
Fee per night: $$.
Management: Forest Service.
Contact: 503-622-7674; 1-800-280-CAMP for reservations.
Finding the campground: From U.S. Highway 26 at Zigzag, go north on Forest Road 18 (Lolo Pass Road) for 4.2 miles. Turn right (east) onto FR 1825, go 1.1 miles, and turn right onto FR 1825.382 for the camp.

About the campground: This quiet camp rests in a mixed-conifer forest at the western foot of Mount Hood, just outside Mount Hood Wilderness Area. Equestrians will find easy access to trails entering the wilderness and linking up with the Pacific Crest Trail. Lost Creek flows past the camp; the sites are mostly shaded. The horse camp is open from late May to late September.

24 Still Creek

Location: About 1 mile southeast of Government Camp.
Sites: 27 basic sites; no hookups.
Maximum length: 25 feet.
Facilities: Tables, grills, vault toilets, drinking water.
Fee per night: $$.
Management: Forest Service.
Contact: 503-622-7674.
Finding the campground: From Government Camp, go 0.5 mile east on U.S. Highway 26, turn right (south) onto Forest Road 2650, and drive 0.3 mile to the camp.

About the campground: This peaceful camp along Still Creek offers comfortable, well-spaced sites in a rich forest of hemlock and fir, with a huckleberry and mixed shrub understory. At the south end of the camp is the Old Barlow Road, which you can follow west on foot across Still Creek. A cedar post at the start indicates that you are on a section of the historic Oregon Trail. If you drive 0.4 mile east on Old Barlow Road, you come to Summit Meadows and a pioneer grave. Fishing and quiet boating are possible at Trillium Lake, only 2 miles east of camp. A day-use fee is charged. Because the Still Creek–Trillium Lake area is popular for cross-country skiing, you may want to scope out the area for winter fun. The campground is open from late May to early September.

25 Tollgate

Location: 3 miles east of Zigzag.
Sites: 15 basic sites; no hookups.
Maximum length: 16 feet.
Facilities: Tables, grills, vault toilets, drinking water, rustic picnic shelter.
Fee per night: $$.
Management: Forest Service.
Contact: 503-622-7674; 1-800-280-CAMP for reservations.
Finding the campground: It is south off U.S. Highway 26, 17 miles east of Sandy and 0.4 mile east of Rhododendron.

About the campground: While fairly close to US 26 and somewhat noisy, this cozy campground occupies a lovely forest of mature firs and cedars on a flat above the Zigzag River. It is also just west of a historic tollgate on Old Barlow Road, which was part of the Oregon Trail. You can reach the interpretive site by hiking east on the Pioneer Bridle Trail from the north end of camp or by driving 0.2 mile east on US 26. The campsites have defined, surfaced parking, but a few are a little awkward to access if you have a longer vehicle, because of the angle of approach and the trees. Special fishing rules apply to the river. If you want to hike and sightsee, you may want to visit the Mount Hood Visitor Information Center in Zigzag, which is on the south side of US 26 west of the camp. The rustic picnic shelter and remaining mossy rock fireplaces add to the camp's charm. The campground is open from late May to late September.

26 Trillium Lake

Location: About 3 miles southeast of Government Camp, on Trillium Lake.
Sites: 57 basic sites; no hookups.
Maximum length: 40 feet.
Facilities: Tables, grills, vault toilets, drinking water, telephone, boat launch, fishing pier.
Fee per night: $$.
Management: Forest Service.
Contact: 503-622-7674; 1-800-280-CAMP for reservations.
Finding the campground: From Government Camp, go 1.7 miles east on U.S. Highway 26 and turn right (south) onto Forest Road 2656. Drive 1.4 miles to the campground entrance on the right.

About the campground: This campground occupies a rich, diverse forest along the east shore of Trillium Lake, which rests in the shadow of Mount Hood. There are superb views and photographic opportunities. From the lake's small dam, you have a direct look at the volcano. Lodgepole pines, cedars, mountain hemlocks, firs, rhododendrons, and beargrass weave an enchanting backdrop for your stay. The quiet alpine lake welcomes family recreation, including non-motorized boating, fishing, and hiking on a lakeside trail. The campground is open from late May to late September.

TIMOTHY LAKE AREA

		Hookup sites	Total sites	Max. RV length	Hookups	Toilets	Showers	Drinking water	Dump station	Recreation	Fee	Can reserve
27	Clackamas Lake		46	32		NF		•		HFR	$$	•
28	Gone Creek		50	32		NF		•		HFBL	$$	•
29	Hoodview		43	32		NF		•		HFBL	$$	•
30	Joe Graham Horse Camp		14	40		NF		•		HFR	$$	•
31	Little Crater Lake		16	22		NF		•		H	$$	•
32	Oak Fork		47	32		NF		•		HFBL	$$	•
33	Pine Point		25	32		NF		•		HFBL	$$	•

Hookups: W = Water E = Electric S = Sewer **Total sites:** T = Tent-only campground **Maximum trailer/RV length** given in feet.
Toilets: F = Flush NF = No Flush **Recreation:** H = Hiking S = Swimming F = Fishing B = Boating L = Boat Launch
O = Off-Highway Driving R = Horseback Riding C = Cycling
Fee: $ = $1-9 $$ = $10-19 $$$ = $20-29 $$$$ = $30-39. If no entry under **Fee**, camping is free.

27 Clackamas Lake

Location: About 20 miles south of Government Camp.
Sites: 46 basic sites (horses allowed in sites 1–19); no hookups.
Maximum length: 32 feet.
Facilities: Tables, grills, vault toilets, drinking water, hitching posts, pioneer cabin monument.
Fee per night: $$.
Management: Forest Service.
Contact: 541-328-6211; 1-800-280-CAMP for reservations.
Finding the campground: From Government Camp, go 11.5 miles southeast on U.S. Highway 26 and turn right onto paved Forest Road 42 (Skyline Road). Follow it another 8.6 miles and turn left. Drive 0.1 mile more to the campground entrance on the left.

About the campground: This campground occupies a forest at the upper edge of Clackamas Meadow, the site of the historic Miller Cabin. A boardwalk path leads to tiny, spring-fed Clackamas Lake, which feeds into the scenic Oak Grove Fork Clackamas River. Campsites are generally shaded amid fir, larch, and mountain hemlock. Outings from camp include following the Miller Trail to the Pacific Crest Trail and visiting Timothy Lake or the Clackamas Historic Ranger Station.

28 Gone Creek

Location: About 21 miles south of Government Camp, on Timothy Lake.
Sites: 50 basic sites; no hookups.
Maximum length: 32 feet.
Facilities: Tables, grills, vault toilets, drinking water, boat launch.
Fee per night: $$.

Management: Forest Service.
Contact: 503-622-7674; 1-800-280-CAMP for reservations.
Finding the campground: From Government Camp, go 11.5 miles southeast on U.S. Highway 26 and turn right onto paved Forest Road 42 (Skyline Road). Follow it for 8.3 miles, turn right onto FR 57, and proceed 1.6 miles to the campground on the right.

About the campground: This campground on the south shore of manmade Timothy Lake sits in a mixed-age conifer forest with several older firs and hemlocks towering above camp. Most sites are only partially shaded. Mount Hood is visible across the reservoir. Camp stays are spent boating (10 miles per hour maximum), fishing, or hiking the Timothy Lake Trail.

29 Hoodview

Location: About 22 miles south of Government Camp, on Timothy Lake.
Sites: 43 basic sites; no hookups.
Maximum length: 32 feet.
Facilities: Tables, grills, vault toilets, drinking water, boat launch.
Fee per night: $$.
Management: Forest Service.
Contact: 503-622-7674; 1-800-280-CAMP for reservations.
Finding the campground: From Government Camp, go 11.5 miles southeast on U.S. Highway 26 and turn right onto paved Forest Road 42 (Skyline Road). Follow it for 8.3 miles, turn right onto FR 57, and proceed 2.6 miles to the campground on the right.

About the campground: On the south shore of manmade Timothy Lake, this campground boasts some big fir and mountain hemlock trees in a mixed-age forest that offers good shade. In early summer, rhododendron pom-poms decorate camp. Premium-priced sites overlook the lake, and Mount Hood is visible across the water to the north. Boating (10 miles per hour maximum), fishing, and the 13-mile Timothy Lake Trail, which circles the reservoir, will keep you occupied.

30 Joe Graham Horse Camp

Location: About 19 miles south of Government Camp.
Sites: 14 basic sites; no hookups.
Maximum length: 40 feet.
Facilities: Tables, grills, vault toilets, drinking water, corrals.
Fee per night: $$.
Management: Forest Service.
Contact: 541-328-6211; 1-800-280-CAMP for reservations.
Finding the campground: From Government Camp, go 11.5 miles southeast on U.S. Highway 26 and turn right onto paved Forest Road 42 (Skyline Road). Follow it another 7.2 miles and turn left onto FR 021 to the horse camp.

About the campground: This campground rests amid beautiful old-growth firs and hemlocks, adjacent to the Oak Grove Fork Clackamas River and picturesque Clackamas Meadow. For the exclusive use of equestrians, this campground has large pole corrals and spacious sites to accommodate horse trailers and camp vehicles. It offers a peaceful, attractive stay and has access to area horse and hiking trails and fishing. The campground is open from mid-May to mid-September.

31 Little Crater Lake

Location: About 18 miles south of Government Camp, on Little Crater Lake.
Sites: 16 basic sites; no hookups.
Maximum length: 22 feet.
Facilities: Tables, grills, vault toilets, drinking water, paved trail to Little Crater Lake.
Fee per night: $$.
Management: Forest Service.
Contact: 541-328-6211; 1-800-280-CAMP for reservations.
Finding the campground: From Government Camp, go 11.5 miles southeast on U.S. Highway 26 and turn right onto paved Forest Road 42 (Skyline Road). Follow it 4.1 miles and turn right onto paved FR 58, heading toward High Rock. Go 2.3 miles and turn left to enter the campground.

About the campground: Little Crater Lake, the star attraction of this camp, is an artesian-fed, remarkably clear lake. Though only an acre in size, it is 45 feet deep and only 34 degrees F. It displays dazzling color and is so clear that you can see silvery logs way at its bottom. The lake's rustic viewing platform is at the end of a pleasant meadow walk from camp; watch for wildlife. Lupine, gentian, and false hellebore color the meadow. The earthen trail beyond the lake links to the Pacific Crest Trail in half a mile, allowing for more strenuous hiking adventures. The campground itself sits in the forest at meadow's edge and has gravel parking and basic amenities.

32 Oak Fork

Location: About 21 miles south of Government Camp, on Timothy Lake.
Sites: 47 basic sites; no hookups.
Maximum length: 32 feet.
Facilities: Tables, grills, vault toilets, drinking water, boat launch, dock.
Fee per night: $$.
Management: Forest Service.
Contact: 541-328-6211; 1-800-280-CAMP for reservations.
Finding the campground: From Government Camp, go 11.5 miles southeast on U.S. Highway 26 and turn right onto paved Forest Road 42 (Skyline Road). Follow it for 8.3 miles, turn right onto FR 57, and proceed 1.4 miles to the campground on the right.

About the campground: This campground on the southeast shore of Timothy Lake has sites set back from the reservoir. It enjoys full shade and has a richer atmosphere than the other lakeside campgrounds. It has gravel parking pads like its neighbors. Some sites have pull-thrus and some have lake views. For recreation, you can go boating (10 miles per hour maximum), fishing, or hiking on the Timothy Lake or Miller Trails.

33 Pine Point

Location: About 23 miles south of Government Camp, on Timothy Lake.
Sites: 25 basic sites; no hookups.
Maximum length: 32 feet.
Facilities: Tables, grills, vault toilets, drinking water, boat launch.
Fee per night: $$.
Management: Forest Service.
Contact: 503-622-7674; 1-800-280-CAMP for reservations.
Finding the campground: From Government Camp, go 11.5 miles southeast on U.S. Highway 26 and turn right onto paved Forest Road 42 (Skyline Road). Follow it for 8.3 miles, turn right onto FR 57, and proceed 3.2 miles to the campground on the right.

About the campground: This campground occupies a second-growth forest on the southwest shore of Timothy Lake, a manmade reservoir with gravelly sand beaches. Timber cutting has made a patchwork of the enfolding hills. Located near the dam, the campground has semi-open sites with gravel pads and some pull-thrus. Several of the sites have lake views. A boating speed limit of 10 miles per hour helps to maintain the quiet of the area; you can also enjoy fishing or hiking on the Timothy Lake Trail, which winds through the forest and along the shore.

ESTACADA–CLACKAMAS RIVER AREA

	Hookup sites	Total sites	Max. RV length	Hookups	Toilets	Showers	Drinking water	Dump station	Recreation	Fee	Can reserve
34 Armstrong		12	16		NF		•		FB	$$	•
35 Carter Bridge		19	28		NF				FBL	$	
36 Fish Creek		24	16		NF		•		FB	$$	•
37 Hideaway Lake		9	16		NF				HFB	$	
38 Indian Henry		86	25		F		•	•	HFB	$$	•
39 Kingfisher		23	16		NF		•		F	$$	•
40 Lake Harriet		13	20		NF		•		FBL	$$	
41 Lazy Bend		21	16		F		•		FB	$$	•
42 Lockaby		30	20		NF		•		FBL	$$	•
43 Metzler County Park	46	70	35	WE	F	•	•	•	HSF	$$	•
44 Milo McIver State Park	44	48	50	WE	F	•	•	•	HFBLRC	$$	•
45 Promontory Park Resort		58	35		F	•	•		FBL	$$	•
46 Raab		27	25		NF				SF	$$	•
47 Rainbow		17	16		NF		•		HF	$$	•
48 Ripplebrook		13	16		NF		•		F	$$	
49 Riverford		9	20		NF				F	$$	•
50 Riverside		16	22		NF		•		HF	$$	•
51 Roaring River		19	16		NF		•		HF	$$	•
52 Shellrock Creek		7	16		NF				HF	$	
53 Sunstrip		9	18		NF		•		FB	$$	•

Hookups: W = Water E = Electric S = Sewer **Total sites:** T = Tent-only campground **Maximum trailer/RV length** given in feet.
Toilets: F = Flush NF = No Flush **Recreation:** H = Hiking S = Swimming F = Fishing B = Boating L = Boat Launch
O = Off-Highway Driving R = Horseback Riding C = Cycling
Fee: $ = $1-9 $$ = $10-19 $$$ = $20-29 $$$$ = $30-39. If no entry under **Fee**, camping is free.

34 Armstrong

Location: About 14 miles southeast of Estacada.
Sites: 12 basic sites; no hookups.
Maximum length: 16 feet.
Facilities: Tables, grills, vault toilets, drinking water.
Fee per night: $$.
Management: Forest Service.
Contact: 503-630-6861; 1-800-280-CAMP for reservations.
Finding the campground: From Estacada, go 14.1 miles southeast on Oregon 224 to enter this camp on the right.

About the campground: Part of the Clackamas Wild and Scenic River lineup of campgrounds, this facility offers sites with gravel parking in a setting of young cedar and maple trees. It sits at the foot of a slope near a bridge and has a grassy bank for easy river access. The campground is open from May to October.

35 Carter Bridge

Location: About 14 miles southeast of Estacada.
Sites: 19 basic sites; no hookups.
Maximum length: 28 feet.
Facilities: Tables, grills, vault toilets. No drinking water.
Fee per night: $.
Management: Forest Service.
Contact: 503-630-6861.
Finding the campground: From Estacada, go 13.6 miles southeast on Oregon 224 to enter this camp on the left.

About the campground: This Clackamas River camp occupies a young forest of cedars, maples, and alders but still enjoys a nice amount of shade. The camp is just downstream from a whitewater launch site and, like most of its overnight counterparts, it offers fishing access to the river. The campground is open from May to October.

36 Fish Creek

Location: About 14 miles southeast of Estacada.
Sites: 24 basic sites; no hookups.
Maximum length: 16 feet.
Facilities: Tables, grills, vault toilets, drinking water.
Fee per night: $$.
Management: Forest Service.
Contact: 503-630-6861; 1-800-280-CAMP for reservations.
Finding the campground: From Estacada, go 14.2 miles southeast on Oregon 224 and turn right onto Fish Creek Road to enter the camp.

About the campground: This campground claims an attractive, forested bench along the Clackamas River. Rhododendrons provide seasonal color. Fishing attracts most river visitors, and fly rods are the most popular weapons. Early in the year, kayaking and rafting lure enthusiasts. The campground is open from May to October.

37 Hideaway Lake

Location: About 41 miles southeast of Estacada, on Hideaway Lake.
Sites: 9 basic sites; no hookups.
Maximum length: 16 feet.
Facilities: Tables, grills, pit toilets. No drinking water.
Fee per night: $.
Management: Forest Service.
Contact: 503-630-4256.
Finding the campground: From Estacada, go 25 miles southeast on Oregon

224 and continue east on Forest Road 57 for another 7.3 miles. Turn left (north) onto FR 58, go 3.1 miles, and turn left (west) onto FR 5830. Proceed another 5.3 miles, and turn left to reach the camp in 0.2 mile.

About the campground: This rustic camp, best suited for tenters, provides access to an idyllic, 12-acre lake tucked away in a hemlock-fir forest. Thirty feet deep, Hideaway Lake naturally produces rainbow and brown trout. Inflatable rafts serve anglers well, because dense vegetation makes shore access difficult. Hikers may follow the Shellrock Trail from the northwest shore of Hideaway Lake to Rock Lakes Basin Loop. This all-day hike or backpacking trip visits additional, remote lakes, which offer solitude and fishing. Serene Lake is the largest of the lakes you can hike to. Views along the trail are few but stretch from Mount Jefferson to Mount Rainier in Washington. The blooms of beargrass and rhododendrons seasonally perk up the forest. The campground is open from mid-June to September.

38 Indian Henry

Location: About 21 miles southeast of Estacada.
Sites: 86 basic sites; no hookups.
Maximum length: 25 feet.
Facilities: Tables, grills, flush toilets, drinking water, dump station.
Fee per night: $$.
Management: Forest Service.
Contact: 503-630-6861; 1-800-280-CAMP for reservations.
Finding the campground: From Estacada, go 20.5 miles southeast on Oregon 224 and bear right on Forest Road 4620 just before the bridge. Continue 0.6 mile to enter the camp on the left; the Clackamas River Trail is on the right.

About the campground: This Clackamas River campground offers paved parking in a tall, old-growth forest of hemlock, cedar, and fir. Rotting logs, vine maples, and ferns contribute to the textured forest setting. You can access the 8-mile river trail across the road from the camp; midway, a spur trail will take you to Pup Falls. Fishing and rafting are the most popular river pursuits. The campground is open from May to October.

39 Kingfisher

Location: About 34 miles southeast of Estacada.
Sites: 23 basic sites; no hookups.
Maximum length: 16 feet.
Facilities: Tables, grills, vault toilets, drinking water.
Fee per night: $$.
Management: Forest Service.
Contact: 503-630-6861; 1-800-280-CAMP for reservations.
Finding the campground: From Estacada, go 25 miles southeast on Oregon 224 to its junction with Forest Road 57 and FR 46. Bear right on FR 46, go 3.5 miles,

and turn right onto FR 63. Drive another 3.5 miles, turn right onto FR 70 toward Bagby Hot Springs, and follow it 1.7 miles to reach the campground on the left.

About the campground: This forest campground sits along the Hot Springs Fork Collawash River and is the closest developed campground to Bagby Hot Springs. Beautiful old-growth firs and cedars and a vibrant midstory contribute to the camp's allure. Gravel bars give anglers access to the river.

40 Lake Harriet

Location: About 32 miles southeast of Estacada, on Lake Harriet.
Sites: 13 basic sites; no hookups.
Maximum length: 30 feet.
Facilities: Some tables, some grills, vault toilets, drinking water.
Fee per night: $$.
Management: Forest Service.
Contact: 503-630-4256.
Finding the campground: From Estacada, go 25 miles southeast on Oregon 224 to its junction with Forest Road 57 and FR 46. Bear left on FR 57, go 6.3 miles, and turn left onto gravel FR 4630. Drive another 1.1 miles to reach the campground.

About the campground: This campground occupies the alder and fir perimeter of a large dirt parking flat where the Oak Grove Fork Clackamas River feeds into Lake Harriet, an elongated reservoir at the foot of steep forest flanks. Sites are primitive and somewhat casually arranged. A sandy boat ramp in the camp allows you to launch a rowboat or raft. No motors are allowed on the lake. Fishing is also popular.

41 Lazy Bend

Location: About 9 miles southeast of Estacada.
Sites: 21 basic sites; no hookups.
Maximum length: 16 feet.
Facilities: Tables, grills, flush toilets, drinking water.
Fee per night: $$.
Management: Forest Service.
Contact: 503-630-6861; 1-800-280-CAMP for reservations.
Finding the campground: From Estacada, go 9.3 miles southeast on Oregon 224 to enter this camp on the right.

About the campground: This campground has paved parking and enjoys a setting of firs, maples, alders, cascaras, filberts, and vine maples alongside the Clackamas River, a wild and scenic waterway. A steep, forested slope rises across the river. Anglers will find an informal riverside path heading upstream from camp. The campground is open from May to October.

42 Lockaby

Location: 14 miles southeast of Estacada.
Sites: 30 basic sites; no hookups.
Maximum length: 20 feet.
Facilities: Tables, grills, vault toilets, drinking water.
Fee per night: $$.
Management: Forest Service.
Contact: 503-630-6861; 1-800-280-CAMP for reservations.
Finding the campground: From Estacada, go 14 miles southeast on Oregon 224. The camp is on the left.

About the campground: This campground is just upstream from a raft put-in site on the Clackamas River. It occupies a narrow forest corridor of cedars, maples, dogwoods, and alders. Several sites are actually located a few strides off the campground road, but they are worth the walk to be along the river. The Clackamas is popular with anglers and provides a relaxing backdrop. The campground is open from May to October.

43 Metzler County Park

Location: About 6 miles southwest of Estacada.
Sites: 46 hookup sites, 24 basic sites; water and electric hookups.
Maximum length: 35 feet.
Facilities: Tables, barbecues, flush toilets, drinking water, showers, dump station, telephone, playground, ball fields, horseshoe pits.
Fee per night: $$.
Management: Clackamas County.
Contact: 503-655-8521.
Finding the campground: From the junction of Oregon 211 and OR 224 in south Estacada, go 3.7 miles south on OR 211, turn right (west) onto South Tucker/South Springwater Road, and continue 0.6 mile. Then turn left onto Metzler Park Road to make a steep descent into the park. Turn right into the campground after 1.8 miles.

About the campground: This charming county park is along Clear Creek, which has three swimming holes to keep campers cool in summer and which supports brook trout for anyone wishing to dunk a fishing line. The basic sites are rustic, nestled in the shade of cedars, firs, and maples closer to the creek, while the hookup sites sit farther back in a stand of younger trees. A nature trail, paired with a plant brochure, suggests a stroll. The park is ideal for family getaways. The campground is open from May 1 to September 30.

44 Milo McIver State Park

Location: About 4 miles west of Estacada.
Sites: 44 hookup sites, 4 basic sites; water and electric hookups.
Maximum length: 50 feet.
Facilities: Tables, grills, flush toilets, drinking water, showers, dump station, telephone, disc golf, boat launch, fish hatchery, picnic shelters.
Fee per night: $$.
Management: Oregon State Parks and Recreation Department.
Contact: 503-630-7150; 1-800-452-5687 for reservations.
Finding the campground: From the junction of Oregon 211 and OR 224 in Estacada, go 1 mile south on OR 211, turn right (west) onto South Hayden Road, and proceed 1.3 miles. Then turn right (north) onto South Springwater Road, go 1.2 miles more, and turn right to enter the park, following the signs to the campground.

About the campground: This large park along the Clackamas River features both groomed and natural areas. Besides its developed, wooded campground, it has sweeping, grassy picnic areas dotted by shade trees and wild, riparian woods crisscrossed by hiking and equestrian trails that suggest wildlife viewing and nature study. A bike path offers campers another way to see the park. The disc golf course covers a good-sized area, but fishing, boating, and rafting are the primary park draws. The campground is open from March 15 to October 31.

45 Promontory Park Resort

Location: 6 miles southeast of Estacada, near North Fork Reservoir.
Sites: 58 basic sites; no hookups.
Maximum length: 35 feet.
Facilities: Tables, grills, flush toilets, drinking water, showers, camp store, playground, children's fishing pond, boat moorage, boat rental, launch, docks.
Fee per night: $$.
Management: Portland General Electric.
Contact: 503-630-7229; 1-800-274-6104 for reservations.
Finding the campground: From the junction of Oregon 211 and OR 224 in south Estacada, go southeast on OR 224 for 6.1 miles and turn right. Make a quick left and follow the signs through the park to the campground.

About the campground: This campground provides access to the 350-acre North Fork Reservoir—a popular place for boating and fishing—and to 1-acre Small Fry Lake, a stocked fishing pond in which youngsters under 14 years old are allowed to catch up to three fish a day. The sites have paved parking and sit fairly close together in a forest of tall Douglas-firs. A few sites overlook the steep bank of the long, narrow reservoir. The campground is open from Memorial Day weekend to October 1.

46 Raab

Location: About 29 miles southeast of Estacada.
Sites: 27 basic sites; no hookups.
Maximum length: 25 feet.
Facilities: Tables, grills, vault toilets. No drinking water.
Fee per night: $$.
Management: Forest Service.
Contact: 503-630-4256; 1-800-280-CAMP for reservations.
Finding the campground: From Estacada, go 25 miles southeast on Oregon 224 to its junction with Forest Road 57 and FR 46. Bear right on FR 46, go 3.5 miles, and turn right onto FR 63. The campground is on the right 0.7 mile farther.

About the campground: Tall firs and cedars and an abundance of rhododendrons enclose these sites on a bluff above the Collawash River. A wire-mesh fence separates the campground from the edge of the bluff; below are enticing deep green pools. If you follow the fence upstream, you will come to an outcrop above a stretch of rushing river, a nice place from which to admire the water's beauty. Access to the river is farther upstream at a gravel bar. The campground has gravel roads and parking pads and is open from late May to early September.

47 Rainbow

Location: About 25 miles southeast of Estacada.
Sites: 17 basic sites; no hookups.
Maximum length: 16 feet.
Facilities: Tables, grills, vault toilets, drinking water.
Fee per night: $$.
Management: Forest Service.
Contact: 503-630-4256; 1-800-280-CAMP for reservations.
Finding the campground: From Estacada, go 25 miles southeast on Oregon 224 to its junction with Forest Road 57 and FR 46. Bear right on FR 46 to enter the campground on the right in less than 0.1 mile.

About the campground: The campground basks in the beauty of a multistoried forest along the Oak Grove Fork Clackamas River, above its confluence with the main Clackamas River. The forest is visually rich with Douglas-fir, cedar, moss-festooned bigleaf maple, vine maple, hazelnut, and an understory of flowers and varied shades of green. Some sites rest along the river, and its rushing current creates a pleasing backdrop throughout the camp. The Riverside Trail travels along both waterways through old-growth forest, passing between Rainbow and Riverside Campgrounds. Fishing is a popular draw. Rainbow Campground is open from May to late September.

48 Ripplebrook

Location: About 25 miles southeast of Estacada.
Sites: 13 basic sites; no hookups.
Maximum length: 16 feet.
Facilities: Tables, grills, vault toilets, drinking water.
Fee per night: $$.
Management: Forest Service.
Contact: 503-630-4256.
Finding the campground: From Estacada, go almost 25 miles southeast on Oregon 224 and turn left to enter the campground; the turn is just prior to the OR 224 junction with Forest Road 57 and FR 46.

About the campground: This campground stretches more than a quarter mile along the Oak Grove Fork Clackamas River. Douglas-firs, cedars, and bigleaf maples shade the campsites, and the understory explodes with greenery. In this linear campground, many sites have engaging riverside locations with exceptional views. Fishing and venturing away from camp to explore prized hiking trails engage visitors. The campground is open from May through September.

49 Riverford

Location: About 29 miles southeast of Estacada.
Sites: 5 basic sites, 4 walk-in tent sites; no hookups.
Maximum length: 20 feet.
Facilities: Tables, grills, vault toilets. No drinking water.
Fee per night: $$.
Management: Forest Service.
Contact: 503-630-4256.
Finding the campground: From Estacada, go 25 miles southeast on Oregon 224 to its junction with Forest Road 57 and FR 46. Bear right on FR 46 and go 3.6 miles to enter the campground on the right. The campground entrance road is 0.1 mile past the junction with FR 63.

About the campground: This small, remote campground is situated on a low bluff above the Clackamas Wild and Scenic River. The sites are shaded by mixed-age trees, and most have river views. The camp is a pleasant retreat for fishing enthusiasts. FR 63 leads toward Bagby Hot Springs and the trails that lead into the Bull of the Woods Wilderness. The campground is open from May to late September.

50 Riverside

Location: About 28 miles southeast of Estacada.
Sites: 11 basic sites, 5 walk-in tent sites; no hookups.
Maximum length: 22 feet.
Facilities: Tables, grills, vault toilets, drinking water.

Fee per night: $$.
Management: Forest Service.
Contact: 503-630-4256; 1-800-280-CAMP for reservations.
Finding the campground: From Estacada, go 25 miles southeast on Oregon 224 to its junction with Forest Road 57 and FR 46. Bear right on FR 46 and go 2.9 miles to the campground entrance on the right.

About the campground: This campground rests on a low bluff above the main Clackamas Wild and Scenic River. Some sites overlook the water, while others are wrapped in glorious forest. Grassy flats claim the forest openings. The campground has a paved road and parking pads. Birds enliven the canopy of trees with movement and song, while wily trout lure anglers. The Riverside Trail is a pleasant place to stroll. The campground is open from mid-May to late September.

51 Roaring River

Location: About 17 miles southeast of Estacada.
Sites: 19 basic sites; no hookups.
Maximum length: 16 feet.
Facilities: Tables, grills, vault toilets, drinking water.
Fee per night: $$.
Management: Forest Service.
Contact: 503-630-6861; 1-800-280-CAMP for reservations.
Finding the campground: From Estacada, go 16.5 miles southeast on Oregon 224 to enter this camp on the left.

About the campground: This campground sits across the road from the Clackamas River, and the picturesque Roaring River races along its western edge. Both rivers have been designated wild and scenic. The camp primarily serves tent campers with sites among old-growth cedars and firs and moss-draped maples. The Roaring River Trail climbs away from the camp. Anglers will probably find the Clackamas River the better bet. The campground is open from May to October.

52 Shellrock Creek

Location: About 33 miles southeast of Estacada.
Sites: 7 basic sites; no hookups.
Maximum length: 16 feet.
Facilities: Tables, grills, vault toilets. No drinking water.
Fee per night: $.
Management: Forest Service.
Contact: 503-630-4256.
Finding the campground: From Estacada, go 25 miles southeast on Oregon 224 to its junction with Forest Road 57 and FR 46. Bear left on FR 57, go 7.3 miles, and turn left onto FR 58. Proceed 0.4 mile to the campground entrance on the left.

About the campground: This small campground is best suited for tent campers. It rests along picturesque Shellrock Creek amid a vital and beautiful forest of firs, cedars, yews, and rhododendrons. Despite the big trees, sites get a mix of sun and shade. Parking is along the graveled, widened road shoulder. Some sites have better tent flats than others. From this quiet campground, you may fish or hike the half-mile Pacific Yew Trail, which starts on the opposite side of the bridge from the camp. The trail may be overgrown in places. The campground is open from mid-June to early September.

53 Sunstrip

Location: About 17 miles southeast of Estacada.
Sites: 9 basic sites; no hookups.
Maximum length: 18 feet.
Facilities: Tables, grills, vault toilets, drinking water.
Fee per night: $$.
Management: Forest Service.
Contact: 503-630-6861; 1-800-280-CAMP for reservations.
Finding the campground: From Estacada, go 17.1 miles southeast on Oregon 224 to enter this camp on the right.

About the campground: This small campground is nestled amid maples, firs, and hemlocks on the bank of the Clackamas River; a few sites overlook the river. Campers have convenient fishing access. A steep canyon slope rises across the water from the campground, which is open from May to October.

OLALLIE LAKE SCENIC AREA

		Hookup sites	Total sites	Max. RV length	Hookups	Toilets	Showers	Drinking water	Dump station	Recreation	Fee	Can reserve
54	Camp Ten		9	16		NF				HFB	$	
55	Lower Lake		8	16		NF				HF		
56	Olallie Meadows		8	16		NF				HR		
57	Paul Dennis		17	16		NF		•		HFB	$–$$	
58	Peninsula		37	24		NF		•		HFB	$	
59	Triangle Lake Equestrian Camp		8	30		NF				HR		

Hookups: W = Water E = Electric S = Sewer **Total sites:** T = Tent-only campground **Maximum trailer/RV length** given in feet.
Toilets: F = Flush NF = No Flush **Recreation:** H = Hiking S = Swimming F = Fishing B = Boating L = Boat Launch
O = Off-Highway Driving R = Horseback Riding C = Cycling
Fee: $ = $1-9 $$ = $10-19 $$$ = $20-29 $$$$ = $30-39. If no entry under **Fee**, camping is free.

54 Camp Ten

Location: About 39 miles northeast of Detroit, on Olallie Lake.
Sites: 9 basic sites; no hookups.
Maximum length: 16 feet.
Facilities: Tables, grills, pit toilets. No drinking water.
Fee per night: $.
Management: Forest Service.
Contact: 503-630-4256.
Finding the campground: From Detroit, drive 25 miles northeast on Forest Road 46. Turn east onto FR 4690 and drive 8.1 miles; the paved road becomes gravel after 6 miles. Turn right onto gravel FR 4220 for Olallie Lake Scenic Area. Go another 6.2 miles to the campground entrance on the left.

About the campground: Located on the southwest shore of Olallie Lake, this campground features closely spaced sites in a forest of lichen-festooned conifers. Parking can be restrictive in some areas. A few sites overlook the big, beautiful, high-mountain lake, as well as Olallie Butte. You can circle Olallie Lake via a hiking trail and a segment of road on the lake's west shore. Huckleberry bushes draw berry pickers in late summer. Fishing and non-motorized boating keep campers busy. The campground is open from mid-June into September.

55 Lower Lake

Location: About 38 miles northeast of Detroit, near Lower Lake.
Sites: 8 basic sites; no hookups.
Maximum length: 16 feet.
Facilities: Tables, grills, pit toilets. No drinking water.
Fee per night: None.
Management: Forest Service.

Contact: 503-630-4256.

Finding the campground: From Detroit, drive 25 miles northeast on Forest Road 46. Turn east onto FR 4690, which begins paved but becomes gravel after 6 miles. Go 8.1 miles and turn right onto gravel FR 4220 for Olallie Lake Scenic Area. Reach the campground on the right after another 4.5 miles.

About the campground: In an alpine forest, this campground offers a quiet retreat. A talus slope abuts one site. A half-mile trail leads from the camp to the scenery, fishing, and huckleberry and blueberry patches at Lower Lake. From the fork in the trail beyond Lower Lake, you can walk 1 mile to Fish Lake, snuggled in a deep, forested basin. Or you can go 3 miles to Red Lake, passing a series of mountain lakes en route. The campground is open from mid-June into September.

56 Olallie Meadows

Location: About 35 miles northeast of Detroit.
Sites: 8 basic sites; no hookups.
Maximum length: 16 feet.
Facilities: Some tables, grills, pit toilets. No drinking water.
Fee per night: None.
Management: Forest Service.
Contact: 503-630-4256.
Finding the campground: From Forest Road 46, 25 miles northeast of Detroit, turn east onto FR 4690, which begins paved but becomes gravel after 6 miles. Go 8.1 miles and turn right onto gravel FR 4220 toward Olallie Lake Scenic Area. The campground is on the left after another 1.4 miles.

About the campground: In a forest of lodgepole pine and spruce, this primitive campground and a rustic cabin sit at the edge of picturesque Olallie Meadows, a rich, moist, textured meadow of grasses, wildflowers, and blueberries. You can occasionally spot deer or even a sandhill crane in the lea. Views from this huge natural opening include Olallie, Sisi, and Badger Buttes. You may tether horses to horse trailers at camp, but the animals are not allowed in the meadow. A trail to Russ Lake begins at the end of the campground and passes two other mountain lakes on the way. Come prepared for mosquitoes. The campground is open from mid-June into September.

57 Paul Dennis

Location: About 39 miles northeast of Detroit, on Olallie Lake.
Sites: 17 basic sites; no hookups.
Maximum length: 16 feet.
Facilities: Tables, grills, vault toilets, drinking water.
Fee per night: $ to $$.
Management: Forest Service.
Contact: 503-630-4256.

Finding the campground: From Forest Road 46, 25 miles northeast of Detroit, turn east onto FR 4690, which begins paved but becomes gravel after 6 miles. Go 8.1 miles and turn right onto gravel FR 4220 toward Olallie Lake Scenic Area. Go another 5.2 miles and turn left to reach the campground in 0.25 mile.

About the campground: Located along the northeast shore of Olallie Lake, next door to rustic Olallie Lake Resort, this campground features sites in a setting of lodgepole pines and mountain hemlocks. Dwarf huckleberry bushes and beargrass grow between the trees and sites. Some sites overlook the big mountain lake, and all lie within easy access of the lake for fishing, non-motorized boating, and admiring. A lakeshore trail nearly circles the lake and provides access to trails radiating through the Olallie Lake Scenic Area. The campground is open from mid-June into September.

58 Peninsula

Location: About 40 miles northeast of Detroit, on Olallie Lake.
Sites: 31 basic sites, 6 walk-in tent sites; no hookups.
Maximum length: 24 feet.
Facilities: Tables, grills, vault toilets, drinking water.
Fee per night: $.
Management: Forest Service.
Contact: 503-630-4256.
Finding the campground: From Forest Road 46, 25 miles northeast of Detroit, turn east onto FR 4690, which begins paved but becomes gravel after 6 miles. Go 8.1 miles, turn right onto gravel FR 4220 toward Olallie Lake Scenic Area, and go 6.6 miles to the campground entrance on the left.

About the campground: This campground occupies a peninsula on the south end of beautiful, blue Olallie Lake. A high-elevation forest of lodgepole pines, mountain hemlocks, true firs, and spruce enfolds the camp. Some sites face the lake, and Olallie Butte towers over it, adding to the view. Huckleberry picking, hiking, fishing, and quiet boating are favorite pastimes at and near the camp. The campground is open from mid-June into September.

59 Triangle Lake Equestrian Camp

Location: About 35 miles northeast of Detroit.
Sites: 8 basic sites; no hookups.
Maximum length: 30 feet.
Facilities: Tables, grills, vault toilets, water for horses, corrals. No drinking water.
Fee per night: None.
Management: Forest Service.
Contact: 503-630-6861.
Finding the campground: From Forest Road 46, 25 miles northeast of Detroit, turn east onto FR 4690, which begins paved but becomes gravel after 6 miles. Go 8.1 miles and turn right onto gravel FR 4220 toward Olallie Lake Scenic Area. The campground is on the right in 2.1 miles.

About the campground: Established for the exclusive use of equestrians, this campground offers tranquil sites in a forest of lodgepole pines and mountain hemlocks. The long gravel parking pads accommodate camp vehicles and horse trailers. Various trails through the Olallie Lake Scenic Area are open to riders, but the short trail to shallow, marshy Triangle Lake is off-limits to horses. Fishing, non-motorized boating, and berry picking are popular pastimes when you choose to leave the horses at camp. The campground is open from mid-June into September.

Willamette Valley and Western Front

Between the Cascade Mountains and the Coast Range stretches this broad, fertile valley fed by the Willamette River, which has its headwater high in the snowy Cascades. The rich soil and mild climate of the Willamette Valley inspired thousands of families in the mid-1800s to make the grueling, 2,000-mile journey west via the Oregon Trail. Their migration rivaled that of the California gold rush, which occurred about the same time.

The valley is prime habitat for a variety of wildlife, including nesting ospreys and herons, geese, ducks, hawks, kingfishers, river otters, muskrats, and beaver (the state animal). It is also crucial habitat for birds migrating on the Pacific Flyway. One of the best and most relaxing ways to watch wildlife is from a raft. The placid Willamette River is well suited to lazy float trips. Contact an outfitter or pick up a copy of *The Willamette River Recreation Guide* from the Oregon State Parks and Recreation Department or a local visitor center. This brochure shows put-ins, stops, and distances, and provides information about river flow and prime float times. Hiking trails offer another means to explore the valley, but learn what poison oak looks like and where it grows. Paved trails along river greenways are ideal for cycling, walking, jogging, and maneuvering a wheelchair or baby stroller.

You need not get your hands dirty to share in the land's bounty. Roadside produce stands teem with baskets, lugs, and bins of fresh fruits, vegetables, and nuts; the variety is amazing. Many produce varieties never reach the grocery store because they are too delicate to transport, but they will delight you with exceptional tastes and textures. If you want a firsthand farm experience, there are also plenty of U-pick farms to put you on your knees or atop a ladder. The Willamette Valley is noted for its berries and for its award-winning wineries, which feature show rooms and tasting tours.

Back roads will take you past covered bridges, river ferries, tulip fields, Christmas tree farms, golf courses, fishing waters, and blackberry brambles. The mid-sized cities of Salem, the capital, and Eugene, a university town, occupy the heart of the valley and lie along the busy artery of Interstate 5. Smaller farm and forest towns hold yesteryear charm.

The climate in the Willamette Valley is mild year-round, allowing for a full calendar of recreation, if you do not mind braving the occasional raindrop. Winter visitors should bring a full suit of rain gear and a sunny disposition. Summer days bask in sunlight, with temperatures climbing into the 90s; humidity is seldom a problem.

This tourism region also incorporates the western front of the central Cascade Mountain Range, with the spectacular scenery and recreational opportunities of the upper Willamette, Santiam, and McKenzie River drainages. Among the attractions are forest byways, hiking trails through old-growth forests, sterling waterfalls, and prized waters for fishing, rafting, canoeing, speed boating, and waterskiing. You can engage in a full lineup of winter sports, explore the historic remains of mining and timber operations, or just kick back at camp and relax.

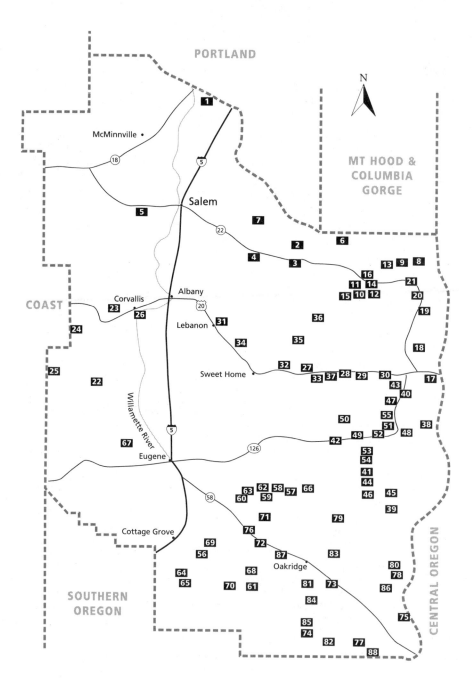

The Cascades experience four distinct seasons, although the climate in the lower elevations remains mild year-round. It typically rains in winter on the lower flanks of the mountains but snows on the passes and peaks. The climate is variable in spring and fall, and afternoon thunderstorms are possible in summer.

SALEM AREA

	Hookup sites	Total sites	Max. RV length	Hookups	Toilets	Showers	Drinking water	Dump station	Recreation	Fee	Can reserve
1 Champoeg State Park	48	106	50	WE	F	•	•	•	HFBC	$$–$$$	•
2 Elkhorn Valley Recreation Site		23	18		NF	•			SF	$	
3 Fisherman's Bend Recreation Site	22	38	40	W	F	•	•	•	HFBL	$$	
4 John Neal Memorial Park		40	25		F	•			FBL	$	
5 Polk County Fairgrounds	100	100	40	WE	F	•	•	•		$–$$	
6 Shady Cove		13	16		NF				HSF	$–$$	
7 Silver Falls State Park	54	110	60	WE	F	•	•	•	HSRC	$$–$$$	

Hookups: W = Water   E = Electric   S = Sewer   **Total sites:** T = Tent-only campground   **Maximum trailer/RV length** given in feet.
Toilets: F = Flush   NF = No Flush   **Recreation:** H = Hiking   S = Swimming   F = Fishing   B = Boating   L = Boat Launch
O = Off-Highway Driving   R = Horseback Riding   C = Cycling
Fee: $ = $1-9 $$ = $10-19 $$$ = $20-29 $$$$ = $30-39. If no entry under **Fee,** camping is free.

1 Champoeg State Park

Location: About 30 miles north of Salem.
Sites: 48 hookup sites, 46 tent sites (availability depends on weather), 12 walk-in tent sites, 6 yurts; water and electric hookups.
Maximum length: 50 feet.
Facilities: Tables, grills, flush toilets, drinking water, showers, dump station, telephone, dock, visitor center, museum, picnic pavilions, amphitheater.
Fee per night: $$ to $$$.
Management: Oregon State Parks and Recreation Department.
Contact: 503-633-8107; 1-800-452-5687 for reservations.
Finding the campground: From Exit 278 of Interstate 5, 5 miles south of Wilsonville, head west on Ehlen Road/Yergen Road for 3.6 miles. Turn right onto Case Road, which later merges into Champoeg Road (bear left). Drive 5.8 miles to the park entrance on the right. The route is well signed.

About the campground: This park beside the sleepy Willamette River captivates campers with its sweeping green pastures, scenic oak groves, and comfortable, clean campsites. The park occupies the site where Oregon's first provisional government—the Northwest's first pro-American government–was born. A pageant depicting this historic event is held every summer in the campground amphitheater. This area was also the site of an Indian hunting and gathering camp, a fur-trading post, and a steamboat landing. Interpretive signs on the park grounds and at the visitor center help tell the tales. For the active, the park offers fishing, birding, a 10-mile bicycle path, and a 1.5-mile riverside hiking trail. The park is well located if you want a base from which to explore the valley back roads, visit U-pick farms, or take in the attractions of Portland, including concerts, museums, shops, gardens, and the Oregon Zoo. The campground is open year-round.

2 Elkhorn Valley Recreation Site

Location: About 30 miles east of Salem.
Sites: 23 basic sites; no hookups.
Maximum length: 18 feet.
Facilities: Tables, grills, vault toilets, drinking water.
Fee per night: $.
Management: Bureau of Land Management.
Contact: 503-375-5646.
Finding the campground: From Oregon 22 at Mehama, 22 miles east of Salem, turn northeast onto Forest Road 2209 (North Fork Road) toward Little North Fork Recreation Area and go 8.4 miles to reach this campground on the left.

About the campground: This pleasant camp sits in an old-growth forest beside the clear, blue-green waters of the Little North Fork Santiam River. It offers relaxation, swimming, fishing, and short hikes on riverside trails. The camp is also a fine base from which to explore a host of area trails that follow the river, pass swimming holes, and wander into the mountains of the Opal Creek Scenic Recreation Area. Upstream from camp on North Fork Road is a golf course, suggesting an alternative means for whiling away the day. The campground is open from May 15 to October.

3 Fisherman's Bend Recreation Site

Location: 28 miles east of Salem.
Sites: 22 hookup sites, 16 basic sites; water hookups.
Maximum length: 40 feet.
Facilities: Tables, grills, flush toilets, drinking water, showers, dump station, telephone, playground, ball fields, horseshoes, boat launch (drift boats or rafts), barrier-free trail and fishing dock for individuals with disabilities.
Fee per night: $$.
Management: Bureau of Land Management.
Contact: 503-375-5646.
Finding the campground: From Oregon 22, 28 miles east of Salem and 1.6 miles west of Mill City, turn south to enter the recreation site and camp.

About the campground: This large but friendly camp and day-use area is on the North Santiam River, a popular waterway for fishing, rafting, and drift boating. The camp rests on a wooded flat and has nice-sized sites for comfort and privacy. A network of trails explores the riparian habitat and riverbank. Herons, mergansers, kingfishers, nighthawks, and ospreys travel the river corridor. The campground is open from mid-May to late October.

4 John Neal Memorial Park

Location: In Lyons, about 25 miles east of Salem.
Sites: 40 basic sites; no hookups.
Maximum length: 25 feet.
Facilities: Tables, grills, flush toilets, drinking water, playground, ball field, horseshoe pits, primitive drift boat/raft launch.
Fee per night: $.
Management: Linn County.
Contact: 541-967-3917.
Finding the campground: From Oregon 22, about 22 miles east of Salem, turn south onto OR 226, go 0.9 mile, and continue east off OR 226 on Main Street for 0.5 mile. Turn left onto 13th Street and drive 0.6 mile to the park entrance.

About the campground: Conveniently located along OR 22, this quiet, rustic camp claims a low bluff overlooking the North Santiam River, a popular waterway for fishing and rafting. The sites have earthen parking and are distributed throughout a forest of cedars, firs, maples, and alders. The campground is open from late April to October 1.

5 Polk County Fairgrounds

Location: In Rickreall, about 11 miles southwest of Salem.
Sites: 100 hookup sites, some dry camping, tent camping on open lawn; water and electric hookups.
Maximum length: 40 feet.
Facilities: Flush toilets, drinking water, showers, dump station, playground.
Fee per night: $ to $$.
Management: Polk County.
Contact: 503-623-3048.
Finding the campground: From Salem, drive 10 miles west on Oregon 22. Turn left (south) onto OR 99W and drive 0.8 mile, passing through Rickreall, to find the fairgrounds on the left.

About the campground: You will find these sites, some paved and some gravel, within the parking lot of the main fairgrounds. Power poles signal the hookup sites; tent camping is on the lawn. The camp has no shade but is convenient for travelers, as well as for participants in and attendees of fairground events. Next door is Nesmith County Park, with its picnic tables and inviting lawn and shade trees. You may want to tour the area wineries, starting with the tasting room just across from the fairgrounds. Each year, the state tourism department puts together brochures for winery tours; copies are generally available at the individual wineries, chambers of commerce, and visitor centers. U-pick farms offer another way to spend your time. The campground is open year-round.

Willamette Valley barn.

6 Shady Cove

Location: About 41 miles east of Salem.
Sites: 13 basic sites; no hookups.
Maximum length: 16 feet.
Facilities: Tables, grills, vault toilets. No drinking water.
Fee per night: $ to $$.
Management: Forest Service.
Contact: 503-854-3366.
Finding the campground: From Oregon 22 at Mehama, about 22 miles east of Salem, turn northeast at the sign for Little North Fork Recreation Area and go 19 miles on Forest Road 2209 and FR 2207 to reach this camp at Shady Cove Bridge. The route is part paved, part gravel.

About the campground: This camp sits on a richly forested flat above the Little North Santiam River at Shady Cove Bridge. Because the road to the camp is twisting and sometimes rough, the facility is best suited for tent camping and small RVs. It makes a good base for anglers and hikers. The Little North Fork Santiam River Trail is located across the river from camp, and other area trails visit the Opal Creek Scenic Recreation Area. A series of inviting green pools on the Little North Santiam River attracts swimmers to this canyon. The campground is open from mid-May to late September.

Falls at Silver Falls State Park.

7 Silver Falls State Park

Location: About 28 miles east of Salem.
Sites: 54 hookup sites, 51 basic sites, 5 horse sites; water and electric hookups.
Maximum length: 60 feet.
Facilities: Tables, grills, flush toilets, drinking water, showers, dump station, telephone, nature center, play area, swimming pond, corrals at horse camp.
Fee per night: $$ to $$$.
Management: Oregon State Parks and Recreation Department.
Contact: 503-873-8681.
Finding the campground: From Salem, drive 12 miles southeast on Oregon 22. Take the exit for Silver Falls State Park and follow OR 214 northeast for 15.5 miles to the park. OR 214 follows a weaving course, but signs mark the junctions.

About the campground: In the foothills of the Cascades along Silver Creek, you will find this picturesque family park that boasts 10 major waterfalls. You can visit them all via the Trail of Ten Falls hiking loop, which offers unique perspectives, passing above, below, and behind the misty curtains of water. Visitors who do not hike can still view several of the falls from the picnic area, from the few drive-to overlooks, or by walking a short distance on trails. Elsewhere, bicycle trails and horse trails explore the woodland park, with its old-growth and mature second-growth forest. The tidy campground is set apart from the bustling day-use area but within easy reach. It offers comfortable, easy-to-access sites, some sunny and open; others shaded by evergreens. The campground is open year-round.

DETROIT LAKE AREA

		Hookup sites	Total sites	Max. RV length	Hookups	Toilets	Showers	Drinking water	Dump station	Recreation	Fee	Can reserve
8	Breitenbush		29	40		NF			•	HF	$–$$	
9	Cleater Bend		9	40		NF			•	HF	$	
10	Cove Creek		63	40		F	•		•	SFBL	$$	
11	Detroit Lake State Recreation Area	177	311	60	WES	F	•		•	SFBL	$$–$$$	•
12	Hoover		37	40		F			•	HFSBL	$$–$$$	
13	Humbug		21	40		NF			•	HF	$	
14	Santiam Flats		open	40		NF				FBL	$	
15	Southshore		30	30		NF			•	HSFBL	$$	
16	Upper Arm Recreation Area		5	20		NF				SFB		

Hookups: W = Water E = Electric S = Sewer **Total sites:** T = Tent-only campground **Maximum trailer/RV length** given in feet.
Toilets: F = Flush NF = No Flush **Recreation:** H = Hiking S = Swimming F = Fishing B = Boating L = Boat Launch
O = Off-Highway Driving R = Horseback Riding C = Cycling
Fee: $ = $1-9 $$ = $10-19 $$$ = $20-29 $$$$ = $30-39. If no entry under **Fee,** camping is free.

8 Breitenbush

Location: About 9 miles northeast of Detroit.
Sites: 29 basic sites; no hookups.
Maximum length: 40 feet.
Facilities: Tables, grills, vault toilets, drinking water.
Fee per night: $ to $$.
Management: Forest Service.
Contact: 503-854-3366.
Finding the campground: From Oregon 22 at the west end of Detroit, turn north onto Forest Road 46 and go 9.1 miles to the campground entrance on the right.

About the campground: Hemlocks, cedars, and vine maples envelop this attractive camp along the Breitenbush River, a pristine, rushing water overhung with trees and framed by the riverside greenery. Campers can fish or they can hike the nearby South Breitenbush Gorge Trail, which passes through a lovely old-growth forest and along a rocky chasm that pinches the South Breitenbush River into a fury of rushing water. The camp is also near the private, alternative-lifestyle Breitenbush Hot Springs. The campground is open from mid-April to late September.

9 Cleater Bend

Location: About 9 miles northeast of Detroit.
Sites: 9 basic sites; no hookups.
Maximum length: 40 feet.
Facilities: Tables, grills, vault toilets, drinking water.
Fee per night: $.
Management: Forest Service.

Contact: 503-854-3366.
Finding the campground: From Oregon 22 at the west end of Detroit, turn north onto Forest Road 46 and go 8.6 miles to the campground entrance on the right.

About the campground: This small, compact campground occupies a bend on the Breitenbush River where an island divides the flow. The sites are in a lovely woodland setting of Douglas-firs, cedars, yews, hemlocks, rhododendrons, and alders. Campers may fish or take a hike along the South Breitenbush Gorge Trail; access is northeast of the camp off FR 4685. Detroit Lake is just minutes away. The campground is open from mid-May to late September.

10 Cove Creek

Location: About 6 miles south of Detroit, on Detroit Lake.
Sites: 63 basic sites; no hookups.
Maximum length: 40 feet.
Facilities: Tables, grills, flush toilets, drinking water, coin-operated showers, boat launch, dock.
Fee per night: $$.
Management: Forest Service.
Contact: 503-854-3366.
Finding the campground: From Detroit, go 2.9 miles east on Oregon 22 and turn right (south) onto Forest Road 10 (Blowout Road). Drive 3.5 miles to the campground entrance on the right.

About the campground: On the south shore of Detroit Lake, this large, comfortable campground offers great access to the full lineup of water fun: fishing, boating, swimming, sailing, waterskiing, and just relaxing on the shore. The camp claims a gentle, evergreen-clad slope and offers paved roads and parking and running-water amenities. Hikers can access the Stahlman Point Lookout Trail off Blowout Road, 0.1 mile south of the camp turnoff. The campground is open from mid-May through September.

11 Detroit Lake State Recreation Area

Location: 2 miles southwest of Detroit, on Detroit Lake.
Sites: 177 full and partial hookup sites, 134 basic sites; water, electric, and sewer hookups.
Maximum length: 60 feet.
Facilities: Tables, grills, flush toilets, drinking water, showers, telephone, boat moorage, launch, dock, swimming beach.
Fee per night: $$ to $$$.
Management: Oregon State Parks and Recreation Department.
Contact: 503-854-3346; 1-800-452-5687 for reservations.
Finding the campground: Drive 2 miles southwest of Detroit on Oregon 22. The campground is on the left side of the highway.

About the campground: This large, developed campground features welcoming, fir-forested sites along the north shore of Detroit Lake, a huge reservoir within the North Santiam River Canyon. The reservoir hosts a full range of water sports, from fishing to waterskiing, making it and the state park popular summer destinations. Some sites overlook the water. The campground is open from March 1 to early November.

12 Hoover

Location: About 4 miles southeast of Detroit, on Detroit Lake.
Sites: 37 basic sites; no hookups.
Maximum length: 40 feet.
Facilities: Tables, grills, flush toilets, drinking water, boat launch, barrier-free trail, wheelchair-accessible fishing platforms and 200-foot-long pier.
Fee per night: $$ to $$$.
Management: Forest Service.
Contact: 503-854-3366.
Finding the campground: From Detroit, go east on Oregon 22 for 2.8 miles, turn right onto Forest Road 10 (Blowout Road), and go another 0.8 mile to find the camp entrance on the right.

About the campground: On the North Santiam River Arm of Detroit Lake, this campground is shaded by a rich Douglas-fir forest with an explosive green understory that tantalizes the eye. Campsites are well spaced for privacy and comfort, but water sports are likely to keep you away from camp. Fishing, boating, swimming, and waterskiing all vie for your time. The 0.3-mile Hoover Nature Trail swings a lasso through the forest. The lower leg of the loop is wheelchair accessible and leads to fishing platforms. The campground is open from mid-May through late September.

13 Humbug

Location: About 4 miles northeast of Detroit.
Sites: 21 basic sites; no hookups.
Maximum length: 40 feet.
Facilities: Tables, grills, vault toilets, drinking water.
Fee per night: $.
Management: Forest Service.
Contact: 503-854-3366.
Finding the campground: From Oregon 22 at the west end of Detroit, turn north onto Forest Road 46 and go 4.4 miles to the campground entrance on the right.

About the campground: At this campground on the Breitenbush River, you will find fairly spacious sites in a semi-open forest of firs, hemlocks, and cedars, rimmed by old-growth trees. The Humbug Flat Trail leaves the camp near site 9, passing above the river through a bounty of rhododendrons and a varied forest.

Steep paths plunge toward fishing holes. Anglers can also try fishing from the dam, the shore, or a boat on Detroit Lake, which is a short drive to the south. The campground is open from mid-April to late September.

14 Santiam Flats

Location: About 3 miles east of Detroit, on Detroit Lake.
Sites: From 20 to 100 basic sites; no hookups.
Maximum length: 40 feet.
Facilities: Some tables, chemical toilets, primitive boat launch. No drinking water.
Fee per night: $.
Management: Forest Service.
Contact: 503-854-3366.
Finding the campground: It is south off Oregon 22, 2.5 miles east of Detroit.

About the campground: In an effort to establish order, this austere campground grew up around Santiam Flats, which had long been used by the public for camping and accessing Detroit Lake. The site locations are still fairly random and best suited for self-contained RVs. Santiam Flats can comfortably accommodate 30 to 40 units, but on holiday weekends the number often swells to 100 or more. A few firs and shrubs combined with some willows along the shore are the only significant vegetation. Despite the rough, potholed dirt access road, the campers keep coming. Their goal: to fish and boat Detroit Lake. The campground is open year-round.

15 Southshore

Location: About 7 miles south of Detroit, on Detroit Lake.
Sites: 22 basic sites, 8 walk-in tent sites; no hookups.
Maximum length: 30 feet.
Facilities: Tables, grills, vault toilets, drinking water, boat launch, dock.
Fee per night: $$.
Management: Forest Service.
Contact: 503-854-3366.
Finding the campground: From Detroit, go 2.9 miles east on Oregon 22 and turn right (south) onto Forest Road 10 (Blowout Road). Continue 4.2 miles to the campground entrance on the right.

About the campground: On the south shore of Detroit Lake—a huge reservoir open to recreation—this campground occupies a mixed forest. The towering trees and the lush, diverse understory create a setting as appealing as the lake. Although the campsites all have paved parking, some are not as level as others; they are better suited for tent camping. Swimming, fishing, boating, waterskiing, and sailing will keep water enthusiasts happy. Hikers will find the Stahlman Point Lookout Trail not far from camp. The campground is open from mid-May through late September.

16 Upper Arm Recreation Area

Location: About 1 mile north of Detroit.
Sites: 5 basic sites; no hookups.
Maximum length: 20 feet.
Facilities: Tables, pit and chemical toilets. No drinking water.
Fee per night: None.
Management: Forest Service.
Contact: 503-854-3366.
Finding the campground: From Oregon 22 on the west end of Detroit, turn north onto Forest Road 46 and go 0.9 mile to find this camp on the left.

About the campground: This compact, primitive camp sits on a forested flat above the Upper Breitenbush River Arm of Detroit Lake. Tables hint at the site locations; parking is informal and unimproved. Fires are prohibited, but campers may use their personal charcoal barbecues. Vine maples and rhododendrons embellish the evergreen forest. To reach the reservoir to fish, boat, or swim, you must descend a steep bank. This part of the lake recedes as summer wears on. The campground is open year-round.

MARION FORKS AREA

	Hookup sites	Total sites	Max. RV length	Hookups	Toilets	Showers	Drinking water	Dump station	Recreation	Fee	Can reserve
17 Big Lake and Big Lake West		60	28		F		•		HFBLO	$	
18 Big Meadows Horse Camp		9	40		NF		•		HR	$	
19 Marion Forks		15	22		NF		•		HF	$	
20 Riverside		37	30		NF		•		F	$	
21 Whispering Falls		16	40		F		•		F	$$	

Hookups: W = Water E = Electric S = Sewer **Total sites:** T = Tent-only campground **Maximum trailer/RV length** given in feet.
Toilets: F = Flush NF = No Flush **Recreation:** H = Hiking S = Swimming F = Fishing B = Boating L = Boat Launch
O = Off-Highway Driving R = Horseback Riding C = Cycling
Fee: $ = $1-9 $$ = $10-19 $$$ = $20-29 $$$$ = $30-39. If no entry under **Fee,** camping is free.

17 Big Lake and Big Lake West

Location: About 26 miles southeast of Marion Forks, on Big Lake.
Sites: 49 basic sites, 11 walk-in tent sites; no hookups.
Maximum length: 28 feet.
Facilities: Tables, grills, vault and flush toilets, drinking water, boat ramp.
Fee per night: $.
Management: Forest Service.
Contact: 541-822-3381.
Finding the campground: From U.S. Highway 20 at Santiam Pass, about 22 miles southeast of Marion Forks, turn south onto Forest Road 2690 (Big Lake Road) and go about 4 miles to these campgrounds.

About the campground: The primary campground occupies the north shore of Big Lake, while the walk-in tent sites line the west shore. Big Lake is an aptly named, natural lake below Hayrick and Hoodoo Buttes; Mount Washington overlooks the lake. Sites are nestled in a high-elevation forest of firs, hemlocks, and lodgepole pines; a few snags among the west shore sites have been carved with totems. The lake offers fishing, swimming, boating, and waterskiing, as well as canoeing along the scalloped shoreline. Area trails visit Patjens Lakes and Mount Washington Wilderness Area. The campground is open from mid-June to early September; to October for the walk-in sites.

18 Big Meadows Horse Camp

Location: About 10 miles south of Marion Forks.
Sites: 9 basic sites; no hookups.
Maximum length: 40 feet.
Facilities: Tables, grills, vault toilets, drinking water, corrals, hitching posts, loading ramps, spring-fed trough for stock watering.

Fee per night: $.
Management: Forest Service.
Contact: 503-854-3366.
Finding the campground: From Oregon 22, 27 miles east of Detroit and 5.6 miles west of Santiam Junction (the junction of OR 22 and U.S. Highway 20), turn north onto Forest Road 2267, go 0.9 mile, and turn left onto FR 2257. Drive 0.5 mile to the campground entrance on the left. All roads to the camp are paved; roads in the camp are gravel.

About the campground: Established for horse campers, this campground occupies a welcoming forest of mixed firs, spruce, and mountain hemlock. Pole fences line the roadways and site turnouts, and each site is paired with a four-stall corral. Deer sometimes visit the vacant stalls, seeking leftover hay. Horse trails leave from camp; be sure to obtain a wilderness permit if you plan to enter Mount Jefferson Wilderness Area. Huckleberry picking is a seasonal diversion.

19 Marion Forks

Location: In Marion Forks.
Sites: 15 basic sites; no hookups.
Maximum length: 22 feet.
Facilities: Tables, grills, pit toilets, drinking water.
Fee per night: $.
Management: Forest Service.
Contact: 541-854-3366.
Finding the campground: It is northeast off Oregon 22 at Marion Forks, 16 miles southeast of Detroit. A sign for a hatchery and the forest camp marks the turn.

About the campground: You will find this quiet campground next to Marion Forks Fish Hatchery on the south bank of sparkling Marion Creek. The sites have a rustic charm and are nicely shaded. The creek is not good for fishing, but it is a fine place to cool your ankles. Area trails lead to Independence Rock, Marion Lake, and the remote backcountry lakes and wilds of Mount Jefferson Wilderness Area. The campground is open from mid-May to mid-October.

20 Riverside

Location: About 3 miles north of Marion Forks.
Sites: 37 basic sites; no hookups.
Maximum length: 30 feet.
Facilities: Tables, grills, pit toilets, drinking water.
Fee per night: $.
Management: Forest Service.
Contact: 503-854-3366.
Finding the campground: It is west off Oregon 22, 13.5 miles southeast of Detroit.

About the campground: This campground stretches along the shore of the North Santiam River amid firs, cedars, and alders. In spring, rhododendron and dogwood blooms dress up the forest midstory. Sparkling, clear, and green, the river courses over bedrock and seduces anglers. Some sites overlook the river from shore or from a slight bluff. All sites have surfaced parking. The campground is open from May 1 to October 1.

21 Whispering Falls

Location: About 8 miles northwest of Marion Forks.
Sites: 16 basic sites; no hookups.
Maximum length: 40 feet.
Facilities: Tables, grills, flush toilets, drinking water.
Fee per night: $$.
Management: Forest Service.
Contact: 503-854-3366.
Finding the campground: It is west off Oregon 22, 8 miles southeast of Detroit.

About the campground: Named for the lacy, gentle-voiced waterfall that spills from a side canyon into the North Santiam River across the river from camp, this campground delivers a picturesque stay. It is fully forested and has a lush understory that contributes both beauty and privacy to the campsites. An abrupt bank separates much of the camp from the river, so take the River Trail for shore and fishing access. The campground is open from May 1 to October 1.

CORVALLIS AREA

	Hookup sites	Total sites	Max. RV length	Hookups	Toilets	Showers	Drinking water	Dump station	Recreation	Fee	Can reserve
22 Alsea Falls Recreation Site		16	38		NF		•		HSF	$	
23 Benton County Fairgrounds	open		40	WE	F	•	•		HC	$-$$	
24 Marys Peak		6	T		NF		•		H	$	
25 Salmonberry County Park		20	40		F		•		FBL	$	
26 Willamette Park		15	30		F		•		HSF	$	

Hookups: W = Water E = Electric S = Sewer **Total sites:** T = Tent-only campground **Maximum trailer/RV length** given in feet.
Toilets: F = Flush NF = No Flush **Recreation:** H = Hiking S = Swimming F = Fishing B = Boating L = Boat Launch
O = Off-Highway Driving R = Horseback Riding C = Cycling
Fee: $ = $1-9 $$ = $10-19 $$$ = $20-29 $$$$ = $30-39. If no entry under **Fee,** camping is free.

22 Alsea Falls Recreation Site

Location: About 29 miles southwest of Corvallis.
Sites: 16 basic sites; no hookups.
Maximum length: 38 feet.
Facilities: Tables, grills, vault toilets, drinking water.
Fee per night: $.
Management: Bureau of Land Management.
Contact: 503-375-5646.
Finding the campground: From Corvallis, go 16 miles south on Oregon 99W and turn right (west) onto Alpine Road at the sign for Alpine and Alsea Falls. Drive 12.9 miles, passing through the town of Alpine, to reach the campground. The road is paved and gravel.

About the campground: A wetland of skunk cabbage and mossy old stumps contributes to the character of this campground, set in a forest of tall firs and alders on the Alsea Falls Back Country Byway. Sites are spacious, and the sound of the South Fork Alsea River in the background is relaxing. From the bridge at the camp, a trail leads half a mile down the river to Alsea Falls. A mile-long extension of this trail continues downstream to McBee Park and Peak Creek and then upstream along Peak Creek to Green Peak Falls. McBee Park is a rustic campground managed by the Hull Oakes Lumber Company (reservations required; call 541-424-3112). Green Peak Falls measures 50 feet tall and twice as wide, and because you come upon it suddenly and unexpectedly, the first impression is amplified. The BLM campground is open from May 15 to September 30.

23 Benton County Fairgrounds

Location: In Corvallis.
Sites: Variable number of sites; some water and electric hookups.
Maximum length: 40 feet.

Facilities: Flush toilets, drinking water, showers (seasonally available), telephone (at fairgrounds).
Fee per night: $ to $$.
Management: Benton County.
Contact: 541-757-1521.
Finding the campground: From U.S. Highway 20 at the west end of Corvallis, go north on 53rd Street for 1 mile to reach the fairgrounds on the left; check in at the office.

About the campground: This camping area on the fairgrounds exists primarily to serve fair participants, but when fair events are not ongoing, area travelers may find it a convenient place from which to explore the Corvallis area. Among the attractions are the Willamette River, valley U-pick farms, William L. Finley National Wildlife Refuge, Oregon State University, and Peavy Arboretum. The campground is open year-round.

24 Marys Peak

Location: About 25 miles southwest of Corvallis.
Sites: 6 tent sites; no hookups.
Maximum length: Suitable for tents only.
Facilities: Tables, grills, vault toilets, drinking water.
Fee per night: $.
Management: Forest Service.
Contact: 541-563-3211.
Finding the campground: From Oregon 34, 10 miles west of Philomath, turn north onto Marys Peak Road and proceed 9 miles to the campground entrance on the right.

About the campground: Just below the summit of Marys Peak sits this tiny camp in a semi-open stand of small noble firs. It rests along Parker Creek adjacent to the Meadows Edge Trail, which explores the denser noble-fir forest and open meadow of the upper mountain, delivering views and accessing a summit spur. Other trails explore the east and north flanks of Marys Peak, which is the highest peak in the Coast Range. It is noted for its wildflowers, its winter recreational opportunities, and views that stretch from the Pacific Ocean to the Cascades. Although it is a popular destination, the peak is still wild enough to be inhabited by deer and bobcats. Vultures may be seen soaring overhead. The campground is open from May through October.

25 Salmonberry County Park

Location: About 30 miles southwest of Corvallis.
Sites: 13 basic sites, 7 tent sites; no hookups.
Maximum length: 40 feet.
Facilities: Tables, grills, flush toilets, drinking water, drift/car-top boat launch, barrier-free trail.

Willamette Valley grapes.

Fee per night: $.
Management: Benton County.
Contact: 541-757-6871.
Finding the campground: From Oregon 34, 6.4 miles west of Alsea and 32 miles east of Waldport, turn south onto Salmonberry Road and go 0.3 mile to the park entrance on the left.

About the campground: Occupying an attractive flat above the quiet Alsea River, this campground has sites with gravel pads edging a large, central lawn. Alders shape the camp perimeter. Each site has been constructed to serve wheelchair users, with easy access to table and grill. A 700-foot, cinder-grade gravel trail provides barrier-free access from the camp to the river. Fishing and drift boating are popular pursuits. The camp conveniently serves travelers passing between the Willamette Valley and the coast. The campground is open from May 15 through October 15.

26 Willamette Park

Location: On the southern outskirts of Corvallis.
Sites: 15 basic sites; no hookups.
Maximum length: 30 feet.
Facilities: Tables, fire rings, flush toilets, drinking water.
Fee per night: $.
Management: City of Corvallis.
Contact: 541-757-6918.
Finding the campground: From Oregon 99W at the south end of Corvallis, turn east onto Goodnight Avenue and follow the paved and graveled road 0.6 mile to the campground entrance, which is on the left as you reach Willamette City Park.

About the campground: Adjacent to Willamette City Park with its complement of fields, playgrounds, picnic areas, exercise trails, and natural woods, this campground appeals to both lazy and active campers. The campground sits on a rise above a day-use area; sites rim a broad, grassy flat that is ringed by evergreens, offering you a choice of sun or partial shade during your stay. The Willamette River flows broad, swift, and smooth past the park. Blackberry brambles may entice you to risk the thorns for a tasty nibble. The campground is open from April 1 to November 15.

LEBANON–SWEET HOME AREA

		Hookup sites	Total sites	Max. RV length	Hookups	Toilets	Showers	Drinking water	Dump station	Recreation	Fee	Can reserve
27	Cascadia State Park		25	35		F		•		HSF	$ -$$	
28	Fernview		11	18		NF		•		HSF	$	
29	House Rock		17	16		NF		•		HSF	$	
30	Lost Prairie		10	35		NF		•		H	$	
31	River Park		10	30		F			•	FBL	$	
32	Sunnyside County Park	162	162	40	WE	F	•	•	•	SFBL	$$	
33	Trout Creek		24	22		NF		•		HSF	$-$$	
34	Waterloo County Park	60	60	40	WE	F	•	•	•	SFBL	$$	
35	Whitcomb Creek County Park		35	30		NF		•		SFBL	$$	
36	Yellowbottom		22	20		NF		•		HSF	$	
37	Yukwah		20	30		NF		•		HSF	$-$$	

Hookups: W = Water E = Electric S = Sewer **Total sites:** T = Tent-only campground **Maximum trailer/RV length** given in feet.
Toilets: F = Flush NF = No Flush **Recreation:** H = Hiking S = Swimming F = Fishing B = Boating L = Boat Launch
O = Off-Highway Driving R = Horseback Riding C = Cycling
Fee: $ = $1-9 $$ = $10-19 $$$ = $20-29 $$$$ = $30-39. If no entry under **Fee,** camping is free.

27 Cascadia State Park

Location: 14 miles east of Sweet Home.
Sites: 25 basic sites; no hookups.
Maximum length: 35 feet.
Facilities: Tables, grills, flush toilets, drinking water, horseshoe pits, sports field.
Fee per night: $ to $$.
Management: Oregon State Parks and Recreation Department.
Contact: 541-854-3406.
Finding the campground: From Sweet Home, drive 14 miles east on U.S. Highway 20. The campground is on the north side of the road.

About the campground: In the South Santiam River Valley, you will find this pleasant camp with paved roads and parking, ample lawn, and shade trees. Although the sites are fairly close together, they are set among native vegetation. Trout fishing on the river and hiking the three-quarter-mile trail to Soda Creek Falls top the list of things to do. Foster Reservoir lies west of camp for boating and fishing; Menagerie Wilderness is east of the park for more serious hiking. The campground is open from April to October.

28 Fernview

Location: 24 miles east of Sweet Home.
Sites: 11 basic sites; no hookups.
Maximum length: 18 feet.
Facilities: Tables, grills, vault toilets, drinking water.
Fee per night: $.
Management: Forest Service.
Contact: 541-367-5168.
Finding the campground: From Sweet Home, drive 24 miles east on U.S. Highway 20. Turn south into the campground.

About the campground: This campground on the south bank of the South Santiam River oozes with tranquility. A rich midstory of vine maples creates an attractive canopy over the individual sites; towering hemlocks and firs deepen the shade. The South Santiam River consists of rushing stretches, deep pools for swimming or fishing, gravel bars, and outcrops. The campground lies within easy reach of hiking trails to House Rock, Iron Mountain, the Menagerie Wilderness, and Rooster Rock. The campground is open from May into September.

29 House Rock

Location: About 28 miles east of Sweet Home.
Sites: 17 basic sites; no hookups.
Maximum length: 16 feet.
Facilities: Tables, grills, vault toilets, drinking water.
Fee per night: $.
Management: Forest Service.
Contact: 541-367-5168.
Finding the campground: From Sweet Home, drive 27 miles east on U.S. Highway 20 and turn south onto gravel Squaw Creek Road. Go about 1 mile to the campground.

About the campground: Bigleaf maples, alders, cedars, firs, and hemlocks weave a rich canopy of shade for this campground at the confluence of Squaw and Sheep Creeks. Because the sites lack long parking pads or pull-thrus, camping here is better suited to tents or small rigs. Fishing and hiking draw campers away from the comfort of camp. House Rock, Old Santiam Wagon Road, Iron Mountain, and Rooster Rock are hiking options. The campground is open from May into September.

30 Lost Prairie

Location: 40 miles east of Sweet Home.
Sites: 4 basic sites, 6 walk-in tent sites; no hookups.
Maximum length: 35 feet.
Facilities: Tables, grills, vault toilets, drinking water.
Fee per night: $.
Management: Forest Service.
Contact: 541-367-5168.
Finding the campground: From Sweet Home, drive 40 miles east on U.S. Highway 20. The campground is south of the highway, 4.2 miles west of the junction of US 20 and Oregon 126.

About the campground: This campground rests in a meadow and forested setting along Hackleman Creek. Its walk-in sites are set back among the firs and spruce just a few strides from the paved parking area. Wildflowers embellish the meadow. Just west of the campground is the Hackleman Trail Old Growth Grove. The campground is open from May to October.

31 River Park

Location: In Lebanon.
Sites: 10 basic sites; no hookups.
Maximum length: 30 feet.
Facilities: Tables, grills, flush toilets (available mid-April through November 1; winter camping for self-contained units only), dump station, playground, boat launch (across street at Gill Landing), horseshoe pits, ball field. Bring drinking water.
Fee per night: $.
Management: City of Lebanon.
Contact: 541-451-7442.
Finding the campground: From Main Street in the center of Lebanon, go north on Grant Street for 0.7 mile to reach the park on the left.

About the campground: This park offers a pleasant stay and overlooks the banks of the South Fork Santiam River. It occupies a flat that is mostly grassy, with maples, oaks, and a few conifers for shade. Cottonwoods and blackberry bushes claim the river's edge. If you tire of fishing and boating, it is only a short hop to the city center.

32 Sunnyside County Park

Location: About 7 miles northeast of Sweet Home.
Sites: 162 hookup sites; water and electric hookups.
Maximum length: 40 feet.
Facilities: Tables, grills, flush toilets, drinking water, showers, dump station, telephone, playground, boat dock, launch, moorage, fish-cleaning station, horseshoe pits, volleyball.

Fee per night: $$.
Management: Linn County.
Contact: 541-967-3917.
Finding the campground: From Sweet Home, go 5.5 miles east on U.S. Highway 20. Turn left (north) onto Quartzville Road, a BLM Back Country Byway that heads toward Green Peter Reservoir. Go 1.4 miles to reach the county park on the right.

About the campground: This tidy, attractive campground occupies a vast, trimmed lawn, with cottonwoods and some planted pines and maples providing pockets of shade. It sits between a forested ridge and Foster Reservoir, near a pair of big ponds with stark shores. The camp has paved roads and parking pads and, despite its large size, rolls out a fine welcome mat for your stay. The waters of Foster and Green Peter Reservoirs invite lake recreation. Blackberry bushes bordering Quartzville Road invite berry pickers to stain their fingers and perhaps collect enough for a pie. The campground is open from April through October.

33 Trout Creek

Location: 21 miles east of Sweet Home.
Sites: 24 basic sites; no hookups.
Maximum length: 22 feet.
Facilities: Tables, grills, vault toilets, drinking water.
Fee per night: $ to $$.
Management: Forest Service.
Contact: 541-367-5168.
Finding the campground: From Sweet Home, drive 21 miles east on U.S. Highway 20. The campground is on the south side of the road.

About the campground: This campground on the South Santiam River offers swimming, fishing, and a pleasant stay in a natural woodland setting, though there is some traffic noise. Some of the sites overlook the river and others are very private. The multistoried forest with its many dogwoods is especially appealing early in the camping season. Trails enter the Menagerie Wilderness or follow Falls Creek to Soapgrass Mountain and Gordon Lakes. At the Trout Creek Trailhead, across the road from the camp, a short spur trail leads to an elk-viewing platform, while the main trail enters the wilderness on its way to Rooster Rock. The campground is open from May through September.

34 Waterloo County Park

Location: About 9 miles northwest of Sweet Home.
Sites: 60 hookup sites; water and electric hookups.
Maximum length: 40 feet.
Facilities: Tables, grills, flush toilets, drinking water, showers, dump station, playground, beach area, boat launch, shelter.
Fee per night: $$.

Management: Linn County.
Contact: 541-967-3917.
Finding the campground: From the junction of U.S. Highway 20 and Oregon 228 in Sweet Home, follow US 20 northwest for 8.4 miles and turn right (north) onto Waterloo Drive at the sign for the park. Drive 1 mile through the community of Waterloo to reach the right-hand turn to the park. The campground is at the end of the park road.

About the campground: This extensive riverside campground fronts the broad and glassy South Santiam River and enjoys a relaxing valley location. Expansive lawns, attractive oaks and maples, and browsing deer add to the idyllic scene. Cottonwoods grow along the river. The park offers room to roam, but beware of poison oak. The river is open to boating, swimming, and fishing. Blackberry brambles hold tasty mouthfuls in summer, if you can navigate the thorns.

35 Whitcomb Creek County Park

Location: About 17 miles northeast of Sweet Home, on Green Peter Reservoir.
Sites: 35 basic sites; no hookups.
Maximum length: 30 feet.
Facilities: Tables, grills, vault toilets, drinking water, boat dock, launch.
Fee per night: $$.
Management: Linn County.
Contact: 541-967-3917.
Finding the campground: From Sweet Home, drive 5.5 miles east on U.S. Highway 20 and turn left (north) onto Quartzville Road, a BLM Back Country Byway heading toward Green Peter Reservoir. Go 11.1 miles and turn right to enter the county park. Drive another 0.6 mile to reach the camp entrance on the right; the boat ramp and picnic area lie straight ahead.

About the campground: You will find this campground on the Whitcomb Creek Arm of Green Peter Reservoir, a popular place for speed boating, fishing, and swimming. The county park is situated on terraces on the steep, forested shore of the reservoir. The spacious sites enjoy deep shade, and some are more level than others. Should the campground fill, owners of self-contained units can take advantage of dispersed camping that is allowed along the widened road shoulder of the reservoir outside the park.

36 Yellowbottom

Location: About 29 miles northeast of Sweet Home.
Sites: 22 basic sites; no hookups.
Maximum length: 20 feet.
Facilities: Tables, grills, vault toilets, drinking water.
Fee per night: $.
Management: Bureau of Land Management.
Contact: 503-365-5646.

Finding the campground: From Sweet Home, drive 5.5 miles east on U.S. Highway 20 and turn left (north) onto Quartzville Road, a BLM Back Country Byway heading toward Green Peter Reservoir. You will reach the campground on the left in 23.7 miles.

About the campground: Set in a stand of magnificent old-growth trees interwoven with vine maples, rhododendrons, cascara, and yews is this highly attractive, aesthetically pleasing campground. Across the road are a picnic area and an access trail to Quartzville Creek, an inviting, wild and scenic waterway characterized by boulders, gravel bars, gorgeous swimming holes, and riffles. The creek invites sunbathing, swimming, fishing, and recreational gold panning. Rhododendron Flat Loop offers a 1.2-mile hike. The campground is open from late May to mid-September.

37 Yukwah

Location: About 22 miles east of Sweet Home.
Sites: 20 basic sites; no hookups.
Maximum length: 30 feet.
Facilities: Tables, grills, vault toilets, drinking water.
Fee per night: $ to $$.
Management: Forest Service.
Contact: 541-367-5168.
Finding the campground: From Sweet Home, go 21.5 miles east on U.S. Highway 20. The campground is on the south side of the road.

About the campground: This neighbor of Trout Creek Campground (see above) holds similar attractions, with perhaps a few stouter firs in camp. The sites radiate from the campground loop road into the forest for plenty of privacy. A quarter-mile trail travels along the South Santiam River, providing access. Expect some traffic noise. The campground is open year-round, although services are limited in winter.

BLUE RIVER–MCKENZIE BRIDGE AREA

		Total sites	Max. RV length	Hookups	Toilets	Showers	Drinking water	Dump station	Recreation	Fee	Can reserve
38	Alder Springs	5	T		NF				H		
39	Box Canyon Horse Camp	11	35		NF				HR		
40	Coldwater Cove	35	30		NF			•	HFBL	$-$$	
41	Cougar Crossing	12	25		NF				HSFB	$	
42	Delta	37	35		NF			•	HSFB	$-$$	
43	Fish Lake	6	20		NF			•	H	$	
44	French Pete	17	30		NF			•	HSF	$$	
45	Frissell Crossing	12	35		NF			•	HF	$$	
46	Homestead	7	25		NF				F		
47	Ice Cap	22	16		F			•	HFB	$	
48	Limberlost	12	25		NF				F	$	
49	McKenzie Bridge	20	32		NF			•	FBL	$$	•
50	Mona	23	40		F			•	SFBL	$$	
51	Olallie	17	30		NF			•	HFBL	$	
52	Paradise	64	40		F			•	HFBL	$$	•
53	Slide Creek	16	25		NF			•	SFBL	$-$$	
54	Sunnyside	13	T		NF				SFB	$	
55	Trail Bridge	26	45		F			•	HFBL	$	

Hookups: W = Water   E = Electric   S = Sewer   **Total sites:** T = Tent-only campground   **Maximum trailer/RV length** given in feet.
Toilets: F = Flush   NF = No Flush   **Recreation:** H = Hiking   S = Swimming   F = Fishing   B = Boating   L = Boat Launch
O = Off-Highway Driving   R = Horseback Riding   C = Cycling
Fee: $ = $1-9 $$ = $10-19 $$$ = $20-29 $$$$ = $30-39.   If no entry under **Fee,** camping is free.

38 Alder Springs

Location: About 15 miles east of the community of McKenzie Bridge.
Sites: 5 tent sites; no hookups.
Maximum length: Suitable for tents only.
Facilities: Tables, grills, pit toilets. No drinking water.
Fee per night: None.
Management: Forest Service.
Contact: 541-822-3381.
Finding the campground: From McKenzie Bridge, go 4.6 miles east on Oregon 126 and bear right (east) on OR 242. Drive 10.4 miles to find this campground on the left.

About the campground: This tiny camp sits among the firs on McKenzie Pass Scenic Byway, opposite the trailhead to Linton Lake. Other trails in the area visit Proxy Falls and Scott Mountain. The byway, which passes between Three Sisters and Mount Washington Wilderness Areas, is generally open from July to October.

It is a photographer's wonderland; lava, forest, lakes, and volcanoes all make for spectacular images. Dee Wright Observatory, an outpost built of lava rock atop McKenzie Pass, supplies a unique perspective on the neighborhood and is itself photogenic.

39 Box Canyon Horse Camp

Location: About 30 miles southeast of the community of Blue River.
Sites: 11 basic sites; no hookups.
Maximum length: 35 feet.
Facilities: Tables, grills, vault toilets, corrals. No drinking water.
Fee per night: None.
Management: Forest Service.
Contact: 541-822-3317.
Finding the campground: From Blue River, drive east 4.3 miles on Oregon 126. Turn right (south) onto Forest Road 19 (Aufderheide Forest Drive) toward Cougar Reservoir. In 0.2 mile, turn right to remain on FR 19. Drive another 25.4 miles to the camp on the right (west) side of the road.

About the campground: This peaceful camp sits at the forested foot of Chucksney Mountain, providing a pleasant overnight base for campers with horses. Tall firs, rhododendrons, and ferns dress up the camp. Across the road are a historic guard station and an attractive swath of meadow. Interpretive panels along FR 19 introduce the history of the forest. Trails from the camp lead to Chucksney Mountain and into Three Sisters Wilderness Area. The campground is open from mid-May to mid-September.

40 Coldwater Cove

Location: 18 miles northeast of the community of McKenzie Bridge, on Clear Lake.
Sites: 35 basic sites; no hookups.
Maximum length: 30 feet.
Facilities: Tables, grills, vault toilets, drinking water, boat launch (non-motorized boating).
Fee per night: $ to $$.
Management: Forest Service.
Contact: 541-822-3381.
Finding the campground: From Oregon 126, 18 miles northeast of McKenzie Bridge, turn east at the sign for the camp.

About the campground: This camp occupies a forested slope at the southeast corner of Clear Lake, a frigid, spring-fed lake at the head of McKenzie Wild and Scenic River. A lava flow dotted with vine maples abuts the fir-shaded camp, and a superb trail rings the lake, visiting Great Spring (the source of the icy water) and Clear Lake Resort, where you can rent rowboats. Another exceptional trail follows the river downstream past Sahalie and Koosah Falls, both of which have drive-to viewing areas. Fishing, rowing the length of the lake, and watching ospreys dive for fish are some of the more popular pastimes here. The campground is open from late May to early September.

41 Cougar Crossing

Location: About 14 miles southeast of the community of Blue River, on Cougar Reservoir.
Sites: 12 basic sites; no hookups.
Maximum length: 25 feet.
Facilities: Tables, grills, vault and chemical toilets. No drinking water.
Fee per night: $.
Management: Forest Service.
Contact: 541-822-3317.
Finding the campground: From Blue River, drive 4.3 miles east on Oregon 126. Turn right (south) onto Forest Road 19 (Aufderheide Forest Drive) toward Cougar Reservoir. In 0.2 mile, turn right to remain on FR 19. Drive another 9.3 miles to reach the camp, which is on the right just after you cross the reservoir bridge.

About the campground: This small camp, which is near the reservoir bridge and an information kiosk on Aufderheide Drive, offers camping at the head of Cougar Reservoir. The sites have graveled parking and are open or partially shaded in a setting of maples, willows, cottonwoods, and a sprinkling of firs. Early in the year, the camp is actually on the reservoir. But as the water recedes during the summer, the camp overlooks the stark upper basin of the reservoir and the South Fork McKenzie River. The camp is a good base from which to boat, fish, swim, and water-ski. Terwilliger Hot Springs is 2.2 miles north of the camp on FR 19; the facility charges a user fee.

42 Delta

Location: About 5 miles east of the community of Blue River.
Sites: 37 basic sites, some of which are two party; no hookups.
Maximum length: 35 feet.
Facilities: Tables, grills, vault toilets, drinking water.
Fee per night: $ to $$.
Management: Forest Service.
Contact: 541-822-3317.
Finding the campground: From Blue River, drive 4.3 miles east on Oregon 126. Turn right (south) onto Forest Road 19 (Aufderheide Forest Drive) toward Cougar Reservoir. Go 0.2 mile and turn right to reach the campground after another 0.9 mile.

About the campground: The McKenzie River and its South Fork shape the delta on which this quiet family campground sits. An old-growth forest of firs, cedars, and hemlocks towers over the camp; enormous stumps and logs, as well as dogwoods and ferns, add to the enchanting forest setting. The sites are spacious and well spaced. The barrier-free Delta Nature Trail begins at the end of the campground loop. Fishing, rafting on the McKenzie, a tour along Aufderheide Forest Drive, and boating on Cougar Reservoir are other possible diversions. The campground is open from mid-May to late September.

43 Fish Lake

Location: About 22 miles northeast of the community of McKenzie Bridge.
Sites: 6 basic sites; no hookups.
Maximum length: 20 feet.
Facilities: Tables, grills, vault toilets, drinking water.
Fee per night: $.
Management: Forest Service.
Contact: 541-822-3381.
Finding the campground: It is west off Oregon 126, 22 miles northeast of McKenzie Bridge and 1.5 miles south of the junction of U.S. Highway 20 and OR 126, which in turn is 3 miles south of Santiam Junction.

About the campground: Situated at the edge of seasonal Fish Lake and a lava flow, this campground is shaded by big cottonwoods and firs. When the lake dries up in the summer, eagles visit to feast on fish trapped in small pools. By summer's end, a huge expanse of meadow has replaced the lake. The McKenzie River National Recreation Trail begins nearby, and Clear Lake, the McKenzie River, and Carmen Reservoir allow anglers to wet their lines.

44 French Pete

Location: About 15 miles southeast of the community of Blue River.
Sites: 17 basic sites; no hookups.
Maximum length: 30 feet.
Facilities: Tables, grills, vault toilets, drinking water.
Fee per night: $$.
Management: Forest Service.
Contact: 541-822-3317.
Finding the campground: From Blue River, drive 4.3 miles east on Oregon 126. Turn right (south) onto Forest Road 19 (Aufderheide Forest Drive) toward Cougar Reservoir. In 0.2 mile, turn right to remain on FR 19. Drive another 10.6 miles to the camp on the right.

About the campground: Set among old-growth trees on the scenic South Fork McKenzie River, this linear camp is a gateway to the popular French Pete Trail, which explores a canyon cloaked in old-growth forest as well as a sparkling creek with engaging pools. Other area trails explore nearby peaks and drainages. You may also fish, recreate on Cougar Reservoir downstream from camp, or soak in Terwilliger Hot Springs, 3.5 miles to the north. You must pay a fee to use the hot springs. The campground is open from mid-May to mid-September.

45 Frissell Crossing

Location: About 26 miles southeast of the community of Blue River.
Sites: 12 basic sites; no hookups.
Maximum length: 35 feet.
Facilities: Tables, grills, vault toilets, drinking water.
Fee per night: $$.
Management: Forest Service.
Contact: 541-822-3317.
Finding the campground: From Blue River, drive 4.3 miles east on Oregon 126. Turn right (south) onto Forest Road 19 (Aufderheide Forest Drive) toward Cougar Reservoir. In 0.2 mile, turn right to remain on FR 19. Drive another 21 miles to the camp on the left.

About the campground: This campground rests in an old-growth stand along the South Fork McKenzie River, just upstream from its confluence with the Roaring River. If you continue south past camp a short distance on FR 19, you will be able to view the Roaring River, an exciting whitewater that plunges through a green canyon. The view is well worth the trip. This camp will appeal to anglers, hikers, and camp "slugs." Trails lead upstream along the South Fork and a side creek. Together, the ancient trees, lovely undergrowth, and soothing rush of the river create an ideal backdrop for your stay. The campground is open from mid-May to mid-September.

46 Homestead

Location: About 22 miles southeast of the community of Blue River.
Sites: 7 basic sites; no hookups.
Maximum length: 25 feet.
Facilities: Tables, grills, pit toilets. No drinking water.
Fee per night: None.
Management: Forest Service.
Contact: 541-822-3317.
Finding the campground: From Blue River, drive 4.3 miles east on Oregon 126. Turn right (south) onto Forest Road 19 (Aufderheide Forest Drive) toward Cougar Reservoir. In 0.2 mile, turn right to remain on FR 19. Continue another 17.1 miles to reach the camp on the right.

About the campground: A lovely, old-growth stand of firs, cedars, and bigleaf maples provides the canopy for this linear campground along the South Fork McKenzie River, where special fishing regulations apply. Gravel bars contribute to the river's character as it races past camp. The steep canyon wall across the river enhances the quiet and seclusion of the camp. Boulders outline the parking areas for the well-spaced sites. The campground is open from mid-May to mid-September.

47 Ice Cap

Location: 17 miles northeast of the community of McKenzie Bridge.
Sites: 14 basic sites, 8 tent sites; no hookups.
Maximum length: 16 feet.
Facilities: Tables, grills, flush toilets, drinking water, waterfall viewing area.
Fee per night: $.
Management: Forest Service.
Contact: 541-822-3381.
Finding the campground: From McKenzie Bridge, drive northeast 17 miles on Oregon 126. The campground is on the west side of the highway.

About the campground: This camp on the McKenzie Wild and Scenic River has waterfall viewing platforms at its upper end and is just north of Carmen Reservoir. The sites rest among firs and cedars and generally are well spaced for comfort and privacy, but RVers may need to shop around for the most level site. Three viewpoints overlook Koosah Falls, a 63-foot rushing beauty. Trails travel both sides of the river here, so you can hike to the reservoir, Sahalie Falls, or Clear Lake, or you can make a loop tour between the upper river bridge above Sahalie Falls and the bridge at Carmen Reservoir. Fishing and quiet boating are possible at the reservoir and Clear Lake, or you can fish the river. The campground is open from late May to early September.

48 Limberlost

Location: About 6 miles east of the community of McKenzie Bridge.
Sites: 12 basic sites; no hookups.
Maximum length: 25 feet.
Facilities: Tables, grills, pit toilets. No drinking water.
Fee per night: $.
Management: Forest Service.
Contact: 541-822-3381.
Finding the campground: From McKenzie Bridge, go 4.6 miles east on Oregon 126 and turn right (east) onto OR 242. Drive 1.4 miles to find the campground on the left.

About the campground: This cozy, rustic camp sits above Lost Creek on the lower end of McKenzie Pass Scenic Byway, which is usually open July through October. Tall, straight trees enclose the closely spaced sites. Pockets of skunk cabbage can be found along the banks of the deep, clear creek. Nearby trails visit Proxy Falls, Linton Lake, and Scott Mountain and explore the Upper McKenzie River. The vine maples that dot the lava flows along the byway make for colorful fall drives; the magnificent Three Sisters, Mount Washington, and the wildernesses named for them are equally scenic. The campground is maintained from late May into September.

49 McKenzie Bridge

Location: Less than 1 mile west of the community of McKenzie Bridge.
Sites: 20 basic sites; no hookups.
Maximum length: 32 feet.
Facilities: Tables, grills, vault toilets, drinking water, primitive boat launch for drift boats and rafts.
Fee per night: $$.
Management: Forest Service.
Contact: 541-822-3381; 1-800-280-CAMP for reservations.
Finding the campground: From the community of McKenzie Bridge, drive 0.4 mile west on Oregon 126. The campground is on the south side of the highway.

About the campground: Campers here can enjoy the fun and relaxation afforded by the McKenzie River. Many of the sites overlook the river, and the camp is encompassed by a full, second-growth forest of firs, cedars, and western hemlocks, with a vibrant understory. Sites have gravel parking and are well spaced. River rafting, fishing, and reclining at camp are all popular. The campground is open from May 15 to September 30.

50 Mona

Location: About 7 miles northeast of the community of Blue River, on Blue River Reservoir.
Sites: 23 basic sites, some of which are two party; no hookups.
Maximum length: 40 feet.
Facilities: Tables, grills, flush toilets, drinking water, boat launch (en route to camp).
Fee per night: $$.
Management: Forest Service.
Contact: 541-822-3317.
Finding the campground: From the Blue River Junction on Oregon 126, go 2.7 miles east on OR 126 and turn north onto Forest Road 15 toward Blue River Reservoir. Go 3.8 miles, crossing a bridge over an arm of the reservoir, to reach the long entrance road to camp.

About the campground: This campground overlooks Blue River Reservoir from a forested plateau. A few old-growth monarchs rise amid the otherwise second-growth forest of the camp. The camp is well organized for comfort, with both pull-thru and back-in camp spaces. Roads and parking pads are paved. The large lake is open to fishing, swimming, boating, and waterskiing. The campground is open from mid-May to late September.

51 Olallie

Location: 11 miles northeast of the community of McKenzie Bridge.
Sites: 17 basic sites; no hookups.
Maximum length: 30 feet.
Facilities: Tables, grills, vault toilets, drinking water, boat launch (drift boat or raft).
Fee per night: $.
Management: Forest Service.
Contact: 541-822-3381.
Finding the campground: From McKenzie Bridge, drive 11 miles northeast on Oregon 126. The campground is on the west side of the highway.

About the campground: At the confluence of Olallie Creek and the McKenzie Wild and Scenic River sits this two-tiered camp. Some lower sites are right along the shore, while upper-level sites overlook the river. The sites are spacious and set in a semi-open forest. The McKenzie River National Recreation Trail is across the river. You can access it via Forest Road 2654 (Deer Creek Road), downstream from camp. Fishing, rafting, and drift boating are popular diversions. The campground is open from late May to early September.

52 Paradise

Location: About 4 miles east of the community of McKenzie Bridge.
Sites: 64 basic sites; no hookups.
Maximum length: 40 feet.
Facilities: Tables, grills, flush toilets, drinking water, primitive boat launch for rafts.
Fee per night: $$.
Management: Forest Service.
Contact: 541-822-3381; 1-800-280-CAMP for reservations.
Finding the campground: From McKenzie Bridge, go 3.8 miles east on Oregon 126 and turn left to enter the campground.

About the campground: One of a handful of idyllic McKenzie River campgrounds, this facility serves rafters, anglers, and hikers. The McKenzie National Recreation Trail follows the wild and scenic river upstream 24 miles to Clear Lake and its headwater spring, passing Sahalie and Koosah Falls en route. If your time is limited or your feet unwilling, you can also reach the lake and falls via OR 126. Sites have paved parking and sit in rich, multistoried old-growth forest. The campground is open from May 15 to September 30.

53 Slide Creek

Location: About 15 miles east of the community of Blue River, on Cougar Reservoir.
Sites: 16 basic sites, some of which are two party; no hookups.
Maximum length: 25 feet.
Facilities: Tables, grills, pit toilets, drinking water, paved boat launch.
Fee per night: $ to $$.
Management: Forest Service.
Contact: 541-822-3317.
Finding the campground: From Blue River, go 4.3 miles east on Oregon 126. Turn right (south) onto Forest Road 19 (Aufderheide Forest Drive) toward Cougar Reservoir. In 0.2 mile, bear right to remain on FR 19, and follow it another 9.3 miles. After crossing the reservoir bridge, turn left onto gravel FR 500, which heads north along the east shore. Proceed 1.4 miles to the campground entrance on the left.

About the campground: This popular east-shore campground is at the spot where Slide Creek feeds into Cougar Reservoir. The attractive, long green lake invites fishing, swimming, boating, and waterskiing, and this camp is an ideal gateway to the fun. The ragged skyline and the steep canyon walls, rocky and forested, add to the beauty of the setting. The campsites feature developed, off-shoulder parking and are shaded by fir, maple, and dogwood trees. Trailheads and a hot springs lie within short drives of the camp. The campground is open from mid-May to late September.

54 Sunnyside

Location: About 15 miles southeast of the community of Blue River, on Cougar Reservoir.
Sites: 13 tent sites; no hookups.
Maximum length: Suitable for tents only.
Facilities: Tables, grills, chemical toilets. No drinking water.
Fee per night: $.
Management: Forest Service.
Contact: 541-822-3317.
Finding the campground: From Blue River, drive 4.3 miles east on Oregon 126. Turn right (south) onto Forest Road 19 (Aufderheide Scenic Drive) toward Cougar Reservoir. In 0.2 mile, bear right to remain on FR 19 and follow it another 9.3 miles. After crossing the reservoir bridge, turn left onto gravel FR 500 and proceed about 0.8 mile to the campground entrance on the left. The entry road to the camp is steep.

About the campground: On the east shore of Cougar Reservoir sits this improved dispersed camp, with gravel parking spurs and basic site amenities. Plenty of shade will help to ensure your comfort. Boaters typically put in at Slide Creek Campground about half a mile north, but moor their boats along shore here at Sunnyside. The lake invites fishing, swimming, boating, and waterskiing. Trailheads and a hot springs lie within short drives of the camp. The campground is open from mid-May to late September.

55 Trail Bridge

Location: 13 miles northeast of the community of McKenzie Bridge, on Trail Bridge Reservoir.
Sites: 26 basic sites; no hookups.
Maximum length: 45 feet.
Facilities: Tables, grills, flush and vault toilets, drinking water, boat launch.
Fee per night: $.
Management: Forest Service.
Contact: 541-822-3381.
Finding the campground: From McKenzie Bridge, drive 13 miles northeast on Oregon 126. The campground is on the west side of the highway.

About the campground: This camp offers forested sites along Trail Bridge Reservoir, where the McKenzie River is harnessed for power generation. Additional camping for RVs is available on the open flat beside the reservoir. This is an area where human influence is strongly apparent and nature is overshadowed, but the reservoir offers fishing and boating and there is convenient access to the McKenzie River National Recreation Trail. McKenzie Pass Scenic Drive follows OR 126 and OR 242 for a possible outing away from camp. The campground is open from May to early September.

EUGENE–COTTAGE GROVE AREA

		Hookup sites	Total sites	Max. RV length	Hookups	Toilets	Showers	Drinking water	Dump station	Recreation	Fee	Can reserve
56	Baker Bay		48	35		NF	•	•	•	SFBL	$$	
57	Bedrock		19	20		NF		•		HF	$-$$	
58	Big Pool		5	T		NF		•		HF	$	
59	Broken Bowl		16	20		F		•		HF	$	
60	Cascara		56	35		NF		•	•	SFBL	$	
61	Cedar Creek		8	16		NF				HSF	$	
62	Dolly Varden		5	T		NF				HF	$	
63	Fisherman's Point		8	35		NF		•		FB	$	
64	Pine Meadows		92	40		F	•	•	•	FBL	$	
65	Primitive		15	40		NF		•		FBL	$	
66	Puma		11	16		NF		•		HF	$	
67	Richardson County Park	50	50	60	WE	F	•	•	•	SFBL	$$	•
68	Rujada		11	22		F		•		HF	$	
69	Schwartz		82	40		F	•	•	•	FB	$$	
70	Sharps Creek Recreation Area		11	30		NF		•		SF	$	
71	Winberry		7	small		NF		•		HF	$	

Hookups: W = Water E = Electric S = Sewer **Total sites:** T = Tent-only campground **Maximum trailer/RV length** given in feet.
Toilets: F = Flush NF = No Flush **Recreation:** H = Hiking S = Swimming F = Fishing B = Boating L = Boat Launch
O = Off-Highway Driving R = Horseback Riding C = Cycling
Fee: $ = $1-9 $$ = $10-19 $$$ = $20-29 $$$$ = $30-39. If no entry under **Fee**, camping is free.

56 Baker Bay

Location: About 7 miles east of Cottage Grove, on Dorena Lake.
Sites: 48 basic sites; no hookups.
Maximum length: 35 feet.
Facilities: Tables, grills, flush and vault toilets, drinking water, showers, dump station, telephone, boat rental, boat launch, dock, food concession.
Fee per night: $$.
Management: Lane County.
Contact: 541-682-6940.
Finding the campground: From Interstate 5 in Cottage Grove, take Exit 174 and go east 4.4 miles on Row River Road. Bear right on South Shore Road, following signs for Dorena Lake. Go another 2.7 miles and turn left into the camp.

About the campground: This campground and day-use recreation area faces Baker Bay, part of manmade Dorena Lake, which is contained in an attractive basin of rolling, wooded hills. The camp occupies a pleasant setting of lawn and shade trees, with some big, charismatic oaks for accent. Most sites allow at least a glimpse of the lake. This place bustles on summer weekends, but midweek stays are calmer. Waterskiing, a half-mile walk along shore, or a walk or bicycle ride on the Row River Rail Trail are possible diversions. The campground is open from April to mid-October.

57 Bedrock

Location: About 16 miles northeast of Lowell.
Sites: 13 basic sites, 6 tent sites; no hookups.
Maximum length: 20 feet.
Facilities: Tables, grills, vault toilets, drinking water.
Fee per night: $ to $$.
Management: Forest Service.
Contact: 541-937-2129.
Finding the campground: From Oregon 58, 13 miles east of Interstate 5 and 23 miles west of Oakridge, turn north onto Jasper-Lowell Road and drive 2.8 miles, following the signs through Lowell to Unity. Turn right (east) onto Big Fall Creek Road toward Winberry and North Shore, go 0.4 mile, and bear left to remain on Big Fall Creek Road for another 13.8 miles. The campground entrance is on the left.

About the campground: This camp along Fall Creek occupies a richly vegetated Douglas-fir forest with a midstory of vine maples, hazels, and cascaras. From camp you can easily access the Fall Creek National Recreation Trail to follow the creek in either direction. Nearby nature trails expand the hiking options. Fishing and taking in the recreation at Fall Creek Reservoir are also available. The campground is open from May to October.

58 Big Pool

Location: About 14 miles northeast of Lowell.
Sites: 5 tent sites; no hookups.
Maximum length: Suitable for tents only.
Facilities: Tables, grills, vault toilets, drinking water.
Fee per night: $.
Management: Forest Service.
Contact: 541-937-2129.
Finding the campground: From Oregon 58, 13 miles east of Interstate 5 and 23 miles west of Oakridge, turn north onto Jasper-Lowell Road and drive 2.8 miles, following the signs through Lowell to Unity. Turn right onto Big Fall Creek Road toward Winberry and North Shore, go 0.4 mile, and bear left to remain on Big Fall Creek Road for another 10.9 miles. The campground entrance is on the right.

About the campground: Sandwiched between the road and Fall Creek, this camp rests in the rich vegetation of a low-elevation Douglas-fir forest. Fall Creek National Recreation Trail (NRT) travels the opposite shore of Fall Creek but can be easily accessed in either direction from camp. To the east, Johnny Creek and

Clark Creek Nature Trails connect with the NRT or provide good tours of their own. Fishing and taking in the recreation at Fall Creek Reservoir are also available. The campground is open from May to mid-September.

59 Broken Bowl

Location: About 13 miles northeast of Lowell.
Sites: 6 basic sites, 10 tent sites; no hookups.
Maximum length: 20 feet.
Facilities: Tables, grills, flush toilets, drinking water.
Fee per night: $.
Management: Forest Service.
Contact: 541-937-2129.
Finding the campground: From Oregon 58, 13 miles east of Interstate 5 and 23 miles west of Oakridge, turn north onto Jasper-Lowell Road and go 2.8 miles, following the signs through Lowell to Unity. Turn right onto Big Fall Creek Road toward Winberry and North Shore, go 0.4 mile, and bear left to remain on Big Fall Creek Road for another 10.2 miles.

About the campground: This campground and day-use area along Fall Creek occupies a lush, low-elevation forest of Douglas-firs and western hemlocks and provides visitors with access to Fall Creek National Recreation Trail, as well as water play at the creek. A paved trail leads from the day-use area to Fall Creek. Fall Creek Reservoir offers fishing. The campground is open from mid-May to mid-September.

60 Cascara

Location: About 10 miles northeast of Lowell, on Fall Creek Reservoir.
Sites: 50 basic sites, 6 walk-in tent sites; no hookups.
Maximum length: 35 feet.
Facilities: Tables, grills, pit toilets, drinking water, dump station, telephone, improved boat ramp, dock, security gate at night.
Fee per night: $.
Management: U.S. Army Corps of Engineers.
Contact: 541-937-2131.
Finding the campground: From Oregon 58, 13 miles east of Interstate 5 and 23 miles west of Oakridge, turn north onto Jasper-Lowell Road and follow the signs for 2.8 miles through Lowell to Unity. Turn right on Big Fall Creek Road toward Winberry and North Shore, go 0.4 mile, and bear left to remain on Big Fall Creek Road for another 7.2 miles. Now turn right onto Peninsula Road and go 0.3 mile to the campground entrance on the right.

About the campground: This comfortable family camp along Fall Creek Reservoir offers some sites that are fully shaded and others that receive a mix of sun and shade. The sites have gravel parking and are well spaced for privacy among the firs, alders, and tangled understory. Campers enjoy convenient access to the reservoir for fishing and boating. A designated area serves swimmers. The campground is open from mid-May to early September.

61 Cedar Creek

Location: 23 miles east of Cottage Grove.
Sites: 8 basic sites; no hookups.
Maximum length: 16 feet.
Facilities: Tables, grills, vault toilets. No drinking water.
Fee per night: $.
Management: Forest Service.
Contact: 541-942-5591.
Finding the campground: From Interstate 5 in Cottage Grove, take Exit 174 and go east on Row River Road and Brice Creek Road for 23 miles. The camp is on the north side of Brice Creek Road.

About the campground: At the foot of the Calapooya Mountains, this small camp enjoys a rich, low-elevation forest setting and overlooks scenic Brice Creek, a clear stream punctuated by cascades and pools. On the opposite shore from the camp, the 5.5-mile Brice Creek Trail offers a fine tour along the creek and through old-growth stands; it is open to hikers and mountain bikers. A bridge at the camp accesses the trail; spur trails lead to waterfalls on Trestle Creek. The pools of the creek may inspire you to swim or perhaps dance a fly-line over to them.

62 Dolly Varden

Location: About 12 miles northeast of Lowell.
Sites: 5 tent sites; no hookups.
Maximum length: Suitable for tents only.
Facilities: Tables, grills, vault toilets. No drinking water.
Fee per night: $.
Management: Forest Service.
Contact: 541-937-2129.
Finding the campground: From Oregon 58, 13 miles east of Interstate 5 and 23 miles west of Oakridge, turn north onto Jasper-Lowell Road and follow the signs 2.8 miles through Lowell to Unity. Turn right onto Big Fall Creek Road toward Winberry and North Shore, go 0.4 mile, and bear left to remain on Big Fall Creek Road for another 9.7 miles.

About the campground: Like its counterparts farther upstream, this Fall Creek campground occupies a rich forest setting. It is also next to the lower trailhead for the14-mile Fall Creek National Recreation Trail (NRT), which pursues the creek upstream, sometimes tracing the canyon wall. The NRT can be fragmented for more manageable short hikes, and Johnny Creek and Clark Creek Nature Trails (both short drives east from the camp) offer fine strolls. Fishing, wading, and taking in the recreation at Fall Creek Reservoir are also potential pastimes. The campground is open from May to mid-September.

63 Fisherman's Point

Location: About 10 miles northeast of Lowell, on Fall Creek Reservoir.
Sites: 8 basic sites; no hookups.
Maximum length: 35 feet.
Facilities: Some tables and grills, chemical toilets, drinking water.
Fee per night: $.
Management: U.S. Army Corps of Engineers.
Contact: 541-937-2131.
Finding the campground: From Oregon 58, 13 miles east of Interstate 5 and 23 miles west of Oakridge, turn north onto Jasper-Lowell Road and follow the signs for 2.8 miles through Lowell to Unity. Turn right onto Big Fall Creek Road toward Winberry and North Shore, go 0.4 mile, and bear left to remain on Big Fall Creek Road for another 7.3 miles. The campground is on the left, 0.1 mile past the intersection with Peninsula Road.

About the campground: This camp overlooks Fall Creek at the head of Fall Creek Reservoir. Sites dot the meadow and forest edge, and a couple offer views of the creek. Blackberries are common in camp and tempting in summer. Reservoir fishing and boating are popular draws. The campground is open from May to September.

64 Pine Meadows

Location: About 7 miles south of Cottage Grove, on Cottage Grove Lake.
Sites: 92 basic sites; no hookups.
Maximum length: 40 feet.
Facilities: Tables, fire rings, flush toilets, drinking water, showers, dump station, telephone, playground, nearby boat launch.
Fee per night: $.
Management: U.S. Army Corps of Engineers.
Contact: 541-942-8657.
Finding the campground: From Interstate 5, about 4 miles south of Cottage Grove, take Exit 170 and follow London Road south along the east side of the freeway for 3 miles. Turn left onto Cottage Grove Reservoir Road and go another 2.5 miles to the campground entrance on the right.

About the campground: This large, developed campground stretches along a fair piece of the east shore of Cottage Grove Lake. The camp feels much like a city park with its lovely, groomed lawns and pine and fir shade trees. An open meadow extends to the lake. The campground has paved parking and some pull-thru sites. The large reservoir offers fishing, boating, and waterskiing, but the boat launch is located at Wilson Creek Day-Use Area, 0.6 mile south of camp. Late in the year, the reservoir may be drawn down. The campground is closed in winter.

65 Primitive

Location: About 8 miles south of Cottage Grove, on Cottage Grove Lake.
Sites: 15 basic sites; no hookups.
Maximum length: 40 feet.
Facilities: Tables, fire rings, nonflush toilets, drinking water, nearby boat launch.
Fee per night: $.
Management: U.S. Army Corps of Engineers.
Contact: 541-942-8657.
Finding the campground: From Interstate 5, about 4 miles south of Cottage Grove, take Exit 170 and follow London Road south along the east side of the freeway for 3 miles. Turn left onto Cottage Grove Reservoir Road and go another 3 miles to the campground entrance on the right.

About the campground: These primitive campsites are scattered across a broad meadow dotted by trees and wildflowers on the east shore of Cottage Grove Lake. A few sites sit closer to the open, grassy shore. Geese, ducks, and herons are camp companions. The reservoir hosts fishing, boating, and waterskiing, with access available at Wilson Creek Day-Use Area, 0.1 mile south of camp. The campground is closed in winter.

66 Puma

Location: About 18 miles northeast of Lowell.
Sites: 8 basic sites, 3 tent sites; no hookups.
Maximum length: 16 feet.
Facilities: Tables, grills, vault toilets, drinking water.
Fee per night: $.
Management: Forest Service.
Contact: 541-937-2129.
Finding the campground: From Oregon 58, 13 miles east of Interstate 5 and 23 miles west of Oakridge, turn north onto Jasper-Lowell Road and follow the signs for 2.8 miles through Lowell to Unity. Turn right onto Big Fall Creek Road toward Winberry and North Shore, go 0.4 mile, and bear left to remain on Big Fall Creek Road for another 15.4 miles.

About the campground: At this Fall Creek campground, the sites are fairly close together, but the forest setting is appealing. Fall Creek National Recreation Trail leads hikers through the canyon; the creek welcomes water play and the occasional dip of a fishing line. The campground is open from May to October.

67 Richardson County Park

Location: About 20 miles northwest of Eugene, on Fern Ridge Lake.
Sites: 50 hookup sites; water and electric hookups.
Maximum length: 60 feet.

Facilities: Tables, grills, flush toilets, drinking water, showers, dump station, telephone (at marina), playground (in day-use area), dock, launch, marina with 286 mooring slips, concession stand.
Fee per night: $$.
Management: Lane County.
Contact: 541-682-6940; 541-935-2005 for reservations.
Finding the campground: From Oregon 126 at Veneta, 15 miles west of Eugene, turn north onto Territorial Road and go 4.7 miles. Turn right onto Clear Lake Road and drive 0.2 mile to the park on the right.

About the campground: Covering 157 acres on the northwest shore of Fern Ridge Lake (a large valley reservoir), this park has lots of room to explore. The campground has a dual personality, with one group of sites in the valley trees and the others spread across open lawn among planted conifers. You will find paved roads and parking pads, with several pull-thru sites. The park has areas for sunning or resting in the shade, romping, swimming, boating, and fishing. The campground is open from April 15 to October 15.

68 Rujada

Location: About 20 miles east of Cottage Grove.
Sites: 11 basic sites; no hookups.
Maximum length: 22 feet.
Facilities: Tables, grills, flush and vault toilets, drinking water, softball field and horseshoe pits at picnic area.
Fee per night: $.
Management: Forest Service.
Contact: 541-942-5591.
Finding the campground: From Interstate 5 in Cottage Grove, take Exit 174 and go east on Row River Road for 18.3 miles. Turn left onto Forest Road 17 (Layng Creek Road) and continue 1.8 miles to reach this campground and picnic area.

About the campground: This is a highly pleasant campground along Layng Creek. Beneath the hemlocks and firs of the camp grows a lush midstory of maple, hazel, cascara, and dogwood. The sites are roomy and well spaced, with tent pads and adequate parking. The 1.5-mile Swordfern Trail begins at the picnic area parking lot and leads along silty Layng Creek. If you go 10.5 miles east of camp via Forest Roads 17, 1790, 1702, 1702.728, and 1702.203, you will reach a half-mile trail to 125-foot Moon Falls. The campground is open from late May to late September.

69 Schwartz

Location: About 5 miles east of Cottage Grove.
Sites: 82 basic sites; no hookups.
Maximum length: 40 feet.
Facilities: Tables, grills, flush toilets, drinking water, showers, dump station, playground, horseshoe pits.

Fee per night: $$.
Management: U.S. Army Corps of Engineers.
Contact: 541-942-5631.
Finding the campground: From Interstate 5 in Cottage Grove, take Exit 174 and go east on Row River Road for 4.4 miles. Bear right on South Shore Road, following signs for Dorena Lake. Drive another 0.4 mile to the camp.

About the campground: This quiet family campground stretches along the Row River Valley below the dam that created Dorena Lake. The camp is grassy, with maples, firs, oaks, and cottonwoods providing shade. An ash swale claims a part of the camp. The facility has paved roads and parking and convenient access to Dorena Lake for fishing and boating. The Row River Rail Trail is available to hikers and mountain bikers. The campground is open from late April to late September.

70 Sharps Creek Recreation Area

Location: About 18 miles southeast of Cottage Grove.
Sites: 11 basic sites; no hookups.
Maximum length: 30 feet.
Facilities: Tables, grills, vault toilets, drinking water (hand pump located on Sharps Creek Road).
Fee per night: $.
Management: Bureau of Land Management.
Contact: 541-683-6981.
Finding the campground: From Interstate 5 in Cottage Grove, take Exit 174 and go east on Row River Road for about 15 miles. Turn right (south) onto Sharps Creek Road and go 3.2 miles to the campground entrance on the right.

About the campground: The small campground is situated among tall, second-growth fir trees on the opposite side of Sharps Creek Road from Sharps Creek and a few bluff-top picnic sites. Despite the camp's proximity to the road, it remains relatively quiet in this lightly traveled area. A field stretches along the other side of the camp. Sharps Creek is a picturesque union of sparkling water, gravel bars, and deep blue-green pools cupped in rocky outcrops. One especially deep pool makes a good swimming hole. Sharps Creek is open to recreational gold panning except from March 1 to May 31. The campground is open from May 15 to September 30.

71 Winberry

Location: About 12 miles northeast of Lowell.
Sites: 2 basic sites, 5 tent sites; no hookups.
Maximum length: Small units only.
Facilities: Tables, grills, vault toilets, drinking water, Adirondack-style shelters at some sites.
Fee per night: $.
Management: Forest Service.

Contact: 541-937-2129.

Finding the campground: From Oregon 58, 13 miles east of Interstate 5 and 23 miles west of Oakridge, turn north onto Jasper-Lowell Road and follow the signs for 2.8 miles through Lowell to Unity. Turn right onto Big Fall Creek Road toward Winberry and North Shore, go 0.4 mile, and turn right onto Forest Road 1802 (Winberry Creek Road). Proceed 9 miles to this camp on the right.

About the campground: Along the shore of crystalline Winberry Creek sits this ideal camp for tenters. Tall firs and bigleaf maples; an effusive understory of vine maple, hazel, thimbleberry, and cascara; and a couple of rustic, Adirondack-style shelters add to the camp's appeal. The three-sided, A-frame shelters have earthen floors and tiered bunks ready to hold your sleeping bags. The camp offers tranquility, fishing, and nearby hiking on the 1-mile trail to Station Butte (consult your Willamette National Forest map for the trailhead location). The campground is open from mid-May to October.

OAKRIDGE AREA

	Hookup sites	Total sites	Max. RV length	Hookups	Toilets	Showers	Drinking water	Dump station	Recreation	Fee	Can reserve
72 Black Canyon		72	35		NF		•		HSFBL	$$	
73 Blue Pool		24	25		NF				F	$	
74 Campers Flat		5	18		NF		•		HF	$	
75 Gold Lake		20	25		NF		•		HFBL	$$	
76 Hampton		4	36		NF		•		FBL	$	
77 Indigo Springs		3	18		NF				HF		
78 Islet		55	30		F		•	•	HSBL	$	
79 Kiahanie		19	35		NF		•		F	$	
80 North Waldo		58	30		F		•	•	HSBL	$	
81 Packard Creek		33	28		NF		•		SFBL	$$	
82 Sacandaga		16	20		NF				HF		
83 Salmon Creek Falls		14	40		NF		•		SF	$$	
84 Sand Prairie		20	28		F		•		HF	$-$$	
85 Secret		6	24		NF				SF	$	
86 Shadow Bay		92	30		F		•	•	HSBL	$	
87 Shady Dell		9	T		NF		•		SF	$$	
88 Timpanogas Lake		10	24		NF		•		HFB	$	

Hookups: W = Water E = Electric S = Sewer **Total sites:** T = Tent-only campground **Maximum trailer/RV length** given in feet.
Toilets: F = Flush NF = No Flush **Recreation:** H = Hiking S = Swimming F = Fishing B = Boating L = Boat Launch
O = Off-Highway Driving R = Horseback Riding C = Cycling
Fee: $ = $1-9 $$ = $10-19 $$$ = $20-29 $$$$ = $30-39. If no entry under **Fee**, camping is free.

72 Black Canyon

Location: 6 miles northwest of Oakridge.
Sites: 59 basic sites, 13 tent sites; no hookups.
Maximum length: 35 feet.
Facilities: Tables, grills, vault toilets, drinking water, boat ramp (for canoes and motor boats).
Fee per night: $$.
Management: Forest Service.
Contact: 541-937-2129.
Finding the campground: It is north off Oregon 58, 6 miles west of Oakridge and 22 miles east of Eugene.

About the campground: This camp claims a fir-cedar flat at a bend in the Middle Fork Willamette River just before it empties into Lookout Point Reservoir. The improved sites have level asphalt parking and enjoy the peace and shade that comes from a mature forest setting. The designated tent sites have tent pads to ease the job of setting up camp. Rainbow and cutthroat trout challenge the skills of anglers, while the Black Canyon Nature Trail offers a 1-mile interpretive walk through the forest. The reservoir offers boating, fishing, swimming, and waterskiing. The campground is open from mid-May to October.

73 Blue Pool

Location: 9 miles east of Oakridge.
Sites: 19 basic sites, 5 walk-in tent sites; no hookups.
Maximum length: 25 feet.
Facilities: Tables, grills, vault toilets. No drinking water.
Fee per night: $.
Management: Forest Service.
Contact: 541-782-2283.
Finding the campground: From Oakridge, go 9 miles east on Oregon 58. The campground is on the south side of the highway.

About the campground: A rich forest of fir, cedar, maple, and alder envelops this campground. Some of the well-spaced, private sites overlook Salt Creek, and all have paved parking and are surrounded with greenery: salal, wild rose, Oregon grape, red huckleberry, and more. Salt Creek provides a soothing backdrop, welcomes fishing, and suggests a 14-mile upstream drive to view its 286-foot waterfall, the second tallest in the state. Salt Creek Falls has a developed viewing area and interpretive signs. Hiking and cross-country ski trails radiate from the falls area. The campground is open from mid-May to October.

74 Campers Flat

Location: About 23 miles south of Oakridge.
Sites: 5 basic sites; no hookups.
Maximum length: 18 feet.
Facilities: Tables, barbecues and grills, pit toilets, drinking water.
Fee per night: $.
Management: Forest Service.
Contact: 541-782-2283.
Finding the campground: From Oregon 58, 2 miles east of Oakridge, turn south onto Kitson Springs Road toward Hills Creek Reservoir. Go 0.5 mile and turn right onto Forest Road 21. Follow it for 20 miles to enter the camp on the right.

About the campground: This small camp along the Middle Fork Willamette River features semi-open sites in a setting of cedars and cottonwoods. The river rushes by the camp and features riffles and a deep pool bounded by rock outcrops. Suckers and rainbow and cutthroat trout may tug at your fishing line. An interpretive sign in the camp identifies a portion of the old Oregon Central Military Wagon Road. Hikers can access the Middle Fork Trail near the camp or pick up the 4.1-mile Youngs Rock Trail across the road from the camp entrance. The Youngs Rock Trail also appeals to mountain bikers. The campground is open from late April to mid-October.

75 Gold Lake

Location: About 28 miles southeast of Oakridge, on Gold Lake.
Sites: 20 basic sites; no hookups.
Maximum length: 25 feet.
Facilities: Tables, grills, vault toilets, drinking water, boat launch, wheelchair-accessible canoe dock, picnic shelter.
Fee per night: $$.
Management: Forest Service.
Contact: 541-782-2283.
Finding the campground: From Oakridge, drive 26 miles southeast on Oregon 58. Turn left (north) onto Forest Road 500 and go 2 miles to reach the camp at the end of the road.

About the campground: This attractive, popular camp is found along Gold Lake, a 100-acre, 25-foot-deep mountain lake in an alpine setting of true fir, spruce, white pine, and mountain hemlock. Huckleberry and mountain ash adorn the camp and lakeshore. The lake outlet has its own charm, with its grassy banks, alder clumps, and aquatic wildflowers. The outlet bridge bisects the camp, which has gravel parking, some pull-thru sites, and some lakeside sites. Only fly fishing and non-motorized boating are allowed at the lake. Trailheads at and near the camp open the way to high lakes and peaks for anyone willing to put boot leather to the trail. Some paths double as cross-country ski trails. The campground is open from June through September.

76 Hampton

Location: 9 miles northwest of Oakridge, on Lookout Point Reservoir.
Sites: 4 basic sites; no hookups.
Maximum length: 36 feet.
Facilities: Tables, grills, vault toilets, drinking water, boat launch.
Fee per night: $.
Management: Forest Service.
Contact: 541-782-2283.
Finding the campground: It is north off Oregon 58, 9 miles west of Oakridge and 19 miles east of Eugene.

About the campground: This tiny camp exists primarily to put visitors on Lookout Point Reservoir with a minimum of fuss. It is just off the highway, basic, and not very scenic. However, it does provide access to the reservoir for fishing, boating, and waterskiing.

77 Indigo Springs

Location: About 30 miles southeast of Oakridge.
Sites: 3 basic sites; no hookups.
Maximum length: 18 feet.
Facilities: Tables, fire rings, pit toilets. No drinking water.
Fee per night: None.
Management: Forest Service.
Contact: 541-782-2283.
Finding the campground: From Oregon 58, 2 miles east of Oakridge, turn south onto Kitson Springs Road toward Hills Creek Reservoir. Go 0.5 mile and turn right onto Forest Road 21. Follow it 27 miles to the campground entrance on the left.

About the campground: Across FR 21 from the Middle Fork Willamette River, this tiny campground sits alongside Indigo Creek and a section of the old Oregon Central Military Wagon Road. It enjoys a rich setting of cedars, firs, and hemlocks. From camp, a 500-foot trail loops around the headwater spring that gives birth to Indigo Creek. Campers can also take a few strides along the military wagon road before it becomes too overgrown. You may access the river and a riverside trail on the other side of FR 21. The campground is open from mid-April into November.

78 Islet

Location: About 36 miles east of Oakridge, on Waldo Lake.
Sites: 55 basic sites; no hookups.
Maximum length: 30 feet.
Facilities: Tables, grills, flush and pit toilets, drinking water, dump station (1 mile from camp), boat launch.
Fee per night: $.
Management: Forest Service.
Contact: 541-782-2283.
Finding the campground: From Oakridge, go 23 miles southeast on Oregon 58 and turn left (north) onto Forest Road 5897 toward Waldo Lake. Go 11 miles and bear left on FR 5898 for another 1.5 miles to reach the campground.

About the campground: This camp rests near the north end of Waldo Lake, a large, natural, mountain lake acclaimed for being the fourth clearest lake in the world. The sites sit back from the sandy shore in a forest of hemlocks and firs. Islet Point protrudes 0.1 mile into the lake and gives the camp its name. Benches at the end of the point welcome those who want to meditate or gaze at the sunset. The Shoreline Trail travels 1 mile between Islet and North Waldo Campgrounds; a longer trail system encircles the lake and branches off into Waldo Lake Wilderness. Canoeing and swimming are popular here. Boats are restricted to a speed of 10 miles per hour. Be sure to pack insect repellent, because mosquitoes breed in the pools of snowmelt along the lakeshore. They are most bothersome from June to mid-August. The campground is open from late June through September.

Waldo Lake.

79 Kiahanie

Location: About 22 miles northeast of Oakridge.
Sites: 19 basic sites; no hookups.
Maximum length: 35 feet.
Facilities: Tables, grills, vault toilets, drinking water.
Fee per night: $.
Management: Forest Service.
Contact: 541-782-2283.
Finding the campground: From Oregon 58, just west of Oakridge, turn north at the sign for West Fir. From West Fir, go east on Forest Road 19 (Aufderheide Forest Drive) for 19.7 miles to reach the campground entrance on the left.

About the campground: This camp occupies a mostly uncut forest along the North Fork Middle Fork Willamette Wild and Scenic River on Aufderheide Forest Drive. The camp has a diverse ceiling of fir, cedar, hemlock, yew, vine maple, alder, and bigleaf maple; abundant greenery, huge old stumps, and the crystalline river add to the camp's appeal. The camp has gravel roads and parking and provides river access for fly-fishing. Native fish test anglers' skills. The campground is open from late April to late October.

80 North Waldo

Location: About 35 miles east of Oakridge, on Waldo Lake.
Sites: 58 basic sites; no hookups.
Maximum length: 30 feet.
Facilities: Tables, grills, flush and pit toilets, drinking water, dump station (near Islet Campground), boat launch.
Fee per night: $.
Management: Forest Service.
Contact: 541-782-2283.
Finding the campground: From Oakridge, drive 23 miles southeast on Oregon 58. Turn left (north) onto Forest Road 5897 toward Waldo Lake, go 11 miles, and bear left on FR 5898 for 0.4 mile. Turn right onto FR 5895 and drive 0.5 mile to the camp.

About the campground: This popular camp rests in a high-elevation forest at the north end of Waldo Lake, a 10-square-mile, natural lake with no permanent inlet. This helps to make it one of the purest lakes in the world, although not great for fishing. The deep water at the camp boat launch is perfect for large sailboats. Hikers will find numerous trails starting from the camp, including the 21-mile Waldo Lake Trail and the Shoreline Trail, which leads in 1 mile to Islet Campground (see above). Pack insect repellent, because the mosquitoes can be menacing. The campground is open from late June through September.

81 Packard Creek

Location: About 9 miles southeast of Oakridge, on Hills Creek Reservoir.
Sites: 33 basic sites; no hookups.
Maximum length: 28 feet.
Facilities: Tables, grills and barbecues, vault toilets, drinking water, boat launch, 2 fishing docks (1 barrier free), protected swimming area, sites with individual docks, 2 picnic shelters.
Fee per night: $$.
Management: Forest Service.
Contact: 541-782-2283.
Finding the campground: From Oakridge, go 2 miles east on Oregon 58 and turn south onto Kitson Springs Road toward Hills Creek Reservoir. Go 0.5 mile and turn right onto Forest Road 21. Follow it 6 miles to the campground entrance on the left.

About the campground: This accommodating camp on Hills Creek Reservoir offers forested sites that sit fairly close together. But water sports are what draw most visitors, so they spend lengthy spells away from their sites. Boating, fishing, swimming, and waterskiing are all popular. Expect the camp to fill on summer weekends and holidays. There is a short lakeshore trail at the camp. Beware of poison oak when venturing off trails and roads. The campground is open with full services from late April through September; the boat launch is open year-round.

82 Sacandaga

Location: About 27 miles south of Oakridge.
Sites: 16 basic sites; no hookups.
Maximum length: 20 feet.
Facilities: Tables, grills and barbecues, pit toilets. No drinking water.
Fee per night: None.
Management: Forest Service.
Contact: 541-782-2283.
Finding the campground: From Oregon 58, 2 miles east of Oakridge, turn south onto Kitson Springs Road toward Hills Creek Reservoir. Go 0.5 mile and turn right onto Forest Road 21. Follow it for 24.6 miles to the campground entrance on the right.

About the campground: This campground occupies a mixed forest on a bluff above the Middle Fork Willamette River. The rush of the river echoes through the canyon and contributes to the peacefulness of the camp. A trail leads to a bench seat with a view of the river canyon. Paths lead down to the river if you want to fish or admire the water and rugged riverbank. For longer hikes, you can access the Middle Fork Willamette Trail from the entrance road to the camp. The campground is open from late April to mid-October.

83 Salmon Creek Falls

Location: About 5 miles east of Oakridge.
Sites: 14 basic sites; no hookups.
Maximum length: 40 feet.
Facilities: Tables, grills, vault toilets, drinking water.
Fee per night: $$.
Management: Forest Service.
Contact: 541-782-2283.
Finding the campground: From Oregon 58 in Oakridge, turn north at the light onto Crestview Street toward the Oakridge Business District. Go 0.2 mile and turn right onto 1st Street, which becomes Forest Road 24. Travel 4.9 miles to the campground entrance on the right.

About the campground: A full, mature forest of evergreen and deciduous trees shrouds this camp on a flat above Salmon Creek and Salmon Creek Falls. The abundance of flora further adds to the picturesque setting. Salmon Creek rushes through a tight canyon as it nears the falls and then cascades over 10-foot ledges and sloping bedrock. A misty green pool swirls at the base of the falls, and gravel-bar beaches lie downstream. The viewing area for the falls is at the day-use area. Besides admiring and photographing the falls, you may fish, swim, and kayak. The campground is open from late April to mid-October.

84 Sand Prairie

Location: About 14 miles south of Oakridge.
Sites: 20 basic sites; no hookups.
Maximum length: 28 feet.
Facilities: Tables, grills and barbecues, flush and vault toilets, drinking water.
Fee per night: $ to $$.
Management: Forest Service.
Contact: 541-782-2283.
Finding the campground: From Oregon 58, 2 miles east of Oakridge, turn south onto Kitson Springs Road toward Hills Creek Reservoir. Go 0.5 mile and turn right onto Forest Road 21. Follow it for 11 miles to the campground entrance on the right.

About the campground: This campground on the Middle Fork Willamette River is nicely forested and has comfortably spaced sites. The setting blends towering evergreens with a leafy midstory; the dogwoods are especially pretty when in bloom. The camp marks the start of the 27-mile Middle Fork Trail, the river offers trout fishing, and the upper end of Hills Creek Reservoir is within a short drive of the camp. The campground is open from late April to mid-November.

85 Secret

Location: About 22 miles south of Oakridge.
Sites: 6 basic sites; no hookups.
Maximum length: 24 feet.
Facilities: Tables, grills and barbecues, pit toilets. No drinking water.
Fee per night: $.
Management: Forest Service.
Contact: 541-782-2283.
Finding the campground: From Oregon 58, 2 miles east of Oakridge, turn south onto Kitson Springs Road toward Hills Creek Reservoir. Go 0.5 mile and turn right onto Forest Road 21. Follow it 19 miles to the campground entrance on the right.

About the campground: This camp along the Middle Fork Willamette River feels pleasantly isolated and offers a handful of nicely forested sites. The river's riffles and deep pools draw anglers and summer visitors seeking a refreshing dip; there is a nice pool just upstream from the camp. Cottonwoods reign along the river. The campground is open from late April through October.

86 Shadow Bay

Location: About 32 miles east of Oakridge, on Waldo Lake.
Sites: 92 basic sites; no hookups.
Maximum length: 30 feet.
Facilities: Tables, grills, flush and pit toilets, drinking water, dump station, boat launch (0.5 mile from camp).
Fee per night: $.
Management: Forest Service.
Contact: 541-782-2283.
Finding the campground: From Oakridge, go 23 miles southeast on Oregon 58. Turn left (north) onto Forest Road 5897 toward Waldo Lake, go 6.6 miles, and turn left onto the campground access road. Go about 2 miles to Shadow Bay Campground.

About the campground: On a large, attractive bay at the south end of Waldo Lake, this camp occupies a more humid forest setting than the other lake camps. This means more foliage but also more mosquitoes, so be sure to bring repellent. The camp offers access to the Shoreline Trail (in loop B and near the boat launch) and has a designated swimming area between loops D and E. The sites rest in a mixed-age forest set back from Waldo Lake, Shadow Bay, and a small lily pond. Boats on the lake are restricted to a speed of 10 miles per hour. The campground is open from late June through September.

87 Shady Dell

Location: 5 miles northwest of Oakridge.
Sites: 9 tent sites; no hookups.
Maximum length: Suitable for tents only.
Facilities: Tables, grills, vault toilets, drinking water.
Fee per night: $.
Management: Forest Service.
Contact: 541-937-2129.
Finding the campground: It is south off Oregon 58, 5 miles west of Oakridge and 23 miles east of Eugene.

About the campground: This camp occupies a mature forest featuring old-growth cedars. Tiny Dell Creek threads through camp to join the Middle Fork Willamette River on the opposite side of the highway. You can access the river and Lookout Point Reservoir at Black Canyon Campground 1 mile west. Shady Dell is convenient for through-travelers on OR 58. The campground is open from May to October.

88 Timpanogas Lake

Location: About 45 miles southeast of Oakridge, on Timpanogas Lake.
Sites: 10 basic sites; no hookups.
Maximum length: 24 feet.
Facilities: Tables, grills, pit toilets, drinking water.
Fee per night: $.
Management: Forest Service.
Contact: 541-782-2283.
Finding the campground: From Oregon 58, 2 miles east of Oakridge, turn south onto Kitson Springs Road toward Hills Creek Reservoir. Go 0.5 mile and turn right onto Forest Road 21. Follow FR 21 for 32 miles and turn left onto FR 2154. Drive another 10 miles or so to the campground entrance on the left.

About the campground: Situated below the Cascade Crest in the Oregon Cascades Recreation Area, this is one of the most enchanting spots in the state, but it is guarded by mosquitoes until late in the summer. The sites are spacious, well forested, and spread around lovely, blue Timpanogas Lake, which is rimmed by forest, meadow, and rugged slope. The lake is open to fishing and non-motorized boating. Trails explore the lakeshore and visit Indigo Lake, another high-mountain jewel near which pikas and pine marten dwell. Huckleberry bushes, when weighted with berries, tempt pickers forth with bowls and buckets. The setting offers photographers plenty of subject matter. The campground is open from July to mid-October.

Southern Oregon

The southern region of the state features the spectacular Umpqua and Rogue River drainages, Crater Lake National Park, the wildlife havens of the Klamath Basin, and the rugged wilds and botanical diversity of the Siskiyou Mountains. It encompasses parts of six national forests: Siskiyou, Umpqua, Rogue River, Winema, Fremont, and Deschutes. Campers here will find superb opportunities for outdoor recreation and wildlife observation, but they will also be treated to cultural offerings, including the Shakespeare Festival in Ashland and Favell Museum in Klamath Falls.

This is "Jefferson State" country. For decades now, the residents of southern Oregon and northern California have advocated the creation of a new state as a way to gain a stronger political voice. While they have not succeeded, they continue to maintain their separatist mindset. The major towns of this region are Roseburg, Grants Pass, Medford, Ashland, and Klamath Falls, but much of southern Oregon is lightly inhabited.

The weather can vary greatly in this diverse region. The southern valleys threaded by Interstate 5 typically have mild, wet winters punctuated by a few snowstorms that can close the freeway. Summers are hot and dry. The mountains experience four seasons, with some slopes harboring stubborn snowfields that linger well into summer. The Crater Lake area often has snow banks over 6 feet high when the summer travel season gets under way. Weather in the Klamath Basin is temperamental and varies from season to season. It can be relatively snow free and cold or so snowbound that you would need snowshoes or cross-country skis to enjoy it. Summers are generally warm and dry. Mosquitoes can be annoying, especially in the high lakes region and around the lakes and marshes of Klamath Basin.

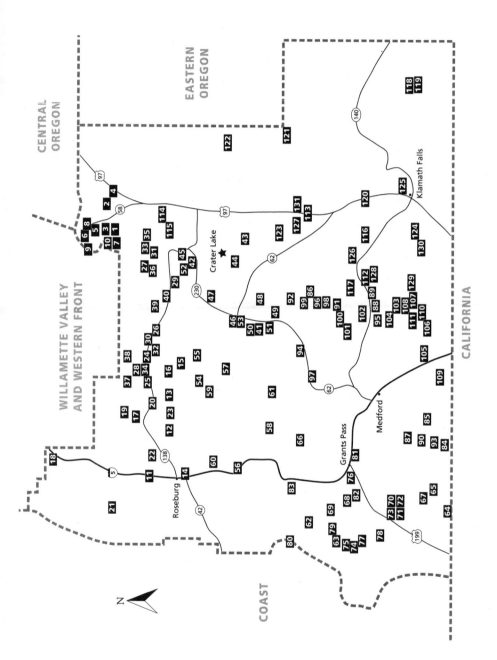

ODELL–CRESCENT LAKES AREA

	Hookup sites	Total sites	Max. RV length	Hookups	Toilets	Showers	Drinking water	Dump station	Recreation	Fee	Can reserve
1 Contorta Point		15	30		NF				SFB		
2 Crescent Creek		10	40		NF		•		F	$	
3 Crescent Lake		47	40		NF		•		HSFBL	$$	•
4 Cy Bingham County Park		12	30		NF		•		FC	$	
5 Odell Creek		22	16		NF				SFB	$	
6 Princess Creek		46	30		NF		•		SFBL	$$	
7 Spring		68	35		NF		•		HSFBL	$$	•
8 Sunset Cove		21	30		NF		•		SFBL	$$	
9 Trapper Creek		32	30		NF		•		HSFBL	$$	
10 Whitefish Horse Camp		17	30		NF		•		HFBR	$-$$	•

Hookups: W = Water E = Electric S = Sewer **Total sites:** T = Tent-only campground **Maximum trailer/RV length** given in feet.
Toilets: F = Flush NF = No Flush **Recreation:** H = Hiking S = Swimming F = Fishing B = Boating L = Boat Launch
O = Off-Highway Driving R = Horseback Riding C = Cycling
Fee: $ = $1-9 $$ = $10-19 $$$ = $20-29 $$$$ = $30-39. If no entry under **Fee,** camping is free.

1 Contorta Point

Location: About 11 miles southwest of the town of Crescent Lake, on Crescent Lake.
Sites: 15 bahsic sites; no hookups.
Maximum length: 30 feet.
Facilities: Tables, fire rings, pit and vault toilets. No drinking water.
Fee per night: None.
Management: Forest Service.
Contact: 541-433-2234.
Finding the campground: From the small community of Crescent Lake on Oregon 58, turn south onto paved Forest Road 60, go 2.3 miles, and turn right to remain on FR 60 another 7.7 miles. Turn left onto FR 280 and drive 0.9 mile to the camp entrance. The final 2.8 miles are on gravel or dusty dirt road.

About the campground: This campground occupies a forest of lodgepole pines on Contorta Point, a peninsula on the south shore of Crescent Lake. The camp serves up some of the best views to be had of Diamond Peak, along with views of Red Top Mountain. The lodgepoles grow tall and thin; the site parking is informal. Afternoon winds and early-summer mosquitoes are common, but the area offers fishing, swimming, sailboarding, and sailing. Trails can be found in nearby Diamond Peak Wilderness and Oregon Cascades Recreation Area. The campground is open from mid-May to October.

2 Crescent Creek

Location: About 7 miles southeast of the town of Crescent Lake.
Sites: 10 basic sites; no hookups.
Maximum length: 40 feet.
Facilities: Tables, grills, pit toilets, drinking water.
Fee per night: $.
Management: Forest Service.
Contact: 541-433-2234.
Finding the campground: From Crescent Lake, drive 3.4 miles east on Oregon 58. Turn left onto Forest Road 61 (Crescent Cutoff Road), go 3.3 miles, and turn right into the camp. Because the sign for the campground is easy to miss, look for the camp entrance 0.1 mile past the intersection of FR 61 with FR 46.

About the campground: This lightly used camp claims a forest of lodgepole and ponderosa pine on a flat along Crescent Creek, a wild and scenic waterway. Bunchgrass, wildflowers, and arid shrubs spread between the sites. In this dry terrain, campers need to be extra careful with campfires. The creek flows deep and clear between banks lined with shrubs and willows, offering anglers a challenge. An access path leads from camp to creek. The campground is open from May to October.

3 Crescent Lake

Location: About 3 miles southeast of the town of Crescent Lake, on Crescent Lake.
Sites: 47 basic sites; no hookups.
Maximum length: 40 feet.
Facilities: Tables, grills, vault toilets, drinking water, boat launch, dock.
Fee per night: $$.
Management: Forest Service.
Contact: 541-433-2234; 1-800-280-CAMP for reservations.
Finding the campground: From the small community of Crescent Lake on Oregon 58, turn south onto paved Forest Road 60, go 2.3 miles, and turn right to remain on FR 60 another 0.4 mile. Turn left to enter the camp.

About the campground: At the north end of Crescent Lake sits this developed campground with paved interior roads and gravel parking. Firs and lodgepole pines shade the terraced camp. Some of the sites overlook the water; the upper sites may require more leveling. The lake is open to swimming, fishing, boating, sailing, sailboarding, and waterskiing. Look for the Fawn Lake Trail, which starts off the campground entrance road. The campground is open from mid-May to October.

4 Cy Bingham County Park

Location: In Crescent.
Sites: 12 basic sites; no hookups.
Maximum length: 30 feet.
Facilities: Some tables and grills, pit toilets, drinking water.
Fee per night: $.
Management: Klamath County.
Contact: 541-883-4696.
Finding the campground: From U.S. Highway 97 in Crescent, head west on the Crescent Cutoff Road for 0.1 mile. Turn right and go a few hundred feet to the campground entrance on the left.

About the campground: Named for an early forester, this is a convenient, no-frills camp just off US 97 and close to the Little Deschutes River. The camp occupies a lodgepole-pine flat. Logs outline the earthen sites, each of which has a table and/or grill. River access is across the road, and a bike path parallels the Crescent Cutoff Road. The campground is closed in winter.

5 Odell Creek

Location: About 2 miles north of the town of Crescent Lake, on Odell Lake.
Sites: 22 basic sites; no hookups.
Maximum length: 16 feet.
Facilities: Tables, grills, vault toilets. No drinking water.
Fee per night: $.
Management: Forest Service.
Contact: 541-433-2234.
Finding the campground: From Oregon 58, 1.9 miles west of the community of Crescent Lake, 5.4 miles east of Willamette Pass, turn south for the East Shore Odell Lake Access and enter the camp within 0.1 mile.

About the campground: This linear campground stretches along the east shore of Odell Lake, an enchanting, 6-mile-long, natural lake with an outstanding fishery of trophy-sized Mackinaw, kokanee, and rainbow trout. Sites enjoy deep shade from a forest of fir and spruce. You can see Lakeview Mountain across the lake and Maiden Peak to the north. Odell Lake invites a full range of water sports, but it receives less traffic than many lakes in the state. Odell Creek, the outlet at the edge of the camp, is scenic in its own right. Across the creek from the camp sits a resort where boat rentals and other services are available. A trail to Fawn Lake begins near the resort. The campground is open from mid-May to October.

6 Princess Creek

Location: About 6 miles northwest of the town of Crescent Lake, on Odell Lake.
Sites: 46 basic sites; no hookups.
Maximum length: 30 feet.
Facilities: Tables, grills, vault toilets, drinking water, boat launch, dock.
Fee per night: $$.
Management: Forest Service.
Contact: 541-433-2234.
Finding the campground: It is south off Oregon 58, 5.6 miles northwest of Crescent Lake.

About the campground: This camp is spread along the north shore of Odell Lake. You can see Diamond Peak across the water. Great concentrations of hemlock, along with fir and spruce, shade the camp and protect it from the lake's notorious afternoon winds. The camp has a paved road, gravel parking, and comfortable sites, but it does get some traffic noise from OR 58 during the day. The lake is prized for its boating, fishing, and swimming. Bald eagles and ospreys also fish this 6-mile-long natural lake. The campground is open from mid-May to October.

7 Spring

Location: About 9 miles southwest of the town of Crescent Lake, on Crescent Lake.
Sites: 68 basic sites; no hookups.
Maximum length: 35 feet.
Facilities: Tables, grills, vault toilets, drinking water, boat launch, dock.
Fee per night: $$.
Management: Forest Service.
Contact: 541-433-2234; 1-800-280-CAMP for reservations.
Finding the campground: From the small community of Crescent Lake on Oregon 58, go south 2.3 miles on paved Forest Road 60 and turn right to remain on FR 60 for another 5.8 miles. Turn left and proceed 0.6 mile to enter camp.

About the campground: This is a developed campground on the south shore of Crescent Lake, a large lake on the outskirts of the Diamond Peak Wilderness. Sites have gravel parking and basic amenities and are partially shaded by lodgepole pines. Campers here enjoy access to the lake for fishing, swimming, boating, waterskiing, sailboarding, and sailing and to the Diamond Peak Wilderness for hiking. A trailhead 0.3 mile west of the camp accesses the Oregon Cascades Recreation Area. Lake visitors should come prepared for mosquitoes at the start of summer. The campground is open from mid-May to October.

8 Sunset Cove

Location: About 3 miles northwest of the town of Crescent Lake, on Odell Lake.
Sites: 21 basic sites; no hookups.
Maximum length: 30 feet.
Facilities: Tables, grills, vault toilets, drinking water, boat launch, dock, wheelchair-accessible jetty for fishing, fish-cleaning station.
Fee per night: $$.
Management: Forest Service.
Contact: 541-433-2234.
Finding the campground: It is south off Oregon 58, 4.7 miles east of Willamette Pass, 2.8 miles west of Crescent Lake Junction.

About the campground: This Odell Lake camp is situated in an evergreen forest punctuated by old-growth trees. Its location on the east shore provides you with front-row seats for sunsets, but it also puts you in the path of the strong afternoon winds, if you venture out of tree cover. Nonetheless, the fishing, boating, swimming, and attractive setting overrule the wind factor, and sailboarders seem more than satisfied with the location's "drawback." The campground is open from mid-May to October.

9 Trapper Creek

Location: About 9 miles northwest of the town of Crescent Lake, on Odell Lake.
Sites: 32 basic sites; no hookups.
Maximum length: 30 feet.
Facilities: Tables, grills, vault toilets, drinking water, boat launch, small dock.
Fee per night: $$.
Management: Forest Service.
Contact: 541-433-2234.
Finding the campground: From Oregon 58, 0.5 mile east of Willamette Pass, 7 miles west of Crescent Lake Junction, turn south onto Forest Road 5810 (Odell Lake West Access Road), go 2 miles, and turn left for the camp.

About the campground: On the west shore of Odell Lake, along pretty Trapper Creek, this camp is tucked away in a fir and spruce forest with a huckleberry understory. A paved road connects the sites, most of which have full shade and are protected from the wind. A few sites overlook Odell Lake, an enormous, natural mountain lake that offers fine views, first-rate fishing, superb boating, and swimming. If you want a change of pace, the Yoran Lake Trail starts near the camp. The campground is open from mid-May to October.

10 Whitefish Horse Camp

Location: About 7 miles south of the town of Crescent Lake, near Crescent Lake.
Sites: 17 basic sites; no hookups.
Maximum length: 30 feet.
Facilities: Tables, grills, vault toilets, drinking water, corrals.
Fee per night: $ to $$.
Management: Forest Service.
Contact: 541-433-2234; 1-800-280-CAMP for reservations.
Finding the campground: From the small community of Crescent Lake on Oregon 58, head south on paved Forest Road 60 for 2.3 miles. Turn right to remain on FR 60 and go another 4.4 miles to the campground entrance on the right.

About the campground: This camp is for the exclusive use of equestrians. It is highly functional, with both ample space between the sites and long, gravel parking pads. Corral size determines the difference in site pricing. The horse camp is set back in a lodgepole pine forest across the road from Crescent Lake, giving visitors the best of two worlds: the quiet of the forest and the recreation of the lake. Nearby day-use areas provide access to the lake. Horse trails leave the camp to enter the Diamond Peak Wilderness. The campground is open from mid-May to October.

ROSEBURG AREA

	Hookup sites	Total sites	Max. RV length	Hookups	Toilets	Showers	Drinking water	Dump station	Recreation	Fee	Can reserve
11 Amacher Park	20	30	35	WES	F	•	•		FBL	$$	
12 Cavitt Creek Recreation Site		8	30		NF		•		S	$	
13 Coolwater		7	24		NF		•		F	$	
14 Douglas County Fairgrounds RV Park	50	50	40	WE	F	•	•	•		$$	
15 Hemlock Lake		13	35		NF				HFBL	$	
16 Lake in the Woods		11	35		F		•		HF	$	
17 Millpond Recreation Site		12	30		F		•		SF	$	
18 Pass Creek County Park	30	40	42	WES	F	•	•		F	$$	
19 Rock Creek Recreation Site		17	30		NF		•		SF	$	
20 Susan Creek Recreation Site		31	30		F	•	•		HFB	$$	
21 Tyee		15	40		NF		•		SF	$	
22 Whistler's Bend Park		23	30		F	•	•		HSFBL	$	
23 Wolf Creek		8	30		F		•		HSF	$	

Hookups: W = Water E = Electric S = Sewer **Total sites:** T = Tent-only campground **Maximum trailer/RV length** given in feet.
Toilets: F = Flush NF = No Flush **Recreation:** H = Hiking S = Swimming F = Fishing B = Boating L = Boat Launch
O = Off-Highway Driving R = Horseback Riding C = Cycling
Fee: $ = $1-9 $$ = $10-19 $$$ = $20-29 $$$$ = $30-39. If no entry under **Fee,** camping is free.

11 Amacher Park

Location: About 3 miles north of Roseburg.
Sites: 20 hookup sites, 10 tent sites; water, electric, and sewer hookups.
Maximum length: 35 feet.
Facilities: Tables, flush toilets, drinking water, showers, telephone, boat launch.
Fee per night: $$.
Management: Douglas County.
Contact: 541-672-4901.
Finding the campground: From Interstate 5, take Exit 129 and head south along the east side of the freeway for 0.5 mile. Turn right to pass under the bridge supports and enter the park.

About the campground: Located along the North Umpqua River and below the freeway and a rail line is this attractive but somewhat noisy park. It has beautiful lawns and big shade trees, and the North Umpqua seldom disappoints anglers and boaters. Any swimming is at your own risk. Look for a beautiful myrtle grove near the day-use area. The campground is open year-round.

12 Cavitt Creek Recreation Site

Location: About 26 miles east of Roseburg.
Sites: 8 basic sites; no hookups.
Maximum length: 30 feet.
Facilities: Tables, grills, vault toilets, drinking water.
Fee per night: $.
Management: Bureau of Land Management.
Contact: 541-440-4930.
Finding the campground: From Roseburg, drive 16.4 miles east on Oregon 138 to Glide. Turn south onto Little River Road (County Road 17). Go 6.6 miles and turn right onto Cavitt Creek Road. Pass through the covered bridge and continue another 3.2 miles to arrive at the campground.

About the campground: This popular, primitive campground is found above Cavitt Creek in a Douglas-fir forest dotted with vine maples and ocean spray. A paved path links the camp with a day-use area and leads to a creek overlook and a stairway to an inviting swimming hole that is fed by a 5-foot cascade. The creek is closed to fishing. Spring wildflowers are varied and many. The campground is open from late May to late October.

13 Coolwater

Location: About 33 miles east of Roseburg.
Sites: 7 basic sites; no hookups.
Maximum length: 24 feet.
Facilities: Tables, grills, pit toilets, drinking water.
Fee per night: $.
Management: Forest Service.
Contact: 541-496-3532.
Finding the campground: From Roseburg, drive 16.4 miles east on Oregon 138 to Glide. Turn south onto Little River Road (County Road 17/Forest Road 27) and go 16.1 miles to this camp.

About the campground: This camp along the Little River enjoys a quiet setting of evergreens and maples. Camp guests may fish or frolic on the river or take the drive to Grotto Falls Trail: Across FR 27 from camp, take the marked turn for the falls on gravel FR 2703, go 4.3 miles, and turn left onto FR 2703.150. Go 2 miles more to reach the trailhead. This quarter-mile trail leads from clearcut to old-growth forest on its way to the 100-foot falls. The trail then wraps behind the falls to a grotto for protected viewing of the misty veil. Just 5.6 miles northwest of the camp on Little River Road is a 1-mile trail through old-growth splendor to Wolf Creek Falls. The campground is maintained from late May through October.

14 Douglas County Fairgrounds RV Park

Location: In Roseburg.
Sites: 50 hookup sites; water and electric hookups.
Maximum length: 40 feet.
Facilities: Some tables, flush toilets, drinking water, showers, dump station, telephone.
Fee per night: $$.
Management: Douglas County.
Contact: 541-440-4505.
Finding the campground: From Interstate 5 at the south end of Roseburg, take Exit 123 to reach the fairgrounds on the east side of the freeway.

About the campground: This clean, serviceable RV park is convenient for those attending fairground events and for travelers on I-5. Sites have gravel pads with lawn meridians on which to place your chair. A few mature trees provide shade, with younger, planted trees promising more in the future. Also on the fairgrounds is the fine Douglas County Museum of History and Natural History. The campground is open year-round.

15 Hemlock Lake

Location: About 47 miles east of Roseburg, on Hemlock Lake.
Sites: 13 basic sites; no hookups.
Maximum length: 35 feet.
Facilities: Tables, grills, vault toilets, boat launch. No drinking water.
Fee per night: $.
Management: Forest Service.
Contact: 541-496-3532.
Finding the campground: From Roseburg, go 16.4 miles east on Oregon 138 to Glide. Turn south onto Little River Road (County Road 17/Forest Road 27) and follow the signs for Hemlock Lake. After traveling 29.6 miles from Glide, turn right off FR 27 onto FR 2700.495 and go another 0.7 mile to the camp.

About the campground: You will find this pleasant campground on a fir-covered slope above the dam that forms Hemlock Lake. The manmade lake is the chief draw, inviting fishing and non-motorized boating. If you prefer to hike, trails explore along the lake and visit Yellow Jacket Glade. Wildflower meadows and stands of old growth complement the trails. The campground is open from June into October.

16 Lake in the Woods

Location: About 42 miles east of Roseburg.
Sites: 11 basic sites; no hookups.
Maximum length: 35 feet.
Facilities: Tables, grills, flush toilets, drinking water.

Fee per night: $.
Management: Forest Service.
Contact: 541-496-3532.
Finding the campground: From Roseburg, go 16.4 miles east on Oregon 138 to Glide. Turn south onto Little River Road (County Road 17/Forest Road 27) and continue another 26 miles to this camp on the right.

About the campground: This out-of-the-way camp offers a shady retreat in the old-growth forest edging Lake in the Woods, a former swamp, horse pasture, and now lake. The shallow lake wears a cap of lilies and a ring of cattails, while rhododendron bushes adorn the forest. A restored historic cabin sits beside the lake. Seventy-foot Yakso Falls and 80-foot Hemlock Falls are only short hikes away. The campground is open from late May through September.

17 Millpond Recreation Site

Location: About 27 miles northeast of Roseburg.
Sites: 12 basic sites; no hookups.
Maximum length: 30 feet.
Facilities: Tables, grills, flush and vault toilets, drinking water, horseshoe pits, playing field, barrier-free trail along the creek, picnic pavilion.
Fee per night: $.
Management: Bureau of Land Management.
Contact: 541-440-4930.
Finding the campground: From Oregon 138, 22.4 miles east of Roseburg (about 6 miles east of Glide), turn left (northeast) onto Rock Creek Road and go 5 miles to the camp.

About the campground: The sites of this Rock Creek campground are distributed among second-growth trees and abundant groundcover. The riprap along the creek creates areas of deeper, faster water; there is one area suitable for swimming. Rock Creek Fish Hatchery, near the junction of OR 138 and Rock Creek Road, is open year-round. You can view juvenile, fingerling, and brood fish, including chinook and coho salmon, steelhead, and rainbow trout. The campground is open from mid-May to mid-October.

18 Pass Creek County Park

Location: About 40 miles north of Roseburg.
Sites: 30 hookup sites, 10 tent sites; water, electric, and sewer hookups.
Maximum length: 42 feet.
Facilities: Tables, grills, flush toilets, drinking water, showers, playground.
Fee per night: $$.
Management: Douglas County.
Contact: 541-942-3281.
Finding the campground: At Exit 163 of Interstate 5, 10 miles south of Cottage Grove, follow frontage Curtin Park Road north along the west side of the freeway into the park.

About the campground: This clean, attractive, 23-acre park is sandwiched between Pass Creek and the freeway on the east and a rail line on the west. Sites have paved parking and are arranged for privacy with shrub dividers. Mature conifer and deciduous trees lend shade. A manmade pond is available for fishing; it supports crappie, bass, bluegill, and some trout. Geese make themselves at home within the wildlife sanctuary of the park. The campground is open year-round.

19 Rock Creek Recreation Site

Location: About 29 miles northeast of Roseburg.
Sites: 17 basic sites; no hookups.
Maximum length: 30 feet.
Facilities: Tables, grills, vault toilets, drinking water, site cabinets.
Fee per night: $.
Management: Bureau of Land Management.
Contact: 541-440-4930.
Finding the campground: From Oregon 138, 22.4 miles east of Roseburg (about 6 miles east of Glide), turn left (northeast) onto Rock Creek Road and go 6.6 miles to the camp entrance.

About the campground: This camp offers a relaxing stay along Rock Creek. Second-growth firs and cedars join bigleaf maples and alders in providing shade for the sites, which are spacious and comfortable. Rock Creek flows wide and shallow, with a few deeper pools for wading. The camp is just a short drive from the Umpqua River, where you can hike, fly fish, raft, kayak, or sightsee. The campground is open from mid-May through October.

20 Susan Creek Recreation Site

Location: About 30 miles east of Roseburg.
Sites: 31 basic sites; no hookups.
Maximum length: 30 feet.
Facilities: Tables, grills, flush toilets, drinking water, showers, barrier-free trails, wildlife viewing platform.
Fee per night: $$.
Management: Bureau of Land Management.
Contact: 541-440-4930.
Finding the campground: It is south off Oregon 138, 29.5 miles east of Roseburg (12.5 miles east of Glide).

About the campground: This attractive, popular camp overlooks the North Umpqua River and was designed for the accessibility and convenience of individuals with disabilities. The sites rest in a soothing setting of mature trees along the wild and scenic river, which is open to fly fishing, rafting, and kayaking. A magnificent 79-mile trail follows the river from its headwaters high in the Cascades to the Swiftwater Trailhead, west of the camp. At Susan Creek Recreation Site, short trails lead to the river and a Watchable Wildlife platform. Others link the camp and day-use area, visit 50-foot Susan Creek Falls, and pass rock mounds left long ago by participants in an Indian rite of manhood. The campground is open from May through October.

21 Tyee

Location: About 23 miles northwest of Roseburg.
Sites: 15 basic sites; no hookups.
Maximum length: 40 feet.
Facilities: Tables, grills, vault toilets, drinking water.
Fee per night: $.
Management: Bureau of Land Management.
Contact: 541-440-4930.
Finding the campground: From Interstate 5 at Sutherlin, take Exit 136 and go west on Oregon 138 for 10.6 miles. Cross the river bridge and go 0.2 mile to Bullock Road. Turn right and follow Bullock Road 0.3 mile to the campground on the right.

About the campground: On a plateau above the Umpqua River, you will find camping on either side of a day-use area. A mixed woods of fir, cedar, maple, vine maple, and dogwood lends full shade. Leafy shrubs contribute privacy to the already well-spaced sites. A paved path travels the length of the rim and offers views of the river, while stairs descend for river access. Although regulations prohibit trout fishing, anglers still find sport, and the camp is quiet and restful. The campground is open from May through the first week of October.

22 Whistler's Bend Park

Location: About 15 miles northeast of Roseburg.
Sites: 23 basic sites; no hookups.
Maximum length: 30 feet.
Facilities: Tables, grills, flush and chemical toilets, drinking water, showers, playground (at day-use area), boat launch.
Fee per night: $.
Management: Douglas County.
Contact: 541-673-4863.
Finding the campground: From Roseburg, go east on Oregon 138 for 12 miles and turn left (north) onto Whistler's Park Road. Go 2.7 miles to enter the county park and follow the signs to the camp.

About the campground: This 148-acre park tucked in a bend of the North Umpqua River provides campers with ample room to roam. Because it is managed as a wildlife refuge, the park also offers opportunities to watch birds and wildlife, including the rare Columbia white-tailed deer. Nestled at the foot of a hill, the rustic camp blends with its oak woodland and riverbank setting. The parking is paved. In spring, camas and iris adorn the natural grasses. The river captivates with its blue-green clarity and recreation. Be sure to check current fishing regulations. A river trail invites exercise, but beware of poison oak when exploring. The campground is open year-round.

23 Wolf Creek

Location: About 28 miles east of Roseburg.
Sites: 8 basic sites; no hookups.
Maximum length: 30 feet.
Facilities: Tables, grills, flush toilets, drinking water; volleyball, horseshoe pits, and playing field at day-use area.
Fee per night: $.
Management: Forest Service.
Contact: 541-496-3532.
Finding the campground: From Roseburg, go 16.4 miles east on Oregon 138 to Glide. Then head south on Little River Road (County Road 17/Forest Road 27) for 11.7 miles to enter this camp on the right.

About the campground: This campground along the Little River offers closely spaced sites in a second-growth forest. A nature trail makes a loop through the mixed-tree setting; you can access it at the camp or via the bridge over the river at the day-use area. If you drive 1.2 miles west of the camp, you can walk the 1-mile Wolf Creek Trail, which crosses the crescent-shaped bridge over the Little River to tour a classic low-elevation forest and goes on to Wolf Creek Falls. The trail halts at an outcrop with an impressive view of the 80-foot upper section of the falls; below the viewpoint is the lower chute. The campground is open mid-May through October.

STEAMBOAT–LEMOLO LAKE AREA

		Hookup sites	Total sites	Max. RV length	Hookups	Toilets	Showers	Drinking water	Dump station	Recreation	Fee	Can reserve
24	Apple Creek		8	22		NF				HF	$	
25	Bogus Creek		15	35		F			•	SFBL	$	
26	Boulder Flat		10	24		NF				HSFBL		
27	Bunker Hill		5	small		NF				HFB	$	
28	Canton Creek		5	16		F			•	S	$	
29	Clearwater Falls		5	15		NF					$	
30	Eagle Rock		28	40		NF			•	HF	$-$$	
31	East Lemolo		10	22		NF				FBL	$	
32	Horseshoe Bend		25	35		F			•	HSFBL	$$	
33	Inlet		13	30		NF				HFB	$	
34	Island		7	20		NF				SFB	$	
35	Kelsay Valley Trailhead Camp		16	35		NF				HFR	$	
36	Poole Creek		59	30		NF			•	HSFBL	$$	
37	Scaredman Creek Recreation Site		10	25		NF				S		
38	Steamboat Falls		10	24		NF				S		
39	Toketee Lake		33	25		NF				HFBL	$	
40	Whitehorse Falls		5	25		NF					$	

Hookups: W = Water E = Electric S = Sewer **Total sites:** T = Tent-only campground **Maximum trailer/RV length** given in feet.
Toilets: F = Flush NF = No Flush **Recreation:** H = Hiking S = Swimming F = Fishing B = Boating L = Boat Launch
O = Off-Highway Driving R = Horseback Riding C = Cycling
Fee: $ = $1-9 $$ = $10-19 $$$ = $20-29 $$$$ = $30-39. If no entry under **Fee**, camping is free.

24 Apple Creek

Location: About 5 miles east of Steamboat.
Sites: 8 basic sites; no hookups.
Maximum length: 22 feet.
Facilities: Tables, grills, pit toilets. No drinking water.
Fee per night: $.
Management: Forest Service.
Contact: 541-496-3532.
Finding the campground: It is south off Oregon 138, 4.5 miles east of Steamboat and 25.5 miles east of Glide.

About the campground: This campground rests on a forested bench below OR 138 and along the mesmerizing North Umpqua River. The camp is shaded by a mix of conifer and deciduous trees and has a luxuriant understory. Hikers will find the Panther Trailhead for the 79-mile North Umpqua National Recreation Trail just west of the camp turnoff: Follow Forest Road 4714 south across the river bridge to reach the trailhead. The trail both follows the river and climbs to the upper canyon. The campground is maintained from late May through October.

25 Bogus Creek

Location: 4 miles west of Steamboat.
Sites: 15 basic sites; no hookups.
Maximum length: 35 feet.
Facilities: Tables, grills, flush toilets, drinking water, raft launch.
Fee per night: $.
Management: Forest Service.
Contact: 541-496-3532.
 Finding the campground: It is north off Oregon 138, 4 miles west of Steamboat and about 17 miles east of Glide.

About the campground: Across OR 138 from the North Umpqua River and a public river access, this campground sits beside Bogus Creek in a restful forest setting. Douglas-firs dominate the landscape and the sites are well spaced for comfort. The river is within easy striking distance for rafting, kayaking, or fly fishing. About 1 mile west is the Wright Creek Trailhead for the North Umpqua National Recreation Trail. The campground is maintained from late May through mid-September.

26 Boulder Flat

Location: 16 miles east of Steamboat.
Sites: 10 basic sites; no hookups.
Maximum length: 24 feet.
Facilities: Tables, grills, vault toilets, raft launch. No drinking water.
Fee per night: None.
Management: Forest Service.
Contact: 541-496-3532.
Finding the campground: It is north off Oregon 138, 16 miles east of Steamboat and 37 miles east of Glide.

About the campground: This camp flat across the North Umpqua River from the confluence with Boulder Creek offers well-spaced sites amid firs and maples. There is direct access to the river for fishing and rafting. The camp also lies within reach of the North Umpqua National Recreation Trail (accessed via Marsters Bridge to the west or near Soda Springs Dam 2 miles to the east) and the Boulder Creek Trail (also near Soda Springs Dam). The campground is maintained from late May through mid-September.

27 Bunker Hill

Location: About 60 miles east of Glide, on Lemolo Lake.
Sites: 5 basic sites; no hookups.
Maximum length: Small units only.
Facilities: Tables, grills, pit toilets. No drinking water.
Fee per night: $.
Management: Forest Service.
Contact: 541-498-2531.
Finding the campground: From Oregon 138, 54 miles east of Glide, turn north onto Forest Road 2610 (Birds Point Road) toward Lemolo Lake, go 3 miles to a junction, and proceed straight on FR 2610 for another 2.5 miles. Turn right onto FR 2612, go 0.6 mile, and turn right to enter the camp.

About the campground: Below forested Bunker Hill on the northwest shore of manmade Lemolo Lake sits this small, rustic campground ideally suited for tents. You may spot bald eagles soaring over the camp. Fishing and hiking are popular pastimes here; boating access is available elsewhere on the lake. Look for the North Umpqua National Recreation Trail near the intersection of FR 2610 and FR 2612. OR 138 is part of the Rogue-Umpqua Scenic Byway, should you get the itch to sightsee. The campground is open mid-May through October.

28 Canton Creek

Location: Less than 1 mile northeast of Steamboat.
Sites: 5 basic sites; no hookups.
Maximum length: 16 feet.
Facilities: Tables, grills, flush toilets, drinking water.
Fee per night: $.
Management: Forest Service.
Contact: 541-496-3532.
Finding the campground: From Oregon 138 at Steamboat, 21 miles east of Glide, go 0.3 mile north on Forest Road 38 (Steamboat Creek Road). The campground is on the right.

About the campground: This small, lightly used campground is best suited for tent camping. It occupies a low bluff above Steamboat Creek near the Canton Creek confluence and is a popular place to swim in the summer. Firs, maples, alders, and cedars shade the sites. A day-use area claims the upper end of the camp, and a memorial honors three Douglas County law enforcement officers who lost their lives in 1985 in a helicopter crash nearby. Both Steamboat and Canton Creeks are closed to angling to protect spawning steelhead and salmon, but the North Umpqua River is open for catch-and-release fly fishing. Steamboat Falls, upstream from the camp via FR 38, is worth visiting and photographing. In the fall, you may see spawning chinooks. The campground is maintained from mid-May to mid-October.

29 Clearwater Falls

Location: About 52 miles east of Glide.
Sites: 5 basic sites; no hookups.
Maximum length: 15 feet.
Facilities: Tables, grills, pit toilets. No drinking water.
Fee per night: $.
Management: Forest Service.
Contact: 541-498-2531.
Finding the campground: It is south off Oregon 138, 51.5 miles east of Glide.

About the campground: This campground occupies a slope cloaked in old-growth Douglas-firs and mountain hemlocks above the Clearwater River. It is best suited for tent camping, given the short, uneven parking pads. The camp is within walking distance of Clearwater Falls, a broad, split-stream waterfall accented by mossy boulders and logs. Downstream from the falls, a footbridge spans the river to access a path on the opposite shore; the path leads to the head of the falls and an area of picnic tables. From OR 138, you can reach additional falls and trails, as well as Toketee, Lemolo, and Diamond Lakes. The campground is open from June through October.

30 Eagle Rock

Location: About 12 miles east of Steamboat.
Sites: 28 basic sites; no hookups.
Maximum length: 40 feet.
Facilities: Tables, grills, vault toilets, drinking water.
Fee per night: $ to $$.
Management: Forest Service.
Contact: 541-496-3532.
Finding the campground: It is north off Oregon 138, 11.5 miles east of Steamboat and 32.5 miles east of Glide.

About the campground: This camp on the North Umpqua Wild and Scenic River has paved roads and parking. Sites are well spaced along a forested flat; some are fully shaded by firs while others receive a mixture of sun and shade. The landmark outcrop known as Eagle Rock overlooks this part of the river. Hikers can access the North Umpqua National Recreation Trail at Marsters Bridge to the west. OR 138 serves up a scenic river drive for those who prefer to save the boot leather. The campground is maintained from late May through mid-September.

31 East Lemolo

Location: About 60 miles east of Glide, on Lemolo Lake.
Sites: 10 basic sites; no hookups.
Maximum length: 22 feet.
Facilities: Tables, grills, vault toilets, primitive boat launch. No drinking water.

Fee per night: $.
Management: Forest Service.
Contact: 541-498-2531.
Finding the campground: From Oregon 138, 54 miles east of Glide, turn north onto Forest Road 2610 toward Lemolo Lake. Go 3 miles and turn right onto FR 2614. Go 2.2 miles, turn left onto gravel FR 2614.430, and proceed 0.3 mile to the camp at road's end.

About the campground: This camp overlooks the east shore of Lemolo Lake, a reservoir harnessing the North Umpqua River. The earthen sites are tucked among tightly clustered lodgepole pines. Because the camp is small, most sites offer views of the lake; some are right on the lakeshore. Forested Bunker Hill is visible across the water. Boating is a popular pastime, as is fishing for kokanee and rainbow and brown trout. The campground is open from mid-May through October.

32 Horseshoe Bend

Location: About 8 miles east of Steamboat.
Sites: 25 basic sites; no hookups.
Maximum length: 35 feet.
Facilities: Tables, grills, flush toilets, drinking water, raft put-in.
Fee per night: $$.
Management: Forest Service.
Contact: 541-496-3532.
Finding the campground: From Oregon 138, 7.5 miles east of Steamboat, turn south at the sign for Horseshoe Bend Campground, Raft Launch, and North Umpqua Trail. Go 0.1 mile and turn right onto Forest Road 4750. Drive another 0.8 mile to the camp.

About the campground: This facility has three camp flats: Beaver, Deer, and Otter. Deer Flat is for groups and must be reserved in advance. For wheelchair-accessible sites and accommodations, go to Beaver Flat. The single-party camp-sites have paved parking and are nestled in the woods along the North Umpqua River. The riffles and pools of the river invite fishing, hiking, and rafting; you will find a river access trail in Otter Flat. From the Horseshoe Bend Raft Put-in, it is a 2- to 3-hour float to Gravel Bin Takeout, 6.7 miles downstream. The North Umpqua National Recreation Trail follows the river on the opposite shore; you can access it by backtracking 0.8 mile on FR 4750 and driving across the one-lane bridge to the trailhead. The campground is open late May through late September.

33 Inlet

Location: About 60 miles east of Glide, on Lemolo Lake.
Sites: 13 basic sites; no hookups.
Maximum length: 30 feet.
Facilities: Tables, grills, pit toilets. No drinking water.

Fee per night: $.
Management: Forest Service.
Contact: 541-498-2531.
Finding the campground: From Oregon 138, 54 miles east of Glide, turn north onto Forest Road 2610 toward Lemolo Lake. Go 3 miles to a junction and turn right onto FR 2614. Go 2.6 miles more to the camp entrance on the right.

About the campground: This camp sits across the road from the east shore of Lemolo Lake at the point where the North Umpqua River feeds into the reservoir. Lupine and paintbrush adorn the floor of the lodgepole-pine forest. The camp has gravel roads and parking and offers convenient lake access for fishing. The North Umpqua National Recreation Trail passes nearby. The campground is open from mid-May through October.

34 Island

Location: 1 mile east of Steamboat.
Sites: 7 basic sites; no hookups.
Maximum length: 20 feet.
Facilities: Tables, grills, vault toilets. No drinking water.
Fee per night: $.
Management: Forest Service.
Contact: 541-496-3532.
Finding the campground: It is south off Oregon 138, 1 mile east of Steamboat.

About the campground: This camp is cut into a slope between OR 138 and the North Umpqua Wild and Scenic River, a blue-ribbon fly fishing stream that has attracted the likes of author Zane Grey. Firs, maples, dogwoods, and the song of the river add to the camp's appeal. When river levels are adequate, you can make a 2- to 3-hour float trip between Horseshoe Bend Raft Put-in (6.5 miles east on OR 138) and Gravel Bin Raft Takeout (0.2 mile west of the camp). The campground is maintained from May to October.

35 Kelsay Valley Trailhead Camp

Location: About 62 miles east of Glide.
Sites: 16 basic sites; no hookups.
Maximum length: 35 feet.
Facilities: Tables, grills, vault toilets, corral, hitching posts. No drinking water.
Fee per night: $.
Management: Forest Service.
Contact: 541-498-2531.
Finding the campground: From Oregon 138, 56 miles east of Glide, turn north onto gravel Forest Road 60 (Windigo Pass Road). Go 4.5 miles, turn right onto red-dirt FR 6000.958, and follow it 1.5 miles to the camp and trailhead. You bypass a 2-site camp en route.

About the campground: This camp is designed to serve both families and equestrian campers. Several site spurs are long enough to accommodate horse trailers. The camp rests in a lodgepole pine forest on the outskirts of a wildflower-spangled high meadow threaded by Bradley Creek, a tributary of the North Umpqua River. Hiker/horse trails travel the area. If you follow the North Umpqua Trail upstream, you will eventually reach the river's headwater, Maidu Lake, on the Cascade Crest. Come prepared for mosquitoes. The campground is open from mid-May through September.

36 Poole Creek

Location: About 58 miles east of Glide, on Lemolo Lake.
Sites: 59 basic sites; no hookups.
Maximum length: 30 feet.
Facilities: Tables, grills, vault toilets, drinking water, boat launch, dock.
Fee per night: $$.
Management: Forest Service.
Contact: 541-498-2531.
Finding the campground: From Oregon 138, 54 miles east of Glide, turn north onto Forest Road 2610 toward Lemolo Lake. Go 3 miles to a junction and proceed straight on FR 2610 for another mile to the campground entrance on the right.

About the campground: This camp sits in a dry forest of lodgepole pines, Shasta red firs, and mountain hemlocks on the western shore of Lemolo Lake, which captures the North Umpqua River as it descends from the Cascade Crest. Boating is a chief draw, as is fishing for kokanee and trout: eastern brook, rainbow, and German brown. Hiking trails and a designated swimming beach provide other diversions; waterskiing is allowed on part of the lake. The campground is open from mid-May through October.

37 Scaredman Creek Recreation Site

Location: About 4 miles north of Steamboat.
Sites: 10 basic sites; no hookups.
Maximum length: 25 feet.
Facilities: Tables, grills, pit toilets. No drinking water.
Fee per night: None.
Management: Bureau of Land Management.
Contact: 541-440-4930.
Finding the campground: From Oregon 138 at Steamboat, 21 miles east of Glide, head northeast on Forest Road 38 (Steamboat Creek Road) for 0.5 mile and turn left onto Canton Creek Road. Go another 3.5 miles to enter this camp on the right.

About the campground: You will find this quiet camp in a tall stand of Douglas-firs along Canton Creek, downstream from the confluence with Scaredman Creek. Although Canton Creek is closed to fishing, it will still engage you with its beauty as it riffles over gravel beds and pinches into green pools. This camp is ideal for retreating from civilization or exploring the North Umpqua River corridor. The campground is maintained from May to October.

38 Steamboat Falls

Location: About 6 miles northeast of Steamboat.
Sites: 10 basic sites; no hookups.
Maximum length: 24 feet.
Facilities: Tables, grills, vault toilets. No drinking water.
Fee per night: None.
Management: Forest Service.
Contact: 541-496-3532.
Finding the campground: From Oregon 138 at Steamboat, 21 miles east of Glide, go northeast 5.5 miles on Forest Road 38 (Steamboat Creek Road). Turn right onto FR 3810 and continue another 0.6 mile to the camp entrance.

About the campground: This campground lines a forested bench along Steamboat Creek at Steamboat Falls, a dazzling, multidirectional, multi-tiered waterfall that spans the 70- to 100-foot breadth of the creek. A fish ladder helps salmon bypass the falls as they migrate upstream. Because the creek is a critical spawning ground for salmon and steelhead, it and its tributaries are closed to fishing. The campground is maintained from mid-May into September.

39 Toketee Lake

Location: About 43 miles east of Glide, on Toketee Lake.
Sites: 33 basic sites; no hookups.
Maximum length: 25 feet.
Facilities: Tables, grills, pit toilets, boat launch, dock. No drinking water.
Fee per night: $.
Management: Forest Service.
Contact: 541-498-2531.
Finding the campground: From Oregon 138, 41 miles east of Glide, turn north onto Forest Road 34 (Toketee-Rigdon Road). Go 0.3 mile, turn left to remain on FR 34, and go another 1.2 miles to the campground entrance on the right.

About the campground: This restful camp is located along the upper North Umpqua River where it feeds into manmade Toketee Lake. The river resembles a sparkling, creek-sized ribbon as it races past the camp. Cedars and alders frame the waterway and shade the campsites. The camp has gravel roads and earthen parking, as well as an adjacent boat launch. Campers can boat and fish the reservoir. Hikers will find that the North Umpqua National Recreation Trail passes next to the camp, and the Toketee Lake Trail can be found along FR 34, half a mile south of the campground entrance. The campground is open from mid-April to late October.

40 Whitehorse Falls

Location: About 48 miles east of Glide.
Sites: 5 basic sites; no hookups.
Maximum length: 25 feet.
Facilities: Tables, grills, pit toilets. No drinking water.
Fee per night: $.
Management: Forest Service.
Contact: 541-498-2531.
Finding the campground: It is north off Oregon 138, 48 miles east of Glide.

About the campground: This tiny, lightly used campground rests in a stand of old-growth Douglas-firs above the Clearwater River and Whitehorse Falls. Rhododendrons and chinquapins complement the towering trees. At the camp's small picnic area, a viewing platform overlooks the 12-foot falls. A stair-step series of small cascades precedes the falls, and a deep, tranquil pool collects the plummeting water before it continues downstream. Additional falls along OR 138 may suggest outings, as will Toketee, Lemolo, and Diamond Lakes. The campground is open from June through October.

CRATER LAKE–DIAMOND LAKE AREA

		Hookup sites	Total sites	Max. RV length	Hookups	Toilets	Showers	Drinking water	Dump station	Recreation	Fee	Can reserve
41	Abbott Creek		25	40		NF		•		F	$	
42	Broken Arrow		147	35		F	•	•	•	HSFBLC	$	•
43	Crater Lake National Park: Lost Creek		16	T		NF		•			$$	
44	Crater Lake National Park: Mazama		200	30		F	•	•	•	H	$$	
45	Diamond Lake		238	35		F	•	•	•	HSFBLC	$$	•
46	Farewell Bend		61	40		F		•		HF	$$	
47	Hamaker		10	30		NF		•		HF	$	
48	Huckleberry Mountain		25	25		NF						
49	Mill Creek		8	25		NF				F	D	
50	Natural Bridge		17	40		NF				HF	$	
51	River Bridge		6	30		NF				HF	$	
52	Thielsen View		60	30		NF		•	•	HSFBLC	$	
53	Union Creek		75	30		NF		•		HF	$	

Hookups: W = Water E = Electric S = Sewer **Total sites:** T = Tent-only campground **Maximum trailer/RV length** given in feet.
Toilets: F = Flush NF = No Flush **Recreation:** H = Hiking S = Swimming F = Fishing B = Boating L = Boat Launch
O = Off-Highway Driving R = Horseback Riding C = Cycling
Fee: $ = $1-9 $$ = $10-19 $$$ = $20-29 $$$$ = $30-39. If no entry under **Fee,** camping is free.

41 Abbott Creek

Location: About 10 miles north of Prospect.
Sites: 25 basic sites; no hookups.
Maximum length: 40 feet.
Facilities: Tables, grills, pit toilets, drinking water.
Fee per night: $.
Management: Forest Service.
Contact: 541-560-3400.
Finding the campground: From Oregon 62, 6.2 miles north of Prospect, 6.3 miles south of the junction of OR 62 and OR 230, turn west on Forest Road 68 and go 3.6 miles to reach the camp on the left.

About the campground: This camp flat beside Abbott Creek presents a mosaic of open meadow, clustered shrubs, and pocket groves of pines, firs, and deciduous trees. There are sites to appeal to the sun-seeker, the shade-lover, and even the undecided. The camp is quiet and rustic and offers access to the creek at several points. Because the creek is small, youngsters can fish and explore without getting into too much trouble. The campground is open from the end of May through October.

Wizard Island in Crater Lake.

42 Broken Arrow

Location: On Diamond Lake.
Sites: 147 basic sites; no hookups.
Maximum length: 35 feet.
Facilities: Tables, grills, flush toilets, drinking water, showers, dump station, barrier-free facilities.
Fee per night: $.
Management: Forest Service.
Contact: 541-498-2531; 1-800-280-CAMP for reservations.
Finding the campground: From Oregon 138, 80 miles east of Roseburg, turn west on Diamond Lake Loop/Forest Road 4795 for the north entry to Diamond Lake Recreation Area. At 0.3 mile keep left and continue for another 2.9 miles. There, turn right for the south shore attractions, reaching Broken Arrow on the left after 0.5 mile.

About the campground: At the southeastern corner of Diamond Lake, tucked away from shore in the lodgepole pines, is this camp shared by humans, jays, and golden mantled squirrels. The center of activity is the natural lake, which covers more than 3,000 acres. It offers year-round fun, taking you from goggles and swimsuits to snowshoes and mittens. During the camping season, swimming, boating, and fishing for rainbow trout are all popular. Five boat ramps serve the lake; the speed limit for boats is 10 miles an hour. Next to the camp, South Shore Picnic Area has a designated swimming beach. A paved pedestrian and bicycle trail travels the shoreline, and nearby hiking trails lead to Teal and

Horse Lakes, Silent Creek, and Mount Bailey. The campground is open from late May through September.

43 Crater Lake National Park: Lost Creek

Location: About 3 miles southeast of Crater Lake.
Sites: 16 tent sites; no hookups.
Maximum length: Suitable for tents only.
Facilities: Tables, grills, vault toilets, drinking water.
Fee per night: $$.
Management: National Park Service.
Contact: 541-594-2211.
Finding the campground: From the Rim Drive junction at the south end of Crater Lake, near Crater Lake National Park Headquarters, follow the rim loop counterclockwise. Go about 8 miles on East Rim Drive, turn right toward The Pinnacles and Lost Creek Campground, and continue 3 miles to the camp entrance on the right.

About the campground: Next to Sand Creek Canyon, en route to The Pinnacles, this campground threaded by Lost Creek occupies a quiet, shady stand of lodgepole pines. Although the camp is removed from the main bustle, it is still within easy access of the 33-mile Rim Drive, with its viewpoints, trailheads, and sightseeing opportunities. The camp is also just a short drive from The Pinnacles, an intriguing canyon landscape of sandcastle-like volcanic fumeroles, which beg to be visited repeatedly so you can photograph them in different lights. The Pinnacles are truly one of nature's art galleries. The campground is open from July to mid-September.

44 Crater Lake National Park: Mazama

Location: About 4 miles south of Crater Lake.
Sites: 200 basic sites; no hookups.
Maximum length: 30 feet.
Facilities: Tables, grills, flush toilets, drinking water, showers, dump station, laundry, telephone, food service.
Fee per night: $$.
 Management: National Park Service.
Contact: 541-594-2211 or 541-830-8700.
Finding the campground: This camp is east off the south entrance road to Crater Lake National Park, 0.1 mile north of the south entrance station off Oregon 62, 3.5 miles south of Rim Drive. The vehicle entry fee is good for 7 days.

About the campground: On a plateau of lodgepole pines above the picturesque, deeply eroded drainage of Annie Creek sits this gateway campground to the splendors of Crater Lake National Park. Crater Lake was formed some 7,700 years ago when the ancient volcano Mount Mazama collapsed and filled with water to form the deepest lake in the United States and the clearest lake in the world. The 33-mile Rim Drive explores the crater, with stops for hikes, sightseeing, and photography. The lake's color explores lovely and uncommon shades of blue. From the camp, the Annie Creek Trail descends to the wildflower-strewn banks of Annie Creek. Other park trails top the caldera peaks for panoramic views of the caldera, lake, and Cascades. A narrated boat tour (a fee attraction) leaves from Cleetwood Cove. To board the boat, you must hike 1.1 miles and descend 700 feet in elevation from the rim trailhead to the cove. The campground is open from June to mid-October.

45 Diamond Lake

Location: On Diamond Lake.
Sites: 238 basic sites; no hookups.
Maximum length: 35 feet.
Facilities: Tables, grills, flush toilets, drinking water, showers, dump station, barrier-free facilities, 2 boat ramps, fish-cleaning station, visitor information station (across road from camp).
Fee per night: $$.
Management: Forest Service.
Contact: 541-498-2531; 1-800-280-CAMP for reservations.
Finding the campground: From Oregon 138, 80 miles east of Roseburg, turn west on Diamond Lake Loop/Forest Road 4795 for the north entry to Diamond Lake Recreation Area. At 0.3 mile keep left and continue for another 2.2 miles to enter the camp.

About the campground: Off the Rogue-Umpqua Scenic Drive and along the east shore of 3,000-acre Diamond Lake lies this camping "metropolis." It is surrounded by the Mount Thielsen Wilderness, Oregon Cascades Recreation Area, and the Umpqua National Forest. Recreation on the lake includes fishing, swimming, and boating (10 miles per hour maximum). A paved pedestrian and bicycle trail travels the lakeshore, and the local hiking options range from a short nature trail to the interstate Pacific Crest National Scenic Trail. A full-service lakeside resort with boat and sports equipment rentals is just a short hop away. The campground is open from mid-May through October.

46 Farewell Bend

Location: About 12 miles north of Prospect.
Sites: 61 basic sites; no hookups.
Maximum length: 40 feet.
Facilities: Tables, grills, flush toilets, drinking water, playground.
Fee per night: $$.
Management: Forest Service.
Contact: 541-560-3400.
Finding the campground: It is west off Oregon 62, 12.2 miles north of Prospect and 0.3 mile south of the junction of OR 62 and OR 230.

About the campground: This pleasant, popular campground is contained by a scenic bend of the Upper Rogue River. A few pine trees rise among the Douglas-firs and hemlocks of camp. The sites have trampled, barren earth floors, but the perimeters burst with greenery. The river courses over bedrock, except where a gorge squeezes it into a 4- to 5-foot-wide chute near sites 20 and 21. The campground is ideal for relaxing at the river or for sightseeing, with Crater Lake National Park, Diamond Lake Recreation Area, and the Upper Rogue River-Union Creek country all nearby. Superior hiking trails follow Union Creek and the Upper Rogue River. You may want to take a drive along OR 62 in late spring or early summer to see the dogwood blooms, a signature of the area. The campground is open from the end of May through September.

47 Hamaker

Location: About 26 miles north of Prospect.
Sites: 10 basic sites; no hookups.
Maximum length: 30 feet.
Facilities: Tables, grills, vault toilets, drinking water.
Fee per night: $.
Management: Forest Service.
Contact: 541-560-3400.
Finding the campground: From the junction of Oregon 62 and OR 230, 12.5 miles north of Prospect, head north on OR 230 for 12.2 miles. Turn right (east) onto gravel Forest Road 6530, go 0.6 mile, and bear right on FR 6530.900. Drive another 0.8 mile to the camp entrance.

About the campground: This idyllic campground occupies a bench overlooking the Rogue Wild and Scenic River as it threads out of Crater Lake National Park. Gorgeous, old-growth Shasta red firs and Douglas-firs rise above the camp. The setting is perfect for lounging, but anglers in pursuit of wily trout can try their luck negotiating the shrubs on the riverbank. Hikers might check out a segment of the Upper Rogue Trail, which pursues this prized waterway downstream from Crater Rim Viewpoint (north on OR 230) to Lost Creek Reservoir (southwest of Prospect). Reach the trail upstream from camp at the barricaded river bridge open to pedestrians only. The campground is open from the end of May through October.

48 Huckleberry Mountain

Location: About 22 miles northeast of Prospect.
Sites: 25 basic sites; no hookups.
Maximum length: 25 feet.
Facilities: Tables, fire rings, pit toilets. No drinking water.
Fee per night: None.
Management: Forest Service.
Contact: 541-560-3400.
Finding the campground: From the junction of Oregon 62 and OR 230, 12.5

Ancient Douglas-fir.

miles north of Prospect, head east on OR 62 for 5.7 miles. Turn south on gravel Forest Road 60 at the sign for the campground near milepost 63. Follow FR 60, which is narrow, winding, and steep, for 4.2 miles to enter the camp.

About the campground: This rustic, mountaintop camp is best suited to small units because its access road is steep and narrow. The sites are widespread for ample privacy, but they lack formal parking. The setting is one of old-growth Shasta red firs, meadows of false hellebore, and huckleberry flats. In late summer, as the berries ripen, you will encounter folks with buckets swinging from their belts and blue stains on their fingertips. Altogether, the camp offers a serene, picturesque retreat that also appeals to wildlife. The campground is open from June through October.

49 Mill Creek

Location: About 3 miles north of Prospect.
Sites: 8 basic sites; no hookups.
Maximum length: 25 feet.
Facilities: Tables, grills, vault toilets. No drinking water.
Fee per night: Donation.
Management: Forest Service.
Contact: 541-560-3400.
Finding the campground: From Prospect, go 2 miles north on Oregon 62. Turn right (east) onto Forest Road 6200.030, go 1 mile, and turn left onto FR 6200.035 to enter the camp.

About the campground: This tiny, creekside camp is set among old-growth firs, with a midstory tangle of dogwood, maple, and chinquapin. It offers a quiet base from which to explore the Upper Rogue River Area. The campground is open from April through October.

50 Natural Bridge

Location: About 10 miles north of Prospect.
Sites: 17 basic sites; no hookups.
Maximum length: 40 feet.
Facilities: Tables, grills and rock fireplaces, pit and vault toilets. No drinking water.
Fee per night: $.
Management: Forest Service.
Contact: 541-560-3400.
Finding the campground: From Oregon 62, about 10 miles north of Prospect, 2.8 miles south of the junction of OR 62 and OR 230, head west on Forest Road 6200.300 toward Natural Bridge and go 0.4 mile; bear right for the campground, left for Natural Bridge Viewpoint parking.

About the campground: Set back from OR 62, this quiet campground covers a large forested flat along the Rogue River. It offers spacious sites, many of them riverside. Firs, pines, hemlocks, and dogwoods shade the camp. Fishing, hiking, and sightseeing along the Rogue River lure guests. The Rogue Gorge Trail passes through the camp, while the Upper Rogue National Recreation Trail traces the opposite bank of the Rogue River. You can access the Upper Rogue Trail via the footbridge at Natural Bridge Viewpoint. Even if you are not a hiker, the short trail to the viewpoint is worth taking. It leads to a spectacular basalt gorge where a lava tube swallows the river whole, only to spit it out 200 feet downstream. The campground is open from the end of May to mid-November.

51 River Bridge

Location: About 5 miles north of Prospect.
Sites: 6 basic sites; no hookups.
Maximum length: 30 feet.
Facilities: Tables, grills, pit toilets. No drinking water.
Fee per night: $.
Management: Forest Service.
Contact: 541-560-3400.
Finding the campground: From Prospect, go 4 miles north on Oregon 62. Turn left (west) onto gravel Forest Road 6210 and go 0.9 mile to the camp entrance on the right.

About the campground: This small camp claims a forest flat set back from the Rogue Wild and Scenic River where it takes a wide bend. Tall firs and hemlocks, along with a leafy midstory, create nearly full shade. The river and Upper Rogue National Recreation Trail lie just steps away from your RV or tent. Riffles occasionally break the glassy surface of the river. A lava outcrop reveals a ropelike pattern and allows for bank fishing. The campground is open from the end of May through October.

52 Thielsen View

Location: On Diamond Lake.
Sites: 60 basic sites; no hookups.
Maximum length: 30 feet.
Facilities: Tables, grills, vault toilets, drinking water, dump station, boat ramps.
Fee per night: $.
Management: Forest Service.
Contact: 541-498-2531.
Finding the campground: From Oregon 138, 80 miles east of Roseburg, turn west onto Diamond Lake Loop/Forest Road 4795 for the north entrance to Diamond Lake Recreation Area. At 0.3 mile, go right and continue for another 3 miles to the camp.

About the campground: At the foot of Mount Bailey on the west shore of Diamond Lake, this campground offers a comfortable stay and a magnificent view of Mount Thielsen. The campsites rest in a mixed forest of pine and fir. Annually, the lake is stocked with nearly half a million rainbow trout fingerlings to keep anglers smiling; the blue expanse offers ample room to troll. Bicyclists can ride an 11-mile paved trail around the lake, while hikers can choose from a plethora of destinations in Mount Thielsen Wilderness, Oregon Cascades Recreation Area, and Umpqua National Forest. The campground is open from mid-May to mid-October.

53 Union Creek

Location: In the community of Union Creek, about 11 miles north of Prospect.
Sites: 75 basic sites; no hookups.
Maximum length: 30 feet.
Facilities: Tables, grills, vault toilets, drinking water.
Fee per night: $.
Management: Forest Service.
Contact: 541-560-3400.
Finding the campground: It is west off Oregon 62, 11.2 miles north of Prospect and 1.3 miles south of the junction of OR 62 and OR 230.

About the campground: This engaging camp straddles Union Creek at its confluence with the Upper Rogue River. The sites are well spaced, cozy, and private. Trails explore both banks of the creek and the east shore of the river, but to access the Upper Rogue National Recreation Trail on the west shore, you will need to drive 1.5 miles south to Natural Bridge Campground and Viewpoint Parking, where there is a pedestrian bridge over the river. Hiking, fishing, sightseeing, and nature study are area pursuits. Among the outstanding features are old-growth trees, dogwood blooms, and dramatic unions of volcanic outcrop and clear, racing water. The campground is open from the end of May through September.

MYRTLE CREEK AREA

	Hookup sites	Total sites	Max. RV length	Hookups	Toilets	Showers	Drinking water	Dump station	Recreation	Fee	Can reserve
54 Boulder Creek		8	25		NF				S	donation	
55 Camp Comfort		5	25		NF				S	donation	
56 Charles V. Stanton County Park	20	43	45	WES	F	•	•	•	FBL	$$	
57 Cover		7	22		NF						
58 Devils Flat		3	20		NF				H		
59 Dumont Creek		5	25		NF				S	donation	
60 Millsite RV Park	11	11	50	WES	F	•	•	•		$-$$	
61 Threehorn		5	20		NF						

Hookups: W = Water E = Electric S = Sewer **Total sites:** T = Tent-only campground **Maximum trailer/RV length** given in feet.
Toilets: F = Flush NF = No Flush **Recreation:** H = Hiking S = Swimming F = Fishing B = Boating L = Boat Launch
O = Off-Highway Driving R = Horseback Riding C = Cycling
Fee: $ = $1-9 $$ = $10-19 $$$ = $20-29 $$$$ = $30-39. If no entry under **Fee,** camping is free.

54 Boulder Creek

Location: About 50 miles east of the town of Myrtle Creek.
Sites: 8 basic sites; no hookups.
Maximum length: 25 feet.
Facilities: Tables, grills, pit toilets. No drinking water.
Fee per night: Donation.
Management: Forest Service.
Contact: 541-825-3201.
Finding the campground: From Oregon 227 in Tiller, go northeast on South Umpqua River Scenic Route/Forest Road 28 for 13.6 miles to the camp entrance on the right.

About the campground: This campground rests in a full conifer-maple forest along the South Umpqua River. Boulder Creek flows into the river at the upper end of the camp; paths to the river are a little rough but passable. They allow you to view the river and cool your ankles, but the river is closed to fishing. Waterfalls farther upstream might be worth a visit: Campbell Falls is 0.8 mile northeast; South Umpqua Falls is 6.1 miles northeast. The campground is maintained from May to October.

55 Camp Comfort

Location: About 60 miles east of the town of Myrtle Creek.
Sites: 5 basic sites; no hookups.
Maximum length: 25 feet.
Facilities: Tables, grills, vault toilets. No drinking water.
Fee per night: Donation.
Management: Forest Service.
Contact: 541-825-3201.

Finding the campground: From Oregon 227 at Tiller, go northeast on South Umpqua River Scenic Route/Forest Road 28 for 26 miles to the camp entrance on the right.

About the campground: This attractive camp is nestled in a grove of old-growth trees. Sugar pines, firs, hemlocks, and cedars scratch the sky, with rhododendrons and vine maples filling out the understory. A steep slope lies between the camp and the South Umpqua River, but you can reach the river via the quarter-mile, barrier-free Camp Comfort Trail. Because the end of this trail is relatively steep and topped with loose gravel, wheelchair users will probably want to turn around sooner. The trail leads through lovely woods, offers river overlooks, and ends where the Castle Rock and Black Rock Forks combine to form the river. Downstream from the confluence is a swimming hole, but be careful of the rock ledges along the sides of the pool. You can also take a 6.3-mile drive downstream to view South Umpqua Falls, a combination bedrock waterslide and broken-ledge chute. The campground is maintained from May to October.

56 Charles V. Stanton County Park

Location: About 8 miles south of the town of Myrtle Creek; 2 miles north of Canyonville.
Sites: 20 hookup sites, 23 basic sites; water, electric, and sewer hookups.
Maximum length: 45 feet.
Facilities: Tables, barbecues (at non-hookup sites only), flush toilets, drinking water, showers, dump station, telephone, playground, gravel-bar boat launch.
Fee per night: $$.
Management: Douglas County.
Contact: 541-839-4483.
Finding the campground: From Interstate 5 Southbound, take Exit 101 and go 1 mile south along the frontage road on the east side of the freeway to the park. From I-5 Northbound, take Exit 99 and go 1 mile north on the east frontage road.

About the campground: Along the South Umpqua River on the east side of I-5 is this attractive 22-acre campground shaded by mature firs and oaks. The lower camp flat contains the non-hookup sites and is closer to the river. All sites have paved parking. Beyond the camp are open lawns for those who want to romp or play. Fishing is popular. The campground is open year-round.

57 Cover

Location: About 50 miles east of the town of Myrtle Creek.
Sites: 7 basic sites; no hookups.
Maximum length: 22 feet.
Facilities: Tables, grills, vault toilets. No drinking water.
Fee per night: None.
Management: Forest Service.
Contact: 541-825-3201.

Finding the campground: From Oregon 227 at Tiller, go northeast on South Umpqua River Scenic Route for 5 miles and then continue east on Forest Road 29 about 12 miles to reach this camp.

About the campground: This camp along Jackson Creek offers sites in a semi-open setting of Douglas-firs and bigleaf maples, with alders growing toward the creek. Tiny Jackson Creek is a scenic complement to your stay, as it courses over bedrock and gravel beds. Just 2 miles west of camp is the World's Largest Sugar Pine. The campground is maintained from May through October.

58 Devils Flat

Location: About 40 miles southeast of the town of Myrtle Creek.
Sites: 3 basic sites; no hookups.
Maximum length: 20 feet.
Facilities: Tables, grills, vault toilets. No drinking water.
Fee per night: None.
Management: Forest Service.
Contact: 541-825-3201.
Finding the campground: From Interstate 5, take the Azalea exit (Exit 88) and go east on County Road 36 (Cow Creek Road) for 17 miles to reach this camp on the left.

About the campground: Just upstream from Cow Creek Falls, at the foot of a steep slope, you will find this reduced-services, little-used camp opposite the historic Devils Flat Guard Station, where a circa 1915 ranger cabin and a horse barn still stand. The camp has a gravel road and open grassy sites ringed by cedars. From the guard station, you can access the Cow Creek Falls and Devils Flat Trails. Because the camp is just 10 miles upstream from Galesville Reservoir (which captures Cow Creek), you can also participate in the recreational opportunities there. The campground is open from late May through October.

59 Dumont Creek

Location: About 45 miles east of the town of Myrtle Creek.
Sites: 5 basic sites; no hookups.
Maximum length: 25 feet.
Facilities: Tables, grills, pit toilets. No drinking water.
Fee per night: Donation.
Management: Forest Service.
Contact: 541-825-3201.
Finding the campground: From Oregon 227 at Tiller, go northeast on South Umpqua River Scenic Route/Forest Road 28 for 11.6 miles to enter the camp on the right.

About the campground: This small camp occupies a forest flat of second-growth firs above the South Umpqua River. When making your way to the river, be alert for poison oak. At the upstream end of camp, where the river spills through fingers of basalt, is a deep, inviting swimming hole. Because of the riverbed cobbles intermixed with the sand, you may want to wade or swim in sneakers. At the downstream end of the camp, Dumont Creek empties into the river. For the protection of wild fish, the river and its tributaries are closed to fishing. The campground is maintained from May to October.

60 Millsite RV Park

Location: In the city of Myrtle Creek.
Sites: 11 hookup sites, a few tent sites (as available); water, electric, and sewer hookups.
Maximum length: 50 feet.
Facilities: Tables, flush toilets, drinking water, showers, dump station, telephone, ball field.
Fee per night: $ to $$.
Management: City of Myrtle Creek.
Contact: 541-863-3171.
Finding the campground: From Interstate 5, take Exit 108 and go east into Myrtle Creek. At the west end of town, turn right (south) onto Northwest 4th Avenue and proceed 0.2 mile to the RV park at the far edge of the city park.

About the campground: This is a tidy, convenient little oasis on the I-5 corridor. The sites have paved parking, grassy meridians with tables, and the open park at their back. Campers can choose between sun or partial shade. Trains passing on a track close to the park can rattle you from your slumber. The campground is open year-round.

61 Threehorn

Location: About 50 miles southeast of the town of Myrtle Creek.
Sites: 5 basic sites; no hookups.
Maximum length: 20 feet.
Facilities: Tables, grills, pit toilets. No drinking water.
Fee per night: None.
Management: Forest Service.
Contact: 541-825-3201.
Finding the campground: It is east off Oregon 227, 13 miles south of Tiller and 14.7 miles north of Shady Cove.

About the campground: This small, primitive campground is tucked in a stand of big, attractive sugar pines, cedars, and firs just off OR 227. It offers a relaxing, shady stay or a convenient overnight stop for people traveling this isolated highway. Sites have gravel parking; some are more level than others. The campground is open from late May through October.

GRANTS PASS–CAVE JUNCTION AREA

	Hookup sites	Total sites	Max. RV length	Hookups	Toilets	Showers	Drinking water	Dump station	Recreation	Fee	Can reserve
62 Alameda County Park		23	40		NF		•	•	FBL	$$	
63 Big Pine		14	40		NF		•	•	H	$$	
64 Bolan Lake		12	15		NF				HSFBL		
65 Cave Creek		18	small		NF		•		H	$$	•
66 Elderberry Flat		9	30		NF				O		
67 Grayback		38	40		F		•	•	F	$$	•
68 Griffin County Park	15	19	40	WE	F	•	•	•	FBL	$$	•
69 Indian Mary County Park	68	92	40	WES	F	•	•	•	FBL	$$	•
70 Lake Selmac County Park: Eagle Loop		14	T		NF		•		SFB	$$	•
71 Lake Selmac County Park: Heron & Teal Loops		20	T		NF		•		HSFBL	$$	•
72 Lake Selmac County Park: Mallard Loop	14	26	40	WES	F	•	•	•	HSFBLR	$$	•
73 Lake Selmac County Park: Osprey Loop	23	36	40	WES	F	•	•	•	SFBL	$$	•
74 Sam Brown		36	35		NF		•		H	$	
75 Sam Brown Horse Camp		7	40		NF		•		HR	$	
76 Schroeder County Park	29	31	40	WES	F	•	•		SFBL	$$	•
77 Secret		5	T		NF					$	
78 Spalding Pond		3	T		NF		•		F	$	
79 Tin Can		4	small		NF				H	$	
80 Tucker Flat Recreation Site		8	small		NF				HF		
81 Valley of the Rogue State Park	146	167	75	WE	F	•	•	•	HFBL	$$	•
82 Whitehorse County Park	8	42	40	WE	F	•	•		SFBL	$$	•
83 Wolf Creek County Park	19	35	30	WE	NF		•	•	H	$$	

Hookups: W = Water E = Electric S = Sewer **Total sites:** T = Tent-only campground **Maximum trailer/RV length** given in feet.
Toilets: F = Flush NF = No Flush **Recreation:** H = Hiking S = Swimming F = Fishing B = Boating L = Boat Launch
O = Off-Highway Driving R = Horseback Riding C = Cycling
Fee: $ = $1-9 $$ = $10-19 $$$ = $20-29 $$$$ = $30-39. If no entry under **Fee,** camping is free.

62 Alameda County Park

Location: About 25 miles northwest of Grants Pass.
Sites: 23 basic sites; no hookups.
Maximum length: 40 feet.
Facilities: Some tables and grills, pit toilets, drinking water, dump station, boat ramp.
Fee per night: $$.
Management: Josephine County.
Contact: 541-474-5285.
Finding the campground: From Interstate 5 north of Grants Pass, take Exit 61

and go 3.6 miles northwest to Merlin. From there, proceed west for 14.3 miles on Merlin-Galice Road, passing through Galice, to reach this county campground on the right.

About the campground: This primitive, informal campground occupies a large flat along the Rogue Wild and Scenic River. Random oaks and ponderosa pines along with a few madrones shade the flat. The understory is grassy (dirt where more trampled). This is a popular fishing and summer river recreation site. Camp guests can take advantage of the many outfitter rafting or fishing trips or shuttle services offered along Merlin-Galice Road. Superb riverside hiking trails lie within short drives of the camp. The campground is open from April 1 to September 30.

63 Big Pine

Location: About 30 miles west of Grants Pass.
Sites: 14 basic sites; no hookups.
Maximum length: 40 feet.
Facilities: Tables, grills and barbecues, vault toilets, drinking water, dump station, playground, horseshoe pits.
Fee per night: $$.
Management: Forest Service.
Contact: 541-471-6500.
Finding the campground: From Interstate 5 north of Grants Pass, take Exit 61 and go 3.6 miles northwest to Merlin. From there, proceed west 8.6 miles on Merlin-Galice Road. Turn south onto Forest Road 25 toward Big Pine and Briggs Valley and go 11.9 miles to reach this campground on the right.

About the campground: Stretched across a forested flat along the banks of Myers Creek is this fine family campground. Some magnificent firs and pines tower above the camp, while vine maples and filberts fill out the midstory. The campsites have earthen parking, and a rustic split-rail fence frames the camp meadow. A nature trail explores the forest and visits the area's champion ponderosa pine. Big Pine shoots 250 feet skyward and has a diameter of almost 6 feet. Also from the camp, spur trails lead to the longer trails that traverse the valleys of Taylor and Briggs Creeks.

64 Bolan Lake

Location: About 30 miles southeast of Cave Junction.
Sites: 12 basic sites; no hookups.
Maximum length: 15 feet.
Facilities: Some tables and fire rings, pit and vault toilets. No drinking water.
Fee per night: None.
Management: Forest Service.
Contact: 541-592-2166.
Finding the campground: From the U.S. Highway 199 and Oregon 46 junction in Cave Junction, go south on US 199 for 6.4 miles and turn east on Waldo

Road (a scenic byway), heading for Takilma and Happy Camp. Go 4.8 miles to a four-way intersection and proceed straight; the road name changes to Happy Camp Road. Continue another 12.4 miles and turn left at a sign for the campground, now on gravel Forest Road 4812. Go 4.1 miles to a three-way junction and proceed straight for Bolan Lake on unlabeled FR 040. Remain on FR 040 as it skirts below the north face of Bolan Mountain to enter the camp in 1.6 miles.

About the campground: This primitive campground is spread along the northern half of 15-acre Bolan Lake, a cold, deep mountain lake that occupies a forest and meadow at the foot of Bolan Mountain. The campground is beautiful, and despite its remoteness, it is popular on weekends. A small gravel beach, trout fishing, and non-motorized boating are the lake attractions. Trails from the camp explore the lakeshore and ascend to Bolan Mountain Lookout. The campground is open from July to October 31.

65 Cave Creek

Location: About 15 miles east of Cave Junction.
Sites: 18 basic sites; no hookups.
Maximum length: No trailers or large RVs.
Facilities: Tables, vault toilets, drinking water.
Fee per night: $$.
Management: Forest Service.
Contact: 541-592-2166; 1-800-280-CAMP for reservations.
Finding the campground: From the junction of U.S. Highway 199 and Oregon 46 at Cave Junction, go east on OR 46/Forest Road 46 for 15.3 miles to the campground entrance on the right. (No trailers may proceed past Grayback Campground at 11.1 miles; see 67 on next page.)

About the campground: Along Cave Creek stretches this linear, open-forested campground that provides convenient access to Oregon Caves National Monument (reached via trail or road). The monument offers guided underground tours and has a fine system of nature trails that ties into the more extensive trail network of the region. A record-size Douglas-fir is one of the hiking destinations. The cool of the cave is especially inviting on hot summer days. The campground is open from late May into September.

66 Elderberry Flat

Location: About 35 miles northeast of Grants Pass.
Sites: 9 basic sites; no hookups.
Maximum length: 30 feet.
Facilities: Tables, grills, vault toilets. No drinking water.
Fee per night: None.
Management: Bureau of Land Management.
Contact: 541-770-2200.

Finding the campground: From the city of Rogue River, go north on East Evans Creek Road for 18 miles and turn left onto West Fork Evans Creek Road. Continue another 9 miles to this campground.

About the campground: This out-of-the-way campground serves motorcycle and off-highway-vehicle enthusiasts, so guests can expect it to be loud and dusty. A forest of firs and hemlocks shades the sites. The campground is open from May through September.

67 Grayback

Location: About 11 miles east of Cave Junction.
Sites: 38 basic sites; no hookups.
Maximum length: 40 feet.
Facilities: Tables, barbecues, flush toilets, drinking water, dump station.
Fee per night: $$.
Management: Forest Service.
Contact: 541-592-2166; 1-800-280-CAMP for reservations.
Finding the campground: From the junction of U.S. Highway 199 and Oregon 46 at Cave Junction, go east on OR 46/Forest Road 46 for 11.1 miles to the campground entrance on the right. No trailers may proceed past Grayback Campground.

About the campground: This campground occupies a mixed, multistoried forest of firs, dogwoods, madrones, filberts, and yews. It is contained within a bend of Sucker Creek at its confluence with Grayback Creek. The barrier-free Grayback Interpretive Trail offers views of Sucker Creek and leads to a falls-viewing platform. The campground lies en route to Oregon Caves National Monument and is within an easy drive of a couple of wineries of the Illinois Valley. The campground is open from May 15 to November 30, weather permitting.

68 Griffin County Park

Location: About 7 miles west of Grants Pass.
Sites: 15 hookup sites, 4 tent sites; water and electric hookups.
Maximum length: 40 feet.
Facilities: Tables, grills, flush toilets, drinking water, showers, dump station, telephone, playground, boat ramp.
Fee per night: $$.
Management: Josephine County.
Contact: 541-474-5285.
Finding the campground: From the intersection of U.S. Highway 199 and Riverbanks Road south of Grants Pass, go northwest on Riverbanks Road for 6 miles and turn right at the sign for Griffin Park. Drive 1 mile to the park entrance on the left.

About the campground: You will find this lovely tree-shaded campground on a gentle slope along the south bank of the Rogue River. Lower sites overlook a broad gravel bar to the acclaimed scenic and recreational waterway; fishing, rafting, and swimming are among the enticements. A pair of ospreys nests on the far shore, and swallows circle overhead and dart after flies rising from the water's surface. The campground is open from April 1 to September 30.

69 Indian Mary County Park

Location: About 15 miles northwest of Grants Pass.
Sites: 68 hookup sites, 24 basic sites; water, electric, and sewer hookups.
Maximum length: 40 feet.
Facilities: Tables, grills, flush toilets, drinking water, showers, dump station, telephone, playground, horseshoe pits, volleyball, disc golf, boat ramp.
Fee per night: $$.
Management: Josephine County.
Contact: 541-474-5285.
Finding the campground: From Interstate 5 north of Grants Pass, take Exit 61 and go 3.6 miles northwest to Merlin. From there, proceed west 6.7 miles more on Merlin-Galice Road to reach the campground on the right.

About the campground: This showplace campground on the Rogue River offers sweeping, tidy grounds and great river access. Its three camping areas are spread across a grassy, shaded flat. The tall native pines, oaks, and maples, along with the various planted trees, make reclining at camp inviting, but a full range of river recreation and family activities is right at your elbow. You can be as lazy or as active as you wish. The campground is open from April 1 to October 31.

70 Lake Selmac County Park: Eagle Loop

Location: About 23 miles southwest of Grants Pass, on Lake Selmac.
Sites: 14 tent sites; no hookups.
Maximum length: Suitable for tents only.
Facilities: Tables, grills, pit toilets, drinking water.
Fee per night: $$.
Management: Josephine County.
Contact: 541-474-5285.
Finding the campground: From U.S. Highway 199, 20 miles south of Grants Pass, 7 miles north of Cave Junction, turn east on Lakeshore Drive, go 2 miles, and bear left to stay on Lakeshore Drive for another 0.6 mile. Turn right on McMullin Creek Road and then take a quick right turn off of it. At the junction just ahead, turn right for Eagle Loop.

About the campground: One of five campground loops on 160-acre Lake Selmac, this tent-camping area occupies a wooded plateau above the lake; a couple of sites overlook the water. A steep 50-foot slope separates the lakeshore from the camp, but there is nearby access for boating (10 miles per hour maximum) and swimming. Bass, crappie, and trout may tug at your fishing lines. The campground is open from April 1 to September 30.

71 Lake Selmac County Park: Heron and Teal Loops

Location: About 23 miles southwest of Grants Pass, on Lake Selmac.
Sites: 5 tent sites at Heron, 15 tent sites at Teal; no hookups.
Maximum length: Suitable for tents only.
Facilities: Tables, grills, pit toilets, drinking water (both camp loops); boat launch, dock, fish-cleaning station (Teal).
Fee per night: $$.
Management: Josephine County.
Contact: 541-474-5285.
Finding the campgrounds: From U.S. Highway 199, 20 miles south of Grants Pass, 7 miles north of Cave Junction, turn east on Lakeshore Drive, go 2 miles, and bear right on Reeves Creek Road. Go 0.8 mile, bear left on South Shore Road, and go 0.2 mile to Heron Loop or 0.4 mile to Teal Loop.

About the campgrounds: Among the flock of campground loops on Lake Selmac, these two tent areas occupy a plateau of firs, pines, and madrones. Some sites offer parking above the lake with a table right on shore. You can see rolling, wooded hills across the lake. Fishing, boating, swimming, and hiking occupy campers here. Watch for ospreys, swans, and coots. A grassy spit at each of the camps gives shore anglers a casting edge. The campgrounds are open from April 1 to September 30.

72 Lake Selmac County Park: Mallard Loop

Location: About 23 miles southwest of Grants Pass, on Lake Selmac.
Sites: 14 hookup sites, 12 basic sites; water, electric, and sewer hookups.
Maximum length: 40 feet.
Facilities: Tables, grills, flush toilets, drinking water, showers, dump station, telephone, playground, ball field, boat launch.
Fee per night: $$.
Management: Josephine County.
Contact: 541-474-5285.
Finding the campground: From U.S. Highway 199, 20 miles south of Grants Pass, 7 miles north of Cave Junction, turn east on Lakeshore Drive, go 2 miles, and bear left to stay on Lakeshore Drive for another 0.6 mile. Turn right on McMullin Creek Road and take a quick right turn off of it. At the next junction, proceed straight 0.5 mile to Mallard.

About the campground: One of five campground loops on 160-acre Lake Selmac, this loop offers a choice of grassy or wooded sites set back from the lake. You will find a horse staging area and trails leaving camp, as well as the various lake recreations: boating (10 miles per hour maximum); fishing for bass, crappie, and trout; and swimming. Lake Selmac sits in a pretty, wooded basin. The campground is open from April 1 to September 30.

73 Lake Selmac County Park: Osprey Loop

Location: About 23 miles southwest of Grants Pass.
Sites: 23 hookup sites, 13 basic sites; water, electric, and sewer hookups.
Maximum length: 40 feet.
Facilities: Tables, grills, flush toilets, drinking water, showers, dump station, telephone, playground, boat launch, fishing dock.
Fee per night: $$.
Management: Josephine County.
Contact: 541-474-5285.
Finding the campground: From U.S. Highway 199, 20 miles south of Grants Pass, 7 miles north of Cave Junction, turn east on Lakeshore Drive, go 2 miles, and bear right on Reeves Creek Road. Go 0.5 mile to reach Osprey Loop on the right.

About the campground: Occupying a gentle, wooded slope, this campground is separated from Lake Selmac by Reeves Creek Road. The glimmer of the lake is nonetheless a vital part of the camp ambiance, and guests may boat, fish, or swim. Ospreys sometimes circle over Lake Selmac, giving credence to the loop's name. The shady setting of the camp provides a welcome retreat from the fun in the sun. The campground is open from April 1 to September 30.

74 Sam Brown

Location: About 30 miles west of Grants Pass.
Sites: 36 basic sites; no hookups.
Maximum length: 35 feet.
Facilities: Tables, grills, vault toilets, drinking water, picnic shelters.
Fee per night: $.
Management: Forest Service.
Contact: 541-471-6500.
Finding the campground: From Interstate 5 north of Grants Pass, take Exit 61 and go 3.6 miles northwest to Merlin. From there, proceed west 8.6 miles on Merlin-Galice Road. Turn left (south) on Forest Road 25 toward Big Pine and Briggs Valley, and go 12.8 miles more. Turn right on FR 2512 and go 0.3 mile to enter the campground on the left.

About the campground: The campsites are arranged in two loops at the perimeter of a fenced meadow: Loop A is forested; loop B occupies the lower meadow toward the creek and is sunnier. The sites have gravel parking and are well spaced for privacy and comfort. The trails that follow Briggs, Taylor, and Dutchy Creeks can all be accessed at or near the camp.

75 Sam Brown Horse Camp

Location: About 30 miles west of Grants Pass.
Sites: 7 basic sites; no hookups.
Maximum length: 40 feet.

Facilities: Tables, grills, vault toilets, drinking water, corral at each site.
Fee per night: $.
Management: Forest Service.
Contact: 541-471-6500.
Finding the campground: From Interstate 5 north of Grants Pass, take Exit 61 and go 3.6 miles northwest to Merlin. From there, proceed west 8.6 miles on Merlin-Galice Road. Turn left (south) on Forest Road 25 toward Big Pine and Briggs Valley and go 12.8 miles more. Turn right on FR 2512, go 0.1 mile, and again turn right to reach the horse camp in another 0.2 mile.

About the campground: This accommodating horse camp occupies a semi-open forest flat, giving campers and their animals plenty of space and convenient access to the area's multiple-use trails. Taylor, Dutchy, and Briggs Creeks all have companion trails to explore. The rustic corrals blend with the setting.

76 Schroeder County Park

Location: On the western outskirts of Grants Pass.
Sites: 29 hookup sites, 2 tent sites; water, electric, and sewer hookups.
Maximum length: 40 feet.
Facilities: Tables, grills, flush toilets, drinking water, showers, telephone, playground, ball fields and courts, boat launch.
Fee per night: $$.
Management: Josephine County.
Contact: 541-474-5285.
Finding the campground: From the junction of U.S. Highway 199 and Oregon 99 in southern Grants Pass, go 0.9 mile south on US 199 and turn right (west) onto Redwood Avenue. Follow it 1.4 miles, turn right onto Willow Lane (signed for the park), and continue 0.8 mile to enter the park.

About the campground: This pleasant campground sits on a tree-shaded flat above a day-use area that actually fronts the Rogue River. The camp offers paved sites; tall, spreading oaks; groomed lawn; some privacy hedges; and mature cottonwoods along the river. Ducks and squirrels sometimes enliven the camp. Fishing, swimming, and boating are the primary onsite activities, but the park sits within easy reach of the urban attractions of Grants Pass. The campground is open year-round.

77 Secret

Location: About 33 miles west of Grants Pass.
Sites: 5 tent sites; no hookups.
Maximum length: Suitable for tents only.
Facilities: Some tables and fire rings, vault toilet, drinking water.
Fee per night: None.
Management: Forest Service.
Contact: 541-471-6500.

Finding the campground: From Interstate 5 north of Grants Pass, take Exit 61 and go 3.6 miles northwest to Merlin. From there, proceed west 8.6 miles on Merlin-Galice Road. Turn left (south) onto Forest Road 25 toward Big Pine and Briggs Valley, go 15.3 miles, and make a left turn followed by a quick right to enter this campground.

About the campground: This tiny, forested campground is tucked along pretty Secret Creek. Because the sites are closely spaced, the parking is sharply angled, and there are no turnarounds, this camp is strictly for tent camping. The trails along Taylor and Briggs Creeks offer welcome outings.

78 Spalding Pond

Location: About 28 miles southwest of Grants Pass.
Sites: 3 tent sites; no hookups.
Maximum length: Suitable for tents only.
Facilities: Tables, fire rings, compost toilets, drinking water, barrier-free path and fishing docks.
Fee per night: $.
Management: Forest Service.
Contact: 541-471-6500.
Finding the campground: From U.S. Highway 199, 16 miles south of Grants Pass; 12 miles north of Cave Junction, take paved Forest Road 25 northwest toward Onion Mountain Lookout. Follow this curving, single-lane road for 7.2 miles and turn left onto unlabeled, gravel FR 2524 (Spalding Mill Road); avoid FR 243. Go 4.3 miles on FR 2524, turn right onto FR 045, and proceed 0.7 mile to the camp.

About the campground: Central to the camp is heart-shaped Spalding Pond, which reflects the green of the surrounding forest as well as the dry slopes dotted with manzanitas. This pond was created to serve Spalding Mill (1933–1936) and later expanded by the Forest Service to its present 3-acre size. The sites are well spaced through the evergreen forest; from them you can see the pond and hear the burble of Soldier Creek. A barrier-free trail leads partway around the pond and accesses fishing docks.

79 Tin Can

Location: About 20 miles west of Grants Pass.
Sites: 4 basic sites; no hookups.
Maximum length: Best suited for tents and pickup campers.
Facilities: Tables, grills, vault toilets. No drinking water.
Fee per night: $.
Management: Forest Service.
Contact: 541-471-6500.
Finding the campground: From Interstate 5 north of Grants Pass, take Exit 61, go 3.6 miles northwest to Merlin, and from there, proceed west 8.6 miles on

Ancient forest trail.

Merlin-Galice Road. Turn left (south) onto Forest Road 25 toward Big Pine and Briggs Valley and go 5 miles to reach this campground on the left.

About the campground: This tiny campground is best suited for tent and pickup camping because of the tight parking angles and lack of turnarounds. It sits along crystalline Taylor Creek and is nestled in a vibrant woods of firs, pines, dogwoods, and vine maples. In spring, giant trilliums adorn the forest floor, while dogwoods flaunt their blooms at eye level. Fish weirs partition Taylor Creek and create artificial cascades. A footbridge spans the waterway, linking the camp to the Taylor Creek Trail, which leads both upstream and downstream from Tin Can. The campground is open year-round.

80 Tucker Flat Recreation Site

Location: About 60 miles northwest of Grants Pass.
Sites: 8 basic sites; no hookups.
Maximum length: Best suited for tents and pickup campers.
Facilities: Some tables and grills or fire rings, pit toilets. No drinking water.
Fee per night: None.
Management: Bureau of Land Management.
Contact: 541-770-2200.
Finding the campground: From Interstate 5 north of Grants Pass, take Exit 61, go 3.6 miles northwest to Merlin, and proceed west on Merlin-Galice Road for

18.2 miles, passing through Galice to Grave Creek. There, cross the Rogue River and bear left on the Grave Creek–Marial BLM Back Country Byway. (Be sure to request a byway brochure from the Medford District Office; it may help you to avoid confusion while navigating the BLM roads.) Follow the byway for 33 miles and bear right past Rogue River Ranch to enter this campground. Watch for byway signs at junctions, especially 20 miles into the tour, where the route drops back into the canyon. It is also advisable to call the BLM about the road conditions before attempting this drive.

About the campground: Although difficult to reach, this recreation site provides a pleasant, primitive camping experience in the Wild Rogue Country. The camp flat above Mule Creek is shaded by fir, tanoak, and live oak. From the camp, the Mule Creek Trail heads upstream and eventually meets the Panther Ridge Trail for a skyline tour of the Wild Rogue Wilderness. You can access the acclaimed Rogue River Trail in the vicinity of Rogue River Ranch, just a short hike away. The ranch is on the National Register of Historic Places and is open for viewing. Fishing, swimming, and wildlife watching further engage campers at Tucker Flat.

81 Valley of the Rogue State Park

Location: About 10 miles southeast of Grants Pass.
Sites: 146 full or partial hookup sites, 21 basic sites, 6 yurts; water and electric hookups.
Maximum length: 75 feet.
Facilities: Tables, grills, flush toilets, drinking water, showers, dump station, telephone, playground, horseshoe pits, boat launch, meeting hall.
Fee per night: $$.
Management: Oregon State Parks and Recreation Department.
Contact: 541-582-1118; 1-800-452-5687 for reservations.
Finding the campground: From Interstate 5, south of the city of Rogue River, take Exit 45. Locate the state park north of the rest area here.

About the campground: Although you may hear the drone of traffic on the freeway, this long, sprawling, attractive campground borders a scenic mile along the Rogue River. Altogether, the state park claims a 3-mile stretch of river and offers ample recreational access. The campsites are spacious, with paved parking. Native pines, oaks, and cedars, along with a variety of landscape trees, contribute to the shade and beauty of the camp. You can fish, boat, or walk the 1.1-mile River Edge Trail. You can even arrange for a shuttle pickup at the park for a jet-boat tour. The campground is open year-round.

82 Whitehorse County Park

Location: About 7 miles west of Grants Pass.
Sites: 8 hookup sites, 34 basic sites; water and electric hookups.
Maximum length: 40 feet.
Facilities: Tables, some barbecues and grills, flush toilets, drinking water, showers, telephone, playground, horseshoe pits, volleyball, paved boat ramp.
Fee per night: $$.
Management: Josephine County.
Contact: 541-474-5285.
Finding the campground: From 6th Street in Grants Pass, go west on G Street, which later becomes Upper River Road and then Lower River Road, to enter the park after 7.3 miles.

About the campground: This fine campground sits on a gentle, wooded hillside above the north bank of the Rogue River. A day-use area claims the lower portion of the park, closer to the river. Attractive lawn and ponderosa pines and oaks lend character to the camp, while cottonwoods grow toward the river. The park is also a bird sanctuary, so naturalists will enjoy the companionship of herons, geese, ospreys, wood ducks, and songbirds. Fishing, rafting, swimming, and riverside nature walks keep visitors delightfully busy. The campground is open from April 1 to September 30.

83 Wolf Creek County Park

Location: In the community of Wolf Creek, about 20 miles north of Grants Pass.
Sites: 19 hookup sites, 16 basic sites; water and electric hookups.
Maximum length: 30 feet.
Facilities: Tables, grills, pit toilets, drinking water, dump station, playground, disc golf, baseball field, horseshoe pits.
Fee per night: $$.
Management: Josephine County.
Contact: 541-474-5285.
Finding the campground: From Interstate 5, take Exit 76 and head west into the town of Wolf Creek. From there, follow the signs for the park, which lies at the end of Main Street, 0.3 mile past the historic Wolf Creek Tavern (or Wolf Creek Inn).

About the campground: This quiet, wooded campground sits just outside the small town of Wolf Creek. The town's historic tavern, a state heritage site, was a stagecoach stop on the Oregon-California line. The campsites are snuggled amid the tall firs, pines, and madrones and have earthen parking. A full, green understory helps to ensure privacy. Only an intermittent train whistle or a big game at the ball field disturbs the quiet. A foot trail links the camp with a viewpoint and the summit of London Peak. The campground is open year-round.

MEDFORD AREA

	Hookup sites	Total sites	Max. RV length	Hookups	Toilets	Showers	Drinking water	Dump station	Recreation	Fee	Can reserve
84 Applegate Lake Recreation Areas		48	40		F		•		HSFBL	$-$$	
85 Beaver-Sulphur		10	18		NF		•			$	
86 Big Ben		2	18		NF				H		
87 Cantrall-Buckley County Park		35	25		NF	•	•		SF	$$	
88 Doe Point		30	32		F		•		HSFBL	$$	
89 Fish Lake		17	32		F		•		HSFBL	$$	
90 Flumet Flat		23	40		F		•		HSF	$	
91 Fourbit Ford		7	20		NF		•		F	$	
92 Imnaha		4	20		NF				H		
93 Jackson		8	T		F		•		SF	$	
94 Joseph Stewart State Park	151	201	80	WE	F	•	•	•	HSFBLC	$$	
95 North Fork		9	30		NF		•		HF	$	
96 Parker Meadows		9	25		NF		•			$	
97 Rogue Elk County Park	16	36	35	WE	F	•	•	•	SFBL	$$	
98 Snowshoe		6	20		NF						
99 South Fork		6	18		NF		•		HF	$	
100 Whiskey Spring		34	30		NF		•		H	$	
101 Willow Lake Recreation Area	37	63	25	WES	F	•	•	•	SFBL	$$	
102 Willow Prairie Horse Camp		10	40		NF		•		HR	$	

Hookups: W = Water E = Electric S = Sewer **Total sites:** T = Tent-only campground **Maximum trailer/RV length** given in feet.
Toilets: F = Flush NF = No Flush **Recreation:** H = Hiking S = Swimming F = Fishing B = Boating L = Boat Launch
O = Off-Highway Driving R = Horseback Riding C = Cycling
Fee: $ = $1-9 $$ = $10-19 $$$ = $20-29 $$$$ = $30-39. If no entry under **Fee,** camping is free.

84 Applegate Lake Recreation Areas

Location: About 30 miles southwest of Medford, on Applegate Reservoir.
Sites: 15 RV spaces at Hart-tish; 33 total walk-in tent sites at Carberry, French Gulch, and Watkins; no hookups.
Maximum length: 40 feet.
Facilities: Tables, grills, flush toilets (Hart-tish), vault toilets (walk-in camps), drinking water (all), boat launch (Hart-tish).
Fee per night: $$ (Hart-tish); $ (walk-in camps).
Management: Forest Service.
Contact: 541-899-1812.
Finding the campground: From Jacksonville, take Oregon 238 west toward Grants Pass, going 7.4 miles to Ruch. There, turn south onto Applegate Road toward Applegate Dam and Star Ranger Station. Go 14.5 miles to the reservoir: Hart-tish, Watkins, and Carberry Recreation Areas dot the west shore; French Gulch is across Applegate Dam on Forest Road 1075.

About the campground: These camps serve visitors to Applegate Reservoir and the surrounding mountains. Fishing and boating (10 miles per hour maximum) are popular draws, especially when the reservoir is high, but the area also boasts superb hiking trails. The Collings Mountain Trail offers a challenging skyline hike and bypasses a trap built for Bigfoot. Other trails wander the reservoir shore or introduce the region's mining past. For each of the camps, parking is in an open lot, with tables and amenities just strides away. The campgrounds are open from May into October.

85 Beaver-Sulphur

Location: About 30 miles southwest of Medford.
Sites: 10 basic sites; no hookups.
Maximum length: 18 feet; best suited for tents.
Facilities: Tables, grills, pit toilets, drinking water.
Fee per night: $.
Management: Forest Service.
Contact: 541-899-1812.
Finding the campground: From Jacksonville, take Oregon 238 west toward Grants Pass. Go 7.4 miles to Ruch and turn left (south) onto Applegate Road toward Applegate Dam and Star Ranger Station. Go 8.9 miles and turn left onto Beaver Creek Road. Continue 2.7 miles to the campground on the right.

About the campground: This is a pleasant, primitive camp tucked among the firs and live oaks beside Beaver Creek. The gentle murmur of the creek provides a soothing backdrop. Site parking is either in gravel spaces or on the shoulder of the camp road. Recreational gold panning is allowed at a designated area within the camp, but a permit is required; secure your permit and information at Star Ranger Station, which is passed en route to the camp. Hiking trails and Applegate Reservoir are within easy reach. The campground is maintained from May 1 to October 15.

86 Big Ben

Location: About 50 miles northeast of Medford.
Sites: 2 basic sites; no hookups.
Maximum length: 18 feet.
Facilities: Tables, grills, pit toilets. No drinking water.
Fee per night: None.
Management: Forest Service.
Contact: 541-865-2700.
Finding the campground: Start from Butte Falls, which is reached some 30 miles northeast of Medford via signed routes off OR 62 or OR 140. From 1 mile east of the town of Butte Falls, turn north onto Butte Falls–Prospect Road, go 8.5 miles, and turn right onto Lodgepole Road/Forest Road 34. Continue 7.8 miles more to the junction with FR 37 and follow FR 37 right for 0.8 mile to reach the camp on the left.

About the campground: Across the road from the South Fork Rogue River, you will find this tiny, quiet camp in a forest of ponderosa pines, firs, and chinquapins. Near the junction of FR 37 and FR 34, you can access the South Fork Rogue River Trail. The campground is open from the end of May to October.

87 Cantrall-Buckley County Park

Location: About 18 miles southwest of Medford.
Sites: 30 basic sites, 5 walk-in tent sites; no hookups.
Maximum length: 25 feet.
Facilities: Tables, barbecues, vault toilets, drinking water, coin-operated showers (at day-use area), playground, volleyball, horseshoe pits.
Fee per night: $$.
Management: Jackson County.
Contact: 541-776-7001.
Finding the campground: From Oregon 238, 25 miles east of Grants Pass, 8.5 miles west of Jacksonville, turn south on Hamilton Road to reach the campground entrance on the right at 1 mile.

About the campground: In an 89-acre woodland of pines, oaks, madrones, and firs sits this county park complex with 1.75 miles of Applegate River frontage. The rustic camp claims a knoll above the river; its companion day-use area is open only on weekends and holidays. Deer are common here, and birding is popular. Trout fishing and swimming will keep you entertained, or you may want to head east into historic Jacksonville. This town traces its origins to the placer gold discoveries of 1851–1852. It retains its old-town charm and welcomes strolling with its museums and shops. The campground is open from April 15 to October 15.

88 Doe Point

Location: About 38 miles east of Medford, on Fish Lake.
Sites: 25 basic sites, 5 walk-in tent sites; no hookups.
Maximum length: 32 feet.
Facilities: Tables, grills, flush toilets, drinking water.
Fee per night: $$.
Management: Forest Service.
Contact: 541-482-3333.
Finding the campground: From Oregon 140, 37.5 miles east of Medford, 6.5 miles west of Lake of the Woods, turn south at the sign for Doe Point Campground on Forest Road 810 and go 0.5 mile to enter the camp.

About the campground: This attractive camp fronts the north shore of Fish Lake, a big, sparkling mountain lake enlarged by a dam on the North Fork Little Butte Creek. The sites are well spaced and shaded by firs. Across the lake from the camp rises Brown Mountain (elevation 7,311 feet). This is a shield volcano, and the lava flow it spewed is one of the most recent in the Cascades. Brown

Mountain Lava Field covers 13 square miles and measures some 250 feet thick. If you hike the Fish Lake Trail to the Pacific Crest Trail and walk south along the PCT, you can visit the outskirts of the lava field or traverse it. However, fishing and swimming keep most guests at the lake. The campground is open from May 1 to October 15.

89 Fish Lake

Location: About 39 miles east of Medford, on Fish Lake.
Sites: 17 basic sites; no hookups.
Maximum length: 32 feet.
Facilities: Tables, grills, flush toilets, drinking water, boat launch, dock, fish-cleaning building.
Fee per night: $$.
Management: Forest Service.
Contact: 541-482-3333.
Finding the campground: From Oregon 140, 38 miles east of Medford, 6 miles west of Lake of the Woods, turn south for Fish Lake, go 0.6 mile, and bear right to enter the camp.

About the campground: This comfortable camp is on the north shore of Fish Lake, a scenic mountain lake enlarged by a dam; the natural lake was only a third this size. From the camp, you can view volcanic Brown Mountain across the water. Fish Lake is open to fishing, swimming, and boating (10 miles per hour maximum or self-propelled). Along its shore is the Fish Lake Trail, which ultimately connects with the Pacific Crest Trail for longer hikes. Sites have paved or earthen parking and double-wide spaces for trailers. Ospreys and eagles may soar overhead. The campground is open from May 1 to October 15.

90 Flumet Flat

Location: About 25 miles southwest of Medford.
Sites: 23 basic sites; no hookups.
Maximum length: 40 feet.
Facilities: Tables, grills, flush toilets, drinking water, horseshoe pits.
Fee per night: $.
Management: Forest Service.
Contact: 541-899-1812.
Finding the campground: From Jacksonville, take Oregon 238 west toward Grants Pass. Go 7.4 miles to Ruch and turn south onto Applegate Road toward Applegate Dam and Star Ranger Station. Go 8.6 miles, bear right on Palmer Creek Road, and go another 0.8 mile to the camp entrance on the right.

About the campground: This comfortable campground along the Applegate River is shaded by pines, madrones, and oaks. It offers a tranquil base for exploring this dry southern valley and the framing Siskiyou Mountains. Area activities include boating and fishing at Applegate Reservoir; recreational gold panning;

McKee Covered Bridge.

and hiking the historic, interpretive Gin Lin Trail, which starts next to the camp. Gin Lin was a Chinese miner who succeeded in drawing more than a million dollars in gold out of this Siskiyou Mountains site. For your gold panning, you must pay a small fee and secure a permit from Star Ranger Station, passed en route to the camp. Along with the permit, you will receive a map showing where you can pan without claim jumping. McKee Covered Bridge about 1 mile northeast makes a good photo opportunity. The campground is maintained from May 1 to October 15.

91 Fourbit Ford

Location: About 34 miles northeast of Medford.
Sites: 7 basic sites; no hookups.
Maximum length: 20 feet.
Facilities: Tables, grills, vault toilets, drinking water.
Fee per night: $.
Management: Forest Service.
Contact: 541-865-3581.
Finding the campground: From Oregon 140, 26 miles east of Medford, go 6 miles north on County Road 821 to Forest Road 3065. From Butte Falls, travel 10 miles south on County 821 to FR 3065. Turn east and follow FR 3065 for 1.4 miles to enter the camp on the left; the final 1.1 miles are on gravel.

About the campground: This pleasant campground overlooks Fourbit Creek. Pines and firs shade the camp; the well for the camp sits in a meadow. The campsites are nicely spaced but have relatively short parking spurs. Although you can fish in the creek, this is mainly a spot to retreat from daily concerns and enjoy the natural surroundings. The campground is open from May 1 to October 15.

92 Imnaha

Location: About 60 miles northeast of Medford.
Sites: 4 basic sites; no hookups.
Maximum length: 20 feet.
Facilities: Tables, grills, pit toilets. No drinking water.
Fee per night: None.
Management: Forest Service.
Contact: 541-865-2700.
Finding the campground: From Prospect, go east on Butte Falls–Prospect Road for 2.8 miles. Turn left onto Bessie Creek Road/Forest Road 37, go 8.2 miles, and turn left into the camp. All but the last mile is paved.

About the campground: Near Imnaha Guard Station, this tiny camp sits at the edge of a meadow. Paths from the camp lead to a big fir and Imnaha Springs; the creek that emerges from the springs threads past the camp. The fir has a 7-foot diameter and could easily feel at home among California's sequoia redwoods. At the far side of the guard station, a gate opens to a boardwalk and path leading to an enchanting, hummocky meadow flat drained by the silver rivulets of Imnaha Springs. Mosses, wildflowers, greenery-coated logs, and clumps of aquatic vegetation contribute to the richness of the scene. En route to the camp, you will have passed the Middle Fork Rogue Trail, which enters Sky Lakes Wilderness. The campground is open from the end of May to October 31.

93 Jackson

Location: About 25 miles southwest of Medford.
Sites: 8 tent sites; no hookups.
Maximum length: Suitable for tents only.
Facilities: Tables, barbecues, flush toilets, drinking water.
Fee per night: $.
Management: Forest Service.
Contact: 541-899-1812.
Finding the campground: From Jacksonville, take Oregon 238 west toward Grants Pass. Go 7.4 miles to Ruch and turn south onto Applegate Road toward Applegate Dam and Star Ranger Station. Go 9.5 miles and turn right to enter this campground.

About the campground: Primarily for tent campers, this campground offers a central parking area and walk-to sites along the Applegate River. Pines, cedars, and madrones lend shade. Swimming is at your own risk. Hiking and the recreational opportunities created by Applegate Reservoir are close by. The campground is maintained from May 1 to October 15.

94 Joseph Stewart State Park

Location: About 35 miles northeast of Medford, on Lost Creek Reservoir.
Sites: 151 hookup sites, 50 basic sites; water and electric hookups.
Maximum length: 80 feet.
Facilities: Tables, grills, flush toilets, drinking water, showers, dump station, telephone, playground, store, marina, boat rental, boat launch, dock.
Fee per night: $$.
Management: Oregon State Parks and Recreation Department.
Contact: 541-560-3334.
Finding the campground: It is north off Oregon 62, 10 miles southwest of Prospect and about 35 miles northeast of Medford.

About the campground: In Rogue River Country, along the southeast shore of Lost Creek Reservoir, stretches this attractive, developed park, with a sweeping groomed lawn, young pines, and some leafy shade trees. Lost Creek Reservoir captures the Rogue, creating a wonderful playground for swimming, fishing, boating, and sailing. Where the river flows free, rafting extends the to-do list. Hiking the area trails or cycling a 6-mile bike path provides a different lake perspective. Cole M. Rivers Fish Hatchery, near the Lost Creek dam, is the largest hatchery in the state and is open for tours. The campground is open from mid-April to late October.

95 North Fork

Location: About 37 miles east of Medford.
Sites: 9 basic sites; no hookups.
Maximum length: 30 feet.
Facilities: Tables, grills, vault toilets, drinking water.
Fee per night: $.
Management: Forest Service.
Contact: 541-482-3333.
Finding the campground: From Oregon 140, 36 miles east of Medford, 8 miles west of Lake of the Woods, turn south on Forest Road 37 to reach the camp on the right in 0.5 mile. Or, from Dead Indian Memorial Road 23.4 miles east of Ashland, turn north on FR 37 and go 7.2 miles to reach the camp on the left.

About the campground: On North Fork Little Butte Creek, the outlet of Fish Lake, this camp offers a rustic camping experience. The North Fork flows broad and clear between grassy banks. A tall, rich fir forest with chinquapin understory and the outskirts of Brown Mountain Lava Field contribute to the setting. The parking spaces are gravel, but only one site offers pull-thru parking. By hiking the Fish Lake Trail, you can reach the dam at 0.6 mile, a resort at 3 miles, and the Pacific Crest Trail at 5 miles. Fish Lake (accessible by trail or road) offers fishing, boating, and swimming. The campground is maintained from May 1 to October 15.

96 Parker Meadows

Location: About 70 miles northeast of Medford.
Sites: 9 basic sites; no hookups.
Maximum length: 25 feet.
Facilities: Tables, grills, pit toilets, drinking water, Adirondack shelter.
Fee per night: $.
Management: Forest Service.
Contact: 541-865-2700.
Finding the campground: From Prospect, go east on Butte Falls–Prospect Road for 2.8 miles and turn left onto Bessie Creek Road/Forest Road 37, which begins paved but becomes gravel. Continue 20 miles and turn right onto an unmarked gravel road to enter the camp in 0.25 mile.

About the campground: This isolated camp rests in a forest of big firs and hemlocks with a huckleberry understory. While it has the amenities of a basic forest camp, the location has a wilderness feeling about it; nature and wildlife are right at your doorstep. The rustic A-frame shelter is at site 9. Not far from the camp is the trail along the South Fork Rogue River that leads into Sky Lakes Wilderness. The campground is open from the end of May to October 31.

97 Rogue Elk County Park

Location: About 25 miles northeast of Medford.
Sites: 16 hookup sites, 20 tent sites; water and electric hookups.
Maximum length: 35 feet.
Facilities: Tables, barbecues, flush and vault toilets, drinking water, showers, dump station, telephone, playground, boat launch.
Fee per night: $$.
Management: Jackson County.
Contact: 541-776-7001.
Finding the campground: It is south off Oregon 62, 4.8 miles northeast of Shady Cove.

About the campground: This shaded and landscaped camp fronts the Rogue River downstream from Lost Creek Reservoir. The overflow tent area occupies a more natural forest setting. The Rogue entertains and enchants with fishing, boating, and swimming. The campground is open from April 15 to October 15.

98 Snowshoe

Location: About 37 miles east of Medford.
Sites: 6 basic sites; no hookups.
Maximum length: 20 feet.
Facilities: Tables, grills, pit toilets. No drinking water.
Fee per night: None.
Management: Forest Service.

Contact: 541-865-3581.
Finding the campground: From Oregon 140, 26 miles east of Medford, go 6 miles north on County Road 821 to Forest Road 3065. From Butte Falls, travel 10 miles south on CR 821 to FR 3065. Turn east and follow FR 3065 for 4.8 miles to the camp entrance on the left; the final 4.5 miles are on gravel.

About the campground: This campground off the beaten track delivers quiet and full shade beneath pines, cedars, and firs. Bring a lounge chair and a good book and relax. The campground is open from May 1 to October 15.

99 South Fork

Location: About 45 miles east of Medford.
Sites: 6 basic sites; no hookups.
Maximum length: 18 feet.
Facilities: Tables, grills, pit toilets, drinking water.
Fee per night: $.
Management: Forest Service.
Contact: 541-865-2700.
Finding the campground: Start from Butte Falls, which is reached some 30 miles northeast of Medford via signed routes off OR 62 or OR 140. From 1 mile east of the town of Butte Falls, turn north onto Butte Falls–Prospect Road, go 8.5 miles, and turn right onto Lodgepole Road/Forest Road 34. Continue 7.3 miles more to enter the camp on the right.

About the campground: This campground occupies a pine- and fir-covered bench above the road and the South Fork Rogue River. Half a mile east of camp, near the junction of FR 37 and FR 34, you can access the South Fork Rogue River Trail. Other trails in the area venture into the Sky Lakes Wilderness. The campground is open from the end of May to October.

100 Whiskey Spring

Location: About 32 miles east of Medford.
Sites: 34 basic sites; no hookups.
Maximum length: 30 feet.
Facilities: Tables, grills, vault toilets, drinking water.
Fee per night: $.
Management: Forest Service.
Contact: 541-865-3581.
Finding the campground: From Oregon 140, 26 miles east of Medford, go 6 miles north on County Road 821 to Forest Road 3065. From Butte Falls, travel 10 miles south on CR 821 to FR 3065. Turn east and follow FR 3065 for 0.3 mile to enter the camp on the left.

About the campground: This campground occupies a large flat of pine trees, with a few cedars and firs sprinkled through the ranks. RVers will find several long, gravel parking pads, as well as some pull-thru sites. Adjacent to the camp are a spring-fed beaver pond and Whiskey Creek, a trout stream. In season, spring peepers enliven the night forest; at other times it is an owl sounding. Squirrels, deer, beavers, woodpeckers, and wood ducks can be spied. A 1-mile, barrier-free trail with a cinder surface visits the beaver pond, Whiskey Creek, and Whiskey Spring, while touring a rich woodland seasonally decorated with colorful wildflowers. The campground is open from May 1 to October 15.

101 Willow Lake Recreation Area

Location: About 35 miles east of Medford, on Willow Lake.
Sites: 37 full or partial hookup sites, 26 tent sites, 7 cabins; water, electric, and sewer hookups.
Maximum length: 25 feet.
Facilities: Tables, grills, flush and vault toilets, drinking water, showers (at beach), dump station, telephone, boat rentals, launch, dock, fish-cleaning station, store, restaurant.
Fee per night: $$.
Management: Jackson County.
Contact: 541-865-3229.
Finding the campground: From Oregon 140, 26 miles east of Medford, go 8 miles north on County Road 821 to Willow Lake Road. From the town of Butte Falls, go 8 miles south on CR 821 to Willow Lake Road. Turn west and follow Willow Lake Road 0.4 mile to the recreation area.

About the campground: This campground-resort complex occupies more than 900 acres on the west shore of Willow Lake, a large reservoir rimmed by forest. Cross-lake views find Mount McLoughlin. This is a busy place: swimming, fishing, and canoeing are popular, and a section of the lake is set aside for waterskiing. The RV area features sites with gravel or earthen parking. The tent area claims a mildly rolling, pine-clad slope, with some sites overlooking the water. The campground is open from April to November.

102 Willow Prairie Horse Camp

Location: About 29 miles east of Medford.
Sites: 10 basic sites; no hookups.
Maximum length: 40 feet.
Facilities: Tables, grills, pit toilets, drinking water, corrals.
Fee per night: $.
Management: Forest Service.
Contact: 541-865-2700.
Finding the campground: From Oregon 140, 26 miles east of Medford, 8 miles west of Lake of the Woods, turn north on County Road 821, heading for Butte Falls. Go 1.6 miles and turn left on Forest Road 3738. Go another 1.2 miles and bear left on FR 3735 to enter the camp on the right in 0.2 mile.

About the campground: This fine horse camp sits next to a prairie meadow threaded by the West Branch Willow Creek. Douglas-firs and grand firs supply shade to the well-spaced sites, which are both accommodating and comfortable. Horse trails allow you to explore from camp. The meadow, a reclaimed beaver pond, now has a new population of beavers, which are again raising the water level. Buttercup, lupine, and false hellebore add a touch of color to the soggy area. Overlooking the lea is the restored Willow Prairie Cabin, which is on the National Register of Historic Places; an antler door handle provides admittance. The campground is maintained from May 15 to the end of September.

ASHLAND AREA

		Hookup sites	Total sites	Max. RV length	Hookups	Toilets	Showers	Drinking water	Dump station	Recreation	Fee	Can reserve
103	Beaver Dam		4	20		NF				HF	$	
104	Daley Creek		6	25		NF				HF	$	
105	Emigrant Lake Recreation Area		42	30		F	•	•	•	SFBL	$$	
106	Hyatt Lake Recreation Site		55	35		F	•	•	•	HFBL	$$	
107	Klum Landing		32	25		NF		•		SFBL	$$	
108	Lily Glen Horse Camp		25	30		NF		•		FR	$$	
109	Mount Ashland		8	small		NF				H		
110	Wildcat		12	20		NF				FBL	$	
111	Willow Point		40	35		NF		•		HSFBL	$$	

Hookups: W = Water E = Electric S = Sewer **Total sites:** T = Tent-only campground **Maximum trailer/RV length** given in feet.
Toilets: F = Flush NF = No Flush **Recreation:** H = Hiking S = Swimming F = Fishing B = Boating L = Boat Launch
O = Off-Highway Driving R = Horseback Riding C = Cycling
Fee: $ = $1-9 $$ = $10-19 $$$ = $20-29 $$$$ = $30-39. If no entry under **Fee,** camping is free.

103 Beaver Dam

Location: About 25 miles northeast of Ashland.
Sites: 4 basic sites; no hookups.
Maximum length: 20 feet.
Facilities: Tables, grills, pit toilets. No drinking water.
Fee per night: $.
Management: Forest Service.
Contact: 541-482-3333.
Finding the campground: From Ashland, go 23.4 miles east on Dead Indian Memorial Road. Turn left (north) onto paved Forest Road 37, go 1.4 miles, and turn right into the camp.

About the campground: This small, primitive campground occupies a forest of Douglas-fir, grand fir, lodgepole pine, and spruce along the willow-lined banks of Beaver Dam Creek. It serves as a quiet retreat. For streamside exploration and trout fishing, a foot trail links this camp to Daley Creek Campground and continues about 2 miles beyond. Howard Prairie and Hyatt Lakes are a short drive southwest from the camp. The campground is maintained from May 1 to October 15.

104 Daley Creek

Location: About 25 miles northeast of Ashland.
Sites: 6 basic sites; no hookups.
Maximum length: 25 feet.
Facilities: Tables, grills, vault toilets. No drinking water.

Fee per night: $.
Management: Forest Service.
Contact: 541-482-3333.
Finding the campground: From Ashland, go 23.4 miles east on Dead Indian Memorial Road. Turn left (north) onto paved Forest Road 37, go 1.6 miles, and turn left into the camp.

About the campground: This quiet hideaway occupies a slight knoll at the confluence of Beaver Dam and Daley Creeks. It rests in a mixed forest and has two sites set aside for wheelchair users. Beaver Dam Trail links this camp to Beaver Dam Campground and allows for a couple of miles of exploring along Beaver Dam Creek. Both creeks are wonderfully clear with a series of small pools. Along the banks, grassy openings between the willows provide access to the pools. The campground is maintained from May 1 to October 15.

105 Emigrant Lake Recreation Area

Location: About 4 miles southeast of Ashland, on Emigrant Lake.
Sites: 42 sites; no hookups.
Maximum length: 30 feet.
Facilities: Tables, grills, flush toilets, drinking water, showers, dump station, telephone, playground, ball field, horseshoe pits, water slide, boat rental, two boat ramps, food concession.
Fee per night: $$.
Management: Jackson County.
Contact: 541-776-7001.
Finding the campground: From Interstate 5 in Ashland, take Exit 14 and go southeast on Oregon 66 for 3.2 miles. Turn left at the sign for Emigrant Lake Recreation Area and continue about a mile to the camp entrance on the left.

About the campground: This campground occupies an oak-studded, grassy hillside above popular Emigrant Lake, a large, horseshoe-shaped reservoir hugged by arid valley foothills. All sites are paved, but some require more RV leveling than others. Recreational opportunities center on the lake, where you can swim, boat, fish, sail, water ski, and sailboard. A water slide is open Memorial Day through Labor Day; there is a fee to use it. The campground is open from March 15 to October 15.

106 Hyatt Lake Recreation Site

Location: About 20 miles east of Ashland, on Hyatt Lake.
Sites: 30 basic sites in the main overnight area, 18 drive-in tent sites, 7 walk-in tent sites; no hookups.
Maximum length: 35 feet.
Facilities: Tables, grills and barbecues, flush toilets, drinking water, showers, dump station, telephone, playground, volleyball, horseshoe pits, 2 boat launches, dock, fish-cleaning station, boat trailer parking.

Fee per night: $$.
Management: Bureau of Land Management.
Contact: 541-770-2200.
Finding the campground: From Oregon 66, 17 miles east of Ashland, 44 miles west of Klamath Falls, turn north on East Hyatt Road at the sign for the reservoir. Go 3 miles and proceed straight for the recreation site as the main road curves left and becomes Hyatt Prairie Road. In 0.1 mile, turn left for Hyatt Lake Recreation Site.

About the campground: This star in the portfolio of BLM campgrounds occupies a gentle, forested slope above Hyatt Lake, a popular boating and fishing reservoir. Mount McLoughlin looms to the north. Ospreys sometimes dive for fish. The sites are mostly shaded by Douglas-firs and grand firs. The Pacific Crest Trail passes through the area not far from the camp. The campground is open from April 25 through October.

107 Klum Landing

Location: About 27 miles east of Ashland, on Howard Prairie Lake.
Sites: 32 basic sites; no hookups.
Maximum length: 25 feet.
Facilities: Tables, grills, vault toilets, drinking water, boat launch, playground.
Fee per night: $$.
Management: Jackson County.
Contact: 541-776-7001.
Finding the campground: From Ashland, drive 19 miles east on Dead Indian Memorial Road. Turn right (south) onto Hyatt Prairie Road, go 4.6 miles, and turn left onto Howard Prairie Dam Road. Drive 3 miles farther to reach the camp on the left.

About the campground: This primitive campground spreads across 156 acres of pine- and fir-forested slope at the southern end of Howard Prairie Lake, a huge, elongated reservoir that offers swimming, fishing, and boating. The campsites are well shaded, a welcome change from the sun-drenched lake. Because all sites are back-ins and some have difficult approaches, this campground is inappropriate for large RV units. The Pacific Crest Trail offers hiking. The campground is open from April 15 to November 1.

108 Lily Glen Horse Camp

Location: About 20 miles east of Ashland, on Howard Prairie Lake.
Sites: 25 basic sites; no hookups.
Maximum length: 30 feet.
Facilities: Tables, grills, vault toilets, drinking water, corrals.
Fee per night: $$.
Management: Jackson County.
Contact: 541-776-7001.

Finding the campground: From Ashland, drive 20 miles east on Dead Indian Memorial Road. Turn right (south) to enter the camp. (The turn is 1 mile east of Hyatt Prairie Road.)

About the campground: This camp occupies a flat shaded by ponderosa pines along the shallow north end of Howard Prairie Reservoir. Boating is popular on much of the lake, but there is no launch here. Because of that, this camp tends to offer a quieter stay. A rustic barn and water tower contribute to the atmosphere of camp. You can access horse trails nearby, and fishing is popular. The campground is open from April 15 to November 1.

109 Mount Ashland

Location: About 20 miles south of Ashland.
Sites: 8 basic sites; no hookups.
Maximum length: Best suited for tents.
Facilities: Tables, barbecues, pit toilets. No drinking water.
Fee per night: None.
Management: Forest Service.
Contact: 916-468-5351.
Finding the campground: From Interstate 5 south of Ashland, take Exit 6 and head west, following the signs for Mount Ashland. Go 0.7 mile, turn right on Mount Ashland Road/Forest Road 20 and follow it for 9.3 miles to reach the campground. The final 0.4 mile is on gravel; the campground is 0.7 mile past the ski area.

About the campground: The campsites—primarily walk-in sites—radiate from both sides of FR 20. Campers enjoy the spectacular high-elevation tapestry of the south flank of Mount Ashland: clusters of big-diameter firs, alpine meadows, grassland, and rocky jumbles. Views from the camp are of the rocky crest of Mount Ashland to the north and the snowy crown of 14,000-foot Mount Shasta (in California) to the south. You may spy grouse, juncos, or jays. This camp is close to the Pacific Crest National Scenic Trail, where it follows the crest of the Siskiyou Mountains. The campground is maintained from July into October.

110 Wildcat

Location: About 22 miles east of Ashland, on Hyatt Lake.
Sites: 12 basic sites; no hookups.
Maximum length: 20 feet.
Facilities: Tables, grills, vault toilets, horseshoe pits, boat launch. No drinking water.
Fee per night: $.
Management: Bureau of Land Management.
Contact: 541-770-2200.
Finding the campground: From Oregon 66, 17 miles east of Ashland, 44 miles west of Klamath Falls, turn north on East Hyatt Road at the sign for the

reservoir. Go 3 miles and proceed straight on East Hyatt Road as the main road curves left and becomes Hyatt Prairie Road. Go another 2 miles to Wildcat.

About the campground: Campers will enjoy ample shoreline at this small campground that sits on a forested peninsula stretching into Hyatt Lake. Ponderosa pines rise among the mixed firs of the camp, creating partial to full shade. The road through the camp and site parking are all gravel. Fishing, boating, hiking, and relaxing are the main diversions here. The campground is open from April 25 through October.

111 Willow Point

Location: About 24 miles east of Ashland, on Howard Prairie Lake.
Sites: 40 basic sites; no hookups.
Maximum length: 35 feet.
Facilities: Tables, grills, vault toilets, drinking water, boat launch, fish-cleaning station.
Fee per night: $$.
Management: Jackson County.
Contact: 541-776-7001.
Finding the campground: From Ashland, head east 19 miles on Dead Indian Memorial Road. Turn right (south) onto Hyatt Prairie Road, go 4.6 miles, and turn left onto Howard Prairie Dam Road. Go 0.5 mile to the campground entrance on the left.

About the campground: Situated on 59 acres along Willow Creek and the southwest shore of Howard Prairie Lake is this forested campground with views of Mount McLoughlin. Fishing, boating, swimming, and sailing are the primary draws of the area, but the Pacific Crest National Scenic Trail passes the south end of the reservoir for anyone interested in hiking. The campground is open from April 15 to November 1.

KLAMATH FALLS–KLAMATH BASIN AREA

		Hookup sites	Total sites	Max. RV length	Hookups	Toilets	Showers	Drinking water	Dump station	Recreation	Fee	Can reserve
112	Aspen Point		60	40		F		•	•	HSFBL	$$	•
113	Collier Memorial State Park	50	68	60	WES	F	•	•	•	HF	$$	
114	Corral Springs		6	40		NF						
115	Digit Point		64	30		F		•	•	HSFBL	$	
116	Eagle Ridge Park		7	30		NF		•		FBL		
117	Fourmile Lake		25	22		NF		•		HSFBL	$-$$	
118	Gerber Reservoir: North		18	35		NF		•	•	SFBL	$	
119	Gerber Reservoir: South		26	40		NF		•	•	SFBL	$	
120	Hagelstein Park		13	30		F		•		FBL	$	
121	Head of the River		5	40		NF				F		
122	Jackson Creek		12	25		NF				F		
123	Jackson F. Kimball State Recreation Site		10	45		NF				F	$	
124	Keno Recreation Area		26	35		F	•	•	•	SFBL	$$	
125	Klamath County Fairgrounds	12	12	40	WE	F	•	•			$	
126	Odessa Creek		5	20		NF				FBL		
127	Spring Creek		5	30		NF		•		F		
128	Sunset		67	40		F		•		HSFBL	$$	•
129	Surveyor Recreation Site		5	25		NF						
130	Topsy Recreation Site		15	40		NF		•		FBL	$	
131	Williamson River		10	30		NF		•		F	$	

Hookups: W = Water E = Electric S = Sewer **Total sites:** T = Tent-only campground **Maximum trailer/RV length** given in feet.
Toilets: F = Flush NF = No Flush **Recreation:** H = Hiking S = Swimming F = Fishing B = Boating L = Boat Launch
O = Off-Highway Driving R = Horseback Riding C = Cycling
Fee: $ = $1-9 $$ = $10-19 $$$ = $20-29 $$$$ = $30-39. If no entry under **Fee,** camping is free.

112 Aspen Point

Location: About 35 miles northwest of Klamath Falls, on Lake of the Woods.
Sites: 60 basic sites; no hookups.
Maximum length: 40 feet.
Facilities: Tables, grills, flush toilets, drinking water, dump station, boat launch, boat rentals nearby.
Fee per night: $$.
Management: Forest Service.
Contact: 541-885-3400; 1-800-280-CAMP for reservations.
Finding the campground: From Oregon 140, 34 miles west of Klamath Falls and 44 miles east of Medford, turn south onto Forest Road 3704, go 0.7 mile, and turn right for the campground.

About the campground: This forested campground occupies the northeast shore of Lake of the Woods, a lovely mountain lake that invites swimming, casting a fishing line, trolling along shore, or sailing the lake's length. Brown Mountain and Mount McLoughlin punctuate the skyline. Trails in the area follow the shoreline, lead to neighboring lakes, and meet up with the Pacific Crest Trail. The campground is open from late May to late September.

113 Collier Memorial State Park

Location: 5 miles north of Chiloquin.
Sites: 50 hookup sites, 18 basic sites; water, electric, and sewer hookups.
Maximum length: 60 feet.
Facilities: Tables, grills, flush toilets, drinking water, showers, dump station, telephone, logging museum, pioneer village, gift shop.
Fee per night: $$.
Management: Oregon State Parks and Recreation Department.
Contact: 541-783-2471.
Finding the campground: It is east off U.S. Highway 97, 5 miles north of Chiloquin and 30 miles north of Klamath Falls.

About the campground: An open-air logging museum and the Spring Creek–Williamson River confluence are the headline attractions at this park in the Klamath Basin. The closely spaced sites are nestled in a second-growth forest of ponderosa and lodgepole pines; bitterbrush and currant bushes dot the needle-strewn forest floor. The camp is located above the Williamson River, across US 97 from Spring Creek and the museum. A pedestrian underpass allows for safe passage between the camp and the day-use area. Fishing, hiking the short trails along Spring Creek, and wandering the red cinder paths among the logging museum exhibits are activities you can pursue at the camp. Not far from the park, Agency and Upper Klamath Lakes beckon with boating, canoeing, fishing, and birding. The campground is open from mid-April to late October.

114 Corral Springs

Location: About 5 miles north of Chemult.
Sites: 6 basic sites; no hookups.
Maximum length: 40 feet.
Facilities: Tables, grills, pit toilets. No drinking water.
Fee per night: None.
Management: Forest Service.
Contact: 541-365-7001.
Finding the campground: From U.S. Highway 97, 2.8 miles north of Chemult, 5.3 miles south of the US 97 and Oregon 58 junction, turn west onto gravel Forest Road 9774 and go 2 miles to enter this camp on the right.

About the campground: This improved campground has gravel roads and long, gravel parking spaces. It is set in a lodgepole pine forest with small meadow clearings. It offers a quiet retreat or a traveler's stop and lies along the historic Old Klamath Trail, which was used by Indians and early explorers. Early in the year, come prepared for mosquitoes. The campground is open from May 15 to October 15.

115 Digit Point

Location: About 13 miles west of Chemult, on Miller Lake.
Sites: 64 basic sites; no hookups.
Maximum length: 30 feet.
Facilities: Tables, grills, flush and vault toilets, drinking water, dump station, boat ramp.
Fee per night: $.
Management: Forest Service.
Contact: 541-365-7001.
Finding the campground: From U.S. Highway 97, 1 mile north of Chemult, turn west onto gravel Forest Road 9772 and go 12 miles to enter this camp on the right.

About the campground: More than a mile above sea level, this campground claims a broad peninsula on the southwest shore of Miller Lake, an attractive, natural lake on the eastern side of the Cascade Crest. Mixed conifers frame the sites and provide shade. A fine 4-mile trail rings the lake, offering a chance to view wildlife. Boating, fishing, and swimming are also popular. From the west end of the Miller Lakeshore Trail, hikers can take a spur to the Pacific Crest National Scenic Trail or cross over the crest to Maidu Lake. The latter is the head of the North Umpqua Wild and Scenic River and marks the start of the North Umpqua National Recreation Trail. Come prepared for mosquitoes at these high lakes. The campground is open from mid-June through September.

116 Eagle Ridge Park

Location: About 22 miles northwest of Klamath Falls.
Sites: 7 basic sites; no hookups.
Maximum length: 30 feet.
Facilities: Tables, fire rings, pit toilets, drinking water, boat launch, dock.
Fee per night: None.
Management: Klamath County.
Contact: 541-883-4696.
Finding the campground: From the junction of U.S. Highway 97 and Oregon 140 at Klamath Falls, head west on OR 140 for 17.2 miles and turn right (east) for the park. Follow the park and wildlife viewing signs along the gravel road for 4.4 miles to reach the camp.

About the campground: On Shoalwater Bay on Upper Klamath Lake, this camp occupies a small, open flat at the western foot of pine-and-juniper-clad Eagle Ridge. The sites have basic amenities and gravel parking, but a shade source can improve your stay. At night, the lapping of the lake against the shore ensures a tranquil sleep. By day, the lake invites fishing, boating, and bird watching for eagles, grebes, cormorants, and geese. Although the road beyond the camp is unsuitable for trailers and passenger vehicles, you can hike or mountain bike for 2 miles along it to the tip of the peninsula, where you will find a knoll; additional birding and fishing; and views of the lake, Pelican Butte, and the Mountain Lakes Wilderness. The campground is open from May to November.

117 Fourmile Lake

Location: About 40 miles northwest of Klamath Falls, on Fourmile Lake.
Sites: 25 basic sites; no hookups.
Maximum length: 22 feet.
Facilities: Tables, grills, vault toilets, drinking water, boat ramp.
Fee per night: $ to $$.
Management: Forest Service.
Contact: 541-885-3400.
Finding the campground: From Oregon 140, 34.6 miles west of Klamath Falls, turn north on gravel Forest Road 3661. Follow it 5.5 miles to Fourmile Lake and the campground.

About the campground: The sites of this camp are distributed among lodgepole pines on the shore of Fourmile Lake, which has been enlarged by a small dam. A few sites overlook the water and the attractive lake basin. This area is a gateway to the Sky Lakes Wilderness; a single trailhead serves as the jumpoff point. Trout fishing, swimming, and boating engage guests closer to camp. The campground is open from June to late September.

118 Gerber Reservoir: North

Location: About 45 miles east of Klamath Falls, on Gerber Reservoir.
Sites: 18 basic sites; no hookups.
Maximum length: 35 feet.
Facilities: Tables, grills, vault toilets, drinking water, dump station, boat launch, dock, fish-cleaning station.
Fee per night: $.
Management: Bureau of Land Management.
Contact: 541-883-6916.
Finding the campground: From Klamath Falls, go 18 miles east on Oregon 140 to Dairy, turn right onto OR 70, and go 7 miles southeast to Bonanza. From there, bear right on East Langell Valley Road, go another 10.5 miles, and turn left onto Gerber Road. Proceed 8.1 miles and turn right toward Gerber Reservoir Recreation Site. You will reach a junction in 0.6 mile. Keep left and go another 0.6 mile to the campground.

About the campground: This popular BLM camp rests amid the ponderosa pines and scraggly junipers on the western shore of Gerber Reservoir, which was created to provide irrigation. Sites near the water are more closely spaced. You may see waterfowl, bald eagles, and ospreys. The potholes northwest of the reservoir attract other birds, including sandhill cranes. Bass, crappie, catfish, and perch are among the game fish here, and the lake is popular with boaters. During World War II, the U.S. military used an island in this reservoir for bombing practice. Today, ospreys and pelicans are the only bombers of Gerber Reservoir. The campground is open from May 1 to October 31.

119 Gerber Reservoir: South

Location: About 45 miles east of Klamath Falls, on Gerber Reservoir.
Sites: 26 basic sites; no hookups.
Maximum length: 40 feet.
Facilities: Tables, grills, vault toilets, drinking water, dump station, boat launch, fish-cleaning station.
Fee per night: $.
Management: Bureau of Land Management.
Contact: 541-883-6916.
Finding the campground: From Klamath Falls, go 18 miles east on Oregon 140 to Dairy, turn right onto OR 70, and go 7 miles southeast to Bonanza. From there, bear right on East Langell Valley Road, go another 10.5 miles, and turn left onto Gerber Road. Proceed 8.1 miles and turn right toward Gerber Reservoir Recreation Site. You will reach a junction in 0.6 mile. Go right 0.4 mile to the campground.

About the campground: Gerber Reservoir is a 3,830-acre playground for campers. Fishing, swimming, boating, and birding are all popular. Near the dam, this camp is generally quieter and has roomier sites set farther from shore than its northern counterpart. Ponderosa pines supply the shade, while a basalt-studded, sage prairie fans out from the camp. Watch the skies for bald eagles, which nest at the north end of the lake. The campground is open from May 1 to October 31.

120 Hagelstein Park

Location: About 10 miles north of Klamath Falls.
Sites: 13 basic sites; no hookups.
Maximum length: 30 feet.
Facilities: Tables, grills, flush toilets, drinking water, boat launch, dock.
Fee per night: $.
Management: Klamath County.
Contact: 541-883-4696.
Finding the campground: It is east off U.S. Highway 97, 10 miles north of the US 97 and Oregon 39 junction at the north end of Klamath Falls, 15 miles south of Chiloquin.

About the campground: This campground lies beside a small, spring-fed pond and inlet of Upper Klamath Lake. Yellow wildflowers emblazon the juniper- and basalt-covered slope of Naylox Mountain, which overshadows the camp. The camp layout includes groomed lawns, site amenities, and natural trees and shrubs for partial shade. Parking is on the gravel shoulder of the camp road. Swallows nest under the pond footbridge, and schools of fish can sometimes be seen. The camp makes an attractive base and provides boating access to Upper Klamath Lake, where anglers will want to try for the prized rainbow trout. The campground is open year-round, but only self-contained RVs are permitted from December through February.

121 Head of the River

Location: About 30 miles northeast of Chiloquin.
Sites: 5 basic sites; no hookups.
Maximum length: 40 feet.
Facilities: Tables, grills, pit toilets. No drinking water.
Fee per night: None.
Management: Forest Service.
Contact: 541-783-4001.
Finding the campground: From Chiloquin, head northeast on Sprague River Highway for 5.4 miles and turn left onto paved Williamson River Road. Follow it for 7.6 miles and then turn left to remain on Williamson River Road for another 16.8 miles. Turn left onto dirt Forest Road 4648, go 0.4 mile, and turn left to enter the camp.

About the campground: This small campground is tucked away in a lodge-pole-pine forest beside the spring-launched Head of Williamson River, an acclaimed, crystalline water with a prized trout fishery downstream. Pole fencing defines the road and sites of the camp, while egresses in the fence provide access to the headwater spring and its river. Ponderosa pines cluster at the headwater, and clumps of aquatic plants dress the spring and contrast with the dried grasses of the forest floor. The camp provides a quiet retreat from society, putting you in the company of deer, mergansers, kingfishers, and songbirds. In fall, the camp serves as a hunter's base. The campground is maintained from May to September.

122 Jackson Creek

Location: About 48 miles northeast of Chiloquin.
Sites: 12 basic sites; no hookups.
Maximum length: 25 feet.
Facilities: Tables, grills, pit toilets. No drinking water.
Fee per night: None.
Management: Forest Service.
Contact: 541-365-7001.
Finding the campground: From U.S. Highway 97, 24 miles south of Chemult, 21 miles north of Chiloquin, turn east on Silver Lake Highway (County Road 676), go 22 miles, and turn right on cinder Forest Road 49 at the sign for the

campground. Go another 4.6 miles and turn left on FR 4900.740 to enter the campground in 0.3 mile.

About the campground: This primitive, out-of-the-way campground is housed among ponderosa pines on a flat beside alder-lined Jackson Creek. A few old-growth pines tower above the dense stand of young trees. Wildflowers sprinkle the creekside meadows. Hunting, fishing, relaxing, cross-country skiing, and watching for deer and antelope may variously entertain camp guests. The campground is maintained from June into September.

123 Jackson F. Kimball State Recreation Site

Location: About 18 miles northwest of Chiloquin.
Sites: 10 basic sites; no hookups.
Maximum length: 45 feet.
Facilities: Tables, grills, pit toilets. No drinking water.
Fee per night: $.
Management: Oregon State Parks and Recreation Department.
Contact: 541-783-2471.
Finding the campground: From the junction of U.S. Highway 97 and Oregon 62, about 3 miles south of Chiloquin, go west on OR 62 for 12.5 miles and turn right on Sun Mountain Road. Proceed 3 miles to reach the park entrance on the left.

About the campground: This primitive campground occupies a wooded flat at the headwater of Wood River, a spellbindingly beautiful, spring-launched river with water so turquoise that the Crayola company would kill for the color. Aspens and a few ponderosa pines intersperse the firs and lodgepole pines of the camp. Parking is on the gravel road shoulder, and the site tables and grills are a few strides away; as a result the camp may be better suited for tenting. You may spy a beaver lodge on the riverbank. Mosquitoes can sometimes be annoying. From the camp, you can venture out to Fort Klamath Museum, Crater Lake National Park, or the Pacific Crest Trail. The campground is open from mid-April to late October.

124 Keno Recreation Area

Location: In Keno, about 11 miles southwest of Klamath Falls.
Sites: 26 basic sites; no hookups.
Maximum length: 35 feet.
Facilities: Tables, grills, flush toilets, drinking water, showers, dump station, playground, boat launch, dock.
Fee per night: $$.
Management: Pacific Power and Light Company.
Contact: 503-464-6666.
Finding the campground: From the junction of U.S. Highway 97 and Oregon 66 in southwest Klamath Falls, go west on OR 66 for 9.8 miles. Turn right at the sign for Keno Recreation Area at the west end of Keno. Go 0.7 mile on the gravel road to enter the camp.

About the campground: This campground rests on a low, broad knoll above a Klamath River reservoir in a pleasant setting of pine, juniper, sage, bitterbrush, and bunchgrass. Beyond camp stretches arid prairie inhabited by quail and jackrabbits. You may fish, boat, and waterski; swimming is restricted to a designated site inside the boom area. Near the dam, cormorants commonly line up on the boom. Elsewhere, white pelicans, great blue herons, egrets, night herons, ospreys, swallows, and ducks may cause you to raise your binoculars. The campground is open from May through October.

125 Klamath County Fairgrounds

Location: In Klamath Falls.
Sites: 12 hookup sites; water and electric hookups.
Maximum length: 40 feet.
Facilities: Flush toilets, drinking water, showers, telephone, playground (across street).
Fee per night: $.
Management: Klamath County.
Contact: 541-884-0088.
Finding the campground: It is east off 6th Street, at the corner of Altamont Drive and South 6th Street in Klamath Falls. Make arrangements to stay here at the Fairgrounds Office.

About the campground: In an open field at the north end of the fairgrounds is this designated overnight area for RVs. You simply back your rig up against a fence to the hookup post. While not fancy or aesthetic, the sites serve visitors on the go, whether they are involved with fair events or taking in the museums, country music, and natural and historical attractions of Klamath Falls. No dogs are allowed between July 10 and 30.

126 Odessa Creek

Location: About 23 miles northwest of Klamath Falls.
Sites: 5 basic sites; no hookups.
Maximum length: 20 feet.
Facilities: Tables, grills, pit toilets, primitive boat launch. No drinking water.
Fee per night: None.
Management: Forest Service.
Contact: 541-885-3400.
Finding the campground: From the junction of U.S. Highway 97 and Oregon 140 in Klamath Falls, go west on OR 140 for 21.8 miles and turn right (northeast) onto Forest Road 3639. Drive another 0.8 mile into the camp.

About the campground: Where Odessa Creek empties into Upper Klamath Lake, you will find this small, primitive camp among the ponderosa pines and thick understory of aspen, dogwood, wild rose, cherry, and other flowering shrubs. The sites have earthen parking and provide a front-row seat to the marshy channels and areas of open water for birding, fishing, canoeing, and boating. You may spot bald eagles, beavers, kingfishers, grebes, frogs, deer, and water snakes. The trout fishing on Upper Klamath Lake is renowned, with 5- and 6-pounders not uncommon.

127 Spring Creek

Location: About 12 miles north of Chiloquin.
Sites: 5 basic sites; no hookups.
Maximum length: 30 feet.
Facilities: Tables, grills, vault toilets, drinking water.
Fee per night: None.
Management: Forest Service.
Contact: 541-783-4001.
Finding the campground: From Chiloquin, take U.S. Highway 97 north for about 7.5 miles and turn left (west) onto gravel Forest Road 9732 toward Oux Kanee Viewpoint and Spring Creek. Go 4 miles to reach the camp.

About the campground: This small, quiet camp rests in the forest above attractive, aquamarine Spring Creek, whose chilly, freshwater springs percolate up through the pumiceous sands of its stream bed. Besides the percolating sands, you may view a rare form of algae known as "Mare's Egg." Short nature trails explore the banks. On the basalt rim above the camp is Oux Kanee Viewpoint, from which you can see the enchanting Spring Creek Valley and the distant Cascades. Vultures roost on the nearby trees and soar the thermals. But occasionally the broad-winged bird you see in flight may be a golden eagle. The campground is maintained from mid-May to November.

128 Sunset

Location: About 35 miles northwest of Klamath Falls, on Lake of the Woods.
Sites: 67 basic sites; no hookups.
Maximum length: 40 feet.
Facilities: Tables, grills, flush toilets, drinking water, boat launch, docks, boat rental nearby.
Contact: 541-885-3400; 1-800-280-CAMP for reservations.
Fee per night: $$.
Management: Forest Service.
Finding the campground: From Oregon 140, 33 miles west of Klamath Falls, 45 miles east of Medford, turn south on Dead Indian Memorial Highway, go 2.5 miles, and turn right to enter the camp.

About the campground: This popular campground on the east side of Lake of the Woods allows you to escape to the cool shade of the firs and pines when you are not out on the lake fishing, swimming, and boating. Mount McLoughlin can be seen from shore. The 1-mile Sunset Trail links the camp and Rainbow Bay. Longer trails in the vicinity lead to Fourmile Lake and its entourage of smaller lakes. Hard-core hikers can journey into one of the neighboring wilderness areas. The campground is open from June to mid-September.

129 Surveyor Recreation Site

Location: About 30 miles west of Klamath Falls.
Sites: 5 basic sites; no hookups.
Maximum length: 25 feet.
Facilities: Tables, grills, vault toilets. No drinking water.
Fee per night: None.
Management: Bureau of Land Management.
Contact: 541-883-6916.
Finding the campground: From the junction of U.S. Highway 97 and Oregon 66 in southwest Klamath Falls, go west on OR 66 for 15.7 miles. Turn right on the paved Keno Access Road (BLM 39-7E-31) for Buck Lake and Spencer Creek. Go 14.1 miles and turn left for the camp. Or, from Dead Indian Memorial Road, 0.5 mile east of Howard Prairie Lake, turn south on Keno Access Road and go 13 miles before turning right into the camp.

About the campground: This primitive camp is an ideal place for quiet reflection. It is set in an old-growth forest setting of firs. Logs are scattered across the forest floor, which is covered by ferns and delicate blossoms of prince's pine, starflower, and trillium. The camp has dirt roads and parking and gets light use. The campground is open from mid-May through Labor Day weekend.

130 Topsy Recreation Site

Location: About 16 miles southwest of Klamath Falls.
Sites: 15 basic sites; no hookups.
Maximum length: 40 feet.
Facilities: Tables, grills, vault toilets, drinking water, boat launch, barrier-free dock and fishing pier.
Fee per night: $.
Management: Bureau of Land Management.
Contact: 541-883-6916.
Finding the campground: From the junction of U.S. Highway 97 and Oregon 66 in southwest Klamath Falls, go west on OR 66 for 15.3 miles. Turn left onto gravel Topsy Road as you reach John C. Boyle Reservoir. Follow the signs about 1 mile to the camp entrance on the right.

About the campground: This terraced camp is both pretty and functional, blending into its natural pine setting above John C. Boyle Reservoir. All sites have level, gravel parking pads, but some also offer tent platforms. From almost anywhere in the camp, you can admire the sparkling water. You can also watch birds and wildlife right from your lawn chair; an osprey nest overlooks the shore. Crappie, bass, catfish, and panfish tug at the lines of anglers, and the reservoir is open to boating. The campground is open from mid-May through Labor Day weekend.

131 Williamson River

Location: About 7 miles north of Chiloquin.
Sites: 10 basic sites; no hookups.
Maximum length: 30 feet.
Facilities: Tables, grills, pit toilets, drinking water.
Fee per night: $.
Management: Forest Service.
Contact: 541-783-4001.
Finding the campground: From Chiloquin, go about 5 miles north on U.S. Highway 97 and turn right (east) onto Forest Road 9730 for the Collier and Williamson River Campgrounds. Keep left at the Collier Campground turnoff, going 1.3 miles on FR 9730, a wide, improved surface road. Turn right and go another 0.4 mile to the camp.

About the campground: Removed from US 97, this quiet campground occupies a bench above the Williamson River. Ponderosa and lodgepole pines surround the sites, and dry-land shrubs spot the forest floor. Here, the river is shallow, flowing over waving mats of algae. Willows and grass claim the bank below the camp, while sage rules the opposite shore. This camp offers convenient access to neighboring Collier Memorial State Park, as well as to the sights, sounds, and stops of the Klamath Basin–Upper Klamath Lake Area. The campground is open from mid-May into November.

Central Oregon

Central Oregon includes the eastern slopes of the Central Cascades and the High Lava Plains, which spread out from Bend. The east-central Cascades serve up such outstanding features as the Metolius Wild and Scenic River, the Three Sisters, Mount Bachelor, Tam McArthur Rim, and the Cascade Lakes Area.

Within the High Lava Plains, you will find the Deschutes Wild and Scenic River, Newberry National Volcanic Monument, and Crooked River National Grassland. You can visit ghost towns, rock climb at Smith Rock State Park, hunt for thundereggs in Ochoco National Forest, go speedboating at Cove Palisades, fish at area reservoirs, and stargaze at Pine Mountain Observatory.

The tourist-oriented communities of Bend and Sisters, along with several ranching towns and the river-floating mecca of Maupin, serve travelers.

The Cascade Range—the snowcapped chain of volcanoes that partitions the state and dominates the skyline in much of Central Oregon—was named by noted botanist David Douglas. Two stages of volcanic activity shaped these mountains, with the younger volcanoes in the eastern part of the range. Ponderosa and lodgepole pines, along with a sprinkling of western larch, grow on these dry eastern slopes.

The High Lava Plains feature a textured mosaic of sagebrush and native bunch-grass, juniper and pine forests, lava flows and lava-tube caves, obsidian ridges, cinder cones, and caldera lakes. Newberry Crater, a shield volcano in the center of the state, covers a larger area than any other volcano in Oregon.

Golden and bald eagles, peregrine falcons, ospreys, and night hawks favor these rugged plains, as do bluebirds and western tanagers. The larcenous gray jay is often a companion in the Cascades.

Given the diversity of the region, you should expect a variety of weather. The Cascades host downhill and cross-country skiing in winter and offer partially shaded trails and cool mountain lakes in summer. Do not be deceived by the dusty lodgepole pine forests; snowmelt can create ponds in summer that breed mosquitoes, sometimes in hordes. So be sure to keep a supply of insect repellent handy.

Weather on the arid plains varies from crisp, chilly days in winter to baking temperatures in summer. Outdoor activities are generally possible year-round, with caving, rock climbing, hiking, mountain biking, and horseback riding among the more popular pursuits. Snowmobiling and ice fishing fill out the winter calendar at Newberry Crater.

Throughout Central Oregon, in the mountains and on the high plains, summertime visitors should be prepared for afternoon thunderstorms.

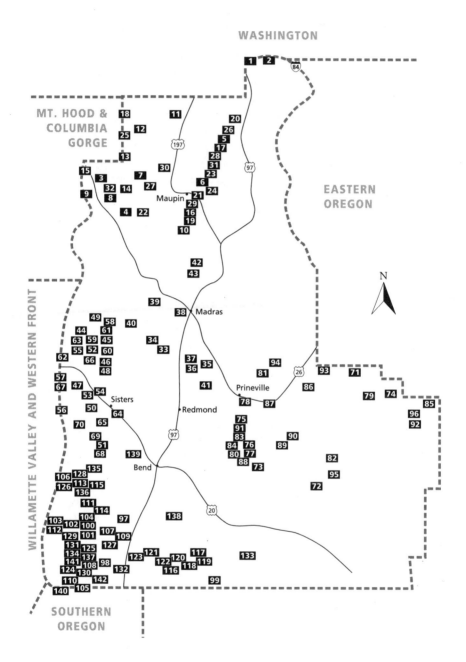

RUFUS AREA

		Hookup sites	Total sites	Max. RV length	Hookups	Toilets	Showers	Drinking water	Dump station	Recreation	Fee	Can reserve
1	Giles French Park		open	40		F		•		FBL		
2	Le Page Park	22	22	40		F		•	•	SFBL	$–$$	

Hookups: W = Water E = Electric S = Sewer **Total sites:** T = Tent-only campground **Maximum trailer/RV length** given in feet.
Toilets: F = Flush NF = No Flush **Recreation:** H = Hiking S = Swimming F = Fishing B = Boating L = Boat Launch
O = Off-Highway Driving R = Horseback Riding C = Cycling
Fee: $ = $1-9 $$ = $10-19 $$$ = $20-29 $$$$ = $30-39. If no entry under **Fee,** camping is free.

1 Giles French Park

Location: Just northeast of Rufus.
Sites: Open camping; no hookups.
Maximum length: 40 feet.
Facilities: Flush toilets, drinking water, boat launch.
Fee per night: None.
Management: U.S. Army Corps of Engineers.
Contact: 541-296-1181.
Finding the campground: From Interstate 84, about 25 miles east of The Dalles, take Exit 109 for Rufus and follow the frontage road on the north side of the freeway east for 0.5 mile to the campground.

About the campground: The park, which was originally intended for day use only, now has a combined campground/day-use area stretching for 1.7 miles along the Columbia River between the boat launch and John Day Dam. A steep slope plunges from the camp to the rocky riverbank. Overnight parking is allowed on the large gravel- or asphalt-surfaced lots, while tent camping is permitted on the grass. Shade trees are but a few steps away; wind is common in the gorge. Shad and sturgeon fishing, bounty fishing for squaw fish, boating, and visiting John Day Dam and its fish-viewing windows will keep campers on the go. The campground is open year-round.

2 Le Page Park

Location: About 5 miles northeast of Rufus.
Sites: 22 hookup sites, open tent camping; water and electric hookups.
Maximum length: 40 feet.
Facilities: Flush toilets, drinking water, dump station, boat launch, docks.
Fee per night: $ to $$.
Management: U.S. Army Corps of Engineers.
Contact: 541-296-1181.
Finding the campground: It is off Interstate 84 at Exit 114.

About the campground: This landscaped park overlooks the John Day River just as it meets the harnessed Columbia River above John Day Dam. The camp provides boaters and anglers with convenient access to the water, and 3 miles up the John Day River, an 8-site, boat-to camp is available for overnight stays. Black locust trees give some shade to the RV spaces, which directly overlook the water. Tenters can pitch their shelters anywhere on the grass. A beach area serves swimmers. The campground is open year-round.

DUFUR-MAUPIN AREA

		Hookup sites	Total sites	Max. RV length	Hookups	Toilets	Showers	Drinking water	Dump station	Recreation	Fee	Can reserve
3	Barlow Crossing		5	small		NF				F		
4	Bear Springs		21	32		NF		•			$	•
5	Beavertail Recreation Site		17	40		NF		•		FBL	$-$$	
6	Blue Hole Recreation Site		5	40		NF				FB	$-$$	
7	Bonney Crossing		8	16		NF				HF	$	
8	Clear Creek Crossing		7	16		NF				HO		
9	Clear Lake		28	32		NF		•		FBL	$$	
10	Devil's Canyon Recreation Site		3	T		NF				FB	$-$$	
11	Dufur City Park	10	10	40	WES	F	•	•	•	F	$-$$	•
12	Eightmile Crossing		20	30		NF				HC		
13	Fifteenmile Forest Camp		3	16		NF				H		
14	Forest Creek		8	16		NF				F		
15	Frog Lake		33	22		NF		•		HFBL	$$	•
16	Harpham Flat Recreation Site		9	25		NF				FBL	$-$$	
17	Jones Canyon Recreation Site		10	40		NF				FB	$-$$	
18	Knebal Springs Horse Camp		8	22		NF				HR		
19	Long Bend Recreation Site		4	25		NF				FB	$-$$	
20	Macks Canyon Recreation Site		18	40		NF		•		HFBLC	$-$$	
21	Maupin City Park	20	37	40	WES	F	•	•		FBL	$$	•
22	McCubbins Gulch		7	25		NF				O		
23	Oak Springs Recreation Site		5	40		NF				FB	$-$$	
24	Oasis Recreation Site		12	40		NF				FB	$-$$	
25	Pebble Ford		7	16		NF				H		
26	Rattlesnake Canyon Recreation Site		10	40		NF				FB	$-$$	
27	Rock Creek Reservoir		33	18		NF		•		HSFBL	$$	•
28	Twin Springs Recreation Site		7	40		NF				FB	$-$$	
29	Wapinitia Recreation Site		2	25		NF				FBL	$-$$	
30	Wasco County F.G.: Hunt RV Park	150	200	60	WE	F	•	•	•		$$	
31	White River Recreation Site		3	40		NF				FB	$-$$	
32	White River Station		6	small		NF				F		

Hookups: W = Water   E = Electric   S = Sewer   **Total sites:** T = Tent-only campground   **Maximum trailer/RV length** given in feet.
Toilets: F = Flush   NF = No Flush   **Recreation:** H = Hiking   S = Swimming   F = Fishing   B = Boating   L = Boat Launch
O = Off-Highway Driving   R = Horseback Riding   C = Cycling
Fee: $ = $1-9 $$ = $10-19 $$$ = $20-29 $$$$ = $30-39.   If no entry under **Fee,** camping is free.

3 Barlow Crossing

Location: About 17 miles southeast of Government Camp.
Sites: 5 basic sites; no hookups.
Maximum length: Small units only due to road conditions.
Facilities: Tables, grills, vault toilets. No drinking water.
Fee per night: None.
Management: Forest Service.
Contact: 541-352-6002.
Finding the campground: From Oregon 35 at the White River crossing, 2 miles south of Mt. Hood Meadows ski area, 5 miles north of the U.S. Highway 26 and OR 35 junction, follow Forest Road 48 southeast for 8.8 miles. Turn right (west) on FR 43 for 0.6 mile and again turn right on narrow, dirt Old Barlow Road/Forest Road 3530 to reach the camp in 0.2 mile. Turn right, followed by a second right to locate the sites. (Note: Old Barlow Road is closed from December 15 through April 1, and it requires four-wheel-drive past the camp turnoff.)

About the campground: In the fall, hunters use this quiet, rustic camp, which is situated in a forest of firs and lodgepole pines above Barlow Creek, just upstream from its confluence with the White River. The sites have pretty log tables, the parking is undefined, and one site is on a level with the clear, 10-foot-wide creek. Steller's jays color and animate the camp. Nearby interpretive signs tell the story of Barlow Road, an overland segment of the Oregon Trail that linked the Columbia Gorge to the Willamette Valley and allowed emigrants to avoid a treacherous voyage down the Columbia River. Pioneers cached supplies near this site in 1845.

4 Bear Springs

Location: About 24 miles southwest of Maupin.
Sites: 21 basic sites; no hookups.
Maximum length: 32 feet.
Facilities: Tables, grills, vault toilets, drinking water.
Fee per night: $.
Management: Forest Service.
Contact: 541-467-2291; 1-800-280-CAMP for reservations.
Finding the campground: From Oregon 216, 4 miles east of the U.S. Highway 26 and OR 216 junction; 24 miles west of Maupin, turn south at the sign for the campground. Go 0.1 mile to the camp entrance on the right.

About the campground: Above the headwaters of Indian Creek, you will find this pleasant forest campground with a paved road and gravel parking. A good share of the sites are better suited for tents or smaller RV units because of the spur size and parking access; there is one pull-thru site. Grand firs, Douglas-firs, and ponderosa pines shade this compact camp. Bring a good book and settle in. The campground is open from late May through September.

5 Beavertail Recreation Site

Location: About 21 miles north of Maupin.
Sites: 17 basic sites; no hookups.
Maximum length: 40 feet.
Facilities: Tables, vault toilets, drinking water, drift boat/raft launch.
Fee per night: $ to $$.
Management: Bureau of Land Management.
Contact: 541-416-6700.
Finding the campground: From the junction of U.S. Highway 197 and Oregon 216 East at Tygh Valley (7 miles north of Maupin), go east on OR 216, crossing the Deschutes River at Sherars Bridge after 7 miles, and after another 1.1 miles, turn left (north) on gravel Deschutes River Access Road, a BLM Back Country Byway. Go 9.6 miles to reach this camp on the left.

About the campground: This camp rests on a grassy bench at a bend in the Deschutes River. It offers guests convenient access to superb fishing and river floating (a boater's pass is required for the river). A few trees provide spotty shade. Across the river you can see a steep canyon wall. In this fragile, arid canyon, fires and smoking are prohibited from June 1 to October 15. The campground is open year-round.

Camping along the Deschutes River.

6 Blue Hole Recreation Site

Location: About 3 miles northeast of Maupin.
Sites: 5 basic sites; no hookups.
Maximum length: 40 feet.
Facilities: Tables, vault toilets. No drinking water.
Fee per night: $ to $$.
Management: Bureau of Land Management.
Contact: 541-416-6700.
Finding the campground: From U.S. Highway 197 in Maupin, go east on Bakeoven Road to Deschutes River Access Road and proceed north (downstream) 3.4 miles to the camp entrance on the left.

About the campground: On a low bench next to the engaging Deschutes River sits this attractive day-use area and campground. The shade from one or two of the trees at the day-use area may spill over into camp, but mostly it is sunny. The landscape is grassland and sagebrush, the sport is fishing, and an oriole may brighten your stay. In Maupin, signs for river outfitters may entice you to sign up for a float trip. Fires and smoking are prohibited from June 1 to October 15. The campground is open year-round.

7 Bonney Crossing

Location: About 17 miles west of Tygh Valley.
Sites: 8 basic sites; no hookups.
Maximum length: 16 feet.
Facilities: Tables, grills, pit toilets. No drinking water.
Fee per night: $.
Management: Forest Service.
Contact: 541-467-2291.
Finding the campground: From the junction of U.S. Highway 197 and Oregon 216 East at Tygh Valley (7 miles north of Maupin), go west 6 miles on Tygh Valley and Wamic Market Roads to Wamic. From there, continue west for another 6 miles on Rock Creek Dam Road/Forest Road 48. Turn right (north) onto FR 4810, go 2 miles, and turn right again onto FR 4811. Go 1.2 miles, turn right onto dirt FR 2710, and go 1.7 miles to camp.

About the campground: This small campground rests in a transition forest along Badger Creek as it drains out of Badger Creek Wilderness. Douglas-firs, oaks, and ponderosa pines contribute to the character and shade of the camp. The creek is captivating and clear; the Badger Creek Trail starts on its north bank and follows the scenic waterway upstream into the wilderness for prized solitude. You may spot wild turkeys in the oak-grasslands. The campground is open from May through mid-October.

8 Clear Creek Crossing

Location: About 29 miles west of Maupin.
Sites: 7 basic sites; no hookups.
Maximum length: 16 feet.
Facilities: Tables, grills, vault toilets. No drinking water.
Fee per night: None.
Management: Forest Service.
Contact: 541-467-2291.
Finding the campground: From Oregon 216, 2 miles east of the U.S. Highway 26 and OR 216 junction, 26 miles west of Maupin, turn north on Forest Road 2130 at the sign for the campground, go 3 miles, and turn right to enter the camp. Watch out for free-ranging cattle.

About the campground: You will find this campground on Clear Creek within McCubbins Gulch Off-Highway-Vehicle Area, downstream from the McCubbins Gulch diversion. The campsites occupy a mild slope in a setting of tall, mature firs; logs outline the roadway and sites. Clear Creek is aptly named. The log footbridge that spans it leads to Clear Creek Trail, a 5-mile-long link between this camp and the rustic Keeps Mill Campground. OHV trails can be accessed off FR 2130; look for them while en route to camp. The campground is open from May through September.

9 Clear Lake

Location: About 11 miles southeast of Government Camp.
Sites: 28 basic sites; no hookups.
Maximum length: 32 feet.
Facilities: Tables, grills, vault toilets, drinking water, boat launch.
Fee per night: $$.
Management: Forest Service.
Contact: 541-352-6002.
Finding the campground: From Government Camp, go southeast on U.S. Highway 26 for 9.5 miles, turn right onto Forest Road 2630, and go 1.1 miles to the camp entrance.

About the campground: Located on a slope above Clear Lake and shaded by firs and mountain hemlocks, this campground can fill up on summer weekends. All sites have gravel parking, some have pull-thrus, and some have tree-filtered lake views. Chinquapins, kinnikinnick, and rhododendrons grow in sunny forest openings. Boating (10 miles per hour maximum) and fishing fill out campers' days. There are opportunities to hike beyond the camp. The campground is open from late May to early September.

10 Devil's Canyon Recreation Site

Location: About 5 miles south of Maupin.
Sites: 3 tent sites; no hookups.
Maximum length: Suitable for tents only.
Facilities: Tables, pit toilets. No drinking water.
Fee per night: $ to $$.
Management: Bureau of Land Management.
Contact: 541-416-6700.
Finding the campground: From the Deschutes River bridge on U.S. Highway 197 in Maupin, go south on US 197 for 0.2 mile and turn right at the BLM sign for Upper River Access. Drive 5 miles to reach this camp on the right.

About the campground: This primitive campground occupies a sagebrush flat and offers scenic views of a bend in the Deschutes River. A butte rises across the river. Red-winged blackbirds, orioles, mergansers, ducks, swallows, and geese visit the area. Fishing and boating are popular; you will find a launch at Wapinitia Recreation Site, 2 miles downstream. Fires and smoking are prohibited from June 1 to October 15. The campground is open year-round.

11 Dufur City Park

Location: In Dufur.
Sites: 10 hookup sites, some tent camping; water, electric, and sewer hookups.
Maximum length: 40 feet.
Facilities: Flush toilets, drinking water, showers, dump station, playground, volleyball, horseshoe pits, ball field, swimming pool.
Fee per night: $ to $$.
Management: City of Dufur.
Contact: 541-467-2349.
Finding the campground: The campground is at the south end of the city of Dufur; follow signs for the park.

About the campground: Camping is available at the edge of the playing fields at this pleasant city park. The camp rests along Fifteenmile Creek, which offers fishing and nurtures the fully grown trees that provide shade. The camp is a convenient base from which to explore historic Dufur, a quaint farming and ranching community, and the Columbia River Gorge is only minutes away. The campground is open from March to November.

12 Eightmile Crossing

Location: About 17 miles west of Dufur.
Sites: 20 basic sites; no hookups.
Maximum length: 30 feet.
Facilities: Tables, grills, vault toilets. No drinking water.
Fee per night: None.

Management: Forest Service.
Contact: 541-467-2291.
Finding the campground: From U.S. Highway 197, take the exit for Dufur; at the south end of town, turn west on Dufur Valley Road/Forest Road 44. Follow it for 17 miles, then turn right (north) on FR 4430; enter the campground on the right in 0.3 mile. From Oregon 35, 16 miles northeast of Government Camp, 26 miles south of Hood River, turn east on FR 44 and go 9.8 miles to reach FR 4430. Proceed north to the camp.

About the campground: You will find this quiet camp in a mixed-age conifer forest along the upper reaches of Eightmile Creek. The sites are comfortably spaced and fully or partially shaded. At the camp is a trailhead for the 6.2-mile, hike or bike Eightmile Loop Trail. A half-mile, barrier-free trail pursues Eightmile Creek downstream to Lower Eightmile Forest Camp. For an alternative place to stay, Lower Eightmile Forest Camp (also called Lower Crossing Campground) has three closely spaced sites (16-foot maximum length) with similar facilities. You can reach it by going half a mile east on FR 44 from its junction with FR 4430 and then 1 mile north on FR 4440. Both campgrounds are open from June to mid-October.

13 Fifteenmile Forest Camp

Location: About 23 miles southwest of Dufur.
Sites: 3 basic sites; no hookups.
Maximum length: 16 feet.
Facilities: Tables, grills, vault toilets. No drinking water.
Fee per night: None.
Management: Forest Service.
Contact: 541-467-2291.
Finding the campground: From U.S. Highway 197, take the exit for Dufur; at the south end of town, turn west on Dufur Valley Road/Forest Road 44 and go 18.5 miles. Turn south on FR 4420 for Flag Point Lookout, go 2.1 miles, and proceed another 1.9 miles south on FR 2730 to reach this campground on the left. When arriving from Oregon 35, go 8.3 miles east on FR 44 and turn south on FR 4420, following the remaining directions to the camp.

About the campground: This closely grouped trio of sites sits in an open stand of huge ponderosa pines along Fifteenmile Creek. Across the creek is the Badger Creek Wilderness; this camp is a gateway to the wilderness trail system. Riffling Fifteenmile Creek cuts a deep drainage at the camp. The campground is open from June to mid-October.

14 Forest Creek

Location: About 25 miles west of Tygh Valley.
Sites: 8 basic sites; no hookups.
Maximum length: 16 feet.

Facilities: Tables, grills, pit toilets. No drinking water.
Fee per night: None.
Management: Forest Service.
Contact: 541-467-2291.
Finding the campground: From the junction of Oregon 216 East and U.S. Highway 197 at Tygh Valley, go west on Tygh Valley and Wamic Market Roads for 6 miles to Wamic. From there, continue west on Rock Creek Dam Road/Forest Road 48 for 18 miles, turn left (south) on gravel FR 4885, go 1 mile, and turn left on FR 3530 to enter the camp in 0.2 mile. The road beyond the camp is not maintained for passenger cars.

About the campground: Historically a wayside stop for pioneers, this small, quiet camp is set among ponderosa pines, spruce, hemlocks, cedars, and firs. It rests along Forest Creek on Old Barlow Road, part of the Oregon Trail. Barlow was an overland toll road that allowed emigrants to bypass the treacherous voyage on the Columbia River to reach the fertile farmland of the Willamette Valley. The campground is open from late May through October.

15 Frog Lake

Location: About 8 miles southeast of Government Camp.
Sites: 33 basic sites; no hookups.
Maximum length: 22 feet.
Facilities: Tables, grills, vault toilets, drinking water, boat launch.
Fee per night: $$.
Management: Forest Service.
Contact: 541-352-6002; 1-800-280-CAMP for reservations.
Finding the campground: From Government Camp, go southeast on U.S. Highway 26 for 7 miles and turn left on Forest Road 2610 to enter this camp in 0.5 mile.

About the campground: This popular campground occupies a forest of hemlocks and firs along the shore of quiet Frog Lake. You can see Mount Hood peeking over the trees, especially from the south end of the day-use area. The camp is a fine base for outdoor recreation: You can fish or take your non-motorized boat out on the lake or hike nearby trails to Frog Lake Buttes and Twin Lakes. You also have easy access to the Pacific Crest National Scenic Trail. The campground is open from mid-June to mid-September.

16 Harpham Flat Recreation Site

Location: About 4 miles south of Maupin.
Sites: 9 basic sites; no hookups.
Maximum length: 25 feet.
Facilities: Tables, vault toilets, boat launch. No drinking water.
Fee per night: $ to $$.
Management: Bureau of Land Management.
Contact: 541-416-6700.

Finding the campground: From the Deschutes River bridge on U.S. Highway 197 in Maupin, go south on US 197 for 0.2 mile and turn right at the BLM sign for Upper River Access. Drive 3.5 miles to reach the campground entrance on the right.

About the campground: Adjacent to a popular raft put-in, this campground bustles with activity. It occupies a broad, sunny flat where the river canyon broadens; campers should bring a good shade source and ample water. Fishing, boating, rafting, and sightseeing keep Deschutes River guests returning again and again. Fires and smoking are prohibited from June 1 to October 15. The campground is open year-round.

17 Jones Canyon Recreation Site

Location: About 19 miles north of Maupin.
Sites: 10 basic sites; no hookups.
Maximum length: 40 feet.
Facilities: Tables, vault and pit toilets, boat launch (downstream at Beavertail). No drinking water.
Fee per night: $ to $$.
Management: Bureau of Land Management.
Contact: 541-416-6700.
Finding the campground: From the junction of U.S. Highway 197 and Oregon 216 East at Tygh Valley (7 miles north of Maupin), go east on OR 216, crossing the Deschutes River at Sherars Bridge after 7 miles, and after another 1.1 miles, turn left (north) on gravel Deschutes River Access Road, a BLM Back Country Byway. Go 7.7 miles to reach this camp on the left.

About the campground: Tall clumps of sagebrush isolate the sites of this tree-less camp above the Deschutes River, downstream from Jones Canyon. The camp serves up river-canyon views, world-class fishing, and nearby access for boats and rafts. The Deschutes is a prized wild and scenic river. Boaters need permits and should find out where and when motorized boats are permissible. You may spot river otters here. Fires and smoking are prohibited from June 1 to October 15. The campground is open year-round.

18 Knebal Springs Horse Camp

Location: About 25 miles west of Dufur.
Sites: 8 basic sites; no hookups.
Maximum length: 22 feet.
Facilities: Tables, fire rings, vault toilets, horse-loading ramp, hitching rail, corrals, trough. No drinking water.
Fee per night: None.
Management: Forest Service.
Contact: 541-467-2291.
Finding the campground: From Forest Road 44, 21.7 miles west of Dufur (at

the south end of town) and 5.1 miles east of Oregon 35, turn north on the paved FR 17, go 0.5 mile, and bear right on FR 1720. Go 2.6 miles more to enter the campground via gravel FR 150 on the right. The entry is not marked from this direction, so be alert for the turnoff.

About the campground: This serviceable, comfortable campground is intended for equestrian campers. The campsites are partially shaded by firs, pines, and larches. Forest Service Trail 474, the Knebal Springs Trail, passes the camp and connects with other horse trails in the area. The springs at the camp are fenced. The campground is open from June to October.

19 Long Bend Recreation Site

Location: About 5 miles south of Maupin.
Sites: 4 basic sites; no hookups.
Maximum length: 25 feet.
Facilities: Tables, pit toilets. No drinking water.
Fee per night: $ to $$.
Management: Bureau of Land Management.
Contact: 541-416-6700.
Finding the campground: From the Deschutes River bridge on U.S. Highway 197 in Maupin, go south on US 197 for 0.2 mile and turn right at the BLM sign for Upper River Access. Drive another 4.4 miles to reach the campground entrance on the right.

About the campground: This linear camp claims a narrow strip of shoreline along the Deschutes River. White alders line the riverbank, and hackberry grows at the upper edge of the camp. Across the river you can see cliffs, rims, and an active rail line. The Deschutes River provides fishing and boating, but strong undercurrents make swimming dangerous. Fires and smoking are prohibited from June 1 to October 15. The campground is open year-round.

20 Macks Canyon Recreation Site

Location: About 29 miles north of Maupin.
Sites: 18 basic sites; no hookups.
Maximum length: 40 feet.
Facilities: Tables, vault toilets, drinking water, boat launch.
Fee per night: $ to $$.
Management: Bureau of Land Management.
Contact: 541-416-6700.
Finding the campground: From the junction of U.S. Highway 197 and Oregon 216 East at Tygh Valley (7 miles north of Maupin), go east on OR 216, crossing the Deschutes River at Sherars Bridge after 7 miles, and after another 1.1 miles, turn left (north) on gravel Deschutes River Access Road, a BLM Back Country Byway. Go 17 miles to reach this camp.

About the campground: This camp is at a site where prehistoric Indian tribes wintered in pit houses more than 2,000 years ago. Present-day campers are similarly attracted to the mostly open river flat because of its convenient access to the Deschutes River and superb fishing and boating. The abandoned railroad grade on this side of the canyon serves hikers and bicyclists. It extends from the north end of the camp downstream to Deschutes River State Recreation Area. The trail offers fine river views and occasional river access, but beware of rattlesnakes in rocky reaches and if you venture off trail. Fires and smoking are prohibited June 1 to October 15; boaters should familiarize themselves with river rules. The campground is open year-round.

21 Maupin City Park

Location: In Maupin.
Sites: 20 hookup sites, 17 tent sites; water, electric, and sewer hookups.
Maximum length: 40 feet.
Facilities: Some tables, flush toilets, drinking water, showers, telephone, fee docking and launch, community building with kitchen for rent, no campfires.
Fee per night: $$.
Management: City of Maupin.
Contact: 541-395-2252.
Finding the campground: The park is off Bakeoven Road in Maupin, on the east shore of the Deschutes River.

About the campground: Across the bridge from Maupin, this city park provides a lovely overnight camping facility. The hookup sites have concrete two-tracks on which to park, a lawn shaded by locust trees, and superb river views. You can reach the tent area by crossing a footbridge over Bakeoven Creek. The tent sites are on a big, open lawn edged by locusts and alders; there is shade late in the day. A grain elevator on the opposite side of Bakeoven Road adds to the rural atmosphere. Geese browse the park lawn in the morning. This is a fine place to relax, watch the rafters float by, join a river trip yourself, or fish, boat, or sightsee. The campground is open from April 1 to October 31.

22 McCubbins Gulch

Location: About 24 miles southwest of Maupin.
Sites: 7 basic sites; no hookups.
Maximum length: 25 feet.
Facilities: Tables, grills, vault toilets. No drinking water.
Fee per night: No camping fee, but Trail Park Pass required.
Management: Forest Service.
Contact: 541-467-2291.
Finding the campground: From Oregon 216, 5 miles east of the U.S. Highway 26 and OR 216 junction, 23 miles west of Maupin, turn north on Forest Road 2110 at the sign for the campground, go 1.1 miles, and turn right on gravel FR 230. Continue another 0.3 mile to the campground entrance on the right.

About the campground: This off-highway-vehicle (OHV) campground claims a mild slope and flat along McCubbins Gulch, a diversion of Clear Creek. The silt-bottomed stream flows along the lower edge of the camp; a bridge across it leads to one of the OHV trails in the area. Others start near the camp entrance. The camp floor is somewhat rolling, rutted, and barren, but the tall firs and pines are pleasant. Dust and noise are part of the deal, so if you are not an OHV enthusiast, avoid this camp. The campground is open from May through September.

23 Oak Springs Recreation Site

Location: About 4 miles north of Maupin.
Sites: 5 basic sites; no hookups.
Maximum length: 40 feet.
Facilities: Tables, vault toilets. No drinking water.
Fee per night: $ to $$.
Management: Bureau of Land Management.
Contact: 541-416-6700.
Finding the campground: From U.S. Highway 197 in Maupin, go east on Bakeoven Road to Deschutes River Access Road. Turn left (north) and proceed downstream 4 miles to the campground entrance on the left.

About the campground: This camp on the Deschutes River has a central, gravel parking area with tables set up around it. At the south end of the camp, a basalt outcrop grades to the river. A few residences dot the opposite arid slope, while Oak Springs provides a splash of uncharacteristic green. Fishing, boating, rafting, and relaxing are the pursuits of campers. Undercurrents in the river make swimming dangerous. Fires and smoking are prohibited from June 1 to October 15. The campground is open year-round.

24 Oasis Recreation Site

Location: About 1 mile north of Maupin.
Sites: 12 basic sites; no hookups.
Maximum length: 40 feet.
Facilities: Tables, vault toilets. No drinking water.
Management: Bureau of Land Management.
Fee per night: $ to $$.
Contact: 541-416-6700.
Finding the campground: From U.S. Highway 197 in Maupin, go east on Bakeoven Road to Deschutes River Access Road. Turn left (north) and proceed 1.2 miles downstream to the campground entrance on the left.

About the campground: One of the larger BLM camps along the Lower Deschutes River, Oasis occupies a long stretch of shore. Native grasses grow in the camp, while sagebrush grows at the periphery and willows and alders along the bank. Here, the canyon lacks the wild and rocky disposition it reveals downstream, but the river still hosts boating and fishing and captivates onlookers. For whitewater excitement, schedule a float trip with one of the outfitters in Maupin. Fires and smoking are prohibited from June 1 to October 15. The campground is open year-round.

25 Pebble Ford

Location: About 18 miles west of Dufur.
Sites: 7 basic sites; no hookups.
Maximum length: 16 feet.
Facilities: Tables, grills, vault toilets. No drinking water.
Fee per night: None.
Management: Forest Service.
Contact: 541-467-2291.
Finding the campground: From Forest Road 44, 17.5 miles west of Dufur (at the south end of town) and 9.3 miles east of Oregon 35, turn south on the gravel road indicated for this campground and continue 0.1 mile to find the entrance.

About the campground: In a setting of firs, cedars, and ponderosa pines, this small campground straddles a tributary; a footbridge links the camp halves. Sites have gravel parking, and most have tables and grills. Trails explore the surrounding forest. The campground is open from June to mid-October.

26 Rattlesnake Canyon Recreation Site

Location: About 23 miles north of Maupin.
Sites: 10 basic sites; no hookups.
Maximum length: 40 feet.
Facilities: Tables, vault toilets, boat launch (upstream at Beavertail). No drinking water.
Fee per night: $ to $$.
Management: Bureau of Land Management.
Contact: 541-416-6700.
Finding the campground: From the junction of U.S. Highway 197 and Oregon 216 East at Tygh Valley (7 miles north of Maupin), go east on OR 216, crossing the Deschutes River at Sherars Bridge after 7 miles, and after another 1.1 miles, turn left (north) on gravel Deschutes River Access Road, a BLM Back Country Byway. Go 10.5 miles to reach this camp on the left.

About the campground: This camp is on a slight bench above the Deschutes Wild and Scenic River; its sites blend into the expanse of sagebrush and rabbitbrush. Trees grow closer to the river, a cliff overlooks the camp, and a tableland is across the river. Fishing, boating, and rafting are the primary diversions. The river canyon funnels various birds past the camp; bats may be active at dusk. Boaters should familiarize themselves with river rules, and a dangerous undercurrent makes swimming dangerous. Fires and smoking are prohibited June 1 to October 15. The campground is open year-round.

27 Rock Creek Reservoir

Location: About 13 miles west of Tygh Valley, on Rock Creek Reservoir.
Sites: 33 basic sites; no hookups.
Maximum length: 18 feet.
Facilities: Tables, grills, pit toilets, drinking water, ramp for non-motorized boats.
Fee per night: $$.
Management: Forest Service.
Contact: 541-467-2291; 1-800-280-CAMP for reservations.
Finding the campground: From the junction of Oregon 216 East and U.S. Highway 197 at Tygh Valley, go west on Tygh Valley and Wamic Market Roads for 6 miles to Wamic. From there, continue west on Rock Creek Dam Road/ Forest Road 48 for 6.5 miles, turn right (west) on FR 4820, go 0.2 mile, and turn right on FR 120. Go another 0.2 mile to the camp.

About the campground: You will find this camp on the south side of the dam that captures Rock Creek and creates the reservoir. A picnic area is on the north side. Oaks and small ponderosa pines grow in the basin. The lake offers trout fishing, swimming, and non-motorized boating. The campground is open from mid-April to early October.

28 Twin Springs Recreation Site

Location: About 16 miles north of Maupin.
Sites: 7 basic sites; no hookups.
Maximum length: 40 feet.
Facilities: Tables, vault toilets. No drinking water.
Fee per night: $ to $$.
Management: Bureau of Land Management.
Contact: 541-416-6700.
Finding the campground: From the junction of U.S. Highway 197 and Oregon 216 East at Tygh Valley (7 miles north of Maupin), go east on OR 216, crossing the Deschutes River at Sherars Bridge after 7 miles, and after another 1.1 miles, turn left (north) on gravel Deschutes River Access Road, a BLM Back Country Byway. Go 4 miles to reach this camp on the left.

About the campground: This shadeless camp occupies a low, sagebrush-covered plateau above the Deschutes River. Basalt cliffs rise across the river. The railroad track that traverses the opposite shore represents the victor in a battle to see which railroad would serve the canyon. The abandoned grade on this side is used now by hikers and bicyclists; you can access the grade at Macks Canyon, at the north end of Deschutes River Access Road. Fishing, boating, and rafting are the river pursuits; undercurrents make swimming dangerous. Fires and smoking are prohibited from June 1 to October 15. The campground is open year-round.

29 Wapinitia Recreation Site

Location: About 3 miles south of Maupin.
Sites: 2 basic sites; no hookups.
Maximum length: 25 feet.
Facilities: Tables, vault toilets, boat launch. No drinking water.
Fee per night: $ to $$.
Management: Bureau of Land Management.
Contact: 541-416-6700.
Finding the campground: From the Deschutes River bridge on U.S. Highway 197 in Maupin, go south on US 197 for 0.2 mile and turn right at the BLM sign for Upper River Access. Drive 3 miles to the campground entrance on the right.

About the campground: This campground fronts the Deschutes River where its canyon is lined by bald, rounded ridges. Junipers dot the opposite slope, and white alders edge the river. Fishing, boating, rafting, and enjoying the remote canyon quiet are reasons to visit. Fires and smoking are prohibited from June 1 to October 15. The campground is open year-round.

30 Wasco County Fairgrounds: Hunt RV Park

Location: In Tygh Valley.
Sites: 150 hookup sites, 50 tent sites; water and electric hookups.
Maximum length: 60 feet.
Facilities: Flush toilets, drinking water, showers, dump station, telephone, horse stalls for rent.
Fee per night: $$.
Management: Wasco County.
Contact: 541-483-2288.
Finding the campground: From the junction of U.S. Highway 197 and Oregon 216 East at Tygh Valley (7 miles north of Maupin), go west on Tygh Valley Road for 0.3 mile and turn right onto Main Street. Follow it for 0.1 mile and turn right onto Fairgrounds Road. Follow Fairgrounds Road 1.8 miles to arrive at the fairgrounds and Hunt RV Park.

About the campground: You will find this pleasant wayside on a flat surrounded by the bald, rolling hills of the Plateau Country. Mature trees shade the camp's groomed lawns. When events are not taking place at the fairgrounds, the camp can be quite restful. Otherwise, you will find a bustling mini-village of RVs and tents.

31 White River Recreation Site

Location: About 5 miles north of Maupin.
Sites: 3 basic sites; no hookups.
Maximum length: 40 feet.
Facilities: Tables, vault toilets. No drinking water.

Fee per night: $ to $$.
Management: Bureau of Land Management.
Contact: 541-416-6700.
Finding the campground: From U.S. Highway 197 in Maupin, go east on Bake-oven Road to Deschutes River Access Road. Turn left (north) and proceed 5.2 miles downriver to the campground entrance on the left.

About the campground: This camp has a gravel parking area partitioned into marked spaces; tables paired with the sites occupy the lot's perimeter. Sagebrush and a few riverside alders are the only vegetation on this otherwise open flat. Like the other camps of the Deschutes River corridor, this one serves up breathtaking river and canyon views and great fishing. The White River confluence is across the Deschutes from the camp. Maupin is the base for several river-running outfitters, should you seek a livelier look at the Deschutes. Fires and smoking are prohibited from June 1 to October 15. The campground is open year-round.

32 White River Station

Location: About 18 miles southeast of Government Camp.
Sites: 6 basic sites; no hookups.
Maximum length: Small units only due to narrow, bumpy entry road.
Facilities: Tables, grills, vault toilets. No drinking water.
Fee per night: None.
Management: Forest Service.
Contact: 541-467-2291.
Finding the campground: From Oregon 35 at the White River crossing, 2 miles south of Mt. Hood Meadows ski area, 5 miles north of the U.S. Highway 26 and OR 35 junction, follow Forest Road 48 southeast for 8.8 miles and turn right (west) on FR 43 for 0.6 mile. Turn left on narrow, dirt Old Barlow Road/Forest Road 3530 to reach the camp on the left in 1.2 miles. Old Barlow Road is closed from December 15 through April 1.

About the campground: First used by pioneers on the Oregon Trail, this quiet camp occupies a semi-open flat along the White River. A few big firs rise among the lodgepole pines, while alders and cottonwoods grow beside the river. The sites are spacious and widely spaced; they have log tables and undefined parking. Interpretive signs introduce the history of the area. The White River originates from glaciers on Mount Hood and rolls turbulent, cloudy, and fast past camp.

MADRAS-REDMOND AREA

		Hookup sites	Total sites	Max. RV length	Hookups	Toilets	Showers	Drinking water	Dump station	Recreation	Fee	Can reserve
33	The Cove Palisades State Park: Crooked River	91	91	60	WE	F	•	•	•	SFBL	$$	•
34	The Cove Palisades State Park: Deschutes River	87	181	60	WES	F	•	•		HSFBL	$$-$$$	•
35	Haystack		24	30		F		•		FBL	$	
36	Haystack Reservoir: South Shore		20	T		NF				FB		
37	Haystack Reservoir: West Shore		25	30		NF				FBL		
38	Jefferson County Fairgrounds	65	65	60	WES	F	•	•	•		$$	•
39	Pelton Park		80	40		F	•	•		SFBL	$$	•
40	Perry South		63	40		NF		•		SFBL	$	
41	Skull Hollow		40	25		NF						
42	South Junction Recreation Site		6	T		NF				F	$	
43	Trout Creek Recreation Site		23	25		NF				HFBLC	$-$$	

Hookups: W = Water E = Electric S = Sewer **Total sites:** T = Tent-only campground **Maximum trailer/RV length** given in feet.
Toilets: F = Flush NF = No Flush **Recreation:** H = Hiking S = Swimming F = Fishing B = Boating L = Boat Launch
O = Off-Highway Driving R = Horseback Riding C = Cycling
Fee: $ = $1-9 $$ = $10-19 $$$ = $20-29 $$$$ = $30-39. If no entry under **Fee**, camping is free.

---

33 The Cove Palisades State Park: Crooked River

Location: About 10 miles southwest of Madras, about 25 miles northwest of Redmond.
Sites: 91 hookup sites; water and electric hookups.
Maximum length: 60 feet.
Facilities: Tables, grills, flush toilets, drinking water, showers, dump station, telephone, boat launch (at day-use area).
Fee per night: $$.
Management: Oregon State Parks and Recreation Department.
Contact: 541-546-3412; 1-800-452-5687 for reservations.
Finding the campground: From U.S. Highway 97/26 in Madras, take Culver Highway southwest at the sign for Cove Palisades and go 7.1 miles. Turn right (west) onto Gem Lane and follow the signs for the state park through a series of turns to reach this campground on the left in 2.5 miles. From Redmond, go north on US 97 for 16 miles, turn left (west) at the sign for the park, and continue to follow the park signs another 8.5 miles to enter this campground on the left.

About the campground: This campground claims a high plateau above the Crooked River Arm of Lake Billy Chinook, but it lacks lake overlooks. It does provide views of Mount Jefferson and Three Fingered Jack. The flat is land-scaped with lawn and trees that offer some shade, and the sites have paved parking. For lake recreation, just take the short drive downhill into the core of the park. The turnoff for the marina and restaurant is a mile from the camp. The day-use boat launch, picnic area, and swimming area are 1.1 miles away. The campground is open year-round.

Lake Billy Chinook at The Cove Palisades State Park.

34 The Cove Palisades State Park: Deschutes River

Location: About 14 miles southwest of Madras, 29 miles northwest of Redmond.
Sites: 87 hookup sites, 94 basic sites, cabins and houseboats; water, electric, and sewer hookups.
Maximum length: 60 feet.
Facilities: Tables, grills, flush toilets, drinking water, showers, telephone, store, playground, boat launch (at day-use area), fish-cleaning station.
Fee per night: $$ to $$$.
Management: Oregon State Parks and Recreation Department.
Contact: 541-546-3412; 1-800-452-5687 for reservations.
Finding the campground: From U.S. Highway 97/26 in Madras, take Culver Highway southwest at the sign for Cove Palisades and go 7.1 miles. Turn right (west) onto Gem Lane and follow the signs for the state park through a series of turns to reach this campground on the left in another 7 miles. From Redmond, go north on US 97 for 16 miles, turn left (west) at the sign for the park, and continue to follow the signs another 13 miles to the campground.

About the campground: This campground occupies a canyon just removed from the Deschutes River Arm of Lake Billy Chinook. Native junipers, along with locusts, cottonwoods, and willows, shade the developed camp. Nature trails lead to Ship Rock and to the day-use swimming area. A longer hiking trail climbs to and then traverses the summit plateau of The Peninsula, which overlooks the camp. This landmark shaped by the Deschutes and Crooked River Arms of Lake Billy Chinook dishes up fine views of the lake and another area landmark, The Island. You can access the lake at the park's day-use areas on either side of the camp. Billy Chinook is one of the state's premier recreational waters for boating, fishing, swimming, and waterskiing. The campground is open year-round.

35 Haystack

Location: About 12 miles south of Madras, 22 miles north of Redmond, on Haystack Reservoir.
Sites: 24 basic sites; no hookups.
Maximum length: 30 feet.
Facilities: Tables, grills, flush and vault toilets, drinking water, boat launch, covered picnic tables (at Haystack Reservoir).
Fee per night: $.
Management: Crooked River National Grassland.
Contact: 541-475-9272; 541-416-6640.
Finding the campground: From U.S. Highway 97, 8 miles south of Madras and 18 miles north of Redmond, turn east onto Jericho Lane, go 1.2 miles, and turn right onto Haystack Road. Continue 2.1 miles to reach the campground entrance road. Follow it left for 0.5 mile to the camp.

About the campground: This campground is on a juniper- and sagebrush-covered slope above the east shore of Haystack Reservoir. It has paved roads and parking and presents views of Haystack and Juniper Buttes, Mount Jefferson, and the surrounding high desert and distant Cascades. Because of the wind and sun, keep the sunscreen handy. The lake is regularly stocked with fish. Sailboards, boats, and geese ply the sun-spangled water. The campground is open from mid-May through September.

36 Haystack Reservoir: South Shore

Location: About 10 miles south of Madras and 20 miles north of Redmond, on Haystack Reservoir.
Sites: 20 tent sites; no hookups.
Maximum length: Suitable for tents only.
Facilities: Chemical toilets. No drinking water.
Fee per night: None.
Management: Crooked River National Grassland.
Contact: 541-475-9272; 541-416-6640.
Finding the campground: From U.S. Highway 97, 8 miles south of Madras and 18 miles north of Redmond, turn east onto Jericho Lane, go 1.2 miles, and turn right onto Haystack Road. Continue 1.1 miles to reach this camp on the left.

About the campground: This dry-weather camp consists of a maze of rough dirt roads and primitive overnight spots scattered across the gentle, juniper-dotted south slope of Haystack Reservoir. While this area is better suited for tent camping and the west shore (see below) is better for RVs, you may encounter some of both here. However, RVers, in particular, should avoid this area during times of heavy rain and mud. Views to the north are of Mount Hood; views to the west are of Mount Jefferson. As the reservoir recedes in summer, visitors drive across the growing beach/dry lakebed to reach the open water for their fun and sport. The lake attracts boaters, anglers, sailboarders, and swimmers.

37 Haystack Reservoir: West Shore

Location: About 10 miles south of Madras and 20 miles north of Redmond, on Haystack Reservoir.
Sites: 25 primitive RV sites; no hookups.
Maximum length: 30 feet.
Facilities: Chemical toilets, paved boat launch. No drinking water.
Contact: 541-475-9272; 541-416-6640.
Fee per night: None.
Management: Crooked River National Grassland.
Finding the campground: From U.S. Highway 97, 8 miles south of Madras and 18 miles north of Redmond, turn east onto Jericho Lane, go 1.2 miles, and turn right onto Haystack Road. Continue 0.6 mile to reach this camp on the left.

About the campground: This camp claims a narrow strip of shoreline on the west side of Haystack Reservoir. Views from the camp are of the arid, juniper-dotted hills; the open expanse of Crooked River National Grassland; and Haystack and Juniper Buttes. The camp is basically an undeveloped parking lot, but its lake access for boating, fishing, and sailboarding wins over guests. The campground is open year-round.

38 Jefferson County Fairgrounds

Location: In Madras.
Sites: 65 hookup sites; water, electric, and sewer hookups.
Maximum length: 60 feet.
Facilities: Tables, flush toilets, drinking water, showers, dump station, telephone.
Fee per night: $$.
Management: Jefferson County.
Contact: 541-475-4460.
Finding the campground: From U.S. Highway 97/26 at the south end of Madras, turn west onto Fairgrounds Road, go 0.1 mile, and turn right toward the RV camp entrance.

About the campground: This RV camp occupies an open, gravel flat at the eastern edge of the Jefferson County Fairgrounds. It offers a clean, orderly layout, with a table at each site, and it is highly convenient for event participants or attendees. Make reservations well in advance. The open lawn adjacent to the RV spaces welcomes repose.

39 Pelton Park

Location: About 13 miles northwest of Madras, on Lake Simtustus.
Sites: 80 basic sites; no hookups.
Maximum length: 40 feet.
Facilities: Tables, fire rings, flush toilets, drinking water, showers, laundry, telephone, camp store, snack bar, volleyball, horseshoe pits, swimming area, boat rental, moorage, launch, fish-cleaning station, community kitchen for rent.
Fee per night: $$.
Management: Portland General Electric.
Contact: 541-475-0517, 503-464-8515.
Finding the campground: From the junction of U.S. Highway 97 and US 26 West in Madras, go north on US 26W for 9.4 miles and turn left at Pelton Junction onto Pelton Dam Road. Continue 3.3 miles to enter the park on the right.

About the campground: This campground and its accompanying day-use area, owned and leased by Portland General Electric, occupy half a mile of the Lake Simtustus shore for a full lineup of wet fun. The canyon junipers provide welcome shade. Across the water, you can see a basalt-rimmed canyon wall. The camp has paved parking, dry lawns, picturesque junipers, and a few natural boulders and outcrops; some sites overlook the lake. Much of Lake Simtustus has a maximum boat speed of 10 miles per hour, but there is an area designated for speed craft. Kokanee, steelhead, rainbow and brown trout, and small-mouthed bass haunt the blue waters and make for excellent fishing and, later, dining. You need both a valid state fishing license and a Warm Springs Indian Reservation license; you can buy the latter at the camp store. About 1 mile from camp, an abandoned railroad grade that leads into Madras makes a good hiking trail. The campground is open from April 1 to October 31.

40 Perry South

Location: About 30 miles southwest of Madras, on Lake Billy Chinook.
Sites: 59 basic sites, 4 walk-in tent sites; no hookups.
Maximum length: 40 feet.
Facilities: Tables, grills, pit toilets, drinking water, boat launch, dock, fish-cleaning station.
Fee per night: $.
Management: Forest Service.
Contact: 541-549-2111.
Finding the campground: From U.S. Highway 97/26 in Madras, take Culver Highway southwest at the sign for Cove Palisades and go 7.1 miles. Turn right (west) onto Gem Lane and follow the signs for the state park through a series of turns, remaining on the main road to and through the park. Eventually, the route becomes Forest Road 64. After going 20.3 miles from the Culver Highway turn-

off, you will come to the junction of FR 64 and FR 1170; stay on FR 64 and drive another 2.5 miles to reach the camp. (Carrying a Deschutes National Forest map can help you track your progress.)

About the campground: This camp straddles FR 64 and occupies a narrow draw above the Metolius River Arm of Lake Billy Chinook. A dry forest of pines, cedars, and firs houses the sites. There are some big pines and a spring at the lower camp. The lower camp is closer to the lake, but the upper camp promises the quieter retreat. Boating, swimming, fishing, and waterskiing entertain guests. You must have both a state license and a Warm Springs Indian Reservation license to fish the Metolius River Arm of Lake Billy Chinook. Nesting bald eagles are treated to a mandated quiet on this part of the lake until April 15 each year. By the time this campground opens in May, the success of their nests is secured; keep an eye on the skies. The campground is open from May through September.

41 Skull Hollow

Location: About 13 miles northeast of Redmond.
Sites: 40 basic sites; no hookups.
Maximum length: 25 feet.
Facilities: Vault toilets. No drinking water.
Fee per night: None.
Management: Crooked River National Grassland.
Contact: 541-475-9272; 541-416-6640.
Finding the campground: From Redmond, drive 3 miles north on U.S. Highway 97 and turn right (east) at the sign for O'Neil and Lone Pine. Follow O'Neil Road for 4.8 miles, turn left onto Lone Pine Road, and continue another 5.3 miles. Turn left onto Forest Road 5710, go 0.1 mile, and turn left to enter the camp.

About the campground: This amazing camp, seemingly in the middle of nowhere and with little to recommend it, blossoms into a tent city on weekends. The reason is Smith Rock State Park to the southwest, a world-renowned rock climbing area on the Crooked River. The camp also lies within easy reach of the Gray Butte Trail for hiking and mountain biking, the Endurance Trail for horseback riding, and the wide-open spaces of Crooked River National Grassland. A loop road and vault toilets alone define this minimalist camp on the juniper-dotted sage-grassland. In this fragile, dry landscape, pay heed to fire restrictions and use common sense when parking: Use established turnouts and avoid vegetated areas. The campground is open year-round.

42 South Junction Recreation Site

Location: About 36 miles north of Madras.
Sites: 6 tent sites; no hookups.
Maximum length: Suitable for tents only.
Facilities: Tables, pit toilets. No drinking water.

Fee per night: $.
Management: Bureau of Land Management.
Contact: 541-416-6700.
Finding the campground: From the junction of U.S. Highway 197 and US 97 at Shaniko Junction (21 miles south of Maupin, 26 miles north of Madras), go west on South Junction Road, which begins paved and becomes gravel. Follow it 9.2 miles to a fork, bear right, and go another 0.4 mile to enter the camp via a narrow dirt road.

About the campground: Located on the east shore of the Deschutes River, across from Warm Springs Indian Reservation and the Warm Springs River confluence, these campsites are well spaced along a juniper- and sagebrush-studded grassland slope. Each site features a shade tree or two. The river, a strong enticement to anglers and daydreamers, is 0.1 mile from camp, across a BLM fence and a railroad track. A stile allows for an easy passage over the fence; be alert when crossing the tracks. Fires and smoking are prohibited from June 1 to October 15. The campground is open year-round.

43 Trout Creek Recreation Site

Location: About 16 miles north of Madras.
Sites: 23 basic sites; no hookups.
Maximum length: 25 feet.
Facilities: Tables, vault toilets, boat launch. No drinking water.
Fee per night: $ to $$.
Management: Bureau of Land Management.
Contact: 541-416-6700.
Finding the campground: From Madras, go 3 miles north on U.S. Highway 97. Turn left onto Cora Lane and then immediately left again onto Clark Drive. Proceed 8 miles to Gateway (the road name changes en route). In Gateway, turn right onto Clemmens Drive toward Trout Creek. Drive 4.3 miles, passing through a narrow tunnel with 14-foot clearance and down a steep gravel road to the base of the canyon. Turn left and continue 0.3 mile to the recreation site. The road is not recommended for trailers.

About the campground: This BLM recreation site occupies a pretty canyon along the Deschutes River. Sites claim a broad flat of native grasses, sage, and rabbitbrush, with a light sprinkling of junipers. In this sun-drenched canyon, the juniper-shaded sites are quickly snapped up. Just downstream looms an impressive butte. An abandoned railroad grade/multiple-use trail journeys upstream to Mecca Flat, offering views of, and occasional access to, the river. Fishing and boating are popular draws. Fires and smoking are prohibited from June 1 to October 15. The campground is open year-round.

SISTERS AREA

		Hookup sites	Total sites	Max. RV length	Hookups	Toilets	Showers	Drinking water	Dump station	Recreation	Fee	Can reserve
44	Abbott Creek		4	18		NF						
45	Allen Springs		20	30		NF		•		HF	$$	
46	Allingham		10	40		NF		•	•	HF	$$	
47	Blue Bay		25	30		NF		•		HFBL	$$	•
48	Camp Sherman		15	35		NF		•		HF	$$	
49	Candle Creek		7	25		NF				HF		
50	Cold Springs		23	40		NF		•		H	$	
51	Driftwood		17	16		NF				HSFB	$	
52	Gorge		18	40		NF		•		HF	$$	
53	Graham Horse Camp		13	40		NF		•		HR	$	
54	Indian Ford		25	40		NF		•			$	
55	Jack Creek		11	40		NF				HR		
56	Lava Camp Lake		10	22		NF				HF		
57	Link Creek		33	40		NF		•		HSFBL	$$	•
58	Lower Bridge		12	22		NF		•		HF	$$	
59	Lower Canyon Creek		5	18		NF				HF		
60	Pine Rest		8	T		NF		•		HF	$$	
61	Pioneer Ford		20	40		NF		•		HF	$$	
62	Round Lake		5	T		NF				HFBL		
63	Sheep Springs Horse Camp		10	30		NF		•		HR	$	•
64	Sisters City Park		60	40		F		•			$	
65	Sisters Cow Camp Horse Camp		5	40		NF				HR		
66	Smiling River		38	40		NF		•		HF	$$	
67	South Shore		38	30		NF		•		HSFBL	$$	•
68	Three Creek Lake		10	25		NF				HSFB	$	
69	Three Creek Meadow		20	40		NF				HFR	$	
70	Whispering Pines Horse Camp		9	40		NF				HR	$	•

Hookups: W = Water E = Electric S = Sewer **Total sites:** T = Tent-only campground **Maximum trailer/RV length** given in feet.
Toilets: F = Flush NF = No Flush **Recreation:** H = Hiking S = Swimming F = Fishing B = Boating L = Boat Launch
O = Off-Highway Driving R = Horseback Riding C = Cycling
Fee: $ = $1-9 $$ = $10-19 $$$ = $20-29 $$$$ = $30-39. If no entry under **Fee,** camping is free.

44 Abbot Creek

Location: About 23 miles northwest of Sisters.
Sites: 4 basic sites; no hookups.
Maximum length: 18 feet.
Facilities: Some tables and grills, vault toilets. No drinking water.
Fee per night: None.
Management: Forest Service.

Contact: 541-549-2111.
Finding the campground: From Sisters, go west on U.S. Highway 20 for 12 miles, turn right (north) onto Forest Road 12, and follow it for 10.7 miles. (FR 12 begins paved but becomes gravel.) Turn left onto FR 900 and go 0.4 mile to the camp.

About the campground: This is a no-frills, primitive camp for the do-it-your-selfer. Sites are mostly shaded by firs and ponderosa pines. Abbot Creek babbles in the background. Mainly this is a camp at which to kick back, but you can also sightsee, fish, and hike. The campground is open from May to October.

45 Allen Springs

Location: About 20 miles northwest of Sisters.
Sites: 17 basic sites, 3 walk-in tent sites; no hookups.
Maximum length: 30 feet.
Facilities: Tables, grills, vault toilets, drinking water (in season).
Fee per night: $$.
Management: Forest Service.
Contact: 541-549-2111.
Finding the campground: From Sisters, go west on U.S. Highway 20 for 9.3 miles, turn right (north) onto paved Forest Road 14, and follow it for 11.1 miles to the campground entrance on the left.

About the campground: One of a string of choice family campgrounds along the Metolius Wild and Scenic River, this camp occupies a bend of the river. Most of the sites sit amid fir, cedar, and ponderosa pine trees, but the walk-in sites occupy a meadow at the downstream end of camp. Because river trails explore both the west and east banks, you can make a 6-mile loop hike between Lower Bridge (downstream) and the bridge at Wizard Falls Fish Hatchery (upstream). Fly fishing lines often dance over the stunning water, while geese dwell in the quiet afforded by the bend. The campground is open year-round, but there are no services provided after the summer season.

46 Allingham

Location: About 16 miles northwest of Sisters.
Sites: 10 basic sites; no hookups.
Maximum length: 40 feet.
Facilities: Tables, grills, vault toilets, drinking water, dump station.
Fee per night: $$.
Management: Forest Service.
Contact: 541-549-2111.
Finding the campground: From Sisters, go west on U.S. Highway 20 for 9.3 miles, turn right (north) onto paved Forest Road 14, and follow it for 6 miles. Turn left onto FR 1419 at the sign that reads "To Camp Sherman," go 0.2 mile, and turn right onto paved FR 900, which is signed for campgrounds. Go 0.7 mile to reach this camp on the left.

About the campground: This Metolius River campground has several pull-thru sites and is well suited for RVs and large trailers. Ponderosa pines and bitterbrush set the stage for your stay. Views are of the glassy, deep river; its green banks; and the cabins on the opposite bank. Fly fishing, hiking trails, the Camp Sherman fish-feeding platform, and the Wizard Island Fish Hatchery are area attractions. The campground is open from May to October.

47 Blue Bay

Location: About 14 miles northwest of Sisters, on Suttle Lake.
Sites: 25 basic sites; no hookups.
Maximum length: 30 feet.
Facilities: Tables, grills, vault toilets, drinking water, boat launch, fish-cleaning station.
Fee per night: $$.
Management: Forest Service.
Contact: 541-549-2111; 1-800-280-CAMP for reservations.
Finding the campground: From U.S. Highway 20, 13 miles west of Sisters, 6.5 miles east of Santiam Pass, turn south onto paved Forest Road 2070 toward Suttle and Blue Lakes (the east access road). Go 1 mile to the campground entrance on the right.

About the campground: In a select-cut forest of firs and ponderosa pines, this campground offers semi-sunny sites along the south shore of Suttle Lake, a big, natural lake that boasts a full range of lake recreation. Vine maples claim the lower story. The campground has paved roads and gravel parking pads, some of which are pull-thrus. Entertainment here includes boating, fishing, waterskiing, and hiking the 3.25-mile Shoreline Trail. Elsewhere on the lake, you will find suitable swimming areas. On most days, boaters and anglers must contend with a strong afternoon wind. The campground is open from mid-April to late September.

48 Camp Sherman

Location: About 16 miles northwest of Sisters.
Sites: 15 basic sites; no hookups.
Maximum length: 35 feet.
Facilities: Tables, grills, vault toilets, drinking water (in season), picnic shelter.
Fee per night: $$.
Management: Forest Service.
Contact: 541-549-2111.
Finding the campground: From Sisters, go west on U.S. Highway 20 for 9.3 miles, turn right (north) onto paved Forest Road 14, and follow it for 6 miles. Turn left onto FR 1419 at the sign that reads "To Camp Sherman," go 0.2 mile, and turn right onto paved FR 900 (signed for campgrounds). Go 0.2 mile to reach this camp on the left.

About the campground: This campground occupies a flat of mixed-age ponderosa pines; the mature pines parade reddish-yellow trunks. A grassy meadow extends to the river, while bitterbrush claims the roadside. Wildflower-decorated islands and banks contribute to the charm of the river. Relaxing, birding, hiking, fly fishing, and sightseeing are among the pastimes here. The campground is open year-round, but there are no services provided after the summer season.

49 Candle Creek

Location: About 16 miles northwest of Sisters.
Sites: 7 basic sites; no hookups.
Maximum length: 25 feet.
Facilities: Tables, grills, vault toilets. No drinking water.
Fee per night: None.
Management: Forest Service.
Contact: 541-549-2111.
Finding the campground: From Sisters, go west on U.S. Highway 20 for 9.3 miles, turn right (north) onto paved Forest Road 14, and follow it for 13.6 miles to Lower Bridge, where the road becomes gravel and its number changes to FR 12. Go another mile on FR 12 and turn right onto FR 980. Proceed 1.5 miles to the campground.

About the campground: This peaceful campground sits on a forested bluff above the Metolius River at the Candle Creek confluence. Many of the sites overlook the river, and although no fee is charged, the camp features established parking at each site. Alders and vine maples grow along the swift waterway, which is open to fly fishing only. You can access the West Metolius Trail from the camp; it leads along the river. The campground is open from May to October.

50 Cold Springs

Location: 4 miles west of Sisters.
Sites: 23 basic sites; no hookups.
Maximum length: 40 feet.
Facilities: Tables, grills, vault toilets, drinking water.
Fee per night: $.
Management: Forest Service.
Contact: 541-549-2111.
Finding the campground: From the junction of U.S. Highway 20 and Oregon 242 at the west end of Sisters, go west on OR 242 for 4 miles to reach this camp.

About the campground: Lovely ponderosa pines and an aspen grove create a soothing setting for your stay. There are both pull-thru and back-in gravel parking spurs. Spring Trail begins near the campground entrance and leads a quarter of a mile through mixed woods and across a spring to a lava outcrop. You can scramble to the top of the outcrop for a new perspective on the area or follow an old jeep trail away from the site to extend your journey. The area is particularly appealing in early October, when the aspens turn yellow and jet-black ravens pass between the trees. Birding is popular here. The campground is open from May to mid-October.

51 Driftwood

Location: About 16 miles southwest of Sisters, on Three Creek Lake.
Sites: 17 basic sites; no hookups.
Maximum length: 16 feet.
Facilities: Tables, grills, vault toilets. No drinking water.
Fee per night: $.
Management: Forest Service.
Contact: 541-549-2111.
Finding the campground: From U.S. Highway 20 in Sisters, turn south at the sign for Three Creek Lake onto South Elm, which later becomes Forest Road 16. Go 15.7 miles to the campground entrance on the right. The final 1.6 miles are on gravel.

About the campground: On the north shore of Three Creek Lake, you will find this campground in a forest of lodgepole and whitebark pines and true firs. Half of the sites are pull-in; parking for the remaining sites is along the widened road shoulder. The campsites are strung along the shore of this shimmering manmade lake at the foot of Tam McArthur Rim. Drift logs ring the lake, hinting at the camp's name. The sites receive only partial shade, and you should come prepared for mosquitoes. Fishing, non-motorized boating, and hiking the trails to Tam McArthur Rim and Little Three Creek Lake engage guests. The campground is open from July to mid-September.

52 Gorge

Location: About 17 miles northwest of Sisters.
Sites: 18 basic sites; no hookups.
Maximum length: 40 feet.
Facilities: Tables, grills, vault toilets, drinking water.
Fee per night: $$.
Management: Forest Service.
Contact: 541-549-2111.
Finding the campground: From Sisters, go west on U.S. Highway 20 for 9.3 miles, turn right (north) onto paved Forest Road 14, and follow it for 6 miles. Turn left onto FR 1419 at the sign pointing "To Camp Sherman," go 0.2 mile, and turn right onto paved FR 900 (signed for campgrounds). Go 1.8 miles to reach this camp on the left.

About the campground: This Metolius River campground occupies a ponderosa-pine flat, with bitterbrush growing in the understory. Sites are partially sunny, and a number of them offer pull-thru parking, which will appeal to visitors with larger rigs. The banks of the Metolius here are grassy, and fly fishing is the order of the day. The campground is open from May to October.

53 Graham Horse Camp

Location: About 7 miles northwest of Sisters.
Sites: 13 basic sites; no hookups.
Maximum length: 40 feet.
Facilities: Tables, grills, pit toilets, drinking water, central partitioned corral, horse-loading chute, corrals at 4 sites, hitching rails.
Fee per night: $.
Management: Forest Service.
Contact: 541-549-2111; no reservations accepted.
Finding the campground: From the junction of U.S. Highway 20 and Oregon 242 at the west end of Sisters, go 4 miles west on US 20 and turn left onto gravel Forest Road 1012 toward the Cold Springs Cut-off and Graham Corral. Go 1 mile, turn right onto FR 1012.300, and go another mile. Turn right onto FR 340 and go 0.6 mile to the camp.

About the campground: Along the lengthy Metolius-Windigo National Recreation Trail, this horse camp sits where numerous roundups were held from the late 1800s to the early 1900s. Here, sheep and cows that ranged the Cache Mountain–Metolius River area were gathered and counted; the central corral seen and used today re-creates the historic scene. Campers today enjoy a spacious facility in a beautiful setting of ponderosa pines and bitterbrush. To the north above the treetops, you may glimpse Black Butte.

54 Indian Ford

Location: About 6 miles northwest of Sisters.
Sites: 25 basic sites; no hookups.
Maximum length: 40 feet.
Facilities: Tables, grills, vault toilets, drinking water.
Fee per night: $.
Management: Forest Service.
Contact: 541-549-2111.
Finding the campground: From Sisters, go 5.6 miles west on U.S. Highway 20 and turn right onto Forest Road 11. Immediately make a second right turn into the camp.

About the campground: This camp sits beside a narrow creek in a tranquil setting of big ponderosa pines, aspens, bunchgrass, and sagebrush. The ford at this location was mentioned in the journals of 19th-century explorer John C. Fremont. The camp is convenient for through-travelers on US 20. You can watch birds right at your site, but there is traffic noise. With this camp as a base, you can hike to the top of Black Butte or fly fish the Metolius Wild and Scenic River. The frontier village of Sisters holds a different appeal, with its galleries and boutiques. The campground is open from May to mid-October.

Black Butte Summit.

55 Jack Creek

Location: About 17 miles northwest of Sisters.
Sites: 11 basic sites; no hookups.
Maximum length: 40 feet.
Facilities: Tables, grills and fire rings, vault toilets. No drinking water.
Fee per night: None.
Management: Forest Service.
Contact: 541-549-2111.
Finding the campground: From Sisters, go west on U.S. Highway 20 for 12 miles, turn right (north) onto paved Forest Road 12, and follow it for 4.4 miles. Turn left onto FR 1230, go 0.6 mile, cross a bridge, and turn left onto FR 1232. Go another 0.2 mile to reach the campground entrance on the left.

About the campground: This campground has a random, informal layout, with tables and grills hinting at the site locations. Big, impressive pines rise above camp, but the *pièce de résistance* is Jack Creek, one of the prettiest creeks in the country. Cold and crystalline, Jack Creek originates from a spring and wends its way around logs and around islands capped with mosaics of fern, giant lupine, grass, and young trees. A trail leads upstream from the camp to the spring, Head of Jack Creek. The hike is worthwhile; every few strides reveal a scene worth photographing. Near the FR 1230 bridge, you can access the Metolius-Windigo Trail, a long-distance trail. Jack Creek is closed to angling. The campground is open from May to October.

56 Lava Camp Lake

Location: About 14 miles southwest of Sisters.
Sites: 10 basic sites; no hookups.
Maximum length: 22 feet.
Facilities: Tables, grills, pit toilets. No drinking water.
Fee per night: None.
Management: Forest Service.
Contact: 541-549-2111.
Finding the campground: From the junction of U.S. Highway 20 and Oregon 242 at the west end of Sisters, go west on OR 242 for 14 miles and turn left onto red-cinder Forest Road 900. Go 0.4 mile to the camp, bypassing a parking lot for the Pacific Crest Trail.

About the campground: You will find this rustic camp just off McKenzie Pass Scenic Highway (OR 242) next to tiny, mud-bottomed Lava Camp Lake. The sites rest on a terrace above the lake and along the shoreline in a mixed forest of lodgepole pines, mountain hemlocks, and firs. Half a mile west on OR 242, Dee Wright Observatory serves up fine views of the Three Sisters and Mount Washington Wilderness Areas, the Cascade volcanoes, and the mosaic of forest and lava flow. The fortress-like observatory is constructed of volcanic rock and perched atop a crusty flow; it is itself a good photo subject. The arrangement of the open-air windows allows you to pinpoint landmarks. You will find other spectacular wilderness views, as well as access to the Pacific Crest and a host of other trails, from the twisting scenic highway. In the fall, the red blush of the vine maples suggests a drive. The campground is open from June through September.

57 Link Creek

Location: About 15 miles northwest of Sisters, on Suttle Lake.
Sites: 33 basic sites; no hookups.
Maximum length: 40 feet.
Facilities: Tables, grills, vault toilets, drinking water (in season), boat dock, launch, fish-cleaning station.
Fee per night: $$.
Management: Forest Service.
Contact: 541-549-2111; 1-800-280-CAMP for reservations.
Finding the campground: From U.S. Highway 20, 13 miles west of Sisters, 6.5 miles east of Santiam Pass, turn south onto paved Forest Road 2070 toward Suttle and Blue Lakes (the east access road). Go 2.3 miles to the campground entrance on the right.

About the campground: This campground sits next to Link Creek on the southwest shore of Suttle Lake. Mixed pines and firs tower above the camp, while sticky laurel bushes grow in the more open areas. The campground has paved roads, and the sites feature either gravel or paved parking pads, some of them pull-thrus. Several sites overlook the huge, natural lake. Boating, fishing, waterskiing, swimming, and hiking the 3.25-mile Shoreline Trail keep campers entertained. Afternoon winds commonly wash over the lake. In the fall, look for kokanee spawning in Link Creek. The campground is open year-round, but there are no services provided after the summer season.

58 Lower Bridge

Location: About 23 miles northwest of Sisters.
Sites: 12 basic sites; no hookups.
Maximum length: 22 feet.
Facilities: Tables, grills, vault toilets, drinking water.
Fee per night: $$.
Management: Forest Service.
Contact: 541-549-2111.
Finding the campground: From Sisters, go west on U.S. Highway 20 for 9.3 miles, turn right (north) onto paved Forest Road 14, and follow it for 13.5 miles to this campground. The entrance is on the right as you arrive at Lower Bridge.

About the campground: This pleasant, shady camp sits downstream of Lower Bridge, where fishing with barbless hooks and lures is allowed on a short stretch of the Metolius Wild and Scenic River. Elsewhere on the river, only fly fishing is allowed. The sites occupy a terraced forest slope above the river. Western tanagers sometimes decorate the tree branches. Foot trails trace both riverbanks in both directions. Upstream, a 6-mile loop hike is possible with a river crossing on the Wizard Falls Fish Hatchery bridge. The campground is open from May to October.

59 Lower Canyon Creek

Location: About 18 miles northwest of Sisters.
Sites: 5 basic sites; no hookups.
Maximum length: 18 feet.
Facilities: Tables, grills, vault toilets. No drinking water.
Fee per night: None.
Management: Forest Service.
Contact: 541-549-2111.
Finding the campground: From Sisters, go west on U.S. Highway 20 for 9.3 miles, turn right (north) onto paved Forest Road 14, and follow it for 2.6 miles. Turn left onto FR 1419 at the sign for Camp Sherman, go 1.3 miles, and proceed straight on FR 1420, following the signs for Sheep Springs Horse Camp. Follow FR 1420 for 4 miles (the road eventually becomes gravel), turn right onto FR 1420.400, and go 0.7 mile to the campground.

About the campground: At the convergence of Canyon Creek and the Metolius River, you will find this small, pleasant campground in a setting of ponderosa pines, bitterbrush, and bunchgrass. At the end of the campground loop, the West Metolius Trail departs on a 9-mile journey down the river to Candle Creek.

You will enjoy spectacular scenes of sun-gilded riffles, channels, and deep pools; grassy islands showy with wildflowers; families of geese and mergansers; nesting ospreys overhead; and the dancing lines of the fly anglers. The color of the river ranges from icy blue to satiny black.

60 Pine Rest

Location: About 17 miles northwest of Sisters.
Sites: 8 tent sites; no hookups.
Maximum length: Suitable for tents only.
Facilities: Tables, grills, vault toilets, drinking water (in season), picnic shelter.
Fee per night: $$.
Management: Forest Service.
Contact: 541-549-2111.
Finding the campground: From Sisters, go west on U.S. Highway 20 for 9.3 miles, turn right (north) onto paved Forest Road 14, and follow it for 6 miles. Turn left onto FR 1419 at the sign for Camp Sherman, go 0.2 mile, and turn right onto paved FR 900 (signed for campgrounds). Go 1.5 miles to reach this camp on the left.

About the campground: For tent campers, this area offers a pleasant stay along the Metolius River. Sites are spread across a shrub and meadow flat beneath ponderosa pines, firs, and larches. On the opposite shore, a few cabins overlook the river. The rustic stone and log picnic shelter is an attractive camp structure. You may well want to try your hand at fly fishing. The campground is open year-round, but there are no services provided after the summer season.

61 Pioneer Ford

Location: About 22 miles northwest of Sisters.
Sites: 18 basic sites, 2 walk-in sites; no hookups.
Maximum length: 40 feet.
Facilities: Tables, grills, vault toilets, drinking water, picnic shelter.
Fee per night: $$.
Management: Forest Service.
Contact: 541-549-2111.
Finding the campground: From Sisters, go west on U.S. Highway 20 for 9.3 miles, turn right (north) onto paved Forest Road 14, and follow it for 12.6 miles to this campground on the left.

About the campground: Part of the Metolius River line-up of popular family campgrounds, Pioneer Ford provides convenient access to fly fishing, riverside trails, the Wizard Falls Fish Hatchery, the Head of the Metolius (the originating spring for this spectacular river), and other area attractions. The sites occupy an attractive flat cloaked in cedars, firs, and pines. The campground is open from May to October.

Head of the Metolius River.

62 Round Lake

Location: About 19 miles northwest of Sisters, on Round Lake.
Sites: 5 basic sites; no hookups.
Maximum length: Tents and small units only.
Facilities: A few tables and grills, pit toilet, primitive boat launch. No drinking water.
Fee per night: None.
Management: Forest Service.
Contact: 541-549-2111.
Finding the campground: From U.S. Highway 20, 12 miles west of Sisters and 7.5 miles east of Santiam Pass, head north on paved Forest Road 12 (Jack Lake Road). Go 1.1 miles and bear left on gravel FR 1210 toward Round Lake. Drive 5.6 miles farther to reach the camp.

About the campground: This primitive campground sits on the shore of Round Lake, a shallow mountain lake with views across the water of Three Fingered Jack. Rough dirt roads access the no-frills sites, which are set in a semi-open forest of firs and pines. Alders, willows, and dogwoods rim the lake. Angling and non-motorized boating are the diversions at Round Lake. From the camp vicinity (0.8 mile past the camp on FR 1210), trails lead to Long and Square Lakes and into the splendor of the Mount Jefferson Wilderness. If you plan to hike, before heading to the camp, be sure to acquire a trail park pass at the Sisters Ranger District office or one of the outlets in town; the self-register wilderness permits are typically available at the trailhead.

63 Sheep Springs Horse Camp

Location: About 22 miles northwest of Sisters.
Sites: 10 basic sites; no hookups.
Maximum length: 30 feet.
Facilities: Tables, grills, pit toilets, drinking water (creek for livestock), 40 box stalls (4 per site).
Fee per night: $.
Management: Forest Service.
Contact: 541-549-2111; 541-882-3799 for reservations (which are required).
Finding the campground: From U.S. Highway 20, 12 miles west of Sisters, 7.5 miles east of Santiam Pass, turn north onto Forest Road 12 and follow it for 7.9 miles (FR 12 begins paved but becomes gravel). Turn left onto FR 1260, go 1.1 miles, and turn right onto FR 1260.200. Go another 1.3 miles to the campground entrance on the right.

About the campground: Set aside for the exclusive use of people camping with horses, this campground offers a pleasant, quiet stay in a forest of ponderosa pines and mixed firs. A pole fence separates the camp from Sheep Springs Meadow. Across the road from the camp is the Metolius-Windigo Trail, on which long-distance rides are possible. Deer seeking stray wisps of hay sometimes venture into the camp. The campground is open from May to October.

64 Sisters City Park

Location: In Sisters.
Sites: 60 basic sites, some hike/bike-in sites; no hookups.
Maximum length: 40 feet.
Facilities: Some tables, flush toilets, drinking water, telephone.
Fee per night: $.
Management: City of Sisters.
Contact: 541-549-6022.
Finding the campground: The camp is on the south side of U.S. Highway 20 at the east end of Sisters, just west of the junction of US 20 and Oregon 126 East.

About the campground: This campground occupies a scenic pine flat on the east shore of Squaw Creek; a day-use area claims the west shore. Beneath the big pines, you will find lawn or natural vegetation. The park is convenient for travelers and a fine base from which to explore Sisters, a picturesque little town (ideal for strolling), with frontier storefronts, galleries, shops, and eateries. Sisters rests in the heart of one of the state's most prized recreational areas. From the camp you can easily get to Bend, Smith Rock State Park, Tam McArthur Rim, the Metolius River, the McKenzie River, McKenzie Pass, and the Three Sisters and Mount Washington Wilderness Areas. The campground is open from April 15 to mid-October.

65 Sisters Cow Camp Horse Camp

Location: About 4 miles southwest of Sisters.
Sites: 5 basic sites; no hookups.
Maximum length: 40 feet.
Facilities: Tables, grills, pit toilets, spring water for horses only, large central corral, loading ramp. Bring drinking water.
Fee per night: None.
Management: Forest Service.
Contact: 541-549-2111.
Finding the campground: From Sisters, go west on Oregon 242 for 1.3 miles and turn left (southwest) onto Forest Road 15, a paved and gravel route. Follow it for 2.4 miles and turn left to enter the camp in 0.2 mile.

About the campground: Located on a broad, grassy flat with mature ponderosa pines, the sites of this horse camp encircle a large, partitioned corral. In the 1920s, this camp was a cattle roundup and shipping site; hence the awkward name. The long-distance Metolius-Windigo Trail passes the camp. The campground is open from May to October.

66 Smiling River

Location: About 17 miles northwest of Sisters.
Sites: 38 basic sites; no hookups.
Maximum length: 40 feet.
Facilities: Tables, grills, vault toilets, drinking water (in season).
Fee per night: $$.
Management: Forest Service.
Contact: 541-549-2111.
Finding the campground: From Sisters, go west on U.S. Highway 20 for 9.3 miles, turn right (north) onto paved Forest Road 14, and follow it for 6 miles. Turn left onto FR 1419 at the sign for Camp Sherman, go 0.2 mile, and turn right onto paved FR 900 (signed for campgrounds). Go 1 mile to reach this camp on the left.

About the campground: Of the string of Metolius River camps, this one is well suited for large RVs and trailers. It has many pull-thru sites and offers attractive riverside stays beneath some lovely ponderosa pines. A beautiful meadow and some privately owned cabins are across the glassy river. Standing hip-deep in the river, fly fishers tempt the wild fish with their dancing lines and arsenal of flies. The campground is open year-round, but there are no services provided after te summer season.

67 South Shore

Location: About 14 miles northwest of Sisters, on Suttle Lake.
Sites: 38 basic sites; no hookups.
Maximum length: 30 feet.

Facilities: Tables, grills, vault toilets, drinking water, boat dock, launch, fish-cleaning station.
Fee per night: $$.
Management: Forest Service.
Contact: 541-549-2111; 1-800-280-CAMP for reservations.
Finding the campground: From U.S. Highway 20, 13 miles west of Sisters, 6.5 miles east of Santiam Pass, head south on paved Forest Road 2070 toward Suttle and Blue Lakes (the east access road). Go 1.1 miles to reach this campground on the right.

About the campground: On the south shore of Suttle Lake—a huge, natural lake in a scenic, tree-lined basin—this campground offers the full gamut of water fun. The midday sun can pierce through the canopy of tall firs and big ponderosa pines, but generally campsites enjoy good shade throughout the day. There are paved roads through the camp and gravel or paved parking pads. Lakeside sites are snapped up quickly. Boating, fishing, waterskiing, and swimming, as well as hiking the 3.25-mile Shoreline Trail and just relaxing at camp, should keep everyone in the family happy. To escape having to battle the afternoon winds, shore anglers will want to rise early.

68 Three Creek Lake

Location: 16 miles southwest of Sisters, on Three Creek Lake.
Sites: 10 basic sites; no hookups.
Maximum length: 25 feet.
Facilities: Tables, grills, vault toilets. No drinking water.
Fee per night: $.
Management: Forest Service.
Contact: 541-549-2111.
Finding the campground: From U.S. Highway 20 in Sisters, go south at the sign for Three Creek Lake on South Elm, which later becomes Forest Road 16. Go 16 miles to the campground. The final 1.9 miles are on gravel.

About the campground: Sandwiched between Three Creek Lake and Tam McArthur Rim, this campground sits in the shadow of the towering rim in a setting of firs, mountain hemlocks, and lodgepole pines. Wildflowers speckle the grassy lakeshore. This popular camp offers quiet lake recreation and superb hiking to the top of Tam McArthur Rim, from which there are dizzying views and access to Broken Top. Clark's nutcrackers may visit the treetops. Mosquitoes can be annoying. A tiny, rustic store near the camp entrance sells tackle and bait and rents rowboats. The campground is open from July to mid-September.

69 Three Creek Meadow

Location: About 15 miles southwest of Sisters.
Sites: 11 basic sites; adjacent horse camp with 9 sites; no hookups.
Maximum length: 40 feet.

Facilities: Tables, grills, vault toilets, corrals at horse camp. No drinking water.
Fee per night: $.
Management: Forest Service.
Contact: 541-549-2111.
Finding the campground: From U.S. Highway 20 in Sisters, head south at the sign for Three Creek Lake on South Elm, which later becomes Forest Road 16. Go 14.7 miles to enter the family campground, 14.9 miles to enter the horse camp. The final mile is not paved.

About the campground: This dual campground sits among the lodgepole pines on the fringe of Three Creek Meadow. Deep, sparkling streams thread through the wildflower-dressed meadow. Tam McArthur Rim looms to the south, retaining its snow for much of the year. It makes for a striking view at times with its halo of clouds. At the camp, shade is limited and mosquitoes can be a bother. An open flat serves large camp rigs. Hiking, horseback riding, and fishing engage visitors. The shops, galleries, and eateries of Sisters may also lure you back. The campground is open from July to mid-September.

70 Whispering Pines Horse Camp

Location: About 10 miles southwest of Sisters.
Sites: 9 basic sites; no hookups.
Maximum length: 40 feet.
Facilities: Tables, grills, vault toilets, 4-horse corrals. No drinking water.
Fee per night: $.
Management: Forest Service.
Contact: 541-549-2111.
Finding the campground: From Sisters, go west on Oregon 242 for 5.7 miles and turn left (south) onto gravel Forest Road 1018 toward Whispering Pines. Continue 4.3 miles and turn left onto FR 1520. Drive another 0.2 mile to the campground entrance on the left.

About the campground: This equestrian camp has a meadow floor with an open stand of mature ponderosa pines and a punctuation of clustered firs. The sites are large, comfortable, and functional. Trout Creek flows past the camp. Contact the Sisters Ranger District about horse trails in the area. The campground is open from mid-May through mid-October.

PRINEVILLE AREA

	Hookup sites	Total sites	Max. RV length	Hookups	Toilets	Showers	Drinking water	Dump station	Recreation	Fee	Can reserve
71 Allen Creek Horse Camp		5	24		NF				FR		
72 Antelope Flat Reservoir		25	30		NF				FBL	$	
73 Big Bend Recreation Site		20	25		NF				FBL		
74 Big Springs		6	20		NF						
75 Castle Rock Recreation Site		6	35		NF				F	$-$$	
76 Chimney Rock Recreation Site		20	24		NF		•		HF	$-$$	
77 Cobble Rock Recreation Site		15	25		NF				F	$-$$	
78 Crook County RV Park	81	90	40	WES	F	•	•	•	F	$-$$	•
79 Deep Creek		6	24		NF				F		
80 Devil's Post Pile Recreation Site		8	25		NF				F	$-$$	
81 Dry Creek Horse Camp		5	small		NF				HR		
82 Elkhorn		4	24		NF						
83 Lone Pine Recreation Site		8	25		NF				F	$-$$	
84 Lower Palisades Recreation Site		15	35		NF				F	$-$$	
85 Mud Springs		4	20		NF				HR		
86 Ochoco Forest Camp		6	24		NF		•		HF	$	
87 Ochoco Lake Crook County Park		22	35		F		•		FBL	$$	
88 Poison Butte Recreation Site		6	T		NF				F	$	
89 Prineville Reservoir State Park: Main	45	70	40	WES	F	•	•		SFBL	$$-$$$	•
90 Prineville Reservoir State Park: Jasper Point		29	30		NF		•		SFBL	$$	•
91 Stillwater Recreation Site		11	35		NF				F	$-$$	
92 Sugar Creek		17	24		NF		•			$	
93 Walton Lake		30	30		NF		•		HSFBL	$	
94 Wildcat		17	30		NF		•		HF	$	
95 Wiley Flat		5	24		NF						
96 Wolf Creek		11	24		NF					$	

Hookups: W = Water E = Electric S = Sewer **Total sites:** T = Tent-only campground **Maximum trailer/RV length** given in feet.
Toilets: F = Flush NF = No Flush **Recreation:** H = Hiking S = Swimming F = Fishing B = Boating L = Boat Launch
O = Off-Highway Driving R = Horseback Riding C = Cycling
Fee: $ = $1-9 $$ = $10-19 $$$ = $20-29 $$$$ = $30-39. If no entry under **Fee,** camping is free.

71 Allen Creek Horse Camp

Location: About 44 miles east of Prineville.
Sites: 5 basic sites; no hookups.
Maximum length: 24 feet.
Facilities: Tables, grills, vault toilet, corrals. No drinking water.
Fee per night: None.
Management: Forest Service.
Contact: 541-416-6645.

Finding the campground: From Prineville, go east on U.S. Highway 26 about 17 miles and bear right (northeast) on Ochoco Creek Road/Forest Road 22. Follow it 27 miles to enter the camp on the right.

About the campground: The campground is set up to serve people camping with horses. It is situated in an attractive ponderosa-pine forest along Allen Creek, a picturesque waterway and complement to the camp. The rustic corrals blend with the setting; the old roads leading from the camp invite exploration. Water for stock is available, but you will need to bring water for your own drinking and cooking. The campground is open from May 1 to October 31.

72 Antelope Flat Reservoir

Location: About 44 miles southeast of Prineville, on Antelope Flat Reservoir.
Sites: 25 basic sites; no hookups.
Maximum length: 30 feet.
Facilities: Tables, grills, vault toilets, boat launch. No drinking water.
Fee per night: $.
Management: Forest Service.
Contact: 541-416-6500.
Finding the campground: From the junction of Main Street and U.S. Highway 26 in Prineville, go east on US 26 for 1 mile and turn right (south) toward Paulina on North Combs Flat Road (which becomes Paulina Highway). Go 30.2 miles, turn right onto gravel Forest Road 17, and stay on it. After 10.1 miles, FR 17 turns left onto FR 16, only to quickly veer right away from it. The campground is 2.8 miles farther on FR 17.

About the campground: You will find this campground in a forest of ponderosa pines, junipers, and bunchgrass above Antelope Flat Reservoir. Canoes and fishing boats ply the lake, which is rimmed by low hills clad in pine and sage. Sites have defined parking; those closer to the water tend to be more closely spaced. Paths lead to the shore and to a boat ramp. The camp is generally relaxing, unless it is a bad mosquito season. The campground is open from May 1 to October 31.

73 Big Bend Recreation Site

Location: 19 miles south of Prineville.
Sites: About 20 informal, basic sites; no hookups.
Maximum length: 25 feet.
Facilities: Primitive fire rings, chemical toilets, boat launch (at Prineville Reservoir). No drinking water.
Fee per night: None.
Management: Bureau of Land Management.
Contact: 541-416-6700 (Bureau of Land Management).
Finding the campground: From U.S. Highway 26 in Prineville, head south on Main Street/Oregon 27 (the Crooked River Highway, a BLM Back Country

Byway) and proceed 19 miles to the unmarked turnoff for the camp. Veer downhill to the right on a rough, dirt road that is for dry weather use only.

About the campground: At this primitive recreation site on the Crooked River below Prineville Reservoir, dirt roads lead to previously used camp spots among the junipers. Campers here have easy access to the river for fishing and to the reservoir (1.2 miles upstream) for both fishing and boating. The reservoir looks its best when it is full, blue, and reflecting its arid surroundings. Because of the rough, dirt access road, this recreation site is probably best suited to tent campers and day users, but some RVers still make their way here. Fires and smoking are prohibited from June 1 to October 15.

74 Big Springs

Location: About 55 miles east of Prineville.
Sites: 6 basic sites; no hookups.
Maximum length: 20 feet.
Facilities: A few tables and crude fire rings, pit toilets. No drinking water.
Fee per night: None.
Management: Forest Service.
Contact: 541-477-3713; 541-416-6643.
Finding the campground: From Prineville, go east on U.S. Highway 26 about 17 miles and bear right (northeast) on Ochoco Creek Road/Forest Road 22. Follow it 8 miles to the Ochoco Ranger Station. From there, go east on FR 42 for 28 miles and turn left onto FR 4270. Go 1.5 miles more and turn left onto FR 100 to reach the camp in another 0.1 mile.

About the campground: At this primitive camp, you can recline in a mixed setting of pine forest and meadow and enjoy nature's peace. Wildflowers decorate the meadow, but there are very few parking options for large units when the meadow periphery is wet. The camp's remote locale serves hunters well. The campground is open from May 1 to October 31.

75 Castle Rock Recreation Site

Location: About 12 miles south of Prineville.
Sites: 6 basic sites; no hookups.
Maximum length: 35 feet.
Facilities: Tables, grills, pit toilets. No drinking water.
Fee per night: $ to $$.
Management: Bureau of Land Management.
Contact: 541-416-6700.
Finding the campground: From U.S. Highway 26 in Prineville, head south on Main Street/Oregon 27 (the Crooked River Highway, a BLM Back Country Byway). Proceed 12.3 miles to the camp.

About the campground: Where the Crooked River Canyon broadens, you will find this camp, which is a little drier and sunnier than its upstream counterparts.

Here, the west canyon wall is arid, with an uneven rim; the east canyon wall parades exciting rock features. A single pull-thru site accommodates large units. Fishing is popular. Fires and smoking are prohibited from June 1 to October 15. The campground is open year-round.

76 Chimney Rock Recreation Site

Location: 16 miles south of Prineville.
Sites: 20 basic sites; no hookups.
Maximum length: 24 feet.
Facilities: Tables, vault toilets, drinking water, fishing dock for individuals with disabilities.
Fee per night: $ to $$.
Management: Bureau of Land Management.
Contact: 541-416-6700.
Finding the campground: From U.S. Highway 26 in Prineville, head south on Main Street/Oregon 27 (the Crooked River Highway, a BLM Back Country Byway) and proceed 16 miles to the camp on the right.

About the campground: A fishing dock is center stage at this campground on the Crooked Wild and Scenic River. RVers will likely prefer the upstream end of the camp, which has a broad, gravel parking lot for easy parking. The sites downstream tend to be fairly short, although a few near the turnaround loop are fine for RVs. Swallows nest in the cliffs across the river, and Chimney Rock looms above the camp. You may want to lace on your hiking boots for a closer inspection; the trailhead is across the road from the camp. The Rim Trail travels 1.4 miles and gains 500 feet to reach the saddle of Chimney Rock. From this lofty perspective, you can admire the Central Cascades, the Crooked River, the camp, and the stunning river canyon. Fires and smoking are prohibited from June 1 to October 15. The campground is open year-round.

77 Cobble Rock Recreation Site

Location: 17 miles south of Prineville.
Sites: 15 basic sites; no hookups.
Maximum length: 25 feet.
Facilities: Tables, grills, pit toilets. No drinking water.
Fee per night: $ to $$.
Management: Bureau of Land Management.
Contact: 541-416-6700.
Finding the campground: From U.S. Highway 26 in Prineville, head south on Main Street/Oregon 27 (the Crooked River Highway, a BLM Back Country Byway) and proceed 17 miles to the camp.

About the campground: This campground on the Crooked River has gravel roads and defined road-shoulder or pullout parking. While there are fire rings at this recreation site and the other camps along the river, a strict ban on fires and smoking is in effect from June 1 to October 15 to protect this fragile, dry canyon. Junipers dot the tiered camp, and a few ponderosa pines grow closer to the river. Views include nearby Chimney Rock, columnar buttes and crests, and a palisades just across the river from the camp. When the fish are not biting, you can hike the Rim Trail to Chimney Rock. The trailhead is 1 mile north, across OR 27 from Chimney Rock Recreation Site. The campground is open year-round.

78 Crook County RV Park

Location: In Prineville.
Sites: 81 hookup sites, 9 tent sites, 2 bunkhouses; water, electric, sewer, and cable TV hookups.
Maximum length: 40 feet.
Facilities: Flush toilets, drinking water, showers, dump station, telephone, playground at nearby Crooked River Park.
Fee per night: $ to $$.
Management: Crook County.
Contact: 541-447-2599; 1-800-609-2599 for reservations.
Finding the campground: From U.S. Highway 26 in Prineville, head south on Main Street/Oregon 27 at the sign for the fairgrounds. Go 0.5 mile and turn left to enter the RV park.

About the campground: This comfortable RV park is ideal for campers attending fairground events or sightseeing in Prineville. It has formal tent pads and long, paved parking spaces. Families or groups can rent the bunkhouses. The young trees in the camp have yet to provide much shade, but there are some big cottonwoods and weeping willows in the neighborhood. Following OR 27 south offers a scenic drive on the Crooked River BLM Back Country Byway. Crooked River Park, across the road from the camp, has a playground and offers fishing. The campground is open year-round.

79 Deep Creek

Location: About 50 miles east of Prineville.
Sites: 6 basic sites; no hookups.
Maximum length: 24 feet.
Facilities: Tables, grills, vault toilet. No drinking water.
Fee per night: None.
Management: Forest Service.
Contact: 541-416-6645.
Finding the campground: From Prineville, go east on U.S. Highway 26 about 17 miles and bear right (northeast) on Ochoco Creek Road/Forest Road 22. Follow it 8 miles to the Ochoco Ranger Station. From there, go east on FR 42 for 24 miles and turn right into the camp.

About the campground: Located along the North Fork Crooked River near its confluence with Deep Creek, this rustic camp boasts many big, yellow-bellied pines. The sites enjoy a mix of sun and shade, and most have tables and grills. The river calls to anglers, while the casual rock collector can usually discover an agate or two among the cobbles on the shore. The campground is open from May 1 to October 31.

80 Devil's Post Pile Recreation Site

Location: About 18 miles south of Prineville.
Sites: 8 basic sites; no hookups.
Maximum length: 25 feet.
Facilities: Tables, grills, pit toilets. No drinking water.
Fee per night: $ to $$.
Management: Bureau of Land Management.
Contact: 541-416-6700.
Finding the campground: From U.S. Highway 26 in Prineville, head south on Main Street/Oregon 27 (the Crooked River Highway, a BLM Back Country Byway) and proceed 17.5 miles to the camp.

About the campground: This camp sits amid the junipers at a bend in the Crooked River. It has back-in and pull-thru sites. Camp guests while away their time fishing, relaxing, and admiring the canyon setting. Fires and smoking are prohibited from June 1 to October 15. The campground is open year-round.

81 Dry Creek Horse Camp

Location: About 17 miles northeast of Prineville.
Sites: 5 basic sites; no hookups.
Maximum length: Tents and small RV units.
Facilities: Tables, grills, pit toilet, corrals. No drinking water.
Fee per night: None.
Management: Forest Service.
Contact: 541-416-6500.
Finding the campground: From Prineville, go east on U.S. Highway 26 for 9 miles and turn left onto Mill Creek Road/Forest Road 33. Go 5 miles, turn left onto FR 3370, and continue another 2.4 miles. Turn left onto FR 200 and go 0.1 mile to the camp. The road into the camp is not suitable for large RVs.

About the campground: Established for the equestrian camper, this facility offers convenient, serviceable sites in a forest of pines and firs near Brennan Palisades. There are rustic pole corrals and split-rail fences. Dry Creek is across the road, as is the Giddy-Up-Go Trail, a 12-mile loop ride. The campground is open from April 15 through November.

82 Elkhorn

Location: About 38 miles southeast of Prineville.
Sites: 4 basic sites; no hookups.
Maximum length: 24 feet.
Facilities: Tables, some grills, pit toilets. No drinking water.
Fee per night: None.
Management: Forest Service.
Contact: 541-416-6500.
Finding the campground: From the Paulina Highway, 33 miles east of Prineville; 23 miles west of Paulina, head south on gravel Drake Creek Road/Forest Road 16 and go 4.5 miles to this campground on the left. Although the turnoff is unmarked, the camp is visible from FR 16.

About the campground: Encircled by a rail fence is this small rustic camp in a pine-meadow setting. Arnica and wild roses add seasonal color to the meadow. Hunters and agate collectors sometimes make use of this peaceful outpost. The campground is open from May 1 to October 31.

83 Lone Pine Recreation Site

Location: About 14 miles south of Prineville.
Sites: 8 basic sites; no hookups.
Maximum length: 25 feet.
Facilities: Tables, grills, pit toilets. No drinking water.
Fee per night: $ to $$.
Management: Bureau of Land Management.
Contact: 541-416-6700.
Finding the campground: From U.S. Highway 26 in Prineville, head south on Main Street/Oregon 27 (the Crooked River Highway, a BLM Back Country Byway) and proceed 14.3 miles to camp.

About the campground: This is one of several BLM camps on the east bank of the Crooked River. Lone Pine is set mainly among junipers, although a ponderosa pine here and there lends credence to the camp name. The canyon crest shapes a beautiful skyline. The sites have defined parking, and there is direct fishing access from the camp. Fires and smoking are prohibited from June 1 to October 15. The campground is open year-round.

84 Lower Palisades Recreation Site

Location: About 15 miles south of Prineville.
Sites: 15 basic sites; no hookups.
Maximum length: 35 feet.
Facilities: Tables, fireplaces, vault toilets, 2 small fishing docks for individuals with disabilities. No drinking water.
Fee per night: $ to $$.

Management: Bureau of Land Management.

Contact: 541-416-6700.

Finding the campground: From U.S. Highway 26 in Prineville, head south on Main Street/Oregon 27 (the Crooked River Highway, a BLM Back Country Byway) and proceed 15.3 miles to this riverside camp.

About the campground: This is one of the more developed campgrounds along the Crooked Wild and Scenic River. The sites are well spaced and have good river access, and the junipers create at least some shade at each site. Across the river from the camp rise the bulging, cobbled, palisade cliffs. A barrier-free trail accesses the fishing docks. There is a ban on smoking and fires along the river corridor from June 1 to October 15. The campground is open year-round.

85 Mud Springs

Location: About 87 miles east of Prineville.

Sites: 3 basic sites, 1 horse campsite; no hookups.

Maximum length: 20 feet.

Facilities: Tables, vault toilets, rustic rope corral at horse campsite. No drinking water.

Fee per night: None.

Management: Forest Service.

Contact: 541-477-3713; 541-416-6643.

Finding the campground: From Paulina (56 miles southeast of Prineville), go east on County Road 112 (the Paulina Highway toward Suplee) for 4.2 miles. Turn left onto gravel CR 113/Forest Road 58 and stay on FR 58 (a paved and gravel route) for 20 miles. Turn left onto FR 5840. Go another 6 miles, turn right onto FR 5840.400, and proceed 0.7 mile to the camp.

About the campground: This serene but primitive campground on the southeast flank of Wolf Mountain will appeal to the escapist. It enjoys a setting of big meadows and big pines and allows campers to spread out. False hellebore, widow grass, buttercup, wyethia, violet, and larkspur color the meadow. The dirt roads of the camp can be very rutted; avoid this camp during wet weather. Forest Service Trail 821, the South Prong Trail, provides hiker and horse access to the Black Canyon Wilderness. Hunters use this camp in the fall. The campground is open from May 1 to October 31.

86 Ochoco Forest Camp

Location: About 25 miles northeast of Prineville.

Sites: 6 basic sites; no hookups.

Maximum length: 24 feet.

Facilities: Tables, grills, vault toilet, drinking water, log picnic shelter.

Fee per night: $.

Management: Forest Service.

Contact: 541-416-6645.

Finding the campground: From Prineville, go east on U.S. Highway 26 about 17 miles, bear right on paved Ochoco Creek Road/Forest Road 22, and proceed 8 miles to this campground, which is adjacent to Ochoco Ranger Station.

About the campground: This quiet little camp sits beside pretty Ochoco Creek, which cuts a deep groove through a brushy meadow as it meanders past the camp. Ponderosa pines and alders frame the sites and are interspersed with native grasses and shrubs. Across the road from the camp starts the Lookout Mountain Trail, which leads past magnificent old-growth ponderosa pines and through grasslands decorated with iris in the spring to attain a superb Ochoco Forest vantage atop Lookout Mountain. The campground is open from mid-May to October.

87 Ochoco Lake Crook County Park

Location: 7 miles east of Prineville.
Sites: 22 basic sites, some hike/bike sites; no hookups.
Maximum length: 35 feet.
Facilities: Tables, grills, flush toilets, drinking water, boat launch, fish-cleaning station.
Fee per night: $$.
Management: Crook County.
Contact: 541-447-1209.
Finding the campground: From Prineville, go east on U.S. Highway 26 for 7 miles to reach the park on the right.

About the campground: This park features groomed lawns shaded by junipers on a slope above Ochoco Reservoir, which is open for recreation. Fishing and boating are the chief attractions. Arid, juniper-dotted tablelands and hills shape the basin and view. Blacktop trails allow short strolls along the lake. The campground is open year-round.

88 Poison Butte Recreation Site

Location: About 18 miles south of Prineville.
Sites: 6 tent sites; no hookups.
Maximum length: Suitable for tents only.
Facilities: Tables, fire rings, pit toilets. No drinking water.
Fee per night: $.
Management: Bureau of Land Management.
Contact: 541-416-6700.
Finding the campground: From U.S. Highway 26 in Prineville, head south on Main Street/Oregon 27 (the Crooked River Highway, a BLM Back Country Byway) and go 18.2 miles to the camp.

About the campground: This is one of the smaller camps along the Crooked River. Like others in the area, it is set in a juniper forest, but some big ponderosa pines loom across the river. The river here slows, broadens, and grows shallow enough that anglers can wade across it. White rocks and grassy banks complement the green water, and geese and herons sometimes favor the area with a visit. Fires and smoking are prohibited from June 1 to October 15. The campground is open year-round.

89 Prineville Reservoir State Park: Main

Location: About 16 miles southeast of Prineville, on Prineville Reservoir.
Sites: 45 full or partial hookup sites, 25 basic sites; water, electric, and sewer hookups.
Maximum length: 40 feet.
Facilities: Tables, grills, flush toilets, drinking water, showers, telephone, boat launch, docks, fish-cleaning station.
Fee per night: $$ to $$$.
Management: Oregon State Parks and Recreation Department.
Contact: 541-447-4363; 1-800-452-5687 for reservations.
Finding the campground: From the junction of Main Street and U.S. Highway 26 in Prineville, go east on US 26 for 1 mile, turn right (south) onto North Combs Flat Road, and follow it for 1.2 miles. Turn right onto Juniper Canyon Road and continue 13 miles to a junction. Go right and drive 0.7 mile more to reach the main campground.

About the campground: This developed camp is located on a juniper-canyon slope above Prineville Reservoir; some sites overlook the water and most receive a mix of sun and shade. Noise from the speedboats and jet skis carries across the water, but these recreational activities are among the reasons folks come to the park. Fishing and swimming are two of the quieter pursuits. Big Island adds to the view of this vast, sparkling lake. The campground is open year-round.

90 Prineville Reservoir State Park: Jasper Point

Location: About 18 miles southeast of Prineville, on Prineville Reservoir.
Sites: 29 basic sites; no hookups.
Maximum length: 30 feet.
Facilities: Tables, grills, vault toilets, drinking water, boat launch.
Fee per night: $$.
Management: Oregon State Parks and Recreation Department.
Contact: 541-447-4363; 1-800-452-5687 for reservations.
Finding the campground: From the junction of Main Street and U.S. Highway 26 in Prineville, go east on US 26 for 1 mile, turn right (south) onto North Combs Flat Road, and follow it for 1.2 miles. Turn right onto Juniper Canyon Road and continue 13 miles to a junction. Bear left and go another 2.5 miles to Jasper Point.

About the campground: Set apart from the developed portion of the state park, this camp claims another sun-basked, juniper-studded slope above Prineville Reservoir. It offers direct access to the lake for fishing, boating, waterskiing, and jet skiing. All sites have gravel parking pads; some will require more leveling of the RV than others. The lake boasts excellent fishing, and in this hot climate, swimming is popular. The campground is open year-round.

91 Stillwater Recreation Site

Location: About 13 miles south of Prineville.
Sites: 11 basic sites; no hookups.
Maximum length: 35 feet.
Facilities: Tables, grills, vault toilets. No drinking water.
Fee per night: $ to $$.
Management: Bureau of Land Management.
Contact: 541-416-6700.
Finding the campground: From U.S. Highway 26 in Prineville, head south on Main Street/Oregon 27 (the Crooked River Highway, a BLM Back Country Byway) and go 13.2 miles to the camp.

About the campground: Reached by way of a scenic byway and located along a slow stretch of the Crooked River, you will find this camp cradled between canyon walls of differing character: one rock, the other juniper-grassland. Fishing and water play may engage you, although probably not at the same time. To protect the arid canyon habitat, a ban on fires and smoking is in effect from June 1 to October 15. The campground is open year-round.

92 Sugar Creek

Location: About 70 miles east of Prineville.
Sites: 17 basic sites; no hookups.
Maximum length: 24 feet.
Facilities: Tables, grills, vault toilets, drinking water, barrier-free trail to creek.
Fee per night: $.
Management: Forest Service.
Contact: 541-477-3713; 541-416-6643.
Finding the campground: From Paulina (56 miles southeast of Prineville), go east on County Road 112 (the Paulina Highway toward Suplee) for 4.2 miles. Turn left onto gravel CR 113/Forest Road 58 and continue 8.5 miles to the campground entrance on the right side of FR 58.

About the campground: You will find this relaxing campground in an attractive forest of ponderosa pines on the banks of Sugar Creek. The warbling of songbirds and the telegraphic knocking of woodpeckers are likely to accompany your stay here. Bald eagles have a winter roost nearby. Split-rail fences add charm to the scene, and a barrier-free trail allows for creek viewing. The campground is open from May 1 to October 31.

93 Walton Lake

Location: About 32 miles northeast of Prineville, on Walton Lake.
Sites: 30 basic sites; no hookups.
Maximum length: 30 feet.
Facilities: Tables, grills, vault toilet, drinking water, boat ramp (electric motors permitted but no gas motors), swimming area, barrier-free fishing pier.
Fee per night: $.
Management: Forest Service.
Contact: 541-416-6645.
Finding the campground: From Prineville, go east on U.S. Highway 26 about 17 miles, bear right on paved Ochoco Creek Road/Forest Road 22, and proceed another 15 miles, following the signs to locate this campground.

About the campground: This popular campground is located along the shore of Walton Lake, a former mountain meadow that was transformed into a quiet mountain lake by a small earthen dam. Campsites dot the ponderosa-pine forest on the north and south shores; site parking is either on the roadside or on spurs. The lake is stocked with trout three times each summer, so the fishing is usually pretty good. Quiet boating, swimming, hiking the lakeside trail, watching the antics of otter or muskrat, and just relaxing in camp are other potential activities. The camp also contains a trailhead for the Round Mountain National Recreation Trail, for a more challenging hike. The campground is open from late May to late September.

94 Wildcat

Location: About 19 miles northeast of Prineville.
Sites: 17 basic sites; no hookups.
Maximum length: 30 feet.
Facilities: Tables, grills, vault toilets, drinking water.
Fee per night: $.
Management: Forest Service.
Contact: 541-416-6500.
Finding the campground: From Prineville, go east on U.S. Highway 26 for 9 miles and turn left (north) onto Mill Creek Road/Forest Road 33. Drive another 10.4 miles to the campground entrance on the right. Part of the route is on gravel.

About the campground: A gateway to Mill Creek Wilderness, this popular camp sits beside East Fork Mill Creek on a flat cloaked in firs and ponderosa pines. The East Fork is your guide upstream into the wilderness, a wildflower showcase with areas of recovered burn, thriving forest, and the intriguing forked monolith of Twin Pillars. The trail crisscrosses the sparkling East Fork several times. Although there are often logs or stones, you may still have to ford the creek on occasion. Another fine rock destination is Steins Pillar. To reach its trailhead, go 4 miles south of the camp on FR 33, turn east onto FR 500, and go 2 miles. Steins Pillar is a 350-foot-tall, free-standing column of pinkish stone streaked with black. The campground is open from mid-April to late October.

95 Wiley Flat

Location: About 44 miles southeast of Prineville.
Sites: 5 basic sites; no hookups.
Maximum length: 24 feet.
Facilities: Tables, some grills, pit toilets. No drinking water.
Fee per night: None.
Management: Forest Service.
Contact: 541-416-6500.
Finding the campground: From the Paulina Highway, 33 miles east of Prineville, 23 miles west of Paulina, turn south on gravel Drake Creek Road/Forest Road 16, and go 10.4 miles. There, turn right onto FR 400 and follow the rough road 0.8 mile into the camp.

About the campground: Although this out-of-the-way camp does accommodate large vehicles, the rocky access road promises a rattling ride and the dirt roads in camp are impassable in wet weather. The headwater spring of Wiley Creek sends a silver thread through this quiet meadow dotted with mixed-age pines. Arnica, wild strawberry, wild geranium, violet, and cinquefoil are among the wildflower varieties here. Birds, filtered sunlight, and the rich vanilla scent of pines can contribute to the relaxing atmosphere. In the fall, hunters frequent this area. The campground is open from May 1 to October 31.

96 Wolf Creek

Location: About 70 miles east of Prineville.
Sites: 11 basic sites; no hookups.
Maximum length: 24 feet.
Facilities: Tables, grills, vault toilets. No drinking water.
Fee per night: $.
Management: Forest Service.
Contact: 541-477-3713; 541-416-6643.
Finding the campground: From Paulina (56 miles southeast of Prineville), go east on County Road 112 (the Paulina Highway toward Suplee) for 4.2 miles. Turn left onto gravel CR 113/Forest Road 58 and continue 7.2 miles to the junction of FR 58 and FR 42. Turn left onto FR 42 and go 1.7 miles. Enter the campground upon crossing the Wolf Creek bridge.

About the campground: A rustic, zigzagging rail fence wraps around this campground, which sits beside Wolf Creek in a meadow dotted with ponderosa pines. The murmur of the small, attractive creek is soothing. The campground is maintained from June to September.

BEND AREA

		Hookup sites	Total sites	Max. RV length	Hookups	Toilets	Showers	Drinking water	Dump station	Recreation	Fee	Can reserve
97	Big River		11	22		NF				FBL	$	
98	Bull Bend		12	12		NF				SFBL	$	
99	China Hat		14	30		NF		•				
100	Cow Meadow		21	20		NF				FBL	$	
101	Crane Prairie		146	40		NF		•		FBL	$$	
102	Cultus Corral Horse Camp		11	35		NF		•		R	$	•
103	Cultus Lake		55	22		NF		•		HSFBL	$$	
104	Deschutes Bridge		15	30		NF		•		F	$	
105	East Davis		33	40		NF		•		FB	$	
106	Elk Lake		23	25		NF		•		HSFBL	$	
107	Fall River		10	22		NF				F	$	
108	Gull Point		81	40		F		•	•	FBL	$$	
109	La Pine State Recreation Area	145	145	85	WES	F	•	•	•	HSFBL	$$	•
110	Lava Flow		12	22		NF				FBL		
111	Lava Lake		43	40		NF		•		HFBL	$$	
112	Little Cultus		20	30		NF		•		HFBL	$	
113	Little Fawn		12	25		NF		•		HFBL	$	
114	Little Lava Lake		10	22		NF		•		FBL	$	
115	Mallard Marsh		15	22		NF				FBL	$	
116	Newberry NVM: Chief Paulina Horse		14	30		NF				HFBR	$$	•
117	Newberry NVM: Cinder Hill		110	30		F		•		HFBL	$$	•
118	Newberry NVM: East Lake		29	30		F		•		HSFBL	$$	•
119	Newberry NVM: Hot Springs		52	30		NF		•		HFBL	$$	
120	Newberry NVM: Little Crater		50	30		NF		•		HFBL	$$	•
121	Newberry NVM: McKay Crossing		10	22		NF				HF	$	
122	Newberry NVM: Paulina Lake		69	30		NF		•		HFBL	$$	•
123	Newberry NVM: Prairie		16	30		NF		•		HF	$	•
124	North Davis Creek		17	25		NF		•		FBL	$	
125	North Twin		20	35		NF		•		HSFBL	$	
126	Point		10	22		NF				HSFBL	$	
127	Pringle Falls		6	22		NF				FB	$	
128	Quinn Meadow Horse Camp		25	40		NF		•		HR	$$	•
129	Quinn River		41	40		NF		•		HFBL	$	
130	Reservoir		28	40		NF				FBL	$	
131	Rock Creek		31	40		NF		•		FBL	$	
132	Rosland		10	40		NF		•		F	$	
133	Sand Spring		6	18		NF				O		
134	Sheep Bridge		18	40		NF		•		FBL	$	
135	Soda Creek		7	20		NF				F		
136	South		23	40		NF				FBL	$	
137	South Twin		24	30		F		•		HSFBL	$$	
138	Swamp Wells Horse Camp		6	22		NF				HOR		
139	Tumalo State Park	22	87	44	WES	F	•	•		SF	$$–$$$	•
140	West Davis		25	22		NF		•		FBL	$	
141	West South Twin		24	30		F		•		HSFBL	$$	
142	Wickiup Butte		12	25		NF				FBL	$	

Hookups: W = Water E = Electric S = Sewer **Total sites:** T = Tent-only campground **Maximum trailer/RV length** given in feet.
Toilets: F = Flush NF = No Flush **Recreation:** H = Hiking S = Swimming F = Fishing B = Boating L = Boat Launch
O = Off-Highway Driving R = Horseback Riding C = Cycling
Fee: $ = $1-9 $$ = $10-19 $$$ = $20-29 $$$$ = $30-39. If no entry under **Fee**, camping is free.

97 Big River

Location: About 22 miles southwest of Bend.
Sites: 9 basic sites, 2 tent sites; no hookups.
Maximum length: 22 feet.
Facilities: Tables, grills, vault toilet, boat launch. No drinking water.
Fee per night: $.
Management: Forest Service.
Contact: 541-388-5664.
Finding the campground: From U.S. Highway 97, 17.5 miles south of Bend, 4.9 miles north of the turnoff for La Pine State Recreation Area, turn west for Fall River on Forest Road 42 (labeled Vandevert Road and then South Century Drive). Go 4.6 miles to the camp.

About the campground: This camp is shaded by lodgepole and small ponderosa pines. It overlooks a slow stretch of the Deschutes River. The forest floor is mostly needlemat and grass, interspersed with a few shrubs. The dirt access road can be rutted, so take it easy when entering the camp. Fishing is the main attraction here. The boat ramp is on the opposite side of FR 42. The campground is open from May to October.

98 Bull Bend

Location: About 37 miles southwest of Bend.
Sites: 12 basic sites; no hookups.
Maximum length: 12 feet.
Facilities: Tables, grills, vault toilets, boat launch. No drinking water.
Fee per night: $.
Management: Forest Service.
Contact: 541-388-5664.
Finding the campground: From U.S. Highway 97 at Wickiup Junction, 27 miles south of Bend, go west on County Road 43 for 8 miles. Turn left (south) onto gravel Forest Road 4370 and continue 1.5 miles to the camp.

About the campground: The Deschutes River makes a big horseshoe bend around the peninsula of ponderosa and lodgepole pines that houses this camp. The sites are mostly open; bitterbrush and currant grow beneath the trees. Fishing, swimming, canoeing, and rafting are among the most popular activities here. You can devise a short float trip around the camp peninsula by putting in at the upstream end of the river bend and taking out downstream. The campground is open from May to October.

99 China Hat

Location: About 65 miles southeast of Bend.
Sites: 14 basic sites; no hookups.
Maximum length: 30 feet.
Facilities: Tables, grills, vault toilets, drinking water.

Fee per night: None.
Management: Forest Service.
Contact: 541-388-5664.
Finding the campground: From U.S. Highway 97 at La Pine (about 30 miles south of Bend), head east on Forest Road 22. Go 26.4 miles, turn left (north) onto FR 18, and continue 5.9 miles to the camp entry road on the left.

About the campground: This primitive camp sits south of its namesake peak in a forest that has been greatly thinned to eliminate an insect infestation. The camp offers solitude and bird watching and serves the fall hunter. En route to camp, you will pass South Ice Cave; it is north off FR 22, 1.2 miles west of the intersection with FR 18. The campground is open from May into October.

100 Cow Meadow

Location: About 47 miles southwest of Bend, on Crane Prairie Reservoir.
Sites: 21 basic sites; no hookups.
Maximum length: 20 feet.
Facilities: Tables, grills, vault toilets, boat launch. No drinking water.
Fee per night: $.
Management: Forest Service.
Contact: 541-388-5664.
Finding the campground: From Bend, head southwest on Cascade Lakes Highway, which is also variously labeled Century Drive, County Road 46, or Forest Road 46, depending on jurisdiction. Go 45 miles and turn left onto FR 40. Go 0.4 mile and then turn right onto gravel FR 970. Continue 2 miles on FR 970 and FR 620. The campground entrance is on the right off FR 620 just after you cross the bridge over the Deschutes River.

About the campground: Along the Deschutes River where it feeds into Crane Prairie Reservoir, you will find this quiet camp among the lodgepole pines; a meadow floor spills between the trees. The sites are rustic and open. Boaters are restricted to a speed of 10 miles per hour, while anglers have a choice of dipping their line in the river or the reservoir. Ospreys commonly patrol over the water. The campground is open from May to mid-October.

101 Crane Prairie

Location: About 48 miles southwest of Bend, on Crane Prairie Reservoir.
Sites: 146 basic sites; no hookups.
Maximum length: 40 feet.
Facilities: Tables, grills, vault toilets, drinking water, 2 boat launches, dock, fish-cleaning station.
Fee per night: $$.
Management: Forest Service.
Contact: 541-388-5664.

Finding the campground: From U.S. Highway 97 at Wickiup Junction, 27 miles south of Bend, head west on County Road 43 and then Forest Road 42, traveling a total of 16.5 miles. Turn right (north) onto FR 4270 and proceed 4.2 miles to this camp on the left.

About the campground: The sites of this campground are distributed across a gentle slope of lodgepole pines above and along Crane Prairie Reservoir, which is noted for its nesting ospreys. Despite the size of this camp, the sites are nicely arranged for comfort, and they are partially or fully shaded by the mature trees. Views of the reservoir, its sculpted shore, Mount Bachelor, South Sister, and Broken Top will enhance your stay. Fishing, boating, birding, and relaxing will fill your days. The campground is open mid-April to mid-October.

102 Cultus Corral Horse Camp

Location: About 45 miles southwest of Bend.
Sites: 11 basic sites; no hookups.
Maximum length: 35 feet.
Facilities: Tables, grills, vault toilets, drinking water, community shelter, 4-horse corral at each site.
Fee per night: $.
Management: Forest Service.
Contact: 541-388-5664.
Finding the campground: From Bend, head southwest on Cascade Lakes Highway, which is also variously labeled Century Drive, County Road 46, or Forest Road 46, depending on jurisdiction. Go 45 miles, turn right onto gravel FR 4630, go 0.4 mile, and turn left to enter the camp.

About the campground: This horse camp rests in a cut-over forest of lodgepole pines near the Cultus River. The facility is one of a growing number in the state catering to equestrians. There is a trailhead in the camp, and other horse trails are a short drive away. Check with the Bend Ranger District about specific rides. This particular camp is sunny and dry, so you might want to bring a shade source. The campground is open from late May to mid-October.

103 Cultus Lake

Location: About 48 miles southwest of Bend, on Cultus Lake.
Sites: 55 basic sites; no hookups.
Maximum length: 22 feet.
Facilities: Tables, grills, vault toilets, drinking water, boat launch.
Fee per night: $$.
Management: Forest Service.
Contact: 541-388-5664.
Finding the campground: From Bend, head southwest on Cascade Lakes Highway, which is also variously labeled Century Drive, County Road 46, or Forest

Road 46, depending on jurisdiction. Go 46 miles, turn right onto FR 4635, and go 2 miles to enter the camp.

About the campground: This campground offers pleasant, forested sites just above Cultus Lake, a large, natural lake open to boating, fishing, swimming, waterskiing, sailing, and sailboarding. During the day, the area resounds with the roar of boat motors, laughing voices, and general bustle; by night it quiets down. The camp offers direct access to the Winopee Trail, which leads to Three Sisters Wilderness and a series of tranquil, high-mountain lakes. Other trails lead from Cultus Lake to Deer and Little Cultus Lakes. The campground is open from late May to mid-October.

104 Deschutes Bridge

Location: About 41 miles southwest of Bend.
Sites: 15 basic sites; no hookups.
Maximum length: 30 feet.
Facilities: Tables, grills, vault toilets, drinking water.
Fee per night: $.
Management: Forest Service.
Contact: 541-388-5664.
Finding the campground: From Bend, head southwest on Cascade Lakes Highway, which is also variously labeled Century Drive, County Road 46, or Forest Road 46, depending on jurisdiction. Go 41 miles and turn left (east) onto FR 4270, where you will immediately cross the Deschutes River bridge. Upon crossing, enter the camp on the right.

About the campground: This camp is just off Cascade Lakes Highway in a dense stand of lodgepole pines along a pretty section of the Upper Deschutes River. Here, the river flows narrow, dark, and fast between verdant banks of grass and wildflowers. Giant lupines, false hellebore, bog orchids, and Indian paintbrushes strike a dramatic contrast to the barren ground in the camp. Fishing and birding are popular camp pursuits, and the highway serves as a gateway for sightseers. The campground is open from late May to October.

105 East Davis

Location: About 65 miles southwest of Bend, on Davis Lake.
Sites: 33 basic sites; no hookups.
Maximum length: 40 feet.
Facilities: Tables, grills, vault toilets, drinking water.
Fee per night: $.
Management: Forest Service.
Contact: 541-388-2234.
Finding the campground: From Oregon 58, 3.4 miles east of Crescent Lake, turn northeast onto Crescent Cut-off Road, go 3.2 miles to Forest Road 46, and turn left. From U.S. Highway 97 at Crescent, go about 9 miles west on County

Road 61 (the Crescent Cut-off Road) to FR 46 and turn right. Follow FR 46 north 7.8 miles and turn left onto FR 850. You will come to a T junction in 0.2 mile. Go left on FR 855 and drive 1.9 miles to the camp entrance on the right.

About the campground: This campground on the south shore of Davis Lake sits across Odell Creek from its counterpart, West Davis Campground. The pair share Odell Bay and are linked by a half-mile trail. East Davis rests among lodgepole pines and dry-land shrubs. Some sites overlook the lakeshore. Views also include Maiden Peak, South Sister, Broken Top, and Mount Bachelor. A lava flow formed this lake by damming the creek. The lake undergoes natural fluctuations in water level from year to year. Because the lake is a good food source for birds, naturalists will want to keep their binoculars handy. Only fly fishing is allowed. The campground is open from May to mid-October.

106 Elk Lake

Location: About 31 miles southwest of Bend, on Elk Lake.
Sites: 23 basic sites; no hookups.
Maximum length: 25 feet.
Facilities: Tables, grills, vault toilets, drinking water, boat launch.
Fee per night: $.
Management: Forest Service.
Contact: 541-388-5664.
Finding the campground: From Bend, head southwest on Cascade Lakes Highway, which is also variously labeled Century Drive, County Road 46, or Forest Road 46, depending on jurisdiction. Go 31.1 miles and turn left into the camp.

About the campground: Lodgepole pines enfold this campground on the north shore of Elk Lake. Although the camp has a couple of pull-thru sites, many of the sites offer uneven or otherwise difficult parking, so RVers will need to search for the ideal site. Elk Lake is a 390-acre natural lake that hosts boating (10 miles per hour limit), fishing, and sailboarding. A lakeside resort rents boats. Hiking is also popular here. Across the lake, you can see Mount Bachelor peeking over a ridge. The campground is open from late May to October.

107 Fall River

Location: About 30 miles southwest of Bend.
Sites: 10 basic sites; no hookups.
Maximum length: 22 feet.
Facilities: Tables, grills, vault toilet. No drinking water.
Fee per night: $.
Management: Forest Service.
Contact: 541-388-5664.
Finding the campground: From U.S. Highway 97, 17.5 miles south of Bend, 4.9 miles north of the turnoff for La Pine State Recreation Area, turn west onto Forest Road 42 (labeled Vandevert Road and then South Century Drive) and go 12.2 miles to this camp.

About the campground: This camp rests in a thinned stand of lodgepole and small ponderosa pines; it gets patchy shade. A sparkling, shallow stretch of spring-fed Fall River flows below the camp. It is open to fly fishing only. Fall River Fish Hatchery is 3.2 miles northeast of the camp on FR 42. The campground is open from May to October.

108 Gull Point

Location: About 46 miles southwest of Bend, on Wickiup Reservoir.
Sites: 81 basic sites; no hookups.
Maximum length: 40 feet.
Facilities: Tables, grills, vault and flush toilets, drinking water, dump station, boat launch, fish-cleaning station.
Fee per night: $$.
Management: Forest Service.
Contact: 541-388-5664.
Finding the campground: From U.S. Highway 97 at Wickiup Junction, 27 miles south of Bend, go west on County Road 43 and Forest Road 42 for 15.6 miles. Turn left onto FR 4260 and go 3 miles to the camp entrance on the right.

About the campground: This large camp occupies a peninsula where the Deschutes River Channel meets the main body of Wickiup Reservoir. Davis Mountain and Maiden Peak can be admired from the shore in camp. The sites have a nice complement of natural vegetation, while a few big ponderosa pines draw the eyes skyward. Gulls and ospreys fish the reservoir. At the main reservoir, activities range from fishing and boating to waterskiing, yet the area is wild enough that deer and elk may be seen in the vicinity of the camp. As the water level is drawn down in late summer, marshy areas commingle with open water. The campground is open from mid-April to mid-October.

109 La Pine State Recreation Area

Location: About 27 miles southwest of Bend.
Sites: 145 full or partial hookup sites; water, electric, and sewer hookups.
Maximum length: 85 feet.
Facilities: Tables, flush toilets, drinking water, showers, dump station, meeting hall.
Fee per night: $$.
Management: Oregon State Parks and Recreation Department.
Contact: 541-382-3586; 1-800-452-5687 for reservations.
Finding the campground: From U.S. Highway 97, about 22 miles south of Bend, take the marked turn for the state recreation area and head west. You will reach the campground in just over 5 miles.

About the campground: Site of Oregon's largest ponderosa pine, this state park offers a pleasant, lightly used camp and day-use area along the Deschutes River. It also lies within reach of the sights and activities of Newberry National Volcanic Monument. Above the river, the camp offers developed, easy-to-access sites in an open stand of lodgepole and small ponderosa pines.

The sites with sewers are more closely spaced. Near the camp, a trail explores the rim overlooking the river. A small, gravelly beach at the day-use area is available for unguarded swimming. Because the park terrain does not lend itself to easy river access, anglers may need to do some scouting. A 1,000-foot, paved path descends to Big Tree, the 500-year-old ponderosa pine with a diameter of 8.6 feet. The campground is open year-round.

110 Lava Flow

Location: 65 miles southwest of Bend, on Davis Lake.
Sites: 12 basic sites; no hookups.
Maximum length: 22 feet.
Facilities: Tables, grills, vault toilets, boat ramp. No drinking water.
Fee per night: None.
Management: Forest Service.
Contact: 541-433-2234.
Finding the campground: From Oregon 58, 3.4 miles east of Crescent Lake, turn northeast onto Crescent Cut-off Road, go 3.2 miles to Forest Road 46, and turn left. From U.S. Highway 97 at Crescent, go about 9 miles west on County Road 61 (the Crescent Cut-off Road) to FR 46 and turn right. Follow FR 46 north for 7.8 miles and turn left onto FR 850. You will come to a T junction in 0.2 mile. Go 1.6 miles and turn right to enter Lava Flow Campground.

About the campground: This campground is sometimes closed to protect nesting bald eagles. Although the camp abuts the lava formation that created this large natural lake and bird haven, the impressive expanse of black, molten rock can be better appreciated from FR 46, as you drive north toward Wickiup Reservoir. Davis Lake is open to fly fishing only. Because the lake is shallow and is an essential habitat for wildlife, small, quiet boats are in order. The campground is generally open from September through January.

111 Lava Lake

Location: About 39 miles southwest of Bend, on Lava Lake.
Sites: 43 basic sites; no hookups.
Maximum length: 40 feet.
Facilities: Tables, grills, vault toilets, drinking water, boat launch.
Fee per night: $$.
Management: Forest Service.
Contact: 541-388-5664.
Finding the campground: From Bend, head southwest on Cascade Lakes Highway, which is also variously labeled Century Drive, County Road 46, or Forest Road 46, depending on jurisdiction. Go 38.4 miles and turn left (east) onto FR 4600.500. Go another mile to the camp.

About the campground: Here, on scenic Lava Lake, the campground and day-use area sit next door to rustic Lava Lake Resort. The campsites occupy a thinned stand of lodgepole pines, while the day-use tables overlook an attractive, multihued wetland. The scalloped shore of Lava Lake is well suited for canoeing. In keeping with the tranquil mood of the lake, the boat speed is limited to 10 miles per hour. Near the boat ramp is Lava Lake Trailhead, a gateway to other area lakes and Edison Ice Cave. Views from the shore include South Sister, Broken Top, and Mount Bachelor. The campground is open from May to mid-October.

112 Little Cultus

Location: About 50 miles southwest of Bend, on Little Cultus Lake.
Sites: 20 basic sites; no hookups.
Maximum length: 30 feet.
Facilities: Tables, grills, vault toilets, drinking water, boat launch.
Fee per night: $.
Management: Forest Service.
Contact: 541-388-5664.
Finding the campground: From Bend, head southwest on Cascade Lakes Highway, which is also variously labeled Century Drive, County Road 46, or Forest Road 46, depending on jurisdiction. Go 46 miles and turn right onto FR 4635. Follow it 0.8 mile and turn left onto gravel FR 4630. Stay on it for 1.7 miles, turn right onto FR 4636, and continue 1 mile to the campground.

About the campground: This appealing campground rests among lodgepole pines on the shore of Little Cultus Lake. Logs frame the camp roads and sites, and in places the lupine is quite lovely. This lake offers a quieter recreational experience than its larger companion, Cultus Lake, which is open to waterskiing. At Little Cultus, the pace is typically slower and the crowd more sedate. Boats are restricted to a speed of 10 miles per hour. As you troll the waters, you can lean back and enjoy views of Cultus Butte and the distant High Cascades. Area trails lead to Cultus Lake and to mountain lakes in the Three Sisters Wilderness. The campground is open from late May to mid-October.

113 Little Fawn

Location: About 37 miles southwest of Bend, on Elk Lake.
Sites: 12 basic sites; no hookups.
Maximum length: 25 feet.
Facilities: Tables, grills, vault toilets, drinking water, boat launch.
Fee per night: $.
Management: Forest Service.
Contact: 541-388-5664.
Finding the campground: From Bend, head southwest on Cascade Lakes Highway, which is also variously labeled Century Drive, County Road 46, or Forest Road 46, depending on jurisdiction. Go 35.5 miles and turn left (east) onto FR 4625, a paved and gravel route, to reach the camp entrance road in 1.7 miles.

About the campground: This camp claims a slope on the southeast shore of Elk Lake. A few firs help fill out the lodgepole-pine forest. Although only some of the sites are right along the shore, all are within easy access of this large, natural lake. Among the recreational opportunities are boating (10 miles per hour limit), fishing, sailboarding, and hiking the Elk Lake Trail, which links the lake recreation sites and delivers new perspectives on the area. The campground is open from mid-May to mid-October.

114 Little Lava Lake

Location: About 40 miles southwest of Bend, on Little Lava Lake.
Sites: 10 basic sites; no hookups.
Maximum length: 22 feet.
Facilities: Tables, grills, vault toilets, drinking water, boat launch.
Fee per night: $.
Management: Forest Service.
Contact: 541-388-5664.
Finding the campground: From Bend, head southwest on Cascade Lakes Highway, which is also variously labeled Century Drive, County Road 46, or Forest Road 46, depending on jurisdiction. Go 38.4 miles and turn left (east) onto FR 4600.500. Go 0.7 mile, turn right onto FR 4600.520, and drive another 0.4 mile to reach the camp.

About the campground: Despite its name, Little Lava Lake is good-sized but smaller than neighboring Lava Lake. It appeals to canoeists because of its beautiful wetland shore and views of Broken Top and Mount Bachelor. The campsites are well spaced in a lodgepole-pine forest above the shore. If you enjoy birding, you may spot swallows, ospreys, gulls, ducks, and cormorants at the lake; nuthatches and other woodland varieties in the forest. The campground is open from late May to October.

115 Mallard Marsh

Location: About 37 miles southwest of Bend, on Hosmer Lake.
Sites: 15 basic sites; no hookups.
Maximum length: 22 feet.
Facilities: Tables, grills, vault toilets, canoe launch (electric motors allowed). No drinking water.
Fee per night: $.
Management: Forest Service.
Contact: 541-388-5664.
Finding the campground: From Bend, head southwest on Cascade Lakes Highway, which is also variously labeled Century Drive, County Road 46, or Forest Road 46, depending on jurisdiction. Go 35.5 miles and turn left (east) onto FR 4625. Follow it for 1.2 miles and turn right into the camp.

About the campground: A combination of wetland and open water, Hosmer Lake is a picturesque place to canoe. It is stocked with trout and Atlantic salmon for catch-and-release fly fishing only. Birders and naturalists are drawn here. The upper lobe of the lake is three to four times bigger than the lower lake; Mount Bachelor and Red Crater are reflected in the open water. The camp is in a tranquil forest of lodgepole pines and firs, and Elk Lake is close by (only about 5 miles to the north) for swimming, sailboarding, or watching the sun set from its Sunset View Picnic Area. The campground is open from late May to October.

116 Newberry National Volcanic Monument: Chief Paulina Horse Camp

Location: About 37 miles south of Bend.
Sites: 14 basic sites; no hookups.
Maximum length: 30 feet.
Facilities: Tables, grills, vault toilets, corrals, water for horses. No drinking water.
Fee per night: $$.
Management: Forest Service.
Contact: 541-388-5664; 1-800-280-CAMP for reservations.
Finding the campground: From U.S. Highway 97, 23.5 miles south of Bend, head east on Forest Road 21 for 13.9 miles to enter this camp on the right.

About the campground: Situated across FR 21 from Paulina Lake, this equestrian camp puts you right in the heart of Newberry Crater and gives you easy access to the scenic and recreational opportunities of the area. The camp is in a pleasant, dry-forest setting. Area trail rides include tours of the Newberry Crater, Paulina Peak, and Peter Skene Ogden Trails; find the Newberry Crater Trail where it passes through the camp. You can expect dusty trail conditions. Besides riding, you can also fish and boat at Paulina Lake or its twin, East Lake. The horse camp is open from June into October.

117 Newberry National Volcanic Monument: Cinder Hill

Location: About 42 miles south of Bend, on East Lake.
Sites: 110 basic sites; no hookups.
Maximum length: 30 feet.
Facilities: Tables, grills, vault and flush toilets, drinking water, boat launch.
Fee per night: $$.
Management: Forest Service.
Contact: 541-388-5664; 1-800-280-CAMP for reservations.
Finding the campground: From U.S. Highway 97, 23.5 miles south of Bend, head east on Forest Road 21 for 17.6 miles. Turn left (north) onto FR 2100.700 and go 0.5 mile to the camp.

About the campground: This camp stretches for 0.7 mile through lodgepole-pine forest on the east shore of East Lake. The twin caldera lakes of Newberry Crater—East and Paulina—were formed in much the same manner as Crater Lake, and they are equally blue and clear. At the camp, grassy spits extend into the lake, shaping quiet coves that attract ducks. East Lake is a favorite with boaters and anglers, and a rustic resort nearby rents boats. Newberry National Volcanic Monument boasts a superb trail system for hiking, mountain biking, and horseback riding; birding and sightseeing also engage guests. Pumice and ash domes, obsidian slopes, stone pillars, and waterfalls are among the sights you can see here. The campground is open from late May into October.

118 Newberry National Volcanic Monument: East Lake

Location: About 40 miles southeast of Bend, on East Lake.
Sites: 29 basic sites; no hookups.
Maximum length: 30 feet.
Facilities: Tables, grills, vault and flush toilets, drinking water, boat launch.
Fee per night: $$.
Management: Forest Service.
Contact: 541-388-5664; 1-800-280-CAMP for reservations.
Finding the campground: From U.S. Highway 97, 23.5 miles south of Bend, turn east onto Forest Road 21 and continue 16.6 miles to the camp entrance on the left.

About the campground: On the south shore of 1,000-acre East Lake, these campsites sit close together in a stand of lodgepole pines. East Lake is one of a pair of deep-water lakes contained in the collapsed bowl of Newberry Crater. The lake is popular with boaters and with anglers, who vie for rainbow and German brown trout, kokanee, and Atlantic salmon. A sandy beach is found at the boat launch, and fine trails explore the geologic wonderland of Newberry National Volcanic Monument. The campground is open from late May into October.

Paulina Peak from Paulina Lake.

119 Newberry National Volcanic Monument: Hot Springs

Location: About 41 miles southeast of Bend.
Sites: 52 basic sites; no hookups.
Maximum length: 30 feet.
Facilities: Tables, grills, vault toilets, drinking water.
Fee per night: $$.
Management: Forest Service.
Contact: 541-388-5664.
Finding the campground: From U.S. Highway 97, 23.5 miles south of Bend, turn east onto Forest Road 21, continue 17.2 miles, and turn right into the camp.

About the campground: This campground is nestled among the lodgepole pines at the foot of a lava flow across the road from East Lake. You will find lake access and a boat ramp at a day-use area across FR 21 from the camp. A slight odor of sulfur in the area hints at hot springs at the bottom of the lake. The Newberry Crater Trail is accessible from the camp; other easy-to-access trails explore lake, creek, falls, and volcanic attractions. Carry plenty of water because the trails are dusty. The campground is open late May into October.

120 Newberry National Volcanic Monument: Little Crater

Location: About 39 miles south of Bend, on Paulina Lake.
Sites: 50 basic sites; no hookups.
Maximum length: 30 feet.
Facilities: Tables, grills, vault toilets, drinking water, boat launch (near entry to camp).
Fee per night: $$.
Management: Forest Service.
Contact: 541-388-5664; 1-800-280-CAMP for reservations.
Finding the campground: From U.S. Highway 97, 23.5 miles south of Bend, turn east onto Forest Road 21, go 14.5 miles, and turn left (north) onto FR 2100.570. Drive 0.5 mile to reach this camp.

About the campground: This camp stretches for half a mile through lodgepole pines along the east shore of Paulina Lake, one of two huge, clear, azure-blue lakes cradled in Newberry Crater; East Lake is the other. A shoreline trail rings Paulina Lake, traversing forest, obsidian flow, and slopes dotted with junipers and manzanitas. Besides lake views, the trail serves up fine looks at craggy Paulina Peak on the southern skyline. The Peter Skene Ogden and Paulina Falls Trails explore the banks of the outlet. Boating (10 miles per hour speed limit), fishing, birding, mountain biking, horseback riding, and sightseeing are other potential pastimes. The winding, sometimes rough, drive to the top of Paulina Peak will reward you with jaw-dropping vistas of the Cascade volcanoes, the caldera lakes below, Paulina Pinnacles, and Fort Rock. The campground is open from late May into October.

121 Newberry National Volcanic Monument: McKay Crossing

Location: About 29 miles south of Bend.
Sites: 10 basic sites; no hookups.
Maximum length: 22 feet.
Facilities: Tables, grills, vault toilets. No drinking water.
Fee per night: $.
Management: Forest Service.
Contact: 541-388-5664.
Finding the campground: From U.S. Highway 97, 23.5 miles south of Bend, turn east onto Forest Road 21, continue 3.2 miles, and turn left onto FR 2120. Go another 2.2 miles to reach the camp.

About the campground: This camp offers quiet, fairly private sites in a setting of lodgepole and small ponderosa pines beside Paulina Creek. From the camp, you can access the Peter Skene Ogden National Recreation Trail, which travels upstream 6 miles to Paulina Lake and caters to multiple use: It is open to foot, horse, and mountain bike travel. Lower Paulina Falls, a picturesque, 25-foot falls on the main creek, is only 500 feet from the camp. The many other attractions of Newberry National Volcanic Monument are within easy reach by vehicle. The campground is open from late May into October.

122 Newberry National Volcanic Monument: Paulina Lake

Location: About 36 miles south of Bend, on Paulina Lake.
Sites: 69 basic sites; no hookups.
Maximum length: 30 feet.
Facilities: Tables, grills, vault toilets, drinking water, boat launch.
Fee per night: $$.
Management: Forest Service.
Contact: 541-388-5664; 1-800-280-CAMP for reservations.
Finding the campground: From U.S. Highway 97, 23.5 miles south of Bend, turn east onto Forest Road 21, go 12.9 miles, and turn left into the camp.

About the campground: Below Paulina Peak, on the south shore of picture-pretty Paulina Lake, you will find these closely spaced campsites among the lodgepole pines. This is one of two azure-blue lakes cradled in Newberry Crater; East Lake is the other. From camp, you will enjoy easy access to the Paulina Lake, Peter Skene Ogden, and Paulina Falls Trails, as well as to fishing, sailing, and boating (10 miles per hour limit) on Paulina Lake. Sightseeing stops and short hikes unravel the volcanic story of Newberry Crater. The campground is open from late May into October.

Paulina Pillars at Newberry National Volcanic Monument.

123 Newberry National Volcanic Monument: Prairie

Location: About 27 miles south of Bend.
Sites: 16 basic sites; no hookups.
Maximum length: 30 feet.
Facilities: Tables, grills, vault toilets, drinking water.
Fee per night: $.
Management: Forest Service.
Contact: 541-388-5664; 1-800-280-CAMP for reservations.
Finding the campground: From U.S. Highway 97, 23.5 miles south of Bend, turn east onto Forest Road 21, go 3.1 miles, and turn right into the camp.

About the campground: Situated in a mixed-pine forest, this camp offers nice, big sites overlooking Paulina Prairie and Creek. It is a picturesque place to kick back and relax, but it also offers a base from which to explore Newberry National Volcanic Monument, the Deschutes River, Wickiup Reservoir, and the Bend area. The campground is open from late May into October.

124 North Davis Creek

Location: 56 miles southwest of Bend, on Wickiup Reservoir.
Sites: 17 basic sites; no hookups.
Maximum length: 25 feet.
Facilities: Tables, grills, vault toilets, drinking water, boat launch.

Fee per night: $.
Management: Forest Service.
Contact: 541-388-5664.
Finding the campground: From Bend, head southwest on Cascade Lakes Highway, which is also variously labeled Century Drive, County Road 46, or Forest Road 46, depending on jurisdiction. Go 56 miles and turn left to enter the camp.

About the campground: This campground occupies a stand of young lodgepole pines on a long inlet arm of Wickiup Reservoir. In the late 1980s, the site was logged due to a pine-beetle infestation. Sparkling North Davis Creek merges with the reservoir here. The inlet bay is clear and quickly grows deep, but the sandy shore broadens as the water level drops later in the year. While the sites are mostly sunny, the tight array of trees offers some privacy. Besides fishing and boating, you can lace on your hiking boots and head for Moore Creek Trailhead. Hike destinations include Davis, Bobby, and Charlton Lakes and Gerdine Butte and The Twins. You can reach the trailhead by taking the signed road across the highway from the camp. The campground is open from May to October.

125 North Twin

Location: About 43 miles southwest of Bend, on North Twin Lake.
Sites: 20 basic sites; no hookups.
Maximum length: 35 feet.
Facilities: Tables, grills, vault toilets, drinking water, boat launch.
Fee per night: $.
Management: Forest Service.
Contact: 541-388-5664.
Finding the campground: From the Wickiup Junction on U.S. Highway 97, 27 miles south of Bend, turn west onto County Road 43, go 11 miles, and continue west on Forest Road 42 for another 4.6 miles. Turn left onto FR 4260, go 0.2 mile, and turn left into the camp.

About the campground: This campground sits on the shore of perfectly round North Twin Lake amid small pines and a few big ponderosa pines. The sites have gravel parking and not much privacy, given the open spacing of the trees and the lack of ground vegetation. The postcard-pretty lake edged with grasses and snags invites quiet boating (no motors allowed), swimming, and fishing. A trail leads 1 mile from camp to this lake's mirror image, South Twin Lake. There is a rustic resort at South Twin. North Twin Campground is open from May to October.

126 Point

Location: 34 miles southwest of Bend, on Elk Lake.
Sites: 10 basic sites; no hookups.
Maximum length: 22 feet.
Facilities: Tables, grills, vault toilets, boat launch. No drinking water.
Fee per night: $.

Management: Forest Service.
Contact: 541-388-5664.
Finding the campground: From Bend, head southwest on Cascade Lakes Highway, which is also variously labeled Century Drive, County Road 46, or Forest Road 46, depending on jurisdiction. Go 34 miles and turn left into the camp.

About the campground: This campground claims the forested southwest corner of Elk Lake, a large, natural lake. Across the water, you can see Mount Bachelor, Broken Top, and South Sister. The lake welcomes fishing, swimming, and boating (10 miles per hour maximum). Next door to the camp is Beach Picnic Area, which offers a broad sandy beach and a nice sandy lake bottom for wading, but no lifeguard. At the picnic area, you can access the Elk Lake Trail. The campground is open from late May to October.

127 Pringle Falls

Location: About 35 miles southwest of Bend.
Sites: 6 basic sites; no hookups.
Maximum length: 22 feet.
Facilities: Tables, grills, vault toilet. No drinking water.
Fee per night: $.
Management: Forest Service.
Contact: 541-388-5664.
Finding the campground: From U.S. Highway 97 at Wickiup Junction, 27 miles south of Bend, go west on County Road 43 for 7.4 miles and turn right (north) onto gravel Forest Road 4330.500. Go 0.2 mile, turn left at the camp turnoff, and continue approximately 0.5 mile to the camp.

About the campground: You will find this pine-shaded campground on the Deschutes River, near the parklike stands of ponderosa pines in Pringle Falls Experimental Forest. The river next to the camp is deep, swift, and channel like. Fishing, rafting, and canoeing are popular; you can put in right at camp. According to a sign at the turn onto FR 4330.500, Tetherow Boat Launch is 3 miles downstream. The campground is open from May to October.

128 Quinn Meadow Horse Camp

Location: About 32 miles southwest of Bend.
Sites: 25 basic sites; no hookups.
Maximum length: 40 feet.
Facilities: Tables, grills, vault toilets, drinking water, tie stalls and corrals, community shelter, manure dump.
Fee per night: $$.
Management: Forest Service.
Contact: 541-388-5664; 541-382-9443 for reservations (which are required).
Finding the campground: From Bend, head southwest on Cascade Lakes Highway, which is also variously labeled Century Drive, County Road 46, or Forest

Road 46, depending on jurisdiction. Go 31 miles and turn left (east) onto the camp entrance road. Follow it 0.5 mile into the camp.

About the campground: This beautiful campground caters to equestrians. The sites are dispersed among lodgepole pines, mountain hemlocks, and firs at the edge of Quinn Meadow, a long, broad sweep of grass threaded by Quinn Creek. The sites are ample and private; they encourage reclining at camp. Trails from the camp follow Quinn Creek or lead into the Three Sisters Wilderness and the Horse Lakes Area, offering numerous choices for trail rides. The horse camp is open from late May to October.

129 Quinn River

Location: About 48 miles southwest of Bend, on Crane Prairie Reservoir.
Sites: 41 basic sites; no hookups.
Maximum length: 40 feet.
Facilities: Tables, grills, vault toilets, drinking water, boat launch.
Fee per night: $.
Management: Forest Service.
Contact: 541-388-5664.
Finding the campground: From Bend, head southwest on Cascade Lakes Highway, which is also variously labeled Century Drive, County Road 46, or Forest Road 46, depending on jurisdiction. Go 48.2 miles and turn left into the camp.

About the campground: This camp occupies a lodgepole-pine flat along Quinn River at Crane Prairie Reservoir. The forest is semi-open as a result of a pine-beetle infestation and a winter blow-down. The large boat ramp accesses a snag-riddled section of the reservoir where Quinn River empties into it. Boaters are restricted to a speed of 10 miles per hour, and there is no anchoring within 100 feet of any trees that hold osprey nests. Billy Quinn Historical Trail starts at camp and visits Quinn River Spring (the source of this short river), the Cy Bingham lodgepole pine, and the grave of Billy Quinn, a pioneer sheepman. The trail ends at Osprey Observation Point (which can also be reached by car, less than 1 mile south on Cascade Lakes Highway). More than half of the ospreys in Oregon nest at Crane Prairie Reservoir. The campground is open from mid-April to mid-September.

130 Reservoir

Location: About 60 miles southwest of Bend, on Wickiup Reservoir.
Sites: 28 basic sites; no hookups.
Maximum length: 40 feet.
Facilities: Tables, grills, vault toilets, boat launch. No drinking water.
Fee per night: $.
Management: Forest Service.
Contact: 541-388-5664.

Finding the campground: From Bend, head southwest on Cascade Lakes Highway, which is also variously labeled Century Drive, County Road 46, or Forest Road 46, depending on jurisdiction. Go 58 miles, turn left onto FR 44, and proceed 1.7 miles to the camp.

About the campground: This campground sprawls along a lodgepole-pine flat on the southwest shore of Wickiup Reservoir. Although the pines are small, they grow densely enough to lend privacy to the campsites. But you will need to bring a shade source. If you get a lakeside site, you can moor your boat on the sandy shore right next to your camp. Boating and fishing are the primary draws to this large reservoir; kokanee is among the catch. The campground is open from May to October.

131 Rock Creek

Location: About 50 miles southwest of Bend, on Crane Prairie Reservoir.
Sites: 31 basic sites; no hookups.
Maximum length: 40 feet.
Facilities: Tables, grills, vault toilets, drinking water, boat launch, fish-cleaning station.
Fee per night: $.
Management: Forest Service.
Contact: 541-388-5664.
Finding the campground: From Bend, head southwest on Cascade Lakes Highway, which is also variously labeled Century Drive, County Road 46, or Forest Road 46, depending on jurisdiction. Go 49.8 miles and turn left into the camp.

About the campground: On the west shore of Crane Prairie Reservoir, you will find this camp in a semi-open stand of lodgepole pines and bitterbrush. Cross-reservoir views are of Mount Bachelor and South Sister; Cultus Butte rises to the north. Songbirds animate the trees in the camp, while an osprey's screech may draw your eyes skyward. The camp is just 2.5 miles south of Osprey Observation Point, an interpretive site worth visiting. The snags of the reservoir provide nesting sites for the lake's osprey population. Trout fishing and boating (10 miles per hour maximum) are the primary activities. The campground is open from mid-April to mid-September.

132 Rosland

Location: About 28 miles south of Bend.
Sites: 10 basic sites; no hookups.
Maximum length: 40 feet.
Facilities: Tables, grills, pit toilets, drinking water.
Fee per night: $.
Management: La Pine Parks and Recreation District.
Contact: 541-536-3983.
Finding the campground: From U.S. Highway 97, 2 miles north of La Pine, 27

miles south of Bend, turn west onto Burgess Road toward Wickiup Reservoir and go 1.5 miles to find the campground on the left.

About the campground: Along the winding, willow-lined Little Deschutes River, this campground occupies a habitat of lodgepole pines, bitterbrush, and native grasses. Sites have gravel parking and limited shade. Back in the 1820s, this location was used as a base by trappers. Today, it is lightly trafficked and peaceful. Fishing is the most popular pastime. The campground is open from April 15 to October 15.

133 Sand Spring

Location: About 41 miles southeast of Bend.
Sites: 6 basic sites; no hookups.
Maximum length: 18 feet.
Facilities: Some tables, pit toilets. No drinking water.
Fee per night: None.
Management: Forest Service.
Contact: 541-388-5664.
Finding the campground: From U.S. Highway 20, 22 miles east of Bend, turn south onto County Road 23, go 6 miles, and bear left, proceeding on Forest Road 23, a wide, red-gravel road. Continue 12.8 miles, turn right onto FR 22, and immediately make a second right turn into the camp.

About the campground: Across the road from Sand Spring, which is ringed by pole fence, this primitive camp is truly a place for the do-it-yourselfer. The camp occupies an open flat of lodgepole pines and bunchgrass surrounded by sagebrush. Your stay here can be one of complete silence and uncommon solitude or one paired with engine roars: En route to camp, you may have noticed the signs indicating that you are in the East Fort Rock Off-Highway-Vehicle Area. This camp is an excellent place from which to stargaze, and it is also in the general vicinity of Lavacicle Cave. Access to this cave is restricted; it is only shown by guided tour. To make reservations for a tour, contact the Bend/Fort Rock Ranger District at the phone number listed above.

134 Sheep Bridge

Location: About 43 miles southwest of Bend, on Wickiup Reservoir.
Sites: 18 basic sites; no hookups.
Maximum length: 40 feet.
Facilities: Tables, grills, vault toilets, drinking water, boat launch.
Fee per night: $.
Management: Forest Service.
Contact: 541-388-5664.
Finding the campground: From U.S. Highway 97 at Wickiup Junction, 27 miles south of Bend, go west on County Road 43 and Forest Road 42 for 15.6 miles. Turn left onto FR 4260, go 0.8 mile, and turn right to reach the camp.

About the campground: You will find this small campground in a mixed-age forest of lodgepole pines along the meandering Deschutes River Channel of Wickiup Reservoir. Younger trees crowd the outskirts of the camp; a few bigger pines within the camp afford at least some shade. The heart of the campground is open due to random parking and heavy foot traffic. Boats are limited to 10 miles per hour on the channel. Fishing is popular. The campground is open from May to October.

135 Soda Creek

Location: About 26 miles southwest of Bend, on Sparks Lake.
Sites: 7 basic sites; no hookups.
Maximum length: 20 feet.
Facilities: Tables, grills, vault toilets. No drinking water.
Fee per night: None.
Management: Forest Service.
Contact: 541-388-5664.
Finding the campground: From Bend, head southwest on Cascade Lakes Highway, which is also variously labeled Century Drive, County Road 46, or Forest Road 46, depending on jurisdiction. Go 26 miles and turn left (east) onto FR 400 at the sign for Sparks Lake. Drive 0.1 mile to the camp area.

About the campground: This is an informal, primitive camp at the northern end of Sparks Lake and Meadow, where Soda Creek feeds into the lake. The sites are situated among the pines and firs at the edge of the meadow, which stretches for more than a mile and is almost as wide. The High Cascades contribute to great views. The area is noted for its abundance of wildlife; watch for elk, deer, and birds. Canoeing, fly fishing, and hiking into the Three Sisters Wilderness are ways to enjoy your stay. The campground is open from late May to October.

136 South

Location: About 37 miles southwest of Bend, on Hosmer Lake.
Sites: 23 basic sites; no hookups.
Maximum length: 40 feet.
Facilities: Tables, grills, vault toilets, boat launch (at Mallard Marsh Campground). No drinking water.
Fee per night: $.
Management: Forest Service.
Contact: 541-388-5664.
Finding the campground: From Bend, head southwest on Cascade Lakes Highway, which is also variously labeled Century Drive, County Road 46, or Forest Road 46, depending on jurisdiction. Go 35.5 miles and turn left (east) onto FR 4625. Follow it for 1.2 miles and turn right into the camp.

About the campground: Along with Mallard Marsh Campground (see page 327), this camp provides access to Hosmer Lake, a scenic wetland and open water that is stocked with trout and Atlantic salmon for catch-and-release fly fishing only. The large lake is ideal for canoeing. You can paddle through reeds, grasses, and water lilies; watch for wildlife; and enjoy the watery reflections of Mount Bachelor and Red Crater. Like Mallard Marsh, this camp is situated among the lodgepole pines and firs and is open from late May to October.

137 South Twin

Location: About 45 miles southwest of Bend, on South Twin Lake at Wickiup Reservoir.
Sites: 24 basic sites; no hookups.
Maximum length: 30 feet.
Facilities: Tables, grills, vault and flush toilets, drinking water, boat launches.
Fee per night: $$.
Management: Forest Service.
Contact: 541-388-5664.
Finding the campground: From U.S. Highway 97 at Wickiup Junction, 27 miles south of Bend, go west on County Road 43 and Forest Road 42 for 15.6 miles. Turn left onto FR 4260, go 2 miles, and turn left into the camp.

About the campground: This camp is housed in a mature forest of lodgepole and ponderosa pines along South Twin Lake, a picturesque, circular body of water cupped by forest. Its fortress-like ring of trees differentiates it from North Twin Lake, where a grassy shore holds back the trees. A mile-long trail links the two lakes. Activities at South Twin include fishing, non-motorized boating, and swimming. Across FR 4260 from the camp is a boat launch on the Deschutes River Channel for additional fishing and boating (10 miles per hour maximum). A neighboring resort puts a cup of espresso just strides from the camp. The campground is open from mid-April to mid-October.

138 Swamp Wells Horse Camp

Location: About 18 miles southeast of Bend.
Sites: 6 basic sites; no hookups.
Maximum length: 22 feet.
Facilities: Tables, grills, vault toilets, watering troughs. No drinking water.
Fee per night: None.
Management: Forest Service.
Contact: 541-388-5664.
Finding the campground: From U.S. Highway 97, 4 miles south of Bend, turn east onto Forest Road 18, go 5.4 miles, and turn right (south) onto FR 1810. Continue 5.8 miles, turn left (east) onto FR 1816, and drive another 3 miles to reach this camp.

About the campground: This camp occupies a cut-over stand of pines and offers access to area trails and jeep tracks for horseback riding, hiking, and all-terrain-vehicle travel. Buttes in the area contribute to vistas and make for fairly easy cross-country hikes. Although the terrain appears relatively flat, the camp occupies the skirt of Newberry Crater, which shows a slow, even incline to the caldera rim. Swamp Wells Trail travels 9 miles south to the crater; its northern destination is Horse Butte. If you continue east on FR 18 past its junction with FR 1810, you will come to a series of lava caves that are fun to explore; carry a flashlight and two backup light sources. If you venture into Wind Cave, you will have to scramble over jumbled rock. Wear boots, gloves, and something to protect your head from low arches and lavacicles. The horse camp is open from May through October.

139 Tumalo State Park

Location: About 5 miles northwest of Bend.
Sites: 22 hookup sites, 65 basic sites, 2 tepees, some hike/bike sites; water, electric, and sewer hookups.
Maximum length: 44 feet.
Facilities: Tables, grills, flush toilets, drinking water, showers, telephone, playground.
Fee per night: $$ to $$$.
Management: Oregon State Parks and Recreation Department.
Contact: 541-382-3586; 1-800-452-5687 for reservations.
Finding the campground: From the junction of U.S. Highway 20 and US 97 at the north end of Bend, go west on US 20 for 3.7 miles. Turn south onto the Old McKenzie–Bend Highway at the sign for the park and proceed 1.1 miles to the campground entrance on the left. A day-use area is on the right.

About the campground: This campground rests along the Deschutes River, where the water has been drawn down for irrigation. Picturesque rocks and yellow iris may complement the water. The sites have paved parking; some basic sites will require more RV leveling than others. The camp is set in a juniper forest, with a few aspen trees and grassy plots between the sites. Most sites have partial shade. A designated swimming area in the day-use area is popular in summer. The attractions of Bend may call you away from the camp. The campground is open from March 1 to December 1.

140 West Davis

Location: About 65 miles southwest of Bend, on Davis Lake.
Sites: 25 basic sites; no hookups.
Maximum length: 22 feet.
Facilities: Tables, grills, vault toilets, drinking water.
Fee per night: $.
Management: Forest Service.
Contact: 541-433-2234.
Finding the campground: From Oregon 58, 3.4 miles east of Crescent Lake, turn northeast onto Crescent Cut-off Road, go 3.2 miles to Forest Road 46, and turn left. From U.S. Highway 97 at Crescent, go about 9 miles west on County

Road 61 (the Crescent Cut-off Road) to FR 46 and turn right. Follow FR 46 for 3.4 miles, turn left onto gravel FR 4660, and continue another 2.9 miles. Turn right onto FR 4669 and proceed 1.7 miles to the camp.

About the campground: This camp occupies the south shore of Davis Lake and the west bank of Odell Creek Inlet. Lodgepole pines cloak the shore, providing just a smattering of shade; bitterbrush claims the forest floor. Sites have cinder parking and convenient access to the lakeshore. The lake, formed by a lava flow, undergoes natural fluctuations in water level and is a rich food source for a variety of birds. Only fly fishing is permitted. Views from the camp are of Hamner Butte and Davis Mountain. A half-mile trail links this camp to East Davis Campground (see Campground 105), on the opposite shore of Odell Creek. West Davis is open from May to mid-October.

141 West South Twin

Location: About 45 miles southwest of Bend, on Wickiup Reservoir.
Sites: 24 basic sites; no hookups.
Maximum length: 30 feet.
Facilities: Tables, grills, vault and flush toilets, drinking water, boat launches.
Fee per night: $$.
Management: Forest Service.
Contact: 541-388-5664.
Finding the campground: From U.S. Highway 97 at Wickiup Junction, 27 miles south of Bend, go west on County Road 43 and Forest Road 42 for 15.6 miles. Turn left onto FR 4260, go 2 miles, and turn right into the camp.

About the campground: Located along the Deschutes River Channel of Wickiup Reservoir, this structured campground retains its native ground vegetation, which contributes to the privacy of the sites and the attractiveness of the camp. Lodgepole and ponderosa pines make up the surrounding forest. From camp, you have direct access to the river channel for boating (10 miles per hour maximum) and fishing. Just across FR 4260 is South Twin Lake, where you can engage in non-motorized boating or hike the 1-mile trail that leads north to North Twin Lake. West South Twin is open mid-April to mid-October.

142 Wickiup Butte

Location: About 44 miles southwest of Bend, on Wickiup Reservoir.
Sites: 12 basic sites; no hookups.
Maximum length: 25 feet.
Facilities: Tables, grills, vault toilets, boat launch. No drinking water.
Fee per night: $.
Management: Forest Service.
Contact: 541-388-5664.
Finding the campground: From U.S. Highway 97 at Wickiup Junction, 27 miles south of Bend, go west on County Road 43 for 10.5 miles and turn left onto

gravel Forest Road 4380. Go 3.6 miles, turn left onto FR 4260, and continue 2.7 miles to the boat area (and primitive camping) or 3 miles to the campground.

About the campground: This campground is at the foot of Wickiup Butte and on the shore of Wickiup Reservoir. It has defined sites, earthen parking, and a setting of mixed pines. Views from the camp are of Davis Mountain, Maiden Peak, The Twins, and the broad, open reservoir. The small size of the camp and the gravel access roads help to keep away the crowds. Fishing, boating, birding, and waterskiing on the main reservoir top the list of recreational attractions. The launch is at the boating area you pass en route to camp; there, next to the dam, you will also find a 6-site, no-frills but free camp. The campground is open from May to October.

Eastern Oregon

Eastern Oregon rolls out an exciting canvas for discovery. It unites John Day Fossil Beds; Steens Mountain; the history, beauty, and wildlife of the Blue Mountains; the chiseled, icy grandeur of the Elkhorn and Wallowa Mountains; the harsh beauty of Hells Canyon; a seemingly endless desert plain; vast desert lakes; hot springs; and the weathered orange canyonlands at the southeast corner of the state. It is wide-open country and a lifetime ticket to adventure. It is a land that supports black bears, coyotes, deer, antelope, elk, bighorn sheep, mountain goats, golden and bald eagles, sturgeon, and wild horses. The land wears the tracks of the Oregon Trail and the telltale signs of dashed mining hopes. And to top it all off, the night sky is a glittery vault.

Settlement in the eastern part of the state is light and generally far-scattered. Interstate 84 strings together the larger communities of the northeast corner of the state: Pendleton, La Grande, Baker City, and Ontario. Lakeview and Burns are the "big cities" of the southern extreme. With such light development, travelers need to be a little more self-sufficient and better prepared for the unexpected. Filling gas tanks; having a reliable spare tire, some tools, electrical tape, and other items for emergency repairs; carrying extra water and blankets; and checking on road and weather conditions are cornerstones to safety.

This region typically experiences four seasons (although some are rushed), with extremes of heat and cold often registered. The extent of snow depends largely on elevation and your location, with regard to the storm track. Chilly dry realms or snowy wonderlands can be found in winter. Summer bakes the desert reaches, making the mountain cool all the more welcome.

Hiking, fishing, birding, horseback riding, hunting, whitewater rafting, rock collecting, boating, skiing, snowmobiling, and snowshoeing are among the active pursuits. Museums, rodeos, county fairs, and historic sites expand the area's appeal.

Aneroid Lake in the Wallowa Mountains.

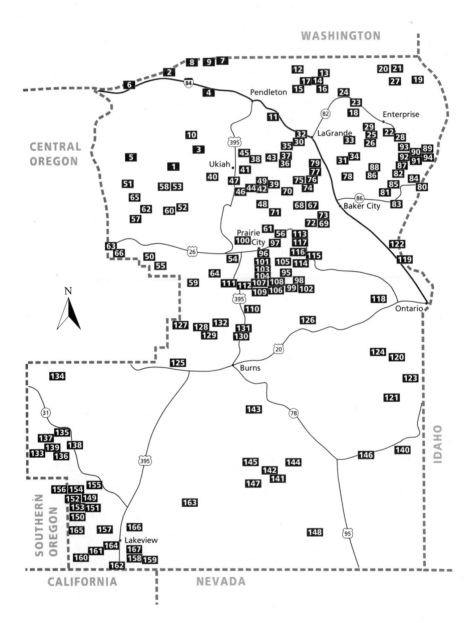

COLUMBIA PLATEAU AREA

		Hookup sites	Total sites	Max. RV length	Hookups	Toilets	Showers	Drinking water	Dump station	Recreation	Fee	Can reserve
1	Anson Wright Memorial Park	16	28	35	WES	F	•	•	•	HF	$	
2	Boardman Marine Park	63	63	80	WES	F	•	•	•	SFBL	$$	
3	Cutsforth County Park	20	40	35	WES	F	•	•		HF	$	
4	The Fort Henrietta RV Park	7	7	40	WES	F	•	•	•		$$	
5	J.B. Burns Park	18	18	30	WE	F	•	•			$	
6	Port of Arlington Marina and RV Park	12	32	40	WES	F		•		FBL	$–$$	
7	Sand Station Recreation Area		14	40		NF				SFB		
8	Umatilla Marina and RV Park	26	36	60	WES	F	•	•	•	SFBL	$$	
9	Warehouse Beach Recreation Site		6	30		NF				SFB		
10	Willow Creek	24	24	40	WES	F	•	•	•	FBL	$	•

Hookups: W = Water E = Electric S = Sewer **Total sites:** T = Tent-only campground **Maximum trailer/RV length** given in feet.
Toilets: F = Flush NF = No Flush **Recreation:** H = Hiking S = Swimming F = Fishing B = Boating L = Boat Launch
O = Off-Highway Driving R = Horseback Riding C = Cycling
Fee: $ = $1-9 $$ = $10-19 $$$ = $20-29 $$$$ = $30-39. If no entry under **Fee,** camping is free.

1 Anson Wright Memorial Park

Location: 25 miles south of Heppner.
Sites: 16 hookup sites, 12 tent sites; water, electric, and sewer hookups.
Maximum length: 35 feet.
Facilities: Tables, fire rings, flush toilets, drinking water, showers, dump station, playground, fishing pond and creek.
Fee: $.
Management: Morrow County.
Contact: 541-676-9061 (ask for parks department).
Finding the campground: It is west off Oregon 207, 25 miles south of Heppner.

About the campground: At the foot of the western slope of Rock Creek Canyon, in ponderosa pine and Douglas-fir shade, this camp extends a quiet stay. The cool nights sometimes catch campers off guard, so keep the blankets handy. Old roads and a planned path offer avenues to walk, and anglers can try their luck in the pond or Rock Creek. A working opal mine (7 miles from the camp) sometimes admits the paying public to dig a bucket of opal; ask the park manager for information. The campground is open from May to mid-November.

2 Boardman Marine Park

Location: In Boardman, on Lake Umatilla.
Sites: 63 hookup sites; water, electric, and sewer hookups.
Maximum length: 80 feet.

Facilities: Tables, flush toilets, drinking water, showers, dump station, telephone, playground, recreation hall, sports field, horseshoe pits, marina, launch, docks.
Fee: $$.
Management: Boardman Parks.
Contact: 541-481-7217.
Finding the campground: From Interstate 84 at Boardman, take Exit 164 and go north to reach the park in less than 1 mile.

About the campground: This camp rests on a grassy Columbia River flat, with leafy shade trees and wind fences at the more open sites. There are both back-in and pull-thru spaces, all paved. Lake Umatilla (the harnessed Columbia River) invites recreation, with a designated swimming area and fishing and boating. Stiff winds common to the Columbia River Gorge may fill the sails of both sailboats and sailboards. At the day-use area, look for petroglyphs rescued from when the dam was built. Binoculars come in handy because McNary and Irrigon wildlife areas and Umatilla National Wildlife Refuge are all in the vicinity. The campground is open from March 1 to December 1.

3 Cutsforth County Park

Location: 20 miles southeast of Heppner.
Sites: 20 hookup sites, 20 basic sites; water, electric, and sewer hookups.
Maximum length: 35 feet.
Facilities: Tables, grills, flush toilets, drinking water, showers, playground, fishing pond, sale of ice and ice cream.
Fee: $.
Management: Morrow County.
Contact: 541-676-9061 (ask for parks department).
Finding the campground: From Oregon 207 at the south end of Heppner, turn east onto Willow Creek Road (the Blue Mountain Scenic Byway) and go 20 miles to reach this park on the right.

About the campground: The main campground is in the eastern half of this park, and its sites are dispersed throughout a mixed forest of pine, spruce, fir, and larch. The pond, a day-use area, and the dry camp claim the western half of the park, which is more open. The pond is stocked with pan-sized trout and is fun for the whole family. In this natural setting, deer, bear, coyote, muskrat, and raccoon have been spied. Campers should cover and safely store food at night to prevent raccoon raids. The campground is open from May to mid-November.

4 The Fort Henrietta RV Park

Location: In Echo, about 10 miles southeast of Hermiston.
Sites: 7 hookup sites, open lawn for tent camping, overflow camping in gravel parking lot; water, electric, and sewer hookups.
Maximum length: 40 feet.
Facilities: Some tables, flush toilets, drinking water, showers, dump station, Oregon Trail interpretive panel.

Fee: $$.
Management: City of Echo.
Contact: 541-376-8411.
Finding the campground: From Interstate 84, take Exit 188 and go south on Old Pendleton River Road for Echo. At 1.1 mile bear right per the trailer emblem, and after another 0.3 mile turn right onto West Main in Echo. Go 0.2 mile to reach the park on the left prior to the Umatilla River bridge.

About the campground: Along the Umatilla River at the western edge of Echo, you will find this small, attractive city park and overnight wayside. The park recalls Oregon's past: Pioneers on the Oregon Trail camped and crossed the river here, and this was the site of the frontier post, Fort Henrietta. The park's replica blockhouse recalls the old fort, as do Henrietta Days, held the second weekend of September. Then, tepees dot the park grounds and people in buckskins mill about. The campground is open year-round.

5 J. B. Burns Park

Location: In Condon.
Sites: 18 hookup sites; water and electric hookups.
Maximum length: 30 feet.
Facilities: Flush toilets, drinking water, showers, picnic pavilion.
Fee: $.
Management: Gilliam County.
Contact: 541-384-3998.
Finding the campground: It is at Gilliam County Fairgrounds, off Oregon 19 at the north end of Condon.

About the campground: This small, open grassy camp serves participants and attendees of Gilliam County Fair and through-travelers (when events are not ongoing); there are not many rival camp accommodations in the area. The park is near the Gilliam County Historical Society Museum, which features a restored 1884 log cabin and a complex of early 1900s buildings.

6 Port of Arlington Marina and RV Park

Location: In Arlington.
Sites: 12 RV hookup sites, 20 RV dry sites, no tent sites; water, electric, and sewer hookups.
Maximum length: 40 feet.
Facilities: Some aluminum tables, flush toilets, drinking water, boat launch.
Fee: $ to $$.
Management: Port of Arlington.
Contact: 541-454-2868.
Finding the campground: From Interstate 84, take Exit 137 and go north to the waterfront in Arlington.

About the campground: This overnight facility is located on a strip of land between the port channel and the main Columbia River. In addition to the assigned hookup sites, dry camping is allowed at the paved parking lot that overlooks the port channel. The area serves as a convenient, although sometimes noisy, overnight stop, and puts boaters and anglers smack in the middle of the Columbia River action.

7 Sand Station Recreation Area

Location: About 12 miles east of Umatilla.
Sites: 4 basic sites, 10 walk-in tent sites, open camping for RVs on gravel flat; no hookups.
Maximum length: 40 feet.
Facilities: Covered tables at basic sites, tables and barbecues at tent sites, vault toilets, telephone. No drinking water.
Fee: None.
Management: U.S. Army Corps of Engineers.
Contact: 541-296-1181.
Finding the campground: From the intersection of Interstate 82 and U.S. Highway 730 in Umatilla, go east on US 730 for 11.5 miles to enter this camp on the left.

About the campground: On the shore of Lake Wallula sits this small, dry camp. A few black locust trees provide modest but treasured shade on this otherwise sun-drenched flat. Cross-lake views are of the steppes and tablelands of Washington State. A designated swimming area and fishing keep camp guests entertained. At night, truck travel on US 730 can break the calm. The campground is open year-round.

8 Umatilla Marina and RV Park

Location: In Umatilla, on Lake Umatilla.
Sites: 26 hookup sites, 6 basic sites, 4 tent sites; water, electric, and sewer hookups.
Maximum length: 60 feet.
Facilities: Tables, flush toilets, drinking water, showers, dump station, telephone, boat launch.
Fee: $$.
Management: Umatilla Marina.
Contact: 541-922-3939.
Finding the campground: From the junction of Interstate 82 and U.S. Highway 730, go west on US 730 for less than 0.1 mile, turn right onto Brownell Boulevard, and continue 0.3 mile. There, turn left onto 3rd Street for another 0.3 mile before turning right onto Quincy to enter the park.

About the campground: This is a split-level facility, with the marina and day-use area fronting the river and the campground on the above plateau. The campground is landscaped, with lawn and planted shade trees that are starting to fill out. Sites have gravel parking and a nice spacing. Superb fishing and boating on the Columbia River (here, Lake Umatilla) attract park guests. In the day-use area, you will find a designated swimming area; elsewhere, trails connect to McNary Nature Trail and McNary National Wildlife Refuge. The campground is open year-round.

9 Warehouse Beach Recreation Site

Location: About 12 miles east of Umatilla.
Sites: 6 basic sites; no hookups.
Maximum length: 30 feet.
Facilities: Covered tables, barbecues, vault toilets, telephone. No drinking water.
Fee: None.
Management: U.S. Army Corps of Engineers.
Contact: 541-296-1181.
Finding the campground: From the intersection of Interstate 82 and U.S. Highway 730 in Umatilla, go east on US 730 for 10.8 miles. Take the exit for Oregon 37 South and Warehouse Beach and quickly turn off the exit to follow a gravel road heading north back under US 730. Stay on it 0.5 mile to the recreation site.

About the campground: Camping is restricted to the six designated sites, which are tucked into a sagebrush slope above a pond and Lake Wallula. Sycamore and olive trees grow at the camp perimeter. A separate day-use area, within an easy walk of the camp, offers a swimming beach. Visitors can fish both the pond and the harnessed Columbia River lake; trails venture through the surrounding arid brush. The campground is open year-round.

10 Willow Creek

Location: Less than 1 mile southeast of Heppner.
Sites: 24 hookup sites (Manager will try to accommodate tent campers.); water, electric, and sewer hookups.
Maximum length: 40 feet.
Facilities: Some tables, flush toilets, drinking water, showers, dump station, telephone, boat launch.
Fee: $.
Management: City of Heppner.
Contact: 541-676-9618.
Finding the campground: From Oregon 207 at the south end of Heppner, turn east onto Willow Creek Road (the Blue Mountain Scenic Byway) and go 0.6 mile to reach this park on the left.

About the campground: This campground terraces an open, grassy slope above Willow Creek Lake, near the dam. The facility has paved roads and sites and just small planted trees. Awnings make for more comfortable stays. The openness allows for views of the lake and its rimming grassland hills and folded terrain. The lake supports trout, crappie, and bass. Besides fishing boats, you may see jet and water skis on the reservoir. Plans call for building a pool. The campground is open from March 1 into November.

NORTHERN BLUE MOUNTAINS

	Hookup sites	Total sites	Max. RV length	Hookups	Toilets	Showers	Drinking water	Dump station	Recreation	Fee	Can reserve
11 Emigrant Springs State Park	18	54	60	WES	F	•	•		HR	$$	•
12 Harris Memorial Park: Gene Palmer	26	31	40	WE	F		•		HFO	$$	•
13 Jubilee Lake		51	40		F		•		HFBL	$$	
14 Target Meadows		20	20		NF		•		H	$	
15 Umatilla Forks		18	30		NF		•		HF		
16 Woodland		8	30		NF						
17 Woodward		18	20		NF		•			$	

Hookups: W = Water E = Electric S = Sewer **Total sites:** T = Tent-only campground **Maximum trailer/RV length** given in feet.
Toilets: F = Flush NF = No Flush **Recreation:** H = Hiking S = Swimming F = Fishing B = Boating L = Boat Launch
O = Off-Highway Driving R = Horseback Riding C = Cycling
Fee: $ = $1-9 $$ = $10-19 $$$ = $20-29 $$$$ = $30-39. If no entry under **Fee,** camping is free.

11 Emigrant Springs State Park

Location: About 26 miles southeast of Pendleton.
Sites: 18 hookup sites, 33 basic sites, 3 horse campsites, 2 covered camper wagons, 1 cabin; water, electric, and sewer hookups.
Maximum length: 60 feet.
Facilities: Tables, grills, flush toilets, drinking water, showers, community building, corrals at horse sites, Oregon Trail exhibit.
Fee: $$.
Management: Oregon State Parks and Recreation Department.
Contact: 541-983-2277.
Finding the campground: From Interstate 84, 25 miles southeast of Pendleton, take Exit 234 for the state park and follow the signs to reach the park on the west side of the freeway in less than 1 mile.

About the campground: This camp rests in a deep-woods setting of fir and spruce just off the interstate and along the historic Oregon Trail. On a wooded rise at the north end of the park, the horse camp is isolated from both the family campground and the day-use area. Horse trails and nature trails invite exploration. Historically, the emigrants of the Oregon Trail camped here, filling their barrels at a spring. South of the park, at the Spring Creek exit, you will find another Oregon Trail site, the Forest Service's Blue Mountain Crossing interpretive site and trail, where you can see actual ruts left by the pioneer wagons. The campground is open from April 15 to late October.

12 Harris Memorial Park: Gene Palmer

Location: About 13 miles southeast of Milton-Freewater.
Sites: 26 hookup sites, 5 tent sites; water and electric hookups.
Maximum length: 40 feet.
Facilities: Tables, grills, flush toilets, drinking water, playground and horseshoe pits (at day-use area).
Fee: $$.
Management: Umatilla County.
Contact: 541-938-5330.
Finding the campground: At the south end of Milton-Freewater, turn east off Oregon 11 (South Main) onto 14th Street, marked for Harris County Park and Upper Walla Walla River; signs will then point you through a couple of quick turns before the road becomes Walla Walla River Road, leaving town. After 5 miles, bear right on South Fork Walla Walla River Road and proceed 7.3 miles more to the park (the final 2 miles are on gravel).

About the campground: Along the South Fork Walla Walla River, below a basalt-tiered, arid-grassland hill is this comfortable county campground, with two camping areas. You may choose between the side-by-side hookup sites along a neatly trimmed lawn or the individual hookup sites (with paved spurs) in the pine-shrub outskirts. Driving 0.4 mile past the camp, you will reach a trailhead for the South Fork Walla Walla River Trail, which dishes up a splendid river-canyon tour; this trail is open to both non-motorized and motorcycle travel. The campground is generally open year-round; self-contained RVs only in winter.

13 Jubilee Lake

Location: About 11 miles north of Tollgate.
Sites: 47 basic sites, 4 tent sites; no hookups.
Maximum length: 40 feet.
Facilities: Tables, grills, flush and vault toilets, drinking water, boat launch.
Fee: $$.
Management: Forest Service.
Contact: 509-522-6290.
Finding the campground: In Tollgate (20.2 miles east of Weston, 21.8 miles west of Elgin), turn north off Oregon 204 onto gravel Forest Road 64, indicated for Target Meadows Campground and Jubilee Lake. Go 11 miles and turn right onto FR 250 to enter the camp.

About the campground: Jubilee Lake is manmade, in a beautiful mountain setting. It welcomes boating (self-propelled or electric motor) and is stocked with trout. Sites claim the high-elevation forest above the lake, with some better suited for RVs than others. Most enjoy good privacy. A 2.5-mile trail, partially paved, encircles the lake, allowing for new perspectives and access for shore fishing. For more avid hikers, the Wenaha-Tucannon Wilderness lies to the lake's northeast. The campground is maintained from June to September.

14 Target Meadows

Location: About 3 miles north of Tollgate.
Sites: 20 basic sites; no hookups.
Maximum length: 20 feet.
Facilities: Tables, grills, vault toilets, drinking water.
Fee: $.
Management: Forest Service.
Contact: 509-522-6290.
Finding the campground: In Tollgate (20.2 miles east of Weston, 21.8 miles west of Elgin), turn north off Oregon 204 onto gravel Forest Road 64, indicated for Target Meadows Campground and Jubilee Lake. Go 0.3 mile and turn left on FR 6401. Go another 1.5 miles, then turn right onto FR 050 to enter the camp in 0.5 mile.

About the campground: This quiet camp occupies the spruce and true-fir perimeter of Target Meadows, a moist, textured meadow expanse, which is especially pretty when the stalks of false hellebore sport creamy floral crowns. Burnt Cabin Trailhead is found at the end of FR 050; the trail from there leads to the South Fork Walla Walla River. From the 1800s to 1906, Target Meadows was used as a U.S. Army firing range; mounds in the area still hold cavalry bullets. The campground is maintained from mid-June to mid-September.

15 Umatilla Forks

Location: About 35 miles east of Pendleton.
Sites: 11 basic sites, 7 tent sites; no hookups.
Maximum length: 30 feet.
Facilities: Tables, grills, pit toilets, drinking water.
Fee: None.
Management: Forest Service.
Contact: 509-522-6290.
Finding the campground: From Mission Junction (2 miles north of Interstate 84, Exit 216), go east on Mission/Umatilla River Road, following the signs to Gibbon, reaching Gibbon at 16.5 miles. Then, continue another 10.5 miles northeast, paralleling the Umatilla River into Umatilla National Forest to reach the campground on the left. (Upon entering the forest, the road becomes Forest Road 32.)

About the campground: Along the South Fork Umatilla River above the North Fork confluence, this linear campground, with a separate tent area, stretches below bald hills and long grassy ridges. A few pines and firs shade the sites, while cottonwoods and alders favor the riverbank. The camp offers quiet and access to trails for hiking and horseback riding; several enter the North Fork Umatilla Wilderness. Wildflowers abound, and wildlife sightings are common. Hunting, fishing, and trail-bike riding (on trails outside the wilderness) are other area pursuits. The campground is maintained from April through mid-October.

Camping in Umatilla National Forest.

16 Woodland

Location: About 5 miles southeast of Tollgate, 17 miles northwest of Elgin.
Sites: 8 basic sites; no hookups.
Maximum length: 30 feet.
Facilities: Tables, grills, vault toilets. No drinking water.
Fee: None.
Management: Forest Service.
Contact: 509-522-6290.
Finding the campground: It is east off Oregon 204, 16.5 miles northwest of Elgin, 5.2 miles southeast of Tollgate.

About the campground: With a single pull-thru site for larger RVs, this small campground occupies a ridge forest of spruce, lodgepole pine, and western larch. Campers may choose between deep shade and partially sunny sites. The camp is convenient for travelers, relatively quiet, and serves as a base for hunters. Umatilla Breaks Viewpoint is not far from the camp. The campground is maintained from mid-June to mid-September.

17 Woodward

Location: West end of Tollgate.
Sites: 18 basic sites; no hookups.
Maximum length: 20 feet.
Facilities: Tables, grills, vault toilets, drinking water, picnic shelter.
Fee: $.

Management: Forest Service.

Contact: 509-522-6290.

Finding the campground: On the west side of Tollgate, this campground is south off Oregon 204 on Forest Road 020. Find the turn 20 miles east of Weston, 22 miles west of Elgin.

About the campground: This camp is in forest along the west shore of marshy-ringed, private Langdon Lake. Although the lake can be admired from the camp, there is no access. Camas favors the moist shore, with grasses grading to the open water. Lichens drape the true fir and spruce. Short paths explore out from sites 1 and 13. The campground is maintained from mid-June to mid-September.

ENTERPRISE AREA

	Hookup sites	Total sites	Max. RV length	Hookups	Toilets	Showers	Drinking water	Dump station	Recreation	Fee	Can reserve
18 Boundary		8	T		NF				HF		
19 Buckhorn		6	T		NF						
20 Coyote		8	20		NF						
21 Dougherty		10	small		NF						
22 Hurricane		8	T		NF				HF		
23 The Lions Park		open	40		NF		•	•		donation	
24 Minam State Park		12	71		NF		•		FBL	$$	
25 Shady		12	16		NF				HF		
26 Two Pan		8	T		NF				HF		
27 Vigne		7	18		NF		•				
28 Wallowa Lake State Recreation Area	121	210	90	WES	F	•	•	•	HSFBLR	$$-$$$	•
29 Williamson		9	15		NF				HF		

Hookups: W = Water E = Electric S = Sewer **Total sites:** T = Tent-only campground **Maximum trailer/RV length** given in feet.
Toilets: F = Flush NF = No Flush **Recreation:** H = Hiking S = Swimming F = Fishing B = Boating L = Boat Launch
O = Off-Highway Driving R = Horseback Riding C = Cycling
Fee: $ = $1-9 $$ = $10-19 $$$ = $20-29 $$$$ = $30-39. If no entry under **Fee,** camping is free.

18 Boundary

Location: About 8 miles south of Wallowa.
Sites: 8 tent sites; no hookups.
Maximum length: Suitable for tents only.
Facilities: Tables, grills, pit toilets. No drinking water.
Fee: None.
Management: Forest Service.
Contact: 541-426-4978.
Finding the campground: From Oregon 82 in Wallowa, go southwest for 0.3 mile on West 1st Street and turn left onto Bear Creek Road/Forest Road 8250, which is paved, then gravel, following it for 7.1 miles. Now, bear right onto FR 8250.040 to pass through the campground in 0.7 mile.

About the campground: Straddling the end of FR 8250.040, prior to the Bear Creek Trailhead, is this rustic camp. Many of the sites line the shore of Bear Creek; most are fully shaded by a mature fir-spruce forest. Although there are gravel parking pads, the narrowness of the road and restricted mobility in the canyon make these sites better suited for tents. Bear Creek courses beautiful and clear; its parallel trail offers a fine introduction to Wallowa-Whitman National Forest and the Eagle Cap Wilderness. The campground is open from May to October.

Bear Creek in Wallowa-Whitman National Forest.

19 Buckhorn

Location: About 40 miles northeast of Enterprise.
Sites: 6 tent sites; no hookups.
Maximum length: Suitable for tents only.
Facilities: Tables, grills, pit toilets. No drinking water.
Fee: None.
Management: Forest Service.
Contact: 541-426-4978.
Finding the campground: From the junction of Oregon 3 and OR 82 in Enterprise, go east on OR 82 toward Joseph; at 3.3 miles, turn north at the sign for Buckhorn Springs onto paved Crow Creek Road. Go 5 miles and turn right onto Zumwalt Road, which begins paved, changes to gravel, and later becomes Forest Road 46 (Wellamotkin Drive). You will remain on Zumwalt Road/FR 46 for 31.6 miles, following the signs for Buckhorn. Here, turn right onto FR 4600.780 for Buckhorn Overlook and go 0.3 mile to a junction. Turn left for the campground; straight ahead 1 mile is the overlook. Watch for free-ranging cattle.

About the campground: This remote, almost-forgotten, primitive campground offers a shady retreat just inside the border of Hells Canyon National Recreation Area. Its neighboring attraction, a deck-ringed observation building at Buckhorn Overlook (elevation 5,333 feet), delivers a stirring Hells Canyon panorama, taking in the crisp lines, folds, and textures of the arid landscape. The view encompasses the "knife-edge" ridges of the Imnaha River drainage and the Idaho side of Hells Canyon, with the Seven Devils high peaks. Nearby hiking trails dive into the canyon or travel ridges. The campground is open from May to October.

20 Coyote

Location: About 41 miles northeast of Enterprise.
Sites: 8 basic sites; no hookups.
Maximum length: 20 feet.
Facilities: Most sites with tables and grills, pit toilets. No drinking water.
Fee: None.
Management: Forest Service.
Contact: 541-426-4978.
Finding the campground: From Enterprise, take Oregon 3 north from town at the sign for Flora and Lewiston; it is Northwest 1st Street in town. Go 14.7 miles and turn right onto Forest Road 46 (Wellamotkin Drive), which begins paved, then becomes gravel. A sign at the turn indicates Starvation and Davis Creeks. Continue 26.3 miles and turn left onto FR 4650 at a sign for the camp. Sites are on the right, 0.1 mile ahead. Be alert for free-ranging cattle along FR 46.

About the campground: This campground out in the "boonies" has a mixed habitat of open grassland and fir-pine groves, with sites well scattered for privacy. Generally, though, your camp companions tend to be wildlife, not humans. When it tests safe, intermittent Coyote Spring can serve as a camp water source, but plan on bringing a drinking supply, because it is a long way back to town. Red

Hill Lookout, passed en route to the camp, offers vistas overlooking the Pevine and Joseph creek drainages. In fall, hunting brings more faces to camp. The campground is open from May to October.

21 Dougherty

Location: About 47 miles northeast of Enterprise.
Sites: 10 sites; no hookups.
Maximum length: Small units, best suited for tents.
Facilities: Some tables or fire rings, pit toilets. No drinking water.
Fee: None.
Management: Forest Service.
Contact: 541-426-4978.
Finding the campground: From Enterprise, take Oregon 3 north from town at the sign for Flora and Lewiston; it is Northwest 1st Street in town. Go 14.7 miles and turn right onto Forest Road 46 (Wellamotkin Drive), which begins paved, then becomes gravel. A sign at the turn indicates Starvation and Davis Creeks. Continue 32.3 miles to enter this campground on the left. Be alert for free-ranging cattle along FR 46.

About the campground: Near Dougherty Spring, this primitive outpost is a great place for solitude, reflection, and nature study. In the fall, it attracts hunting parties. The undeveloped sites dot a broad plateau of meadow and evergreen stands. Wildflowers sprinkle color through the meadow. The campground is open from May to October.

22 Hurricane

Location: About 6 miles south of Enterprise, 4 miles southwest of Joseph.
Sites: 8 tent sites; no hookups.
Maximum length: Suitable for tents only.
Facilities: Some tables, grills, and fire rings; pit toilets. No drinking water.
Fee: None.
Management: Forest Service.
Contact: 541-426-4978.
Finding the campground: From Joseph, turn west off Oregon 82 onto West Wallowa Avenue at the sign for the airport and Hurricane Creek; this road later becomes Airport Lane. Follow it for 2.1 miles. Here, the paved road curves, meeting Hurricane Creek Road. For the campground, turn left onto gravel Hurricane Creek Road and go 1.8 miles to reach the campground (bearing right on paved Hurricane Creek Road takes you into Enterprise).

About the campground: This primitive camp overlooks the impressive waters of Hurricane Creek, a racing, Wallowa-Mountain-fed waterway. The sites are fully forested, snuggled amid the Douglas-firs and true firs, maples, and shrubs. A rough, narrow, gravel-and-rock-studded road stitches together the crude but well-spaced sites. The condition of the camp road, together with the short, uneven parking spaces, makes this primarily a tent camp. Upstream on Hurricane Creek Road (Forest Road 8250), you will find a trailhead for the superb Hurricane Creek Trail and its side trails that explore the Eagle Cap Wilderness. The campground is open from May to October.

23 The Lions Park

Location: In Wallowa.
Sites: Open camping area for at least a dozen units; no hookups.
Maximum length: 40 feet.
Facilities: Few tables and grills, chemical toilets, drinking water, dump station.
Fee: Donation.
Management: The Lions Club.
Contact: No telephone number.
Finding the campground: From Oregon 82 at the west end of Wallowa, turn north onto the truck route and go 0.1 mile to this park on the left.

About the campground: An open lawn and a few dotting pines shape the scene at this convenient travelers' wayside. Willows and cottonwoods edge the camp. The Wallowa County Museum may suggest an outing; among its collection are Nez Perce artifacts. The Wallowa Mountains region is noted for its outdoor recreation. The campground is open from mid-May through October.

24 Minam State Park

Location: At Minam, about 13 miles west of Wallowa.
Sites: 12 basic sites; no hookups.
Maximum length: 71 feet.
Facilities: Tables, grills, pit toilets, drinking water, raft put-in (below the bridge).
Fee: $$.
Management: Oregon State Parks and Recreation Department.
Contact: 541-432-4185.
Finding the campground: From Oregon 82, 15 miles east of Elgin, 13.4 miles west of Wallowa, turn north at the sign for the state park, following a gravel road downstream 1.6 miles to the campground.

About the campground: This canyon campground occupies a plateau above the Wallowa River, downstream from the Minam-Wallowa confluence. It offers groomed lawns, with paved roads and parking. Big ponderosa pines and smaller firs spot shade across the grounds. A fuller wooded slope rises at the back of the camp; cross-river views find a steep canyon wall with a basalt crest. A foot trail and an abandoned jeep trail provide fishing access downstream from the camp. Rafting is popular. The campground is open from mid-April through October.

A Wallowa mountain.

25 Shady

Location: About 17 miles south of Lostine.
Sites: 8 basic sites, 4 tent sites; no hookups.
Maximum length: 16 feet.
Facilities: Tables, grills, pit toilets. No drinking water.
Fee: None.
Management: Forest Service.
Contact: 541-426-4978.
Finding the campground: From Oregon 82 at Lostine, go south on Forest Road 8210 (Lostine River Road) for the Lostine River Campgrounds. The road begins paved, becoming gravel, with sometimes heavy washboard. Reach the campground on the right at 16.6 miles.

About the campground: This camp is paired with the sparkling beauty of the Lostine Wild and Scenic River and trails into the Eagle Cap Wilderness, which leave from the camp and nearby trailheads. Also, outfitters operate along FR 8210 for anyone wanting to get well into the Wallowa Mountains backcountry. Lakes, meadows, pristine streams, alpine forests, and wildlife await. If relaxing at camp is more to your liking, this campground merits a look, with the song of the river and conifer shade. The campground is open from May to October.

26 Two Pan

Location: About 17 miles south of Lostine.
Sites: 2 basic sites, 6 tent sites; no hookups.
Maximum length: Small units, best suited for tents.
Facilities: Tables, grills, pit toilets. No drinking water.
Fee: None.
Management: Forest Service.
Contact: 541-426-4978.
Finding the campground: From Oregon 82 at Lostine, go south on Forest Road 8210 (Lostine River Road) for the Lostine River Campgrounds. The road begins paved, becoming gravel, with sometimes heavy washboard. Reach the campground at road's end at 17.3 miles.

About the campground: This small, rustic campground is often hectic, being a popular gateway to the Eagle Cap Wilderness. A fir-spruce forest houses the camp; the ground is well trampled. Trails from the camp follow the east and west forks of the Lostine River upstream into the high-mountain splendor, with Minam Lake, the Wallowa Lakes Basin, and the Minam River as possible destinations. Besides hiking, fishing is popular. The campground is open from May to October.

27 Vigne

Location: About 40 miles northeast of Enterprise.
Sites: 7 basic sites; no hookups.
Maximum length: 18 feet.
Facilities: Tables, grills, pit toilets, drinking water.
Fee: None.
Management: Forest Service.
Contact: 541-426-4978.
Finding the campground: From Enterprise, take Oregon 3 north from town at the sign for Flora and Lewiston; it is Northwest 1st Street in town. Go 14.7 miles and turn right onto Forest Road 46 (Wellamotkin Drive), which begins paved, then becomes gravel. Go 13.7 miles, turn right onto narrow, paved, sometimes-rough FR 4625, and proceed 11.3 miles to enter the campground on the right. The final 1.5 miles are on gravel; entry to the camp requires a difficult right-hooking turn.

About the campground: This lightly used, rustic campground occupies a corridor of pine, fir, and shrubs along Chesnimnus Creek, a small, shallow creek threading through a pretty canyon. Sites have dirt parking, and the road through the camp is dirt. A turnaround loop helps ease access to and from the sites. The campground is open from May to October.

28 Wallowa Lake State Recreation Area

Location: About 6 miles south of Joseph, on Wallowa Lake.
Sites: 121 hookup sites, 89 basic sites, 1 yurt; water, electric, and sewer hookups.
Maximum length: 90 feet.
Facilities: Tables, flush toilets, drinking water, showers, dump station, telephone, marina, launch, moorage, picnic shelters.
Fee: $$ to $$$.
Management: Oregon State Parks and Recreation Department.
Contact: 541-432-4185; 1-800-452-5687 for reservations.
Finding the campground: From Joseph, drive 5.9 miles south on Oregon 82 and bear right at the fork to reach the state park campground.

About the campground: On the south shore of Wallowa Lake, a large glacial-moraine lake watched over by snowy peaks, sits this popular campground. The lawn-and-forest camp offers comfortable, developed sites within footsteps of the oval lake, its recreation, and prized trails into the Eagle Cap Wilderness. Nearby attractions include Chief Joseph's grave, the steepest vertical-lift gondola in North America (Wallowa Lake Tramway), horse concession trail rides, and Wallowa Loop Scenic Drive. The campground is open from mid-April to late October.

29 Williamson

Location: About 11 miles south of Lostine.
Sites: 9 basic sites; no hookups.
Maximum length: 15 feet.
Facilities: Tables, grills, pit toilets. No drinking water.
Fee: None.
Management: Forest Service.
Contact: 541-426-4978.
Finding the campground: From Oregon 82 at Lostine, go south on Forest Road 8210 (Lostine River Road) for the Lostine River Campgrounds. The road begins paved, then becomes gravel, with sometimes heavy washboard. Reach the campground on the right at 10.8 miles.

About the campground: This primitive campground occupies a wooded slope above the Lostine Wild and Scenic River, one of the prized waterways of the region and state. Lodgepole pine, fir, and larch create partial shade; the parking spaces tend to be small and uneven. Fishing and hiking amuse visitors, with area packers offering an easier way to get into the wilderness. Dispersed sites can be found along FR 8210 for additional camping options. The campground is open from May to October.

LA GRANDE AREA

		Hookup sites	Total sites	Max. RV length	Hookups	Toilets	Showers	Drinking water	Dump station	Recreation	Fee	Can reserve
30	Birdtrack Springs		22	40		NF				F		
31	Catherine Creek State Park		18	30		F		•		F	$$	
32	Hilgard Junction State Park		18	30		F		•		FBL	$$	
33	Moss Springs		14	25		NF				HR		
34	North Fork Catherine Creek		6	small		NF				HFR		
35	Red Bridge State Park		20	30		F		•		F	$	
36	River		13	25		NF		•		F		
37	Spool Cart		16	40		NF				F		

Hookups: W = Water E = Electric S = Sewer **Total sites:** T = Tent-only campground **Maximum trailer/RV length** given in feet.
Toilets: F = Flush NF = No Flush **Recreation:** H = Hiking S = Swimming F = Fishing B = Boating L = Boat Launch
O = Off-Highway Driving R = Horseback Riding C = Cycling
Fee: $ = $1-9 $$ = $10-19 $$$ = $20-29 $$$$ = $30-39. If no entry under **Fee,** camping is free.

30 Birdtrack Springs

Location: About 15 miles west of La Grande.
Sites: 22 basic sites; no hookups.
Maximum length: 40 feet.
Facilities: Tables, grills, vault toilets. No drinking water.
Fee: None.
Management: Forest Service.
Contact: 541-963-7186.
Finding the campground: From Interstate 84 north of La Grande, take Exit 252 and go 5.4 miles west on Oregon 244 to reach this campground on the left. (The camp turnoff is 42 miles east of Ukiah.)

About the campground: This campground enjoys a peaceful setting of tall ponderosa pine, fir, and larch. Wild rose, grass, and currant contribute to the forest's meadow floor. The sites are well spaced, with gravel parking. Songbirds complement a stay. At the camp's west edge is the rail-fenced natural spring captured by a pipe. Although it can supply water when it tests pure, play it safe and bring what you will need. Across OR 244, visitors can access the Grande Ronde River for fishing. The campground is open from early May to late November.

31 Catherine Creek State Park

Location: 8 miles southeast of Union.
Sites: 18 basic sites; no hookups.
Maximum length: 30 feet.
Facilities: Tables, grills, flush toilets, drinking water.
Fee: $$.
Management: Oregon State Parks and Recreation Department.

Contact: 541-983-2277.
Finding the campground: From Union, go 8 miles southeast on Oregon 203; the state park is on the right.

About the campground: Alongside lightly traveled OR 203, this state park picnic area and campground fronts half a mile of the broad, smooth-flowing Catherine Creek. Planted deciduous and native ponderosa pine trees shade the lawns, while cottonwoods tower above the creek. Despite its proximity to OR 203, the location exudes tranquility. Visitors can fish, cool their ankles, or seek out area trails into Wallowa-Whitman National Forest and the Eagle Cap Wilderness. The campground is open from mid-April into October.

32 Hilgard Junction State Park

Location: About 10 miles west of La Grande.
Sites: 18 basic sites; no hookups.
Maximum length: 30 feet.
Facilities: Tables, grills, flush toilets, drinking water, horseshoe pits, rafting access.
Fee: $$.
Management: Oregon State Parks and Recreation Department.
Contact: 541-523-2499.
Finding the campground: From Interstate 84 north of La Grande, take Exit 252 and follow the signs to the park. It is on the west side of the freeway off Oregon 244.

About the campground: This campground occupies a narrow strip between I-84 and the Grande Ronde River. It is a pretty spot but can be noisy when large trucks tackle the interstate grade. Usually, though, the river wins out. Cottonwoods shade the dandelion-sprinkled lawn, with a forested slope rising opposite the camp. This is an Oregon Trail site, and to its northwest off I-84 is Blue Mountain Crossing, a Forest Service interpretive site and trail, where the original wagon ruts can be seen. Fishing and rafting are popular river activities. The campground is open from March 1 to November 30.

33 Moss Springs

Location: About 8 miles east of Cove.
Sites: 11 basic sites, 3 tent sites; no hookups.
Maximum length: 25 feet.
Facilities: Tables, grills, vault toilets, corrals, horse-loading ramp. No drinking water.
Fee: None.
Management: Forest Service.
Contact: 541-962-8589.
Finding the campground: From OR 237 in Cove, turn east onto French Street (opposite the high school) for Moss Springs Campground. French Street then bends into Mill Creek Lane, which later becomes Forest Road 6220. Follow these paved and gravel routes for 8.4 miles to reach the campground.

North Fork Catherine Creek.

About the campground: This camp occupies a high-elevation-forest rim at a popular hiker/horse entryway to the Eagle Cap Wilderness. The sites are well spaced, comfortable, and well used, especially during hunting season. Horse Ranch Trail descends from this Wallowa Mountain plateau, passing through a historic horse ranch at the bottom of the canyon, to meet the pristine Minam River and its trail to discovery. If you visit the ranch area, travel lightly and pitch backpack and horse camps well away from this fragile historical resource. The terrain resembles Hells Canyon as much as the Wallowa high country: View basalt-tiered grassland rims and rocky summits. The campground is open from June into October.

34 North Fork Catherine Creek

Location: About 17 miles southeast of Union.
Sites: 6 basic sites; no hookups.
Maximum length: Best suited for tents and pickup campers.
Facilities: A few tables and fire rings, pit toilets, horse-loading ramp. No drinking water.
Fee: None.
Management: Forest Service.
Contact: 541-962-8589.
Finding the campground: From Union, go 11 miles southeast on Oregon 203 and turn left (east) onto Forest Road 7785 (Catherine Creek Lane). Go 5.7 miles on this gravel, single-lane road to the camp.

About the campground: This rustic creekside camp offers a quiet, no-frills getaway and access to the Eagle Cap Wilderness. The camp has informal parking on a rolling dirt flat; mature conifers offer shade, while wildflowers grow among the grasses. An engaging host, North Fork Catherine Creek is a racing, black satin stream spilling between shrub-lined banks. The North Fork Catherine Creek Trail starts at the camp and heads upstream to cross a creek bridge and swing up-canyon. It visits engaging high meadows and enters wilderness. The campground is open from June into October.

35 Red Bridge State Park

Location: About 16 miles west of La Grande.
Sites: 20 basic sites; no hookups.
Maximum length: 30 feet.
Facilities: Tables, grills, flush toilets, drinking water, horseshoe pits.
Fee: $.
Management: Oregon State Parks and Recreation Department.
Contact: 541-523-2499.
Finding the campground: From Interstate 84 north of La Grande, take Exit 252 and go 7.3 miles west on Oregon 244 to reach this park on the left.

About the campground: At this Grande Ronde River park, previously open for day use only, RVers may now dry camp in the parking area, and tent campers are welcome to walk in and pitch their tents on the grassy, pine-clad river bench at the park's east end. A fee station is at the parking area. The ponderosa pines create a scenic, shady rest; red rosier dogwood grows toward shore. Fishing is the pastime. The campground is open from March 1 to November 30.

36 River

Location: About 31 miles southwest of La Grande.
Sites: 13 basic sites; no hookups.
Maximum length: 25 feet.
Facilities: Tables, grills, pit toilets, drinking water (at picnic area 0.5 mile north).
Fee: None.
Management: Forest Service.
Contact: 541-963-7186.
Finding the campground: From Interstate 84 north of La Grande, take Exit 252 and go 11.7 miles west on Oregon 244 (if following OR 244 from Ukiah, it is 35 miles east). Turn south on Forest Road 51 (Grande Ronde Road), crossing the bridge over the river. Go 10.5 miles to find this camp straddling FR 51.

About the campground: Both parts of this camp overlook the Grande Ronde River; anglers may choose to dunk a line. The west-side sites are rustic, occupy a slope above the river, and have a mix of sun and shade from a pine-larch forest; the east-side sites are equally rustic in a setting of lodgepole pine. The campground is open from early May to late November.

37 Spool Cart

Location: About 25 miles southwest of La Grande.
Sites: 16 basic sites; no hookups.
Maximum length: 40 feet.
Facilities: Tables, grills, vault toilets. No drinking water.
Fee: None.
Management: Forest Service.
Contact: 541-963-7186.
Finding the campground: From Interstate 84 north of La Grande, take Exit 252 and go 11.7 miles west on Oregon 244 (if following OR 244 from Ukiah, it is 35 miles east). Turn south on Forest Road 51 (Grande Ronde Road), crossing the bridge over the river. Go 4.5 miles to find this camp on the right.

About the campground: At this Grande Ronde River campground, large, extra-wide paved parking spaces help get you settled. The camp occupies a relaxing spot on the river for reverie or fishing. The sites are fully or partially shaded by a forest of ponderosa pine, fir, larch, and spruce. The campground is open from early May to late November.

		Hookup sites	Total sites	Max. RV length	Hookups	Toilets	Showers	Drinking water	Dump station	Recreation	Fee	Can re...
38	Bear Wallow		6	35		NF				H	donation	
39	Big Creek		4	small		NF				HFOR		
40	Divide Well		7	40		NF						
41	Drift Fence		5	40		NF						
42	Driftwood		5	small		NF				FB		
43	Frazier		18	40		NF				O		
44	Gold Dredge		6	20		NF				F		
45	Lane Creek		8	40		NF				F		
46	Tollbridge		7	25		NF		•		F		
47	Ukiah-Dale Forest St. Scenic Corridor		22	40		F		•		F	$$	
48	Welch Creek		3	30		NF				F		
49	Winom Creek OHV Campground		7	40		NF				HO		

Hookups: W = Water E = Electric S = Sewer **Total sites:** T = Tent-only campground **Maximum trailer/RV length** given in feet.
Toilets: F = Flush NF = No Flush **Recreation:** H = Hiking S = Swimming F = Fishing B = Boating L = Boat Launch
O = Off-Highway Driving R = Horseback Riding C = Cycling
Fee: $ = $1-9 $$ = $10-19 $$$ = $20-29 $$$$ = $30-39. If no entry under **Fee**, camping is free.

38 Bear Wallow

Location: 11 miles east of Ukiah.
Sites: 6 basic sites; no hookups.
Maximum length: 35 feet.
Facilities: Tables, grills, vault toilets. No drinking water.
Fee: Donation.
Management: Forest Service.
Contact: 541-427-3231.
Finding the campground: From Ukiah, go east on Oregon 244 for 11 miles and turn north to enter this campground.

About the campground: This camp rests at the foot of a spatially open, ponderosa-pine-forested slope; Bear Wallow Creek supplies a pleasant backdrop murmur. The slope shows many of the big, red-trunked pines, with a few right at camp. At the camp, the three-quarter-mile, barrier-free Bear Wallow Creek Interpretive Trail explores the stream habitat; interpretive panels describe habitat management for steelhead. Big larch, false hellebore bogs, and spring wildflowers further recommend a tour. The campground is open from June through October.

39 Big Creek

Location: About 25 miles southeast of Ukiah, 27 miles northwest of Granite.
Sites: 4 basic sites; no hookups.
Maximum length: Small units due to narrow access road.
Facilities: Tables, vault toilets. No drinking water.
Fee: None.
Management: Forest Service.
Contact: 541-427-3231.
Finding the campground: From Forest Road 52, 25 miles southeast of Ukiah, 27 miles northwest of Granite, turn south onto Forest Road 5225 and take a quick right onto FR 020, a single-lane dirt road. Cross Big Creek via a bridge at 0.3 mile and after another 0.1 mile, turn left to enter this camp.

About the campground: This primitive camp beside Big Creek, a pretty, green-flowing stream, escaped the Tower Fire, keeping its quiet, lodgepole-pine setting. The camp is a base for fishing or exploring hiker, horse, or all-terrain-vehicle trails, and it is a jumpoff point for the North Fork John Day Wilderness, a non-motorized area of travel. The campground is open from June through October.

40 Divide Well

Location: About 24 miles west of Ukiah.
Sites: 7 basic sites; no hookups.
Maximum length: 40 feet.
Facilities: Tables, crude fire rings, vault toilets. No drinking water.
Fee: None.
Management: Forest Service.
Contact: 541-427-3231.
Finding the campground: From U.S. Highway 395 near Ukiah, go west on Forest Road 53 for about 14 miles to Four Corners, turn left onto FR 5327, and continue southeast for about 9 miles to enter the camp; expect some heavy washboard.

About the campground: This rustic camp offers a peaceful retreat among the pines and firs, while the large flat gives horse trailers maneuvering room. Generally, the camp is lightly trafficked, serving hunters in the fall and a wagon train in summer, as it retraces history. Mule deer and Rocky Mountain elk dwell in the area of the camp, and 11 miles south via FR 5316 (not suitable for RVs) is Potamus Point, which delivers an overlook of the John Day River drainage and interesting rock formations. The campground is open from June through October.

41 Drift Fence

Location: About 8 miles southeast of Ukiah, 45 miles northwest of Granite.
Sites: 5 basic sites; no hookups.
Maximum length: 40 Feet.

Facilities: Tables, grills, vault toilets. No drinking water.
Fee: None.
Management: Forest Service.
Contact: 541-427-3231.
Finding the campground: From Forest Road 52, 7.5 miles southeast of Ukiah, 44.5 miles northwest of Granite, turn south to enter this camp.

About the campground: This traditional hunter's camp on Blue Mountain Scenic Byway (FR 52) is scheduled for an upgrade. Presently, it offers widespread sites in a full, mature forest of ponderosa pine and larch at the edge of a meadow sprinkled with blue and yellow wildflowers. Bridge Creek Interpretive Trail, located 2.4 miles northwest of the camp (toward Ukiah), offers a half-mile walk on a gravel-surfaced trail to an overlook of the Bridge Creek drainage. The campground is open from June through October.

42 Driftwood

Location: About 20 miles southeast of Ukiah.
Sites: 5 basic sites; no hookups.
Maximum length: Small units.
Facilities: Tables, fire rings, vault toilets. No drinking water.
Fee: None.
Management: Forest Service.
Contact: 541-427-3231.
Finding the campground: From U.S. Highway 395, 1 mile north of Dale, 14 miles south of the junction of US 395 and Oregon 244 near Ukiah, turn east onto gravel Texas Bar Road for Olive Lake. At 0.6 mile, go left onto Forest Road 55, and after another 4.2 miles, turn right to enter the camp.

About the campground: This forest camp on the North Fork John Day Wild and Scenic River affords beautiful views of the river and its downstream canyon, which shows striking basalt rims. Below the camp, a small gravel beach provides easy access to the river, which hosts the only natural run of Chinook salmon in the John Day watershed; special fishing regulations apply. The river also invites rafting, tube floating, and even snorkeling with the steelhead. Ponderosa pines shade the camp. The campground is open from June through October.

43 Frazier

Location: About 18 miles east of Ukiah.
Sites: 18 basic sites; no hookups.
Maximum length: 40 feet.
Facilities: Tables, grills, vault toilets, all-terrain-vehicle loading ramp. No drinking water.
Fee: None.
Management: Forest Service.
Contact: 541-427-3231.

Finding the campground: From Ukiah, go east on Oregon 244 for 17 miles and turn south onto gravel Forest Road 5226 to enter this camp on the left in 0.5 mile.

About the campground: A mix of pine and larch partially shades these well-spaced sites along Frazier Creek. The primary camp user is the all-terrain-vehicle enthusiast. The Butcher Knife ATV Trail leaves from the camp, and a legend at the entry kiosk shows an entire network of ATV tours. Oddly enough, the camp is also rich in wildflowers; even the untrained amateur can detect scores of species. You can pick up a wildflower checklist at the North Fork John Day Ranger District Office in Ukiah. The campground is open from June through October.

44 Gold Dredge

Location: About 22 miles southeast of Ukiah.
Sites: 6 basic sites; no hookups.
Maximum length: 20 feet.
Facilities: Tables, grills, pit toilets. No drinking water.
Fee: None.
Management: Forest Service.
Contact: 541-427-3231.
Finding the campground: From U.S. Highway 395, 1 mile north of Dale, 14 miles south of the junction of US 395 and Oregon 244 near Ukiah, turn east onto gravel Texas Bar Road for Olive Lake. At 0.6 mile, go left onto Forest Road 55, continue 4.8 miles, and from there go straight on FR 5506 for 1.9 miles to reach the campground off FR 030.

About the campground: With a difficult turn into and out of the camp, individuals driving larger units may choose to bypass this facility. The camp extends a shady retreat along the North Fork John Day River, with parking on the grassy river bench. False hellebore adorns the moist meadow reaches, and in spring the camp hawthorn bushes wear white blossoms. Special fishing regulations apply to protect the anadromous fishery of this watershed. Presently, some 9 miles of tailings along this river stretch record the dredge activity of the early 1900s; plans call for the removal of these cobble mounds to enhance and restore fish habitat. The campground is open from June through October.

45 Lane Creek

Location: 10 miles east of Ukiah.
Sites: 8 basic sites; no hookups.
Maximum length: 40 feet.
Facilities: Tables, grills, vault toilets. No drinking water.
Fee: None.
Management: Forest Service.
Contact: 541-427-3231.
Finding the campground: From Ukiah, go east on Oregon 244 for 10 miles and turn north to enter this camp.

About the campground: Tiny Lane Creek flows at the eastern edge of this rustic camp, while towering ponderosa pine and larch riddle the mixed-age forest. The campsites are bathed in a mix of sun and shadow. Fishing on Camas Creek (along OR 244) may divert campers from their leisure; otherwise, this is a typical eat, sleep, yawn-and-stretch destination. The campground is open from June through October.

46 Tollbridge

Location: About 16 miles south of Ukiah.
Sites: 7 basic sites; no hookups.
Maximum length: 25 feet.
Facilities: Tables, fire rings, pit toilets, drinking water.
Fee: None.
Management: Forest Service.
Contact: 541-427-3231.
Finding the campground: From U.S. Highway 395, 1 mile north of Dale, 14 miles south of the junction of US 395 and Oregon 244 near Ukiah, turn east onto gravel Texas Bar Road for Forest Road 10 and Olive Lake. At 0.6 mile, bear right on FR 10, and after another 0.1 mile, turn right to enter the camp.

About the campground: Below FR 10, this camp claims the narrow meadow shore of Desolation Creek just upstream from its confluence with the North Fork John Day River. Hawthorn, box elder, a few conifer, and a lilac bush dot the camp flat. High canyon rims overlook the setting. The camp is a favorite of hunters and fishermen; be sure to check the sportfishing regulations for special rules. The campground is open from June through October.

47 Ukiah-Dale Forest State Scenic Corridor

Location: About 2 miles south of Ukiah.
Sites: 22 basic sites; no hookups.
Maximum length: 40 feet.
Facilities: Tables, grills, flush toilets, drinking water.
Fee: $$.
Management: Oregon State Parks and Recreation Department.
Contact: 541-523-2499.
Finding the campground: It is east off U.S. Highway 395, 1.4 miles south of the junction of US 395 and Oregon 244 near Ukiah, 14 miles north of Dale.

About the campground: This attractive wayside is located along a scenic corridor embracing a 14-mile stretch of Camas Creek, a beautiful, alternately glassy and riffling waterway, with meadow and shrub shores. The creek appeals to anglers, kayakers, and rafters. The camp fills a ponderosa-pine-shaded greenway between Camas Creek and US 395. Cross-creek views are of a rock-and-forest slope. All sites have paved parking; some directly overlook the creek. The camp water source is an artesian well. The campground is open from April 15 to late October.

48 Welch Creek

Location: About 30 miles southeast of Ukiah.
Sites: 3 basic sites; no hookups.
Maximum length: 30 feet.
Facilities: Tables, fire rings, pit toilets. No drinking water.
Fee: None.
Management: Forest Service.
Contact: 541-427-3231.
Finding the campground: From U.S. Highway 395, 1 mile north of Dale, 14 miles south of the junction of US 395 and Oregon 244 near Ukiah, turn east onto gravel Texas Bar Road for Forest Road 10 and Olive Lake. At 0.6 mile, bear right on FR 10, continue another 14 miles, and turn right to enter the camp.

About the campground: This primitive camp occupies an open meadow flat along Desolation Creek, a large, swift-flowing creek. Pine and larch shape a rim to the camp; across the creek rises a congested lodgepole-pine-forested slope, with tightly spaced trees and interlacing logs. The camp is well used by hunters in the fall, and an off-highway-vehicle trail starts to the camp's east, off FR 10. Bird watching and fishing (special regulations apply) are other possible diversions. The campground is open from June through October.

49 Winom Creek Off-Highway-Vehicle Campground

Location: About 25 miles southeast of Ukiah, 29 miles northwest of Granite.
Sites: 7 basic sites; no hookups.
Maximum length: 40 feet.
Facilities: Tables, grills, vault toilets, group picnic shelters, OHV loading ramp. No drinking water.
Fee: None.
Management: Forest Service.
Contact: 541-427-3231.
Finding the campground: From Forest Road 52, 24 miles southeast of Ukiah, 28 miles northwest of Granite, turn south for this campground, following a winding, coarse-grade gravel road 0.7 mile to the camp.

About the campground: At the outskirts of the Tower Fire Zone, this basic forest camp is tucked away in the Winom Creek Valley, in a setting of tall, thin lodgepole pines, with some contrasting big larch. The Tower Fire had a hit-and-miss pattern, sparing the camp but altering its views. This camp is a gateway to the North Fork John Day Wilderness, open to foot and horse travel only, and it is an off-highway-vehicle staging area for the Winom-Frazier OHV Trail System. The campground is open from June through October.

JOHN DAY COUNTRY

		Hookup sites	Total sites	Max. RV length	Hookups	Toilets	Showers	Drinking water	Dump station	Recreation	Fee	Can reserve
50	Barnhouse		6	20		NF						
51	Bear Hollow County Park		13	25		NF					$	
52	Big Bend Recreation Site		4	40		NF				F	$	
53	Bull Prairie Recreation Area		21	40		NF		•	•	HFBL	$	
54	Clyde Holliday State Recreation Site	30	30	60	WE	F	•	•	•	FB	$$	
55	Cottonwood		6	20		NF						
56	Deerhorn		4	25		NF				F		
57	Donnelly Recreation Site		4	40		NF				SFBL	$	
58	Fairview		5	20		NF		•				
59	Frazier		5	20		NF						
60	Lone Pine Recreation Site		4	40		NF				F	$	
61	Middle Fork		10	30		NF				F		
62	Muleshoe Recreation Site		9	35		NF				SFBL	$	
63	Ochoco Divide		28	32		NF		•			$	
64	Oregon Mine		3	22		NF				F		
65	Shelton Wayside State Park		36	35		NF		•		H	$	
66	Wildwood		5	T		NF						

Hookups: W = Water E = Electric S = Sewer **Total sites:** T = Tent-only campground **Maximum trailer/RV length** given in feet.
Toilets: F = Flush NF = No Flush **Recreation:** H = Hiking S = Swimming F = Fishing B = Boating L = Boat Launch
O = Off-Highway Driving R = Horseback Riding C = Cycling
Fee: $ = $1-9 $$ = $10-19 $$$ = $20-29 $$$$ = $30-39. If no entry under **Fee**, camping is free.

50 Barnhouse

Location: About 18 miles southeast of Mitchell.
Sites: 6 basic sites; no hookups.
Maximum length: 20 feet.
Facilities: Tables, a few fire rings, pit toilets. No drinking water.
Fee: None.
Management: Forest Service.
Contact: 541-477-3713; 541-416-6643.
Finding the campground: From U.S. Highway 26, 13 miles east of Mitchell, turn south on Forest Road 12. Go 5 miles, ascending to the camp turnoff on the right.

About the campground: In a full forest of fir, pine, and larch, you will find these primitive campsites, most of which have tables; a few have a grill or fire ring. Parking is where you make it. The buzzing of insects or the knocking of a woodpecker only magnify the quiet. Hiking and hunting can be done nearby. The campground is open from May 1 to October 31.

51 Bear Hollow County Park

Location: About 7 miles southeast of Fossil.
Sites: 13 basic sites; no hookups.
Maximum length: 25 feet.
Facilities: Tables, grills, pit toilets. No drinking water.
Fee: $.
Management: Wheeler County.
Contact: 541-763-2911.
Finding the campground: It is west off Oregon 19, 6.5 miles south of Fossil, 12.5 miles north of the junction of OR 19 and OR 207 South (near Service Creek).

About the campground: This camp has restful appeal, set in a forest of mixed fir, with a meadow floor. Although most of the parking spaces are graveled, they still require some leveling. This park is popular in the fall with hunters and serves John Day Country travelers. The campground is open year-round.

52 Big Bend Recreation Site

Location: 3 miles northeast of Kimberly.
Sites: 4 basic sites; no hookups.
Maximum length: 40 feet.
Facilities: Tables, fire rings (fires and smoking prohibited June to mid-October), vault toilets. No drinking water.
Fee: $.
Management: Bureau of Land Management.
Contact: 541-416-6700.
Finding the campground: The site is south off the Kimberly–Long Creek Highway, 3 miles northeast of Kimberly, 11 miles southwest of Monument.

About the campground: These four well-spaced sites claim a broad river bench where the North Fork John Day River swings a lazy bend. Each site is paired with at least one juniper for shade; parking is on the grassy flat. Opposite from the camp rises a steep, grassy slope, with rimrock tiers and showings of mountain mahogany. You can fish, swim, or explore the John Day Country. Deer sometimes frequent the river. The campground is open year-round.

53 Bull Prairie Recreation Area

Location: About 20 miles north of Spray, on Bull Prairie Reservoir.
Sites: 21 basic sites; no hookups.
Maximum length: 40 feet.
Facilities: Tables, grills, vault and pit toilets, drinking water, dump station, boat launch, wheelchair-accessible fishing platform and trail.
Fee: $.
Management: Forest Service.
Contact: 541-676-9187.

Finding the campground: From Oregon 207, 17 miles north of Spray, 38 miles south of Heppner, turn east onto Forest Road 2039, go 3 miles, and bear right to enter the recreation area.

About the campground: At this relaxing, family retreat, campsites are dispersed throughout the mature, mixed-conifer forest surrounding Bull Prairie Reservoir, a scenic, manmade lake ringed by cattails and stocked with trout. In keeping with the quiet of the setting, the lake is open to non-motorized boating only. The 1.25-mile Lake Shore Trail travels the lake perimeter for a pleasant start or cap to your day. The campground is open from June through October.

54 Clyde Holliday State Recreation Site

Location: 8 miles west of John Day.
Sites: 30 hookup sites; water and electric hookups.
Maximum length: 60 feet.
Facilities: Tables, grills, flush toilets, drinking water, showers, dump station, telephone, horseshoe pits.
Fee: $$.
Management: Oregon State Parks and Recreation Department.
Contact: 541-575-2773.
Finding the campground: It is south off U.S. Highway 26, 8 miles west of John Day.

About the campground: In the shadow of the Blue Mountains, in the heart of John Day Country is this attractive, landscaped John Day River campground. Fishing and sightseeing are popular activities. In John Day, be sure to look for the Kam Wah Chung State Heritage Site, a trading post built between 1866 and 1867 by Chinese merchants; it is shown by guided tour daily (except Friday), May through October. Elsewhere, the units of John Day Fossil Beds National Monument unfold an exciting geologic timeline and spectacular scenery. The John Day River offers rafting opportunities. The campground is open from March through November.

55 Cottonwood

Location: About 27 miles southeast of Mitchell.
Sites: 6 basic sites; no hookups.
Maximum length: 20 feet.
Facilities: A few tables and crude fire rings, pit toilets. No drinking water.
Fee: None.
Management: Forest Service.
Contact: 541-477-3713; 541-416-6643.
Finding the campground: From U.S. Highway 26, 13 miles east of Mitchell, turn south onto Forest Road 12, which begins paved, then becomes gravel, for a hefty ascent. Go 13.5 miles and turn left onto FR 200, proceeding 0.3 mile more to the camp.

About the campground: This is a campground for the do-it-yourself camper. Sites are informal, with perhaps a table or a fire ring marking the spot. The location unites a mature pine-fir forest, false hellebore meadow, and prairie meadow for a pleasant place to kick back and relax. In fall, hunters often base here. The campground is open from May 1 to October 31.

56 Deerhorn

Location: About 22 miles northeast of Prairie City.
Sites: 4 basic sites; no hookups.
Maximum length: 25 feet.
Facilities: Tables, grills, pit toilets. No drinking water.
Fee: None.
Management: Forest Service.
Contact: 541-575-2110.
Finding the campground: From the junction of Main Street and U.S. Highway 26 in Prairie City, go east on US 26 for 15.3 miles, turn north onto Oregon 7 for Sumpter and Baker City, and go another 1.1 miles. There, turn left onto County Road 20 for Susanville and travel 5.1 miles to this camp on the left.

About the campground: This small, rustic camp occupies a transition habitat, where a false hellebore meadow and ponderosa pine forest meet. It rests along the picturesque Middle Fork John Day River and engages guests with fishing, wildlife viewing, and hunting. The campground is maintained from May 30 to mid-October.

57 Donnelly Recreation Site

Location: About 13 miles southwest of Spray.
Sites: 4 basic sites; no hookups.
Maximum length: 40 feet.
Facilities: Tables, vault toilets, primitive boat launch. No drinking water.
Fee: $.
Management: Bureau of Land Management.
Contact: 541-416-6700.
Finding the campground: From the junction of Oregon 19 and Oregon 207 south, near Service Creek (12.3 miles southwest of Spray), turn south on OR 207. Go 0.3 mile to reach the recreation site on the left.

About the campground: Primarily a base for rafters, this camp occupies an arid flat along the John Day River. Only a couple of pines and scattered junipers dot the flat; tables are paired with the trees for a retreat from the sun. The setting is one of basalt-tiered grassland rims, butte-dressed skylines, and river-canyon cliffs. Fishing and swimming are other amusements. The campground is open year-round.

58 Fairview

Location: 39 miles south of Heppner.
Sites: 5 basic sites; no hookups.
Maximum length: 20 feet.
Facilities: Tables, grills, pit toilets, drinking water.
Fee: None.
Management: Forest Service.
Contact: 541-676-9187.
Finding the campground: It is west off Oregon 207, 16 miles north of Spray, 39 miles south of Heppner.

About the campground: On a slope below OR 207, in a ponderosa pine stand with a meadow floor, you will find these five well-spaced campsites. Part of the campground looks out at a burn. The camp is convenient for travelers and welcomes lazing about. The campground is open from June through October.

59 Frazier

Location: About 28 miles northeast of Paulina.
Sites: 5 basic sites; no hookups.
Maximum length: 20 feet.
Facilities: Tables, crude fire rings, pit toilets. No drinking water.
Fee: None.
Management: Forest Service.
Contact: 541-477-3713; 541-416-6643.
Finding the campground: From Paulina (56 miles east of Prineville), go east on County Road 112, the Paulina Highway, for 4.2 miles. Turn left onto gravel CR 113/Forest Road 58, and follow this alternately paved and gravel route for 22.2 miles. Turn left onto narrow, sometimes rough FR 5800.500, continuing another 1.6 miles to the camp.

About the campground: This primitive forest camp provides a quiet escape from everyday demands. It has a pine-meadow setting and well-spaced, informal sites for personal privacy. A grove of aspen with dancing leaves shades a headwater spring of Frazier Creek. The camp is just a short hop away from the South Fork John Day River via FR 58 eastbound, and this camp is another favorite of hunters. The campground is open from May 1 to October 31.

60 Lone Pine Recreation Site

Location: About 2 miles northeast of Kimberly.
Sites: 4 basic sites; no hookups.
Maximum length: 40 feet.
Facilities: Tables, fire rings, vault toilets. No drinking water.
Fee: $.
Management: Bureau of Land Management.

Contact: 541-416-6700.

Finding the campground: It is south off the Kimberly–Long Creek Highway, 1.7 miles northeast of Kimberly.

About the campground: On a flat along the North Fork John Day River, visitors will find this small camp, which lacks improved parking. A grove of cottonwoods shades a pair of sites, while the other two are mostly sunny. Nighttime unites the song of the river and the click of crickets and brings on the erratic flight of bats. Days are filled with fishing, swimming, and exploring the John Day Country and scattered units of John Day Fossil Beds National Monument. The campground is open year-round.

61 Middle Fork

Location: About 23 miles northeast of Prairie City.
Sites: 10 basic sites; no hookups.
Maximum length: 30 feet.
Facilities: Tables, grills, pit toilets. No drinking water.
Fee: None.
Management: Forest Service.
Contact: 541-575-2110.
Finding the campground: From the junction of Main Street and U.S. Highway 26 in Prairie City, go east on US 26 for 15.3 miles, turn north onto Oregon 7 toward Sumpter and Baker City, and go another 1.1 miles. There, turn left onto County Road 20 for Susanville and travel 6.6 miles to the campground on the left.

About the campground: This linear campground stretches alongside the Middle Fork John Day River, with most of its sites overlooking the river and all having gravel parking. The young and middle-aged pines and firs that dress the flat provide at least partial shade for the sites. Alders, a few dogwoods, and meadow vegetation claim the shore. The camp appeals to outdoor interests, with fishing and hunting, and is near Vinegar Hill–Indian Rock Scenic Area. The campground is maintained from May 30 to mid-October.

62 Muleshoe Recreation Site

Location: About 10 miles west of Spray.
Sites: 6 basic sites, 3 walk-in tent sites; no hookups.
Maximum length: 35 feet.
Facilities: Tables, vault toilets, primitive boat launch. No drinking water.
Fee: $.
Management: Bureau of Land Management.
Contact: 541-416-6700.
Finding the campground: From Spray, go 10.3 miles west on Oregon 19 North/ 207 South to reach this camp on the left.

About the campground: This campground rests on a small plateau above the John Day River. The walk-in sites are tucked into a juniper grove; the basic sites have gravel parking spurs and claim an open sagebrush flat for unobstructed river views. The canyon captivates with its folded tableland ridges, cliffs, and rims. Below the camp, hackberry and wild rose grow at the sides of a popular raft put-in/take-out. Fishing, rafting, and swimming attract visitors to this region and camp. The campground is open year-round.

63 Ochoco Divide

Location: 18 miles southwest of Mitchell.
Sites: 28 basic sites, bicycle camp; no hookups.
Maximum length: 32 feet.
Facilities: Tables, grills, vault toilets, drinking water.
Fee: $.
Management: Forest Service.
Contact: 541-416-6645.
Finding the campground: It is east off U.S. Highway 26, 30 miles northeast of Prineville, 18 miles southwest of Mitchell.

About the campground: At Ochoco Pass on US 26, you will find this camp among the old-growth ponderosa pines and firs. The camp primarily caters to the passer-through, so individuals who opt to linger generally enjoy quiet days for birding and relaxing. An old road ventures away from the campground for an easy leg stretch. The Painted Hills Unit of John Day Fossil Beds National Monument is a half-hour drive northwest of the camp. The campground is open from late May through October.

64 Oregon Mine

Location: About 32 miles southwest of John Day.
Sites: 3 basic sites; no hookups.
Maximum length: 22 feet.
Facilities: Tables, grills, pit toilet. No drinking water.
Fee: None.
Management: Forest Service.
Contact: 541-575-2110.
Finding the campground: From U.S. Highway 26, 13 miles east of Dayville, 18 miles west of John Day, turn south onto paved Forest Road 21 (Fields Creek Road). Follow it for 13.4 miles and turn right onto gravel FR 2170 to enter the campground on the left in 0.4 mile.

About the campground: This small, out-of-the-way, primitive campground has great charm, with its shrub-meadow floor, towering ponderosa pines, rustic rail fencing, and shrub-lined Murderers Creek flowing at its back. Deer sometimes visit the camp, and the lilting voices of songbirds invite an early rising. Nearby, a national recreation trail explores a rare Alaskan cedar grove for a 2.2-mile round-trip hike: Return to FR 21 and go 3.5 miles north. There, turn left (west) onto FR 2150, following it 6 miles to find the trailhead on the right. The campground is maintained from May 30 to mid-October.

65 Shelton Wayside State Park

Location: About 10 miles southeast of Fossil.
Sites: 36 basic sites; no hookups.
Maximum length: 35 feet.
Facilities: Tables, grills, pit toilets, drinking water.
Fee: $.
Management: Leased to Wheeler County.
Contact: 541-763-2911.
Finding the campground: It is west off Oregon 19, 10.3 miles south of Fossil, 8.7 miles north of the OR 19 and OR 207 South junction.

About the campground: Service Creek flows through this linear campground, which stretches 1 mile along the foot of a forested ridge. Sites are primitive, with a meadow floor and partial shade from the pine-fir complex. Arnica and mock orange lend seasonal color. A trail traverses the slope above the camp, and the wayside offers a base for exploring the scattered units of John Day Fossil Beds National Monument or participating in the John Day River recreation. The campground is open from April 15 to mid-November.

John Day Fossil Beds National Monument.

66 Wildwood

Location: About 34 miles northeast of Prineville.
Sites: 5 tent sites; no hookups.
Maximum length: Suitable for tents only.
Facilities: Tables, grill, pit toilets. No drinking water.
Fee: None.
Management: Forest Service.
Contact: 541-416-6645.
Finding the campground: From U.S. Highway 26, 27 miles northeast of Prineville, 21 miles southwest of Mitchell, turn east onto gravel Forest Road 2630, go 4 miles, and turn left onto FR 2210. Continue another 3 miles to the camp.

About the campground: Along the old Prineville-Mitchell Highway, this camp has long been a traveler's wayside, although now it is farther off the beaten track for greater relaxation. Its remoteness appeals to great horned owls. The primitive camp occupies a pine-fir slope, with a needle-and-cone strewn floor. It is another place to commune with nature, read a book, or seek out area trails or hunting opportunities. The campground is open from May 1 to October 31.

GRANITE-SUMPTER AREA

	Hookup sites	Total sites	Max. RV length	Hookups	Toilets	Showers	Drinking water	Dump station	Recreation	Fee	Can reserve
67 Deer Creek		6	T		NF						
68 McCully Forks		10	18		NF				F		
69 Millers Lane		7	20		NF				HSFB		
70 North Fork John Day		15	40		NF				HFR	donation	
71 Olive Lake		24	30		NF				HFBL		
72 Southwest Shore		16	35		NF				HSFBL		
73 Union	24	76	40	WES	F	•	•	•	HSFBL	$$	

Hookups: W = Water E = Electric S = Sewer **Total sites:** T = Tent-only campground **Maximum trailer/RV length** given in feet.
Toilets: F = Flush NF = No Flush **Recreation:** H = Hiking S = Swimming F = Fishing B = Boating L = Boat Launch
O = Off-Highway Driving R = Horseback Riding C = Cycling
Fee: $ = $1-9 $$ = $10-19 $$$ = $20-29 $$$$ = $30-39. If no entry under **Fee,** camping is free.

67 Deer Creek

Location: About 12 miles east of Sumpter.
Sites: 6 tent sites; no hookups.
Maximum length: Suitable for tents only.
Facilities: Tables, grills, pit toilets (camp receives minimal maintenance; bring toilet tissue and other necessities). No drinking water.
Fee: None.
Management: Forest Service.
Contact: 541-523-4476.
Finding the campground: From Oregon 7, 3.3 miles east of the Sumpter Junction, 22.7 miles west of Baker City, turn north on the gravel road indicated for Deer Creek Campground (County Road 654/ Forest Road 7240), and proceed straight, avoiding an initial left turn. Go 3.3 miles and turn left onto FR 6510, following it for 1 mile. Now, turn left onto narrow, winding FR 6530 (not recommended for RVs) to find this camp on the left in 1.2 miles.

About the campground: At this rustic camp, half are walk-in tent sites, half have short parking spurs. The camp offers an attractive, soothing, out-of-the-way base and boasts some tremendously big larch in its midst. Ponderosa pine and spruce complete the forest, with cottonwoods growing along Deer Creek. A dramatic canyon wall rises opposite the camp; the creek offers recreational gold panning. Old dredging mounds hint at the area's mining legacy and can be spied en route to the camp. The campground is open from late May to October.

68 McCully Forks

Location: About 3 miles northwest of Sumpter.
Sites: 10 basic sites; no hookups.
Maximum length: 18 feet.
Facilities: Tables, grills, pit toilets. No drinking water.
Fee: None.
Management: Forest Service.
Contact: 541-523-4476.
Finding the campground: From Sumpter (reached from Baker City by going 26 miles southwest on Oregon 7 and 3 miles north on Sumpter Highway), go 2.8 miles north on Sumpter Highway to find this campground on the right.

About the campground: Along Elkhorn Scenic Byway, this small, rustic camp straddles McCully Creek. Fir and spruce shade the sites, with lodgepole pines growing farther from the creek and dogwoods common in the understory. Because of the narrowness of the canyon, parking is constrained, but the camp remains popular, filling up on summer weekends. Recreational gold panning is allowed on the camp stream, but take care to avoid straying (claim jumping). The historic Sumpter Valley Railroad may suggest a side trip. The campground is maintained from late May to October.

69 Millers Lane

Location: About 9 miles southeast of Sumpter, on Phillips Lake.
Sites: 7 basic sites; no hookups.
Maximum length: 20 feet.
Facilities: Tables, grills, vault toilets, boat ramp (at Southwest Shore Campground). No drinking water.
Fee: None.
Management: Forest Service.
Contact: 541-523-4476.
Finding the campground: From Oregon 7, 3.8 miles east of the Sumpter Junction, 22.2 miles west of Baker City, turn south onto paved Hudspeth Lane for Southwest Shore and Millers Lane Campgrounds. Go 1.2 miles and turn left onto gravel Forest Road 2220 to reach this campground on the left after another 1.3 miles.

About the campground: Along the south shore of Phillips Lake, a large, man-made oval platter, you will find this small campground with exceptional cross-lake viewing of the Elkhorns. Sites occupy a ponderosa pine forest, with a rail fence separating the camp from shore. Adjacent to the camp are dry meadows. Fishing, swimming, and boating make this campground popular on summer weekends. A path explores the lakeshore for hiking. The campground is open from May to mid-November.

70 North Fork John Day

Location: About 8 miles north of Granite.
Sites: 8 basic sites, 3 walk-in tent sites, 4 horse sites; no hookups.
Maximum length: 40 feet.
Facilities: Tables, grills, vault toilets, horse feeding station, loading ramp, and corrals. No drinking water.
Fee: Donation.
Management: Forest Service.
Contact: 541-427-3231.
Finding the campground: It is west off Forest Road 52 at its intersection with FR 73, 8.3 miles north of Granite, 39 miles southeast of Ukiah.

About the campground: Along the North Fork John Day Wild and Scenic River at the intersection of the Elkhorn and Blue Mountain Scenic Byways is this pleasant, sunny, lodgepole-pine-forested campground. The North Fork John Day National Recreation Trail leaves one end of the camp and follows the river into the North Fork John Day Wilderness, past tailings, active claims, and old cabins, which unfold the mining legacy. Special fishing regulations protect the anadromous fishery. The campground is open from June through October 31.

71 Olive Lake

Location: 12 miles west of Granite.
Sites: 24 basic sites; no hookups.
Maximum length: 30 feet.
Facilities: Tables, grills, vault toilets, boat dock and launch. No drinking water.
Fee: None.
Management: Forest Service.
Contact: 541-427-3231.
Finding the campground: From Granite, travel 12 miles west on Forest Road 10, a good, wide gravel road, to reach this camp on the left off FR 480. From U.S. Highway 395 north of Dale, follow FR 55 east 0.6 mile to FR 10 and then continue east on FR 10 for another 26.2 miles to reach the campground turnoff.

About the campground: This camp is on the east shore of peaceful Olive Lake; lodgepole pine, fir, spruce, and larch contribute to the forested basin. Enlarged by an earthen dam, the lake invites fishing and boating. Fremont Powerhouse Historic District (8 miles east of camp) makes an interesting side trip; this station powered the gold boom of Eastern Oregon. Its wooden pipeline can be seen in several places throughout the area. Near the camp, trails venture into the North Fork John Day Wilderness and Indian Rock–Vinegar Hill Scenic Area. The campground is open from June to mid-October.

72 Southwest Shore

Location: About 9 miles southeast of Sumpter, on Phillips Lake.
Sites: 16 basic sites; no hookups.
Maximum length: 35 feet.
Facilities: Tables, grills, vault toilets, boat ramp. No drinking water.
Fee: None.
Management: Forest Service.
Contact: 541-523-4476.
Finding the campground: From Oregon 7, 3.8 miles east of the Sumpter Junction, 22.2 miles west of Baker City, turn south on paved Hudspeth Lane for Southwest Shore and Millers Lane Campgrounds. Go 1.2 miles and turn left onto gravel Forest Road 2220 to reach this campground on the left after another 0.5 mile.

About the campground: On the south shore of Phillips Lake, a large, recreational reservoir in the shadow of the Elkhorn Mountains, sits this popular campground with prized views. Sites receive a mix of sun and shade and are generally well spaced across the ponderosa-pine-sagebrush flat. Fishing, boating, swimming, and hiking the south shore trail for photographs and nature study keep guests busy. At the marshy ends of the reservoir are nesting boxes for geese. The campground is open from May to mid-November.

73 Union

Location: About 10 miles southeast of Sumpter, on Phillips Lake.
Sites: 24 hookup sites, 34 basic sites, 18 walk-in tent sites; water, electric, and sewer hookups.
Maximum length: 40 feet.
Facilities: Tables, grills, flush toilets, drinking water, showers, dump station, telephone, docks, paved multilane boat ramp, fish-cleaning station.
Fee: $$.
Management: Forest Service.
Contact: 541-523-4476.
Finding the campground: It is south off Oregon 7, 6.9 miles east of the Sumpter Junction, 19.1 miles west of Baker City.

About the campground: On the north shore of 5-mile-long, 2,450-acre Phillips Lake sits this fully developed Forest Service campground, operated by concession. Sites terrace the pine-forested lake basin slope, with paths leading to the lakeshore, launch, and picnic area. Visitors can enjoy a full day of fun-in-the-sun on the lake and then retreat to the shade of the camp. The roped-off swimming area suggests a refreshing dip, or you can walk the shoreline trail exploring this vast impoundment on the Powder River. Fresh-caught bass or trout may top the dinner menu. Plans call for this campground to become a station on the historic Sumpter Valley Railroad. The campground is open from April 15 to early October.

NORTH POWDER–ANTHONY LAKES AREA

		Hookup sites	Total sites	Max. RV length	Hookups	Toilets	Showers	Drinking water	Dump station	Recreation	Fee	Can reserve
74	Anthony Lakes		37	22		NF		•		HFBL	$	
75	Grande Ronde Lake		8	16		NF		•		HFBL	$	
76	Mud Lake		8	16		NF		•		HFB	$	
77	Pilcher Creek Reservoir Recreation Site		10	40		NF				FBL		
78	Thief Valley Recreation Area		12	30		NF		•		FBL		
79	Wolf Creek–Guy Smith Lake		open	40		NF				FBL		

Hookups: W = Water E = Electric S = Sewer **Total sites:** T = Tent-only campground **Maximum trailer/RV length** given in feet.
Toilets: F = Flush NF = No Flush **Recreation:** H = Hiking S = Swimming F = Fishing B = Boating L = Boat Launch
O = Off-Highway Driving R = Horseback Riding C = Cycling
Fee: $ = $1-9 $$ = $10-19 $$$ = $20-29 $$$$ = $30-39. If no entry under **Fee,** camping is free.

74 Anthony Lakes

Location: About 40 miles northwest of Baker City.
Sites: 16 basic sites, 21 tent sites; no hookups.
Maximum length: 22 feet.
Facilities: Tables, grills, vault toilets, drinking water, boat ramp.
Fee: $.
Management: Forest Service.
Contact: 541-523-1932.
Finding the campground: From Interstate 84, take the North Powder–Anthony Lakes exit (Exit 285) and go west on North Powder River Lane and Forest Road 73 for 20 miles, following the signs to Anthony Lakes. The camp is left off FR 73.

About the campground: This camp occupies a high-elevation forest of small-diameter firs and lodgepole pines along Anthony Lake (elevation 7,100 feet). Campers are treated to a breathtaking setting that pairs the stunning granite peaks of the Elkhorn Crest with this midnight-blue mountain lake. Anthony Lake welcomes trout fishing, human-powered boating, or a shoreline stroll. For more challenging hikes, the options are boundless, with high lakes and the Elkhorn Crest. For windshield sightseeing, this campground is on the 106-mile Elkhorn Loop Drive. The campground is open from July through September.

75 Grande Ronde Lake

Location: About 41 miles northwest of Baker City.
Sites: 8 basic sites; no hookups.
Maximum length: 16 feet.
Facilities: Tables, grills, vault toilets, drinking water, primitive boat ramp.
Fee: $.
Management: Forest Service.

Contact: 541-523-1932.

Finding the campground: From Interstate 84, take the North Powder–Anthony Lakes exit (Exit 285) and go west on North Powder River Lane and Forest Road 73 for 21 miles, following the signs for Anthony Lakes. There, turn right onto FR 43, go 0.2 mile, and bear left to enter the camp.

About the campground: Sites for this camp sit in a high-elevation conifer forest overlooking the broad, wet wildflower meadow that separates this camp from Grand Ronde Lake. The submerged grasses and dotting cow lilies further add to the charm of this small, circular mountain lake, where quiet boating is allowed and the trout fishing can be good. This camp puts visitors within easy access of the Anthony Lake–Elkhorn Crest recreation area, with hiking, sightseeing, photography, and scenic driving. The campground is open from July through September.

76 Mud Lake

Location: About 40 miles northwest of Baker City.
Sites: 5 basic sites, 3 tent sites; no hookups.
Maximum length: 16 feet.
Facilities: Tables, grills, vault toilets, drinking water.
Fee: $.
Management: Forest Service.
Contact: 541-523-1932.
Finding the campground: From Interstate 84, take the North Powder–Anthony Lakes exit (Exit 285) and go west on North Powder River Lane and Forest Road 73 for about 20 miles, following the signs for Anthony Lakes. The camp is on the right.

About the campground: Across the road from Anthony Lake and the Anthony Lakes Ski Area, this camp is set back from Mud Lake, tucked away in the lodgepole pines and spruce. Shallow Mud Lake is ringed by a broad meadow expanse. While the setting is serene, mosquitoes can be bothersome. Visitors enjoy the high-country splendor of the Elkhorn Mountains, with chiseled granite peaks, high lakes, lush meadows, elk herds, Clark's nutcrackers, and wildflower showcases. You can hike, fish, row your boat, and sightsee. The campground is open from July through September.

77 Pilcher Creek Reservoir Recreation Site

Location: About 30 miles northwest of Baker City.
Sites: At least 10 basic sites; no hookups.
Maximum length: 40 feet.
Facilities: Tables, barbecues and fire rings, vault toilets, primitive boat launch. No drinking water.
Fee: None.
Management: Union County.
Contact: 541-963-1001.

Pilcher Creek campsite.

Finding the campground: From Interstate 84, Exit 285 (the North Powder exit), go west on North Powder River Lane, proceeding straight at the junction. At 7.6 miles, turn right onto gravel Tucker Flat Road, go 2 miles, and turn right to enter the camp.

About the campground: Centerpiece for a stay is the broad platter of Pilcher Creek Reservoir, cupped by low, rounded meadow-and-forest rises and a scenic aspen-filled dip. Views include the rugged beauty of the Elkhorn Mountains. The camp offerings are primitive, and the primary activities are boating (5 miles per hour) and fishing. With Elkhorn Wildlife Area bordering this recreation site, deer, elk, and other wildlife can be seen at camp. In spring, balsamroot colors the camp meadow.

78 Thief Valley Recreation Area

Location: About 15 miles south of Union.
Sites: 12 basic sites, plus dispersed camping; no hookups.
Maximum length: 30 feet.
Facilities: Tables, barbecues, chemical and vault toilets, drinking water, boat launch.
Fee: None.
Management: Union County.
Contact: 541-963-1001.
Finding the campground: From Oregon 237, 7.8 miles south of Union, 7.3 miles north of Interstate 84, Exit 285 (the North Powder exit), turn east onto

Telocaset Lane, a good gravel road. After 1.8 miles, turn left to remain on Telocaset Lane and continue 4.2 miles more before turning right for the reservoir. Go 1.5 miles to enter the recreation area.

About the campground: This shadeless flat overlooks the broad, open water of Thief Valley Reservoir, built for irrigation and open to recreation. Low sage-grass ridges shape the reservoir basin. A few willows cluster along the lake rim. The reservoir is open for boating, fishing, swimming, and windsurfing. The jetty offers fishing access for individuals with disabilities. Some big trout are pulled from the reservoir, but by June an algae bloom overtakes the lake, ending the catch. In winter, the lake is open for ice fishing.

79 Wolf Creek–Guy Smith Lake and Dam Recreation Area

Location: About 25 miles northwest of Baker City, on Wolf Creek Lake.
Sites: Open camping near the dam and along the north shore; no hookups.
Maximum length: 40 feet.
Facilities: Some lattice-roofed picnic tables, pit and vault toilets, boat launch, dock. No drinking water.
Fee: None.
Management: Union County.
Contact: 541-963-1001.
Finding the campground: From Interstate 84 north of the community of North Powder, take Exit 283 and go west on Wolf Creek Lane for 4 miles. The recreation area is on the left.

About the campground: This camp abuts a moderate-sized reservoir open to boating, fishing, and waterskiing. Low, rounded sage-grass hills shape the reservoir neighborhood, with the regal Elkhorns or valley farmlands seen in the distance. You may spy ospreys, ducks, geese, goldfinches, and killdeer.

RICHLAND-HALFWAY AREA

		Hookup sites	Total sites	Max. RV length	Hookups	Toilets	Showers	Drinking water	Dump station	Recreation	Fee	Can reserve
80	Copperfield Park	62	72	40	WE	F	•	•	•	SFBL	$-$$	
81	Eagle Forks		12	20		NF		•		HF		
82	Fish Lake		15	15		NF		•		HFBL		
83	Hewitt County Park	38	43	30	WE	F		•		FBL	$$	
84	Lake Fork		10	22		NF		•		HF	$	
85	McBride		19	16		NF		•				
86	Tamarack		24	22		NF		•		F		
87	Twin Lakes		6	15		NF				HF		
88	Two Color		14	22		NF		•		F		

Hookups: W = Water E = Electric S = Sewer **Total sites:** T = Tent-only campground **Maximum trailer/RV length** given in feet.
Toilets: F = Flush NF = No Flush **Recreation:** H = Hiking S = Swimming F = Fishing B = Boating L = Boat Launch
O = Off-Highway Driving R = Horseback Riding C = Cycling
Fee: $ = $1-9 $$ = $10-19 $$$ = $20-29 $$$$ = $30-39. If no entry under **Fee**, camping is free.

80 Copperfield Park

Location: About 17 miles east of Halfway, on the Snake River.
Sites: 62 hookup sites, 10 tent sites; water and electric hookups.
Maximum length: 40 feet.
Facilities: Tables, barbecues and grills, flush toilets, drinking water, showers, dump station, telephone (along Oregon 86 near camp), boat launch (0.6 mile downstream from park).
Fee: $ to $$.
Management: Idaho Power Company.
Contact: 1-800-422-3143, no reservations.
Finding the campground: From Halfway, go east on Oregon 86 for 16.6 miles to enter this park at the river.

About the campground: On the one-time site of the rough-and-tumble mining city of Copperfield, Oregon, sits this pleasant, groomed, developed park, with lots of open lawn and a few big pines. The park offers a swimming area on the broad, harnessed Snake River, with boating access nearby. The river (Hells Canyon Reservoir) is popular with fishermen, with warm-water fish species being the primary catch. North (downstream) from camp, the Hells Canyon Reservoir Trail offers a wonderful canyon walk, with views of the steep-walled canyon and broad, cloudy river. Its trailhead parking, though, is limited and there is no developed turnaround. The campground is open from March 1 to October 31.

81 Eagle Forks

Location: About 10 miles north of Richland.
Sites: 5 basic sites, 7 tent sites; no hookups.
Maximum length: 20 feet.
Facilities: Tables, grills, vault toilets, drinking water.
Fee: None.
Management: Forest Service.
Contact: 541-742-7511.
Finding the campground: At the west edge of Richland, turn north off Oregon 86 at a sign for Sparta, following Sparta Road 2.3 miles to Newbridge. There, continue north on Forest Road 7735 (Eagle Creek Road), which changes to dirt. Go another 7.3 miles and turn left for the campground.

About the campground: On a wooded rise, this camp is threaded by Little Eagle Creek and overlooks Eagle Creek, a wild and scenic waterway. Pine and fir shade the camp, while alder and willows fan Eagle Creek. At the upstream end of the camp, you will find the 7-mile Martin Bridge Trail, which pursues the creek upstream for an engaging water and canyon tour, ending at Martin Bridge, a former stage stop on the Union-Cornucopia Wagon Road that linked this area's historic gold mining districts to Union and Baker City. The creek is open to fishing and to gold panning for a taste of the past. The campground is open from June into October.

82 Fish Lake

Location: About 20 miles north of Halfway, on Fish Lake.
Sites: 15 basic sites; no hookups.
Maximum length: 15 feet; best suited for tents.
Facilities: Tables, grills, vault toilets, drinking water, boat launch (small boats).
Fee: None.
Management: Forest Service.
Contact: 541-742-7511.
Finding the campground: In Halfway, turn north off Halfway-Cornucopia Highway (County Road 413) onto East Pine Creek Road at the sign for Fish Lake. Go 3.2 miles and turn left onto gravel Forest Road 66 (Fish Lake Road), which is indicated for a sno-park. Stay on it for 16.5 miles to enter the campground on the left.

About the campground: At an elevation of 6,600 feet, you will find this inviting mountain lake in a basin of spired trees, meadow, and scree. A small earthen dam has enlarged the lake, a couple of islands contribute to its charm, and avalanche lilies decorate its shore as the snow recedes. The rustic campsites line up along shore just below the road-shoulder parking. Come prepared for mosquitoes and cold nights. For hiking options, you have Fish Creek Trail (2 miles south of the camp), Lake Fork Trail (0.3 mile south), and Clear Creek and Deadman Trails (leaving right near the camp). Fishing, however, remains the big draw. The campground is open from July to September, but bring water in case the water system is not on.

83 Hewitt County Park

Location: About 2 miles east of Richland.
Sites: 38 hookup sites, 5 tent sites; water and electric hookups.
Maximum length: 30 feet.
Facilities: Tables, barbecues, flush toilets, drinking water, telephone, playground, boating and angling docks, boat launch, fish-cleaning station.
Fee: $$.
Management: Baker County.
Contact: 541-523-8219.
Finding the campground: From Richland, go east on Oregon 86 for 0.8 mile and bear right onto the road indicated to Hewitt Park, proceeding 1.5 miles to the park campground at road's end.

About the campground: This campground stretches along the Powder River arm of Brownlee Reservoir, occupying a stunning dry-grass canyon. Primarily a boating and fishing destination, the campground is more functional than aesthetic. The RV area is an extensive paved lot, with numbered sites and accompanying tables and barbecues. The planted shade trees at its perimeter do not yet provide shade. Tent camping is on the tree-and-lawn slope between the camp parking lot and the reservoir; flatter spots for the tent are at the top and bottom margins of the slope. Trophy catfish entice anglers out at night. The campground is open from March 15 to November 15.

84 Lake Fork

Location: About 18 miles northeast of Halfway.
Sites: 10 basic sites; no hookups.
Maximum length: 22 feet.
Facilities: Tables, grills, vault toilets, drinking water.
Fee: $.
Management: Forest Service.
Contact: 541-426-5546.
Finding the campground: From Oregon 86, 10 miles east of Halfway, turn north onto Forest Road 39, the Wallowa Mountain Loop Road, and go 8 miles to reach this camp on the left.

About the campground: This quiet camp along Lake Fork Creek offers well-spaced, shady sites in a multistory forest of fir, larch, and pine. Just north of camp is the Lake Fork Trail for hikes to Big Elk Creek (2 miles) or Fish Lake (11 miles). The camp is conveniently located along Wallowa Mountain Loop Road, which accesses trails and attractions of Wallowa-Whitman National Forest and Hells Canyon National Recreation Area. The campground is open from June to November.

85 McBride

Location: About 16 miles northwest of Halfway.
Sites: 8 basic sites, 11 tent sites; no hookups.
Maximum length: 16 feet.
Facilities: Tables, grills, vault toilets, drinking water.
Fee: None.
Management: Forest Service.
Contact: 541-742-7511.
Finding the campground: From Oregon 86, 6 miles west of Halfway; 47 miles east of Baker City (just west of the summit), turn north onto gravel, washboard Forest Road 77 and follow it for 10.4 miles to enter the camp on the left.

About the campground: Along Brooks Ditch, this camp offers visitors a quiet forest retreat. In fall, hunters may swell the camp's population. Opposite the campground turnoff is FR 7715, which travels 4.5 miles to road's end, Summit Point Trailhead, and a vista; views pan south-southwest. Hiking the Cliff River Trail from there leads past Summit Point Lookout Tower (find its spur at 0.6 mile) to Little Eagle Meadows, Nip and Tuck Passes, and some prized high-mountain lakes, if you are a power hiker or backpacker. Bears frequent the Summit Point area. The campground is open from mid-May through October.

86 Tamarack

Location: About 36 miles northeast of Baker City.
Sites: 12 basic sites, 12 tent sites; no hookups.
Maximum length: 22 feet.
Facilities: Tables, grills, vault toilets, drinking water.
Fee: None.
Management: Forest Service.
Contact: 541-742-7511.
Finding the campground: From Oregon 203 at Medical Springs (20 miles northeast of Baker City), turn southeast onto Collins Road/Eagle Creek Drive for Boulder Park; the road soon becomes wide and gravel. Go 1.6 miles and turn left onto Forest Road 67. Continue 13.5 miles, turn right (east) onto FR 77, and go 0.6 mile to the camp.

About the campground: This campground occupies a sunny location above Eagle Creek, with log-defined parking, grassy sites, and an open forest of larch, spruce, and fir. The creek adds a scenic ribbon and a restful voice. By taking FR 7750 north off FR 77, 0.3 mile west of camp, you can access the Two Color Trail, which travels to Two Color Lake, but you need not walk the entire way to enjoy a leg stretch and a peek at the Wallowa Mountains grandeur. The campground is open from June into October.

87 Twin Lakes

Location: About 25 miles northeast of Halfway.
Sites: 6 basic sites; no hookups.
Maximum length: 15 feet; best suited for tents.
Facilities: Tables, grills, vault toilets. No drinking water.
Fee: None.
Management: Forest Service.
Contact: 541-426-4978.
Finding the campground: In Halfway, turn north off Halfway-Cornucopia Highway (County Road 413) onto East Pine Creek Road for Fish Lake. Go 3.2 miles and turn left onto gravel Forest Road 66 (Fish Lake Road), which is indicated for a sno-park. Stay on it for 21.6 miles to enter this campground on the left.

About the campground: Despite the camp name, there is actually a trio of meadowy ponds that shape a clover leaf about this split-level campground. Lodgepole pine, fir, and larch dress the camp. Russel Mountain presides over the Twin Lakes area. The sites are rustic, and parking is constricted. Twin Lakes and Sugarloaf Trails begin near the camp, with the latter leading to Russel Mountain Lookout. A fire several years ago left a wake of silver snags and logs that continue to be a part of the Twin Lakes mosaic and confuse hikers. At the camp, a ramp spans the meadowy shore to provide fishing access on the open water. The campground is open from July to September.

88 Two Color

Location: About 36 miles northeast of Baker City.
Sites: 14 basic sites; no hookups.
Maximum length: 22 feet.
Facilities: Tables, grills, vault toilets, drinking water.
Fee: None.
Management: Forest Service.
Contact: 541-962-8589.
Finding the campground: From Oregon 203 at Medical Springs (20 miles northeast of Baker City), turn southeast on Collins Road/Eagle Creek Drive for Boulder Park; the road becomes wide and gravel. Go 1.6 miles and turn left onto Forest Road 67. Continue 13.5 miles, turn left (west) on FR 77, and go another 0.7 mile to FR 7755. There, turn right to reach the campground in 0.5 mile. Turnouts are fairly frequent and wide to accommodate RVs.

About the campground: In a mixed-conifer stand, boulders mark off the grassy campsites; some are more level than others. Flowing past the camp is Eagle Creek, wide and clear-rushing, with richly vegetated banks and overhanging logs. Meadows fan out from the camp. By following FR 7755 north to its end, in about 3 miles, you will find Fake Creek and Main Eagle Trails for long-distance hikes, with satisfying scenery and stops for day hikers along the way. The campground is open from June into October.

UPPER IMNAHA RIVER AREA

		Hookup sites	Total sites	Max. RV length	Hookups	Toilets	Showers	Drinking water	Dump station	Recreation	Fee	Can reserve
89	Blackhorse		16	25		NF		•		F	$	
90	Coverdale		9	15		NF		•		F	$	
91	Hidden		10	25		NF		•		F	$	
92	Indian Crossing		15	20		NF		•		HFR	$	
93	Lick Creek		12	25		NF		•			$	
94	Ollokot		12	30		NF		•		F	$	

Hookups: W = Water E = Electric S = Sewer **Total sites:** T = Tent-only campground **Maximum trailer/RV length** given in feet.
Toilets: F = Flush NF = No Flush **Recreation:** H = Hiking S = Swimming F = Fishing B = Boating L = Boat Launch
O = Off-Highway Driving R = Horseback Riding C = Cycling
Fee: $ = $1-9 $$ = $10-19 $$$ = $20-29 $$$$ = $30-39. If no entry under **Fee,** camping is free.

89 Blackhorse

Location: About 36 miles southeast of Joseph.
Sites: 16 basic sites; no hookups.
Maximum length: 25 feet.
Facilities: Tables, grills, pit toilets, drinking water.
Fee: $.
Management: Forest Service.
Contact: 541-426-4978.
Finding the campground: From Oregon 82 in Joseph, turn east onto East Wallowa Avenue at the sign for Imnaha and Halfway; it later becomes the Imnaha Highway. Go 7.8 miles and turn right (south) onto Wallowa Mountain Loop Road. Now, continue 28.6 miles to enter the campground on the left.

About the campground: Along the Imnaha Wild and Scenic River and Wallowa Mountain Loop Road, you will find this camp with well-spaced sites. Meadow openings intersperse the forest of fir, ponderosa pine, and larch, creating a mix of sun and shade. The Imnaha River is captivating: its color, clarity, and overall persona. Besides fishing, camp guests can take a short drive to Hells Canyon Overlook or check out the trails at Indian Crossing (look for the signed turns, south on Wallowa Mountain Loop Road). The campground is open from May to October.

90 Coverdale

Location: About 41 miles southeast of Joseph.
Sites: 9 basic sites; no hookups.
Maximum length: 15 feet; primarily a tent area.
Facilities: Tables, grills, pit toilets, drinking water.
Fee: $.

Management: Forest Service.
Contact: 541-426-4978.
Finding the campground: From Oregon 82 in Joseph, turn east onto East Wallowa Avenue at the sign for Imnaha and Halfway; it later becomes the Imnaha Highway. Go 7.8 miles, turn right (south) onto Wallowa Mountain Loop Road, and continue 29 miles before turning right onto Forest Road 3960. Near milepost 4 on FR 3960, turn left onto FR 100 to enter this unmarked campground.

About the campground: At the edge of a riparian wildflower meadow in an open flat of mixed-age ponderosa pine sits this primitive Imnaha River campground. Sites spread across the untamed, natural setting, which can be overgrown in places. Shrubs edge the clear-rushing river. The rustic camp holds great tranquility, but the mosquitoes can annoy. Fishing, hiking, and horseback riding are area pursuits. The campground is open from May to October.

91 Hidden

Location: About 44 miles southeast of Joseph.
Sites: 10 basic sites; no hookups.
Maximum length: 25 feet.
Facilities: Tables, grills, pit toilets, drinking water.
Fee: $.
Management: Forest Service.
Contact: 541-426-4978.
Finding the campground: From Oregon 82 in Joseph, turn east onto East Wallowa Avenue at the sign for Imnaha and Halfway; it later becomes the Imnaha Highway. Go 7.8 miles, turn right (south) onto Wallowa Mountain Loop Road, and continue 29 miles before turning right onto Forest Road 3960. Go 6.9 miles more to enter this campground on the left.

About the campground: This nicely forested campground has bookend outcrops and footpaths from each site to the Imnaha Wild and Scenic River. Sites enjoy partial to full shade beneath a canopy of fir, pine, and larch. Upstream, the river is braided by meadow islands; downstream, it is fast rushing. You may fish, wildlife watch, or explore an area trail. The campground is open from May to October.

92 Indian Crossing

Location: About 46 miles southeast of Joseph.
Sites: 9 basic sites, 6 horse sites; no hookups.
Maximum length: 20 feet.
Facilities: Tables, grills, vault and pit toilets, drinking water, horse hitching rails, troughs, and ramp.
Fee: $.
Management: Forest Service.
Contact: 541-426-4978.

Finding the campground: From Oregon 82 in Joseph, turn east onto East Wallowa Avenue at the sign for Imnaha and Halfway; it later becomes the Imnaha Highway. Go 7.8 miles, turn right (south) onto Wallowa Mountain Loop Road, and continue 29 miles before turning right onto Forest Road 3960. Go 8.7 miles to reach this campground and trailhead at road's end.

About the campground: A main gateway to the Eagle Cap Wilderness, this open-forest campground is popular with hikers, equestrians, anglers, and hunters. The camp straddles the Imnaha Wild and Scenic River, with the horse camp claiming the north shore; the family sites the south shore. Nearby trails pursue the river upstream into the wilderness and climb the ridge to Duck Lake. The camp road is rough, and the sites are less groomed, with a deep-grass and wildflower floor. The campground is open from May to October.

93 Lick Creek

Location: About 23 miles southeast of Joseph.
Sites: 12 basic sites; no hookups.
Maximum length: 25 feet.
Facilities: Tables, grills, pit toilets, drinking water.
Fee: $.
Management: Forest Service.
Contact: 541-426-4978.
Finding the campground: From Oregon 82 in Joseph, turn east onto East Wallowa Avenue at the sign for Imnaha and Halfway; it later becomes the Imnaha Highway. Go 7.8 miles and turn right (south) onto Wallowa Mountain Loop Road. Continue 15.1 miles to reach this campground.

About the campground: In a meadow setting along Lick Creek, with scattered firs and lodgepole pines, sits this fine campground for the family. The campground has paved roads, with gravel parking, including a couple of small pull-thru sites. Wildflowers spangle the meadow, where deer commonly browse; false hellebore with its showy crown of flowers gives the meadow dimension and texture. Wallowa Mountain Loop Road is the yellow-brick road to many trails and sights in Hells Canyon National Recreation Area and the Eagle Cap Wilderness. The campground is open from May to October.

94 Ollokot

Location: About 37 miles southeast of Joseph.
Sites: 12 basic sites; no hookups.
Maximum length: 30 feet.
Facilities: Tables, grills, vault toilets, drinking water.
Fee: $.
Management: Forest Service.
Contact: 541-426-4978.
Finding the campground: From Oregon 82 in Joseph, turn east onto East

Wallowa Avenue at the sign for Imnaha and Halfway; it later becomes the Imnaha Highway. Go 7.8 miles and turn right (south) onto Wallowa Mountain Loop Road. Continue 29.1 miles to enter the campground on the left.

About the campground: On a low plateau above the Imnaha Wild and Scenic River, this east shore campground occupies a ponderosa-pine stand, with open spacing and a meadow floor. Across the river and above the loop road rises a basalt outcrop, dotted by pines and mountain mahogany, with areas of scree and bunchgrass. The campsites have gravel parking and are generally sunny. Campers can access the river fairly easily for fishing or admiring. Wallowa Mountain Loop Road is the avenue to outward exploration, hiking, and sightseeing. The campground is open from May to October.

PRAIRIE CITY AREA

		Hookup sites	Total sites	Max. RV length	Hookups	Toilets	Showers	Drinking water	Dump station	Recreation	Fee	Can reserve
95	Crescent		4	18		NF				F		
96	Depot Park	20	20	40	WES	F	•	•	•		$–$$	
97	Dixie		11	25		NF		•				
98	Elk Creek		5	T		NF						
99	Little Crane Creek		5	30		NF						
100	Magone Lake		25	16		NF		•		HSFBL		
101	McNaughton Spring		4	22		NF						
102	North Fork Malheur		5	T		NF				HF		
103	Slide Creek Horse Camp	6	30		NF				HR			
104	Strawberry		11	16		NF		•		H		
105	Trout Farm		8	30		NF		•		F		

Hookups: W = Water E = Electric S = Sewer **Total sites:** T = Tent-only campground **Maximum trailer/RV length** given in feet.
Toilets: F = Flush NF = No Flush **Recreation:** H = Hiking S = Swimming F = Fishing B = Boating L = Boat Launch
O = Off-Highway Driving R = Horseback Riding C = Cycling
Fee: $ = $1-9 $$ = $10-19 $$$ = $20-29 $$$$ = $30-39. If no entry under **Fee**, camping is free.

95 Crescent

Location: About 17 miles south of Prairie City.
Sites: 4 basic sites; no hookups.
Maximum length: 18 feet.
Facilities: Tables, grills, pit toilets. No drinking water.
Fee: None.
Management: Forest Service.
Contact: 541-820-3311.
Finding the campground: From U.S. Highway 26 in Prairie City, turn south onto Main Street, go 0.3 mile, and turn left onto Bridge Street, which later becomes County Road 62. Proceed south for 16.6 miles and turn right to enter the campground.

About the campground: Along the John Day River, in a forest of spruce, fir, and lodgepole pine, sits this tiny campground. Sites are partially shaded and have gravel parking. Here, the river spans 5 to 7 feet wide, flows clear, and is fast rushing. It serves up a prized fishery, but no taking of Dolly Varden (bull trout). The campground is maintained from late May to mid-October.

96 Depot Park

Location: In Prairie City.
Sites: 20 RV hookup sites, open lawn for tent camping; water, electric, and sewer hookups.

Maximum length: 40 feet.
Facilities: Tables, flush toilets, drinking water, showers, dump station, telephone, picnic shelter.
Fee: $ to $$.
Management: Prairie City.
Contact: 541-820-3605.
Finding the campground: From U.S. Highway 26 in Prairie City, turn south onto Main Street and go 0.3 mile to find this city park on the left at the intersection with Bridge Street.

About the campground: This charming city park welcomes weary travelers with its neatly trimmed lawns, locust and pine shade, and babbling Strawberry Creek. Sites are available on a first come, first served basis. On the grounds are a 1910 historic depot/museum, railroad boxcar, wagon, rustic statue, gazebo, and picnic shelter. Each RV space has paved parking and a lawn meridian with a table. Tent campers can make use of the picnic shelter when preparing and eating meals. The museum is seasonally open for tours, Thursday through Saturday, and has 10 rooms of pioneer memorabilia. The campground is open from May 1 to October 31.

97 Dixie

Location: About 10 miles east of Prairie City.
Sites: 11 basic sites; no hookups.
Maximum length: 25 feet.
Facilities: Tables, grills, pit toilets, drinking water.
Fee: None.
Management: Forest Service.
Contact: 541-575-2110.
Finding the campground: From the intersection of Main Street and U.S. Highway 26 in Prairie City, go east on US 26 for 9.5 miles and turn left (north) onto Forest Road 2600.848 to enter the camp.

About the campground: At Dixie Summit (elevation 5,000 feet), this campground terraces a forest of lodgepole pine, larch, and fir, but the tall, thin lodgepole pines dominate the look of the camp. Dwarf and true huckleberry grow beneath the trees. Sites are partially shaded, with gravel parking. Set back from US 26, the campground offers a quiet night's sleep. Hunting, berry picking, and a winter sno-park attract visitors to the area. The campground is maintained from late May to mid-October.

98 Elk Creek

Location: About 25 miles southeast of Prairie City.
Sites: 5 basic sites; no hookups.
Maximum length: Best suited for tents and pickup campers.
Facilities: Tables, grills, pit toilets. No drinking water.

Fee: None.
Management: Forest Service.
Contact: 541-820-3311.
Finding the campground: From U.S. Highway 26 in Prairie City, turn south onto Main Street, go 0.3 mile, and turn left onto Bridge Street, which later becomes County Road 62. Proceed south for 7.8 miles and turn left onto Forest Road 13 (an improved-surface and paved route). Continue 15.7 miles to FR 16 and turn right (south) onto FR 16 to reach the camp after another 1.5 miles. From US 395 at Seneca, go east on FR 16 for 40 miles to reach the camp.

About the campground: This small, lightly developed camp is sandwiched by FR 16 and Elk Creek. Ponderosa and lodgepole pines dominate the camp, with a few grand firs and Douglas-firs interwoven. Despite its proximity to FR 16, the camp conveys a feeling of isolation, and it is not far from the hiking at the North Fork Malheur River (southwest of the camp, taking FR 1675 off FR 16) and the Little Malheur River (northeast of the camp off FR 1672). The campground is maintained from late May to mid-October.

99 Little Crane Creek

Location: About 31 miles southeast of Prairie City.
Sites: 5 basic sites; no hookups.
Maximum length: 30 feet.
Facilities: Tables, grills, pit toilets. No drinking water.
Fee: None.
Management: Forest Service.
Contact: 541-820-3311.
Finding the campground: From U.S. Highway 26 in Prairie City, turn south onto Main Street, go 0.3 mile, and turn left onto Bridge Street, which later becomes County Road 62. Proceed south for 7.8 miles and turn left onto Forest Road 13 (an improved-surface and paved route). Continue 15.7 miles to FR 16 and turn right (south) onto FR 16 to reach this camp after another 7 miles. Or, from US 395 at Seneca, go east on FR 16 for 34.5 miles to reach this campground.

About the campground: This quiet retreat is easily accessed off FR 16, has gravel roads and parking spurs, and enjoys a scenic mixed-conifer setting alongside Little Crane Creek. Some large larch can be found in the camp forest. The camp serves anglers and hunters and is close to the hiking at the North Fork Malheur River (east on FR 16 and then south on FR 1675). The campground is maintained from late May to mid-October.

100 Magone Lake

Location: About 19 miles northwest of Prairie City.
Sites: 25 basic sites; no hookups.
Maximum length: 16 feet.
Facilities: Tables, grills, vault/compost toilets, drinking water, dock, boat launch

for human-powered craft. No drinking water.
Fee: None.
Management: Forest Service.
Contact: 541-575-2110.
Finding the campground: From Prairie City, drive west on U.S. Highway 26 for 3.4 miles and turn north onto Bear Creek Road (County Road 18), going 13 miles. Turn left onto Forest Road 3620, follow it 1.5 miles, and turn right onto FR 3618 to reach the campground in another 1.5 miles. (Signs point the way on the paved and gravel route.) An alternative entry is east off U.S. 395, 9 miles north of Mount Vernon: Follow County Road 32/FR 36 and FR 3618 10 miles to the camp.

About the campground: Occupying the forested shore of Magone Lake is this popular campground. In the 1800s a natural landslide captured the waters of Lake Creek to form this 50-acre lake, which now offers swimming, fishing, and quiet boating. Muskrats and duck families inhabit the lake. A 1.5-mile trail encircles the lake, and the 0.5-mile Magone Slide Trail leaves FR 3618 near the day-use area. The campground is maintained from late May to mid-October.

101 McNaughton Spring

Location: About 9 miles south of Prairie City.
Sites: 4 basic sites; no hookups.
Maximum length: 22 feet.
Facilities: Tables, grills, pit toilets. No drinking water.
Fee: None.
Management: Forest Service.
Contact: 541-820-3311.
Finding the campground: From U.S. Highway 26 in Prairie City, turn south onto Main Street, go 0.3 mile, and turn right onto Bridge Street; it begins paved, becomes gravel, and changes name to Forest Road 6001 upon entering the national forest. Reach the camp in 8.4 miles.

About the campground: This semi-primitive camp offers spacious sites in an open forest setting of fir, pine, and larch along Strawberry Creek; the wild-grass floor is dotted by wildflowers. The camp is en route to the Strawberry Mountain Wilderness for some superb hiking and natural sights. Hunters make use of the area. The campground is maintained from late May to mid-October.

102 North Fork Malheur

Location: About 26 miles southeast of Prairie City.
Sites: 5 basic sites; no hookups.
Maximum length: Best suited for tents and small units.
Facilities: Tables, grills, pit toilets. No drinking water.
Fee: None.
Management: Forest Service.

Contact: 541-820-3311.
Finding the campground: From U.S. Highway 26 in Prairie City, turn south onto Main Street, go 0.3 mile, and turn left onto Bridge Street, which later becomes County Road 62. Proceed south for 7.8 miles and turn left onto Forest Road 13 (an improved-surface and paved route). Continue 15.7 miles to FR 16 and turn right (south) onto FR 16 to reach this camp after another 2.2 miles. From US 395 at Seneca, go east on FR 16 for 39.3 miles to reach this campground.

About the campground: Rimmed by fence, this picturesque camp unites a lovely forest of ponderosa pine and larch; a meadowy shore and islands; and the braided, glimmering water of the North Fork Malheur Wild and Scenic River. At either end of the camp, gates provide access to the river, with angler paths to stroll. Following FR 1675 past the camp for less than 1 mile leads to the North Fork Malheur Trailhead (because it has minimal turnaround, leave RVs at the camp and hike FR 1675 to the trail). The trail extends a dozen miles, offers a wonderful river-forest sojourn, and accesses the Crane Creek Trail 2.5 miles downstream. The campground is maintained from late May to mid-October.

103 Slide Creek Horse Camp and Campground

Location: About 9 miles south of Prairie City.
Sites: 3 basic sites; 3 tent sites (Slide Creek Campground); no hookups.
Maximum length: 30 feet.
Facilities: Tables, grills, vault toilets, corrals at horse camp. No drinking water.
Fee: None.
Management: Forest Service.
Contact: 541-820-3311.
Finding the campground: From U.S. Highway 26 in Prairie City, turn south onto Main Street, go 0.3 mile, and turn right onto Bridge Street; it begins paved, becomes gravel, and changes name to Forest Road 6001 upon entering the national forest. Reach the horse camp in another 8.6 miles; the family camp is 0.2 mile farther.

About the campground: These small, rustic camps near the confluence of Slide and Strawberry Creeks have grassy floors and an open-forest look; they serve hunters and hikers, with an entryway to the Strawberry Mountain Wilderness. The Slide Creek Connector Trail heads east off FR 6001 midway between the camps to link up with the wilderness trail network near Slide Lake. The campgrounds are open from mid-May to mid-November.

104 Strawberry

Location: About 11 miles south of Prairie City.
Sites: 11 basic sites; no hookups.
Maximum length: 16 feet.
Facilities: Tables, grills, pit toilets, drinking water.

Fee: None.
Management: Forest Service.
Contact: 541-820-3311.
Finding the campground: From U.S. Highway 26 in Prairie City, turn south onto Main Street, go 0.3 mile, and turn right onto Bridge Street; it begins paved, becomes gravel, and changes name to Forest Road 6001 upon entering the national forest. Reach the camp in another 10.8 miles.

About the campground: At more than 1 mile high, this popular camp is the primary base and entryway to the Strawberry Mountain Wilderness, a prized area of high lakes, snow-patched peaks, cliffs, crags, tinsel-like streams, waterfalls, and wildflower-spangled meadows and crests. A forest of fir, spruce, larch, and lodgepole pine frames the sites; dwarf huckleberry skirts the base of the trees. Trailhead parking is adjacent to the camp, and the Strawberry Basin Trail is your pass to grandeur. The campground is maintained from late May to mid-October.

105 Trout Farm

Location: About 15 miles south of Prairie City.
Sites: 8 basic sites; no hookups.
Maximum length: 30 feet.
Facilities: Tables, grills, vault toilets, drinking water, picnic shelter.
Fee: None.
Management: Forest Service.
Contact: 541-820-3311.
Finding the campground: From U.S. Highway 26 in Prairie City, turn south onto Main Street, go 0.3 mile, and turn left onto Bridge Street, which later becomes County Road 62. Proceed south for 14.9 miles and turn right for the campground.

About the campground: Along the upper John Day River and a small fishing pond sits this tranquil campground in a full fir forest. Often the pond shows a thick vegetation, but small trout and families of ducks still part the water. A barrier-free trail partially rims the pond, providing fishing access for all. The campground is maintained from late May to mid-October.

SENECA–LOGAN VALLEY AREA

	Hookup sites	Total sites	Max. RV length	Hookups	Toilets	Showers	Drinking water	Dump station	Recreation	Fee	Can reserve
106 Big Creek		14	25		NF		•		FC		
107 Canyon Meadows		19	16		NF		•		FB		
108 Murray		5	25		NF				F		
109 Parish Cabin		20	35		NF		•		F		
110 Rock Springs		15	25		NF						
111 Starr		14	30		NF		•				
112 Wickiup		4	22		NF				F		

Hookups: W = Water E = Electric S = Sewer **Total sites:** T = Tent-only campground **Maximum trailer/RV length** given in feet.
Toilets: F = Flush NF = No Flush **Recreation:** H = Hiking S = Swimming F = Fishing B = Boating L = Boat Launch
O = Off-Highway Driving R = Horseback Riding C = Cycling
Fee: $ = $1-9 $$ = $10-19 $$$ = $20-29 $$$$ = $30-39. If no entry under **Fee**, camping is free.

106 Big Creek

Location: About 19 miles northeast of Seneca.
Sites: 14 basic sites; no hookups.
Maximum length: 25 feet.
Facilities: Tables, grills, vault toilets, drinking water.
Fee: None.
Management: Forest Service.
Contact: 541-820-3311.
Finding the campground: From U.S. Highway 395 at Seneca, turn east onto paved Forest Road 16 and go 18.7 miles. Turn left onto gravel FR 815 for the camp.

About the campground: With its closely spaced sites, this campground occupies a flat of ponderosa and lodgepole pine between Big Creek and Logan Valley, an expansive meadow with a kaleidoscope of wildflowers and abundant wildlife. Sightings of deer, antelope, sandhill crane, and coyote are possible. An egress in the camp's rail fence leads to Big Creek, with its alder-lined banks and deep pools. Check the camp information board for the Big Creek Area mountain bike trails, which make use of the seldom-used and closed forest roads in the neighborhood. The campground is maintained from May 30 to October 15.

107 Canyon Meadows

Location: About 29 miles northeast of Seneca, on Canyon Meadows Reservoir.
Sites: 19 basic sites; no hookups.
Maximum length: 16 feet.
Facilities: Tables, grills, vault toilets, drinking water.
Fee: None.
Management: Forest Service.
Contact: 541-575-2110.

Finding the campground: From U.S. Highway 26 at John Day, go south on US 395 for 10.1 miles, and turn left (east) onto paved County Road 65/Forest Road 15 at the sign for Canyon Meadows and Wickiup Campgrounds. Proceed 8.5 miles and turn left onto gravel FR 1520, following it 5 miles to the campground.

About the campground: A southern gateway to the Strawberry Mountain Wilderness, this campground offers a relaxing forest stay along Canyon Meadows Reservoir. Ponderosa pine, western larch, and fir make up the semi-open forest, with sticky laurel punctuating the dry-grass floor. The reservoir allows for fishing, and when it is adequately high, you can launch a small boat, canoe, or raft. Despite the reservoir's exposed, plain-Jane appearance, wildlife finds it a suitable home. North of the camp on FR 1520, the Buckhorn Meadows Trail enters the wilderness. The campground is maintained from May 30 to October 15.

108 Murray

Location: About 20 miles northeast of Seneca.
Sites: 5 basic sites; no hookups.
Maximum length: 25 feet.
Facilities: Tables, grills, pit toilets. No drinking water.
Fee: None.
Management: Forest Service.
Contact: 541-820-3311.
Finding the campground: From U.S. Highway 395 at Seneca, turn east onto paved Forest Road 16 and go 17.2 miles. Turn left onto gravel FR 1600.924 to reach the camp in 2.6 miles. It is on the left before the junction with FR 1648.

About the campground: This informal, primitive camp occupies a semi-open mixed forest along Lake Creek. Within camp, look for a regal, old-growth ponderosa pine that reigns over the area. Lake Creek is a fast-rushing water, with forested shores. Half a mile south of camp near the Lake Creek Organizational Camp, you will find Trail 307, a closed jeep trail to explore. The campground is maintained from May 30 to October 15.

109 Parish Cabin

Location: 11 miles northeast of Seneca.
Sites: 20 basic sites; no hookups.
Maximum length: 35 feet.
Facilities: Tables, grills, vault and pit toilets, drinking water.
Fee: None.
Management: Forest Service.
Contact: 541-575-2110.
Finding the campground: From U.S. Highway 395 at Seneca, turn east onto paved Forest Road 16 and go 11 miles to enter this camp on the left. From US 26 at John Day, go south on US 395 for 10.1 miles, and turn left (east) onto County

Road 65/Forest Road 15 at the sign for Canyon Meadows and Wickiup Campgrounds. Proceed 13.7 miles and turn right onto FR 16 to find the campground on the right in 0.1 mile.

About the campground: This campground occupies a lodgepole-pine-forested flat along picturesque Bear Creek, a meandering clearwater stream with lush meadow banks of grass, wildflowers, and shrubs. The sites have partial shade and gravel parking spaces; a few are pull-thrus. Look for hints of beaver along the creek. The campground is maintained from May 30 to October 15.

110 Rock Springs

Location: About 17 miles southeast of Seneca.
Sites: 15 basic sites; no hookups.
Maximum length: 25 feet.
Facilities: Tables, grills, pit toilets, pipe-captured spring opposite camp entrance. Bring drinking water.
Fee: None.
Management: Forest Service.
Contact: 541-573-7292.
Finding the campground: From U.S. Highway 395, 33 miles north of Burns, 37 miles south of John Day, turn east onto paved Grant County Road 73/Forest Road 17 for Rock Springs. Proceed 4.1 miles, turn right onto FR 1700.054 (a narrow graveled road), and go 0.7 mile more to enter the campground on the left.

About the campground: Amid a meadowy, mixed-age ponderosa pine forest, this rustic camp celebrates quiet and relaxation. The sites are spread across the mildly rolling terrain; some have better defined parking than others, and most receive at least partial shade. During hunting season, the camp draws a few more guests. The campground is maintained from May 30 to October 15.

111 Starr

Location: About 16 miles south of John Day.
Sites: 7 basic sites; 7 tent sites; no hookups.
Maximum length: 30 feet.
Facilities: Tables, grills, pit toilets, drinking water.
Fee: None.
Management: Forest Service.
Contact: 541-575-2110.
Finding the campground: From John Day, go south on U.S. Highway 395 for 15.5 miles to enter the campground on the right at the summit (elevation 5,125 feet).

About the campground: At this campground, the RV sites are in ponderosa-pine forest, while the tent sites rest in a shrub-meadow flat. Across the road from the camp is a winter sports area, with warming hut and sledding hill.

Closed roads allow for hiking, cross-country skiing, or snowshoeing. The camp is near Fall Mountain Lookout, a 20-foot fire tower built in 1933, but it is no longer open to the public. To view this historic tower, north of the campground, take Forest Road 4920 northwest off US 395 to FR 4920.607 and the lookout. Altogether, it is about a 4-mile side trip; the final mile on FR 607 requires high clearance or hiking to the top. Wildflowers and mountain mahogany dress the summit; views are to the east and south. The campground is maintained from May 30 to mid-October.

112 Wickiup

Location: About 23 miles northeast of Seneca.
Sites: 4 basic sites; no hookups.
Maximum length: 22 feet.
Facilities: Tables, grills, vault toilets. No drinking water.
Fee: None.
Management: Forest Service.
Contact: 541-575-2110.
Finding the campground: From U.S. Highway 26 at John Day, go south on US 395 for 10.1 miles, and turn left (east) on paved County Road 65/Forest Road 15 at the sign for Canyon Meadows and Wickiup Campgrounds. Proceed 7.7 miles to reach this camp on the right off FR 1516, which heads to Dry Soda Lookout.

About the campground: Beneath a forested slope, this campground occupies a pine-fir flat along Canyon Creek at the Wickiup confluence. The sparkling water courses over a pebble-and-rock bed, creating a restful backdrop rush. Wild rose and dogwood accent the flat. West of the camp off FR 15 is the trailhead for Table Mountain Loop, and few hikers can resist the call of nearby Strawberry Mountain Wilderness. The campground is maintained from May 30 to October 15.

UNITY AREA

	Hookup sites	Total sites	Max. RV length	Hookups	Toilets	Showers	Drinking water	Dump station	Recreation	Fee	Can reserve
113 Oregon		8	30		NF		•		O		
114 South Fork		12	28		NF				F		
115 Unity Lake State Park	21	43	40	WE	F	•	•	•	SFBL	$$	•
116 Wetmore		12	18		NF		•		H		
117 Yellow Pine		20	25		NF		•		H		

Hookups: W = Water   E = Electric   S = Sewer   **Total sites:** T = Tent-only campground   **Maximum trailer/RV length** given in feet.
Toilets: F = Flush   NF = No Flush   **Recreation:** H = Hiking   S = Swimming   F = Fishing   B = Boating   L = Boat Launch
O = Off-Highway Driving   R = Horseback Riding   C = Cycling
Fee: $ = $1-9 $$ = $10-19 $$$ = $20-29 $$$$ = $30-39.   If no entry under **Fee,** camping is free.

113 Oregon

Location: About 13 miles northwest of Unity.
Sites: 8 basic sites; no hookups.
Maximum length: 30 feet.
Facilities: Tables, grills, vault toilets, drinking water.
Fee: None.
Management: Forest Service.
Contact: 541-446-3351.
Finding the campground: It is north off U.S. Highway 26, 12.7 miles northwest of Unity and 23.6 miles east of Prairie City.

About the campground: Ideal for US 26 travelers, this camp offers fully to partially shaded sites in a ponderosa-pine-fir forest, with a shrub-and-wildflower understory. The sites have gravel parking. From camp, an off-highway-vehicle trail heads north to the bridge outage on North Fork Burnt River. Unity Reservoir, Monument Rock Wilderness, and the historic Sumpter Valley Railroad also suggest outings. The campground is maintained from Memorial Day weekend through Labor Day weekend.

114 South Fork

Location: About 7 miles southwest of Unity.
Sites: 12 basic sites; no hookups.
Maximum length: 28 feet.
Facilities: Tables, grills, pit toilets. No drinking water.
Fee: None.
Management: Forest Service.
Contact: 541-446-3351.
Finding the campground: From U.S. Highway 26 at Unity, go 7.3 miles southwest on South Fork Road (County Road 600/Forest Road 6005) to reach this campground on the left; the final 3.2 miles are on gravel.

About the campground: This quiet camp hugs the pretty South Fork Burnt River; a meadow floor spills beneath the towering pine, fir, and larch. Several of the sites overlook the sparkling river and its alder banks. If you steal up to the water, fishing is possible, and hikers may choose to investigate nearby Monument Rock Wilderness. The campground is maintained from Memorial Day weekend through Labor Day weekend.

115 Unity Lake State Park

Location: About 4 miles north of Unity.
Sites: 21 hookup sites, 22 dry sites; water and electric hookups.
Maximum length: 40 feet.
Facilities: Tables, fire rings, flush toilets, drinking water, showers, dump station, telephone, boat launch, dock.
Fee: $$.
Management: Oregon State Parks and Recreation Department.
Contact: 541-575-2773.
Finding the campground: From Unity, go west on U.S. Highway 26 for 1.7 miles and turn north onto Oregon 245 for Hereford and Baker City. Go another 2.5 miles and turn left at the sign for Unity Lake State Park to proceed into the park.

About the campground: At this landscaped campground, the planted shade trees have yet to reach a size to be considered dependable shade, but the adjoining day-use area is well shaded. Unity Lake harnesses the Burnt River and rests in an arid basin in the Blue Mountains. Views are of the surrounding volcanic-crested sage-grass hills. The blue water is a strong enticement to fish, boat, swim, or windsurf. Best fishing is during the spring and fall, with trout, bass, and crappie. The campground is open from April 15 to late October.

116 Wetmore

Location: About 10 miles northwest of Unity.
Sites: 12 basic sites; no hookups.
Maximum length: 18 feet.
Facilities: Tables, grills, vault and pit toilets, drinking water.
Fee: None.
Management: Forest Service.
Contact: 541-446-3351.
Finding the campground: It is north off U.S. Highway 26, 10.2 miles northwest of Unity and 27.1 miles east of Prairie City.

About the campground: This family campground occupies a rolling terrain of fir, ponderosa pine, and larch, with an understory of mixed shrubs and wild rose that attracts browsing deer. At the west end of the camp, a half-mile, paved barrier-free trail journeys along a gurgling tributary and past old-growth pines and volcanic outcrops to switchback uphill to neighboring Yellow Pine

Campground. Possible car outings include Unity Reservoir or the Sumpter Valley Railroad. The campground is maintained from Memorial Day weekend through Labor Day weekend.

117 Yellow Pine

Location: About 11 miles northwest of Unity.
Sites: 20 basic sites; no hookups.
Maximum length: 25 feet.
Facilities: Tables, grills, pit toilets, drinking water.
Fee: None.
Management: Forest Service.
Contact: 541-446-3351.
Finding the campground: It is north off U.S. Highway 26, 10.8 miles west of Unity and 26.5 miles east of Prairie City.

About the campground: Tucked off US 26, in a gently rolling terrain dotted by mature yellow-bellied ponderosa pines is this pleasant campground. Younger pines and firs fill out the forest. From the east end of the camp, a barrier-free nature trail travels half a mile to Wetmore Campground. Deer sometimes visit the camp. The campground is maintained from Memorial Day weekend through Labor Day weekend.

ONTARIO AREA

	Hookup sites	Total sites	Max. RV length	Hookups	Toilets	Showers	Drinking water	Dump station	Recreation	Fee	Can reserve
118 Bully Creek Reservoir County Park	29	33	40	E	F	•	•	•	SFBL	$	
119 Farewell Bend State Recreation Area	93	140	56	WE	F	•	•	•	SFBL	$$	•
120 Lake Owyhee State Park	33	40	55	WE	F	•	•	•	SFBL	$$	
121 Leslie Gulch–Slocum Creek		8	20		NF				HSFBL		
122 Spring Recreation Site		35	30		NF	•			SFBL	$	
123 Succor Creek State Park		19	small		NF				H		
124 Twin Springs Recreation Site		3	20		NF				O		

Hookups: W = Water E = Electric S = Sewer **Total sites:** T = Tent-only campground **Maximum trailer/RV length** given in feet.
Toilets: F = Flush NF = No Flush **Recreation:** H = Hiking S = Swimming F = Fishing B = Boating L = Boat Launch
O = Off-Highway Driving R = Horseback Riding C = Cycling
Fee: $ = $1-9 $$ = $10-19 $$$ = $20-29 $$$$ = $30-39. If no entry under **Fee**, camping is free.

118 Bully Creek Reservoir County Park

Location: About 11 miles northwest of Vale, on Bully Creek Reservoir.
Sites: 29 hookup sites, 4 basic sites; electric hookups.
Maximum length: 40 feet.
Facilities: Tables, grills, flush toilets, drinking water, showers, dump station, telephone, boat launch, dock.
Fee: $.
Management: Malheur County.
Contact: 541-473-2969.
Finding the campground: From U.S. Highway 20 at the west end of Vale, go northwest on Graham Boulevard for 7 miles and continue northwest on Bully Creek Reservoir Road for another 4 miles to enter the campground on the left.

About the campground: This landscaped campground rests in the grassy-hill basin of Bully Creek Reservoir, the centerpiece to recreation. It offers catches of pan fish, boating, and swimming. The sites have gravel parking, with a few sites shaded by fuller trees. Along the reservoir shore, shade is rare. The campground is open from April to mid-November.

119 Farewell Bend State Recreation Area

Location: About 26 miles northwest of Ontario, on Brownlee Reservoir.
Sites: 93 hookup sites, 43 basic sites, 4 walk-in tent sites, 2 covered camper wagons, 4 tepees; water and electric hookups.
Maximum length: 56 feet.
Facilities: Tables, grills, flush toilets, drinking water, showers, dump station, telephone, playground, sand volleyball, horseshoe pits, fishing docks, boat launch, Oregon Trail exhibit.
Fee: $$.

Management: Oregon State Parks and Recreation Department.
Contact: 541-869-2365; 1-800-452-5687 for reservations.
Finding the campground: From Interstate 84, take Exit 353 (25 miles north-west of Ontario), and go north on U.S. Highway 30 Business toward Huntington to enter the park on the right at 1 mile.

About the campground: Here, along the Snake River, you can camp where the Oregon pioneers did more than 150 years ago, with a couple of notable differences: The accommodations are now first-class, and the river is contained as Brownlee Reservoir. Arid-canyon hills overlook the lawn-and-tree oasis. The hookup sites occupy two distinct areas: one with privacy hedges, mature shade trees, and a central lawn; the other in the arid Snake River Canyon, with open lawn and young trees. Boating, swimming, fishing for bass and catfish, hunting (outside the park), and rockhounding in the outlying area entertain guests. The campground is open year-round.

120 Lake Owyhee State Park

Location: 33 miles southwest of Nyssa.
Sites: 33 hookup sites, 7 basic sites, 2 tepees; water and electric hookups.
Maximum length: 55 feet.
Facilities: Tables, grills, flush toilets, drinking water, showers, dump station, boat launch, dock, fish-cleaning station.
Fee: $$.
Management: Oregon State Parks and Recreation Department.
Contact: 1-800-551-6949.
Finding the campground: The park is right off Owyhee Reservoir Road, 33 miles southwest of Nyssa. From Nyssa, go south on Oregon 201 about 12 miles and turn right for Lake Owyhee, following Owyhee Avenue and Owhyee Reservoir Road the remaining way to the park.

About the campground: In the remote southeast corner of the state, this park's V. W. McCormack Campground offers landscaped sites above Lake Owyhee, an attractive, 52-mile-long, 14,000-acre canyon reservoir open to boating, swimming, and waterskiing, and known for its bass fishing. Attractive reddish cliffs, terraced walls, and unusual geological formations frame the reservoir, adding to boat tours and photographic images. A nearby resort rents boats. The campground is open from mid-April through October.

121 Leslie Gulch–Slocum Creek

Location: About 47 miles southwest of Adrian, on Owyhee Reservoir.
Sites: 8 basic sites; no hookups.
Maximum length: 20 feet.
Facilities: Some tables, vault toilet, boat launch. No drinking water.
Fee: None.
Management: Bureau of Land Management.

Contact: 541-473-3144.
Finding the campground: It is approximately 47 miles southwest of Adrian. From Oregon 201 8 miles south of Adrian; go southwest on Succor Creek Road and then west on Leslie Gulch Road (both are improved-surface roads) to locate this primitive camp on the left prior to reaching the east shore of Owyhee Reservoir.

About the campground: This sun-drenched, barebones camp has limited amenities and informal site parking, but it enjoys a front-row seat to the reservoir and an exciting canyon location. Stargazing is unmatched. The reservoir is noted for its scenery, fishing, and boating. Washes throughout the Leslie Gulch Area prescribe dry-weather hiking trails through the colorful volcanic-ash formations of shields, beehives, and hollows, with opportunities for sightings of bighorn sheep, coyotes, bats, and golden eagles; be alert for snakes. The camp is at the mouth of Slocum Gulch for morning or evening strolls. Bring ample water, hats, sunscreen, and a free-standing shade source. A reservoir dunking is almost always in order. The campground is open in dry weather from April through October.

122 Spring Recreation Site

Location: About 33 miles northwest of Ontario, on Brownlee Reservoir.
Sites: 20 basic sites, 15 tent sites; no hookups.
Maximum length: 30 feet.
Facilities: Tables, grills, vault toilets, drinking water, boat launch, docks, fish-cleaning station.
Fee: $.
Management: Bureau of Land Management.
Contact: 541-473-3144.
Finding the campground: From Interstate 84, take Exit 353 (25 miles northwest of Ontario), and go 5 miles north on U.S. Highway 30 Business to Huntington. There, turn right onto paved Snake River Road for a 3.4-mile winding canyon tour to the camp.

About the campground: Along Brownlee Reservoir on the Snake River, both the tent and RV camping areas rim a gravel parking lot. The tent sites are just a short walk away in an area of established shade trees. The RV spaces are typically paired with smaller trees, but in this narrow, steep-sided canyon, the walls help shadow the camp. Fishing, boating, and swimming attract people to this spot. This campground is open from March 1 to November 30.

123 Succor Creek State Park

Location: About 23 miles southwest of Adrian.
Sites: 19 basic sites; no hookups.
Maximum length: Small units only.
Facilities: Tables, vault toilet. No drinking water.
Fee: None.
Management: Oregon State Parks and Recreation Department.

Succor Creek State Park.

Contact: 1-800-551-6949.
Finding the campground: From Oregon 201, 8 miles south of Adrian, go southwest on improved-surface Succor Creek Road for 15 miles to reach this park.

About the campground: This isolated representative of the state park system serves up a fine dose of solitude in a grand desert-canyon setting. Succor Creek halves the camp, and the sites have small planted trees for some shade. There are no established trails, but the jeep trails and landmarks of the canyon terrain suggest short cross-country outings. Photography, wildlife viewing, stargazing, and relaxing at camp entertain individuals who venture here. When scrambling among the rocks, be alert for snakes. The campground is open in dry weather from March through October.

124 Twin Springs Recreation Site

Location: About 33 miles southwest of Vale.
Sites: 3 basic sites; no hookups.
Maximum length: 20 feet.
Facilities: Tables, grills, vault toilets. No drinking water.
Fee: None.
Management: Bureau of Land Management.
Contact: 541-473-3144.
Finding the campground: From Vale, go 4.6 miles west on U.S. Highway 20 from its junction with US 26 and turn south on paved Russell Road, which is marked for Rock Canyon and Dry Creek. Follow it for 2.2 miles and turn left off

the pavement onto a dirt-and-gravel road marked for Twin Springs and Dry Creek. Go 0.5 mile and turn left, passing through a pair of gates as the road traverses private property; resecure the gates after you. After going another 9 miles, bear left to avoid a jeep road to the right; 3.5 miles farther on, bear right at the sign for Twin Springs. Now, proceed 12.7 miles more to find this campground straddling the road. High clearance is recommended.

About the campground: After a complicated drive on bumpy dirt roads, campers can settle back at this out-of-the-way, spring-fed oasis; shade trees are a rarity in this vast desert. A few free-ranging cows and screeching hawks are your neighbors. The immediate area allows for some motorcycle use, hunting, rock-hounding, and cross-country exploration (for the knowledgeable), but most users seem content just to bask in the solitude and tranquility of the camp. The campground is open in dry weather from May through October.

BURNS AREA

		Hookup sites	Total sites	Max. RV length	Hookups	Toilets	Showers	Drinking water	Dump station	Recreation	Fee	Can reserve
125	Chickahominy Recreation Site		18	35		NF		•		FBL	$	
126	Chukar Park		18	28		NF		•		FBL	$	
127	Delintment Lake		24	30		NF		•		HFBL	$	
128	Emigrant Creek		7	25		NF		•		F	$	
129	Falls		6	22		NF		•		F	$	
130	Idlewild		25	30		NF		•		H		
131	Joaquin Miller Horse Camp		27	35		NF		•		R		
132	Yellowjacket		20	30		NF		•		FBL		

Hookups: W = Water E = Electric S = Sewer **Total sites:** T = Tent-only campground **Maximum trailer/RV length** given in feet.
Toilets: F = Flush NF = No Flush **Recreation:** H = Hiking S = Swimming F = Fishing B = Boating L = Boat Launch
O = Off-Highway Driving R = Horseback Riding C = Cycling
Fee: $ = $1-9 $$ = $10-19 $$$ = $20-29 $$$$ = $30-39. If no entry under **Fee**, camping is free.

125 Chickahominy Recreation Site

Location: 31 miles west of Burns, on Chickahominy Reservoir.
Sites: 18 basic sites, plus lower area of dispersed camping; no hookups.
Maximum length: 35 feet.
Facilities: Tables, fire rings, drinking water, and graveled pull-thru parking at designated areas; vault toilets and boat launch at both areas.
Fee: $.
Management: Bureau of Land Management.
Contact: 541-573-4400.
Finding the campground: It is north off U.S. Highway 20, 31 miles west of Burns, 99 miles east of Bend.

About the campground: This camp rests on the open flat of Chickahominy Reservoir, which holds back the water of Chickahominy Creek. It is a sparkling, big, elongated water body in an arid basin of mixed grasses and sagebrush. Juniper-studded buttes and ridges rise in the backdrop. Bird watching, fishing, and boating are camp pastimes. Some tables have wind-and-sun shelters; sturdy shade sources are a good idea for here. The campground is open year-round.

126 Chukar Park

Location: 6 miles north of Juntura.
Sites: 18 basic sites; no hookups.
Maximum length: 28 feet.
Facilities: Tables, grills, vault toilets, drinking water.
Fee: $.
Management: Bureau of Land Management.
Contact: 541-473-3144.

Finding the campground: From U.S. Highway 20 at Juntura, go 6 miles north on Beulah Reservoir Road.

About the campground: This campground is a pleasing oasis along the North Fork Malheur and rests in a rugged countryside, where the chukar, an introduced gameland partridge, is hunted in the fall. The camp unites lawn and native juniper-grassland vegetation. The 20- to 25-foot-wide North Fork Malheur races past the camp, and scenic cliffs claim the opposite shore. The camp is 9 miles south of Beulah Reservoir for fishing and boating. The campground is open from mid-April into October.

127 Delintment Lake

Location: About 42 miles northwest of Burns/Hines, on Delintment Lake.
Sites: 24 basic sites; no hookups.
Maximum length: 30 feet.
Facilities: Tables, grills, vault toilets, drinking water, boat launch.
Fee: $.
Management: Forest Service.
Contact: 541-573-4300.
Finding the campground: From U.S. Highway 20 at the west end of Hines, turn north onto Burns-Izee Road (County Road 127) for Yellowjacket and Delintment Lakes, go 11.7 miles, and turn left onto Forest Road 41. Proceed 26.2 miles and keep left to remain on FR 41. Reach the lake after another 4 miles, with the camp entrance ahead.

About the campground: This comfortable family campground occupies the treed shore of Delintment Lake, a one-time beaver pond enlarged by an earthen dam to its present 57-acre size. The fishing is good, with average rainbows measuring between 12 and 18 inches. Across the road from the camp, the 5-mile Delintment Creek Trail explores forest and meadow-edge along gurgling, crystalline Delintment Creek. The campground is open from June to mid-October.

128 Emigrant Creek

Location: About 34 miles northwest of Burns/Hines.
Sites: 7 basic sites; no hookups.
Maximum length: 25 feet.
Facilities: Tables, grills, vault toilets, drinking water.
Fee: $.
Management: Forest Service.
Contact: 541-573-4300.
Finding the campground: From U.S. Highway 20 at the west end of Hines, turn north onto Burns-Izee Road (County Road 127) toward Yellowjacket and Delintment Lakes. Go 23.2 miles and bear left onto Forest Road 43. Proceed 9.9 miles more and turn left onto gravel FR 4340, following it 0.3 mile into the campground.

About the campground: This campground is situated among the big ponderosa pines along meadow-banked Emigrant Creek, a picturesque, meandering waterway to explore along or fish. The forest has a lovely meadow-shrub understory, and the sites offer gravel parking. At the edges of the day, deer may be spied as they drift to and from the creek. The campground is open from June to mid-October.

129 Falls

Location: About 32 miles northwest of Burns/Hines.
Sites: 6 basic sites; no hookups.
Maximum length: 22 feet.
Facilities: Tables, grills, vault toilets, drinking water.
Fee: $.
Management: Forest Service.
Contact: 541-573-4300.
Finding the campground: From U.S. Highway 20 at the west end of Hines, turn north onto Burns-Izee Road (County Road 127) for Yellowjacket and Delintment Lakes. Go 23.2 miles and bear left onto Forest Road 43. Proceed 8.2 miles more and turn left onto gravel FR 4300.050 to reach the campsites in 0.2 mile.

About the campground: This campground occupies a ponderosa-pine flat along a bend of Emigrant Creek. The beautiful, towering red-trunked pines complement the green banks and dark, meandering flow of the creek. Above the camp, a few volcanic boulders stud the forest slope. The camp promises a quiet retreat, and a short, rugged trail travels the west shore downstream. The campground is open from June to mid-October.

130 Idlewild

Location: 17 miles north of Burns.
Sites: 25 basic sites; no hookups.
Maximum length: 30 feet.
Facilities: Tables, grills, vault toilets, drinking water, picnic shelter.
Fee: None.
Management: Forest Service.
Contact: 541-573-7292.
Finding the campground: The campground is east off U.S. Highway 395, 17 miles north of Burns, 53 miles south of John Day.

About the campground: At meadow's edge, in a scenic ponderosa-pine forest sits this pleasant campground, a convenient stopover for the US 395 traveler. Planted aspen and natural mountain mahogany vary the look of the forest. The campground roads and parking spaces are paved, with a few pull-thru sites to accommodate longer vehicles. Short hiking trails explore out from the camp: the 1-mile Idlewild Loop and the 2-mile Devine Summit Loop. The campground is maintained from May 30 to October 15.

131 Joaquin Miller Horse Camp

Location: 19 miles north of Burns.
Sites: 27 basic sites; no hookups.
Maximum length: 35 feet.
Facilities: Tables, grills, pit toilets, drinking water, corrals.
Fee: None.
Management: Forest Service.
Contact: 541-573-7292.
Finding the campground: The camp is west off U.S. Highway 395, 19 miles north of Burns, 51 miles south of John Day.

About the campground: At this camp, you will find paved roads and parking and several long pull-thru sites to accommodate the horse camping public. The corrals rest at the far west edge of the camp. The sites are partially shaded by ponderosa pines. Although commonly used horse routes venture away from the camp, there are no formal horse trails. The campground is maintained from May 30 to October 15.

132 Yellowjacket

Location: About 34 miles northwest of Burns/Hines, on Yellowjacket Lake.
Sites: 20 basic sites; no hookups.
Maximum length: 30 feet.
Facilities: Tables, grills, pit toilets, drinking water, primitive boat launch.
Fee: None.
Management: Forest Service.
Contact: 541-573-7292.
Finding the campground: From U.S. Highway 20 at the west end of Hines, turn north onto Burns-Izee Road (County Road 127/Forest Road 47) for Yellow-jacket and Delintment Lakes. Go 30.1 miles and turn right (east) onto FR 37. Go another 2.5 miles and turn right onto gravel FR 3745 to reach the campground on the right in 0.8 mile.

About the campground: This family campground occupies a gentle, pine-clad slope above the west shore of Yellowjacket Lake, an elongated lake at the foot of a low ridge. A small earthen dam harnesses the water. At the lake's north and south ends, willows and marsh claim the shallows, and coots and ducks rear their young. The deeper water toward the lake's center is suitable for fishing tubes and small boats. On summer weekends and holidays, the camp can fill up. The campground is maintained from May 30 to October 15.

SILVER LAKE AREA

	Hookup sites	Total sites	Max. RV length	Hookups	Toilets	Showers	Drinking water	Dump station	Recreation	Fee	Can reserve
133 Antler		9	30		NF		•		HR		
134 Cabin Lake		14	30		NF		•				
135 Duncan Reservoir		7	22		NF		•		FBL		
136 Eastbay		17	40		NF		•		FBL	$	
137 Silver Creek Marsh		15	40		NF		•		HFR		
138 Summer Lake Wildlife Area		20	40		NF				HF		
139 Thompson Reservoir		20	35		NF		•		FBL		

Hookups: W = Water E = Electric S = Sewer **Total sites:** T = Tent-only campground **Maximum trailer/RV length** given in feet.
Toilets: F = Flush NF = No Flush **Recreation:** H = Hiking S = Swimming F = Fishing B = Boating L = Boat Launch
O = Off-Highway Driving R = Horseback Riding C = Cycling
Fee: $ = $1-9 $$ = $10-19 $$$ = $20-29 $$$$ = $30-39. If no entry under **Fee**, camping is free.

133 Antler

Location: About 20 miles southwest of the city of Silver Lake.
Sites: 5 basic sites, 4 walk-in tent sites; no hookups.
Maximum length: 30 feet.
Facilities: Tables, grills, vault toilets, drinking water, corral, hitching posts.
Fee: None.
Management: Forest Service.
Contact: 541-576-2107.
Finding the campground: From Oregon 31, 0.8 mile northwest of Silver Lake, turn south onto paved County Road 4-11/Forest Road 27 for Silver Creek Marsh and Thompson Reservoir and go 9 miles. Turn right onto gravel FR 2804, go 2.5 miles, and turn left onto FR 7645. After another 5.6 miles, turn left onto FR 036, continue 1.5 miles, and then turn right onto FR 038 to reach the camp on the right in 0.6 mile. Some intersection signs help point the way.

About the campground: On Fremont National Recreation Trail, this campground is a gateway to Yamsay Mountain Roadless Area. The sites receive partial shade in a select-cut forest of lodgepole pine and fir. The camp serves hiker and equestrian. Yamsay Mountain—an all-day ride or backpack trip—is an intriguing, volcanic dome, with exceptional views and wild elk herds ranging its flank. The Scenic Rock Loop Trail offers a shorter excursion, touring forest, meadow, and rock near the camp. The campground is open when snow is absent.

134 Cabin Lake

Location: About 32 miles southeast of La Pine.
Sites: 14 basic sites; no hookups.
Maximum length: 30 feet.
Facilities: Tables, grills, vault toilets, drinking water.

Fee: None.
Management: Forest Service.
Contact: 541-388-5664.
Finding the campground: From U.S. Highway 97, at La Pine, turn east onto Forest Road 22, go 26.4 miles, and turn right (south) onto FR 18, continuing 6 miles to reach this camp on the right. From Fort Rock, it is 11 miles north via County Road 511/FR18.

About the campground: This camp claims an attractive stand of mature ponderosa pines at the transition zone between forest and southeastern desert. This little-used camp offers solitude, bird watching, and an opportunity to explore. It takes its name from tiny Cabin Lake, which was located across from the guard station and is now dry. En route to the camp, you will pass South Ice Cave, north off FR 22, 1.2 miles west of FR 18. Suggesting another trip is Fort Rock State Park, a natural rock fortress that rises from the desert floor and has an interesting geological and archaeological story; find its turnoff 9 miles south of the camp off FR 18/CR 511. The campground is open from May into October.

135 Duncan Reservoir

Location: About 10 miles southeast of the city of Silver Lake, on Duncan Reservoir.
Sites: 7 basic sites; no hookups.
Maximum length: 22 feet.
Facilities: Tables, fire rings, vault toilets, boat launch. No drinking water.
Fee: None.
Management: Bureau of Land Management.
Contact: 541-947-2177.
Finding the campground: From Silver Lake, go east on Oregon 31 South for 5.4 miles and turn right onto gravel County Road 4-14 at the sign for Duncan Reservoir. Proceed 0.9 mile and turn right on BLM 6197, a narrow, washboard road; continue 4.1 miles to the camp.

About the campground: This small, primitive camp occupies a juniper-sage shore of Duncan Reservoir, a moderate-sized reservoir cradled in an arid basin. Anglers troll the lake, in hopes of catching evening supper. Stargazing is a pleasant way to cap the day.

136 Eastbay

Location: About 15 miles southwest of the city of Silver Lake, on Thompson Reservoir.
Sites: 17 basic sites; no hookups.
Maximum length: 40 feet.
Facilities: Tables, barbecues, vault toilets, drinking water, boat launch, dock.
Fee: $.
Management: Forest Service.
Contact: 541-576-2107.

Finding the campground: From Oregon 31, 0.3 mile northwest of Silver Lake, turn south onto paved County Road 4-12/Forest Road 28 for Eastbay Campground, go 13.2 miles, and turn right onto FR 014, going another 1.5 miles to enter this campground.

About the campground: On the east shore of 1,532-acre Thompson Reservoir, this comfortable campground borders a quiet cove, offers paved parking, and receives partial shade from its mixed-age pine forest. Thompson Reservoir harnesses Silver Creek for irrigation and has fishing and boating recreation; boat speeds are limited to 10 miles per hour. The lake serves up western views of Yamsay Mountain and has an attractive shoreline when full. The south end of the lake boasts nesting bald eagles, while the lake island is a waterfowl nesting area. The campground is open from early June through October.

137 Silver Creek Marsh

Location: About 11 miles southwest of the city of Silver Lake.
Sites: 15 basic sites; no hookups.
Maximum length: 40 feet.
Facilities: Tables, grills, vault toilets, drinking water, corrals, hitching posts.
Fee: None.
Management: Forest Service.
Contact: 541-576-2107.
Finding the campground: From Oregon 31, 0.8 mile northwest of Silver Lake, turn south onto paved County Road 4-11/Forest Road 27 for Silver Creek Marsh and Thompson Reservoir and go 10 miles to reach this campground on the left.

About the campground: This campground hugs the West Fork Silver Creek, a tiny creek, with a few deep pools for fish. A semi-open pine flat, with big ponderosa pines, houses the camp. The sites have gravel parking, receive a mix of sun and shade, and can serve as a stopover or base for the Fremont National Recreation Trail, which crosses a corner of the camp. Thompson Reservoir, 5 miles southeast, offers more dependable fishing and also boating (10 miles per hour). The campground is open from mid-May to October.

138 Summer Lake Wildlife Area

Location: About 1 mile southeast of the community of Summer Lake.
Sites: 4 camping areas with a total of 20 basic sites; no hookups.
Maximum length: 40 feet.
Facilities: A few tables, nonflush toilets. No drinking water.
Fee: None.
Management: Oregon Department of Fish and Wildlife.
Contact: 541-943-3152.
Finding the campground: At the south end of the community of Summer Lake, turn east off Oregon 31 at the sign for the wildlife area; pick up a refuge

map at the office, and follow the road tour into the wildlife area to the designated camping areas at Windbreak, River, Bullgate, and River Ranch.

About the campground: The refuge offers minimalist camping on broad, gravel flats; comfort is what you bring. Views are of the richly textured refuge lands: open water, channels, marsh, mudflat, and arid brush; to the west rises imposing Winter Ridge. Bird watching and hunting are the chief draws, with the refuge road to drive and the dikes to hike. A cacophony of sound delights, as do the evening stars. Mosquitoes can be villainous, but remember they are part of the food chain sustaining the birds. Insect repellent, hats, scopes, and telephoto lenses should be among your gear.

139 Thompson Reservoir

Location: About 16 miles southwest of the city of Silver Lake, on Thompson Reservoir.
Sites: 20 basic sites; no hookups.
Maximum length: 35 feet.
Facilities: Tables, grills, pit toilets, drinking water, primitive boat launch.
Fee: None.
Management: Forest Service.
Contact: 541-576-2107.
Finding the campground: From Oregon 31, 0.8 mile northwest of Silver Lake, turn south onto paved County Road 4-11/Forest Road 27 for Silver Creek Marsh and Thompson Reservoir. Go 14 miles and turn left onto gravel FR 287 to reach this campground in another 1.1 miles.

About the campground: This rustic campground is on the pine-forested north basin slope of Thompson Reservoir, a large, roundish irrigation reservoir, with a piney rim, treed points, and a riddling of snags. Fishing boats (10 miles per hour) ply the clear, blue water. When the reservoir is full, so is this freebie campground. Look for mergansers, bald eagles, osprey, and migratory shorebirds and waterfowl. The campground is open from mid-May to October.

SOUTHEAST DESERT

		Hookup sites	Total sites	Max. RV length	Hookups	Toilets	Showers	Drinking water	Dump station	Recreation	Fee	Can reserve
140	Antelope Reservoir Recreation Site		4	25		NF				FBL		
141	Fish Lake Recreation Site		20	24		NF		•		FBLR	$	
142	Jackman Park Recreation Site		6	24		NF		•			$	
143	Malheur Field Station	9	9	30	WES	F		•			$–$$	
144	Mann Lake Recreation Site		open	35		NF				FBL		
145	Page Springs Recreation Site		30	24		NF		•		HF	$	
146	Rome Launch Site		6	40		NF		•		FBL		
147	South Steens Recreation Site		36	35		NF		•		HFR	$	
148	Willow Creek Hot Springs Rec. Site		5	small		NF						

Hookups: W = Water E = Electric S = Sewer **Total sites:** T = Tent-only campground **Maximum trailer/RV length** given in feet.
Toilets: F = Flush NF = No Flush **Recreation:** H = Hiking S = Swimming F = Fishing B = Boating L = Boat Launch
O = Off-Highway Driving R = Horseback Riding C = Cycling
Fee: $ = $1-9 $$ = $10-19 $$$ = $20-29 $$$$ = $30-39. If no entry under **Fee**, camping is free.

140 Antelope Reservoir Recreation Site

Location: About 13 miles southwest of Jordan Valley, on Antelope Reservoir.
Sites: 4 basic sites, plus dispersed camping; no hookups.
Maximum length: 25 feet.
Facilities: Tables, grills, vault toilets, primitive boat launch. No drinking water.
Fee: None.
Management: Bureau of Land Management.
Contact: 541-473-3144.
Finding the campground: From U.S. Highway 95, 12 miles west of Jordan Valley, 21 miles east of Rome, go south on gravel Antelope Reservoir Road. At 1.2 miles, reach the campground on the left.

About the campground: On Antelope Reservoir's west shore, this campground occupies points of land on either side of the rocky dam. The reservoir claims a gentle basin, with skyline views of arid rims. Sites dot the barren, shadeless shore; a sage-grassland extends beyond the camp. Fishing and boating engage visitors, and killdeers can animate the shore.

141 Fish Lake Recreation Site

Location: About 78 miles southeast of Burns.
Sites: 20 basic sites; no hookups.
Maximum length: 24 feet.
Facilities: Tables, grills, vault toilets, drinking water, boat ramp.
Fee: $.
Management: Bureau of Land Management.
Contact: 541-573-4400.

Finding the campground: From Frenchglen (61 miles south of Burns on Oregon 205), go east on gravel Steens Mountain Loop Road to enter this campground on the right at about 17 miles.

About the campground: This family campground occupies the shore of a mountain lake, which is large enough to support fishing and motorless boating. Willows claim the shore, with aspens growing on the slope near the camp; the campsites, though, sit mostly in the open. Nearby are corrals for public use. Discovery of Steens Mountain and Malheur National Wildlife Refuge awaits (high-clearance vehicles are necessary at Steens Mountain, with four-wheel drive needed to complete Steens Mountain Loop). The campground is open from June to October 31.

142 Jackman Park Recreation Site

Location: About 80 miles southeast of Burns.
Sites: 6 basic sites; no hookups.
Maximum length: 24 feet.
Facilities: Tables, grills, vault toilets, drinking water.
Fee: $.
Management: Bureau of Land Management.
Contact: 541-573-4400.
Finding the campground: From Frenchglen (61 miles south of Burns on Oregon 205), go east on gravel Steens Mountain Loop Road for almost 20 miles to enter this campground on the right.

About the campground: This small camp has a split-character, with the northern half of the loop showing dry meadows and juniper-mountain-mahogany sagelands and the southern half showing wet meadows and aspen groves. The camp offers a base for exploring Steens Mountain, a rugged, high-clearance-vehicle area. West of camp are Honeymoon and Pate Lakes. The campground is open from July to October 31.

143 Malheur Field Station

Location: About 30 miles southeast of Burns.
Sites: 9 RV sites; water, electric, and sewer hookups.
Maximum length: 30 feet.
Facilities: Toilets, drinking water, telephone, playground, laundry, cabins, restaurant, recreational room, gymnasium.
Fee: $ to $$.
Management: Malheur Field Station.
Contact: 541-493-2629.
Finding the campground: From U.S. Highway 20/395 in Burns, go east on Oregon 78 for 1.7 miles, turn right (south) onto OR 205, and proceed another 24 miles. Turn left onto Princeton-Narrows Road, go just over 3 miles, and turn right onto gravel Central Patrol Road to reach the field station in about 1 mile.

About the campground: Below Coyote Buttes, in an educational center-dormitory setting, you will find this small, austere but serviceable RV camp, the only campground in Malheur National Wildlife Refuge. The RV campground occupies a small area of trimmed-back grass and gravel next to the field station mobile homes. Magnificent birding, refuge sightseeing, and convenient access to area highlights recommend this camp. It is only an hour from Steens Mountain and 30 minutes from Diamond Craters. Driving tours, hiking, fishing, and going in search of the Kiger wild horses may draw you away from your spotting scope. The campground is open from March to October.

144 Mann Lake Recreation Site

Location: About 89 miles southeast of Burns, on Mann Lake.
Sites: Random camping; no hookups.
Maximum length: 35 feet.
Facilities: Vault toilets, 2 primitive boat launches. No drinking water.
Fee: None.
Management: Bureau of Land Management.
Contact: 541-573-4400.
Finding the campground: From U.S. Highway 20/395 in Burns, go east on Oregon 78 for 65 miles, turn right onto the gravel road marked for Andrews, Field, and Denio (Fields-Denio Road). Proceed 23.6 miles and turn right for Mann Lake.

About the campground: Named for an early-day rancher, Mann Lake is a glassy, broad natural platter at the eastern foot of Steens Mountain and centerpiece to your Oregon outback stay. This is a do-it-yourself camping area on the open plain. A shade source is desirable, along with plenty of water and sunscreen. Rainbow and the Mann Lake cutthroat trout survive in this low-oxygen water. Fishing is best early in the year before the algae builds. A wildlife viewing area encompasses the lake, and Alvord Hot Springs can be found some 18 miles south; look for the tin changing cell on the east side of the road. The campground is open year-round.

145 Page Springs Recreation Site

Location: About 64 miles southeast of Burns.
Sites: 30 basic sites; no hookups.
Maximum length: 24 feet.
Facilities: Tables, grills, vault toilets, drinking water.
Fee: $.
Management: Bureau of Land Management.
Contact: 541-573-4400.
Finding the campground: From Frenchglen (61 miles south of Burns on Oregon 205), go east on gravel Steens Mountain Loop Road to enter the campground on the right after about 3 miles.

Fishing on the Donner und Blitzen River.

About the campground: Beneath a basalt rim along the Donner und Blitzen River sits this arid grassland camp, with both sunny and tree-shaded sites. It makes a fine base for visiting its next door neighbor, Malheur National Wildlife Refuge, where you find exceptional birding and natural and cultural discoveries, or for journeying up Steens Mountain, an incredible, alpine fault-block mountain rising from the desert plain (high-clearance vehicles needed). The mountain's chiseled canyons unfold superb scenery and seclude the Kiger wild horses. Page Springs, though, is no ugly stepsister, with the sparkling Donner und Blitzen River, its own birdlife of bluff and tree, and the long-distance Desert Trail passing through the camp. The campground is open from mid-April through mid-November.

146 Rome Launch Site

Location: 33 miles west of Jordan Valley, near Rome.
Sites: 6 basic sites; no hookups.
Maximum length: 40 feet.
Facilities: Tables, vault toilets, drinking water, raft take-out/put-in.
Fee: None.
Management: Bureau of Land Management.
Contact: 541-473-3144.
Finding the campground: It is south off U.S. Highway 95 at the eastern outskirts of Rome, 105 miles southeast of Burns, 33 miles west of Jordan Valley.

About the campground: Here, the sites edge an open, gravel plateau above the Owyhee River and below a sage-grass slope and rocky crest. Planted cottonwoods provide some shade. The Owyhee—one of the originally designated wild and scenic rivers—flows glassy and welcoming; a rafting permit system is in effect. A nearby geologic attraction is the Pillars of Rome. These 100-foot-tall desert white rock towers suggested the ruins of Rome to early-day travelers. The campground is open from March to November.

147 South Steens Recreation Site

Location: About 90 miles southeast of Burns.
Sites: 21 basic sites, 15 horse sites; no hookups.
Maximum length: 35 feet.
Facilities: Tables, grills, vault toilets, drinking water, hitching posts in horse camp.
Fee: $.
Management: Bureau of Land Management.
Contact: 541-573-4400.
Finding the campground: From U.S. Highway 20/395 in Burns, go east on Oregon 78 for 1.7 miles, turn right (south) onto OR 205, and proceed another 69 miles. Turn left onto South Steens Loop Road at the sign for Upper Blitzen. Drive 18.8 miles to the horse camp; 18.9 miles to the family campground.

About the campground: These side-by-side campgrounds occupy the mouth of Big Indian Gorge and offer similar convenience and amenities. Sites are dispersed throughout a juniper sage-grassland and are either sunny or partially shaded. A trail explores Big Indian Gorge, following Big Indian Creek upstream from the camp. With high-clearance vehicles, visitors can drive the Steens Mountain Loop Back Country Byway for stunning vistas and alpine scenery. Wildflowers and wildlife further recommend a visit. The campground is open from June to October.

148 Willow Creek Hot Springs Recreation Site

Location: About 43 miles east of Fields.
Sites: 5 basic sites; no hookups.
Maximum length: Small units only.
Facilities: Vault toilet. No drinking water.
Fee: None.
Management: Bureau of Land Management.
Contact: 541-573-4400.
Finding the campground: From Fields (where services are available, 111 miles south of Burns on Oregon 205), go south on OR 205 for 8.1 miles and turn left onto a wide gravel road heading east across the desert. Where it passes some ranches, bear left; the road narrows. After traveling 32.5 miles from OR 205, veer right near a fence line of Whitehorse Ranch to follow a dirt, dry-weather road for 2.3 miles. There, bear right at an information board to access the recreation site in 0.3 mile.

About the campground: This destination is reserved for the adventurous, who have good map and navigational skills and are comfortable with traveling in an area of few landmarks. The austere camp exists because of two adjoining, modestly developed hot springs pools of different temperature, in a natural outdoor setting of dry-grass and sage. Each of the pools can accommodate up to ten people. The hotter one is clear, with a sandy bottom, and 3 feet deep. The milder pool is cloudy, with a muddy bottom, and 4.5 feet deep. Biting flies can annoy, but the stars dazzle. Dry-weather access only.

PAISLEY–GEARHART MOUNTAIN AREA

	Hookup sites	Total sites	Max. RV length	Hookups	Toilets	Showers	Drinking water	Dump station	Recreation	Fee	Can reserve
149 Campbell Lake		15	25		NF		•		HFBL		
150 Corral Creek Forest Camp		6	30		NF				H		
151 Dairy Point		4	25		NF		•		F		
152 Deadhorse Lake		9	16		NF		•		HFBL		
153 Happy Camp		9	25		NF				F		
154 Lee Thomas		7	20		NF		•		F		
155 Marsters Spring		11	30		NF		•		HF		
156 Sandhill Crossing		5	30		NF		•		F		

Hookups: W = Water E = Electric S = Sewer **Total sites:** T = Tent-only campground **Maximum trailer/RV length** given in feet.
Toilets: F = Flush NF = No Flush **Recreation:** H = Hiking S = Swimming F = Fishing B = Boating L = Boat Launch
O = Off-Highway Driving R = Horseback Riding C = Cycling
Fee: $ = $1-9 $$ = $10-19 $$$ = $20-29 $$$$ = $30-39. If no entry under **Fee,** camping is free.

149 Campbell Lake

Location: About 30 miles southwest of Paisley, on Campbell Lake.
Sites: 15 basic sites; no hookups.
Maximum length: 25 feet.
Facilities: Tables, grills, pit toilets, drinking water, boat launch and dock at day-use area.
Fee: None.
Management: Forest Service.
Contact: 541-943-3114.
Finding the campground: From Oregon 31 at Paisley, turn west on Mill Street, which becomes Forest Road 33. After 20 miles, you will come to a T-junction; turn right onto paved FR 28, go 8.4 miles, and turn left onto FR 033 to reach this campground on the left in 1.8 miles.

About the campground: This inviting campground occupies the lodgepole-pine perimeter of Campbell Lake, a pretty, circular mountain lake below Deadhorse Rim. The tight pine forest affords nearly complete shade, and the sites are well spaced for privacy. The lake is stocked with rainbow trout and open to small fishing boats. Trails from the camp traverse Deadhorse Rim to neighboring Deadhorse Lake. The small pond near the trailhead is sometimes loud with frogs. The campground is open from mid-June to October.

150 Corral Creek Forest Camp

Location: About 30 miles northeast of Bly.
Sites: 6 basic sites; no hookups.
Maximum length: 30 feet.
Facilities: Tables, grills, vault toilets. No drinking water.

Fee: None.
Management: Forest Service.
Contact: 541-353-2427.
Finding the campground: From Oregon 140 at Quartz Mountain (13 miles east of Bly, 30 miles west of Lakeview), turn north onto Forest Road 3660 and go 16 miles to FR 34 and turn right. Continue 0.2 mile more and turn left onto FR 012, going 0.3 mile on the dirt road to reach the camp on the left.

About the campground: At this relaxing getaway, the sites are nicely spaced for privacy in a setting of meadow and lodgepole pine. A rail fence isolates the camp from the picturesque meadow stream of Corral Creek, but an egress provides access for fishing or admiring. You will find wilderness entry and the Gearhart Mountain Trail System at the trailhead at the end of FR 012. The campground is open from June to October.

151 Dairy Point

Location: About 22 miles southwest of Paisley.
Sites: 4 basic sites; no hookups.
Maximum length: 25 feet.
Facilities: Tables, grills, pit toilets, drinking water.
Fee: None.
Management: Forest Service.
Contact: 541-943-3114.
Finding the campground: From Oregon 31 at Paisley, turn west onto Mill Street, which becomes Forest Road 33, following the signs to Marsters Spring and Dairy Creek. After 20 miles, you will come to a T-junction; turn left onto paved FR 28, go 2.1 miles, and again turn left to enter the camp.

About the campground: A rail fence enfolds this small, pleasant flat that edges a meadow and is just removed from Dairy Creek. The camp itself enjoys a setting of meadow and mature ponderosa pine. This is a place to commune with nature or attempt fishing along Dairy Creek. Bird songs and coyote wails are melodies heard at the camp. The campground is open from June to October.

152 Deadhorse Lake

Location: 32 miles southwest of Paisley.
Sites: 9 basic sites; no hookups.
Maximum length: 16 feet.
Facilities: Tables, grills, pit toilets, drinking water, boat launch, dock.
Fee: None.
Management: Forest Service.
Contact: 541-943-3114.
Finding the campground: From Oregon 31 at Paisley, turn west onto Mill Street, which becomes Forest Road 33. After 20 miles, you will come to a T-junction; turn right onto paved FR 28, go 8.4 miles, and turn left onto FR 033 to reach this campground in 3.2 miles.

About the campground: This campground occupies the lodgepole-pine-dressed shore of elongated Deadhorse Lake, one of two attractive mountain lakes below Deadhorse Rim; the other is Campbell Lake. This tranquil mountain retreat welcomes fishing, boating (5 miles per hour), and hiking. The lake is stocked with rainbow trout. Trails travel Deadhorse Rim to Campbell Lake and follow Deadcow Drainage for a nature walk. The campground is open from July to October.

153 Happy Camp

Location: About 24 miles southwest of Paisley.
Sites: 9 basic sites, 3 rustic Adirondack-style shelters; no hookups.
Maximum length: 25 feet.
Facilities: Tables, grills, pit toilets. No drinking water.
Fee: None.
Management: Forest Service.
Contact: 541-943-3114.
Finding the campground: From Oregon 31 at Paisley, turn west onto Mill Street, which becomes Forest Road 33, following the signs to Marsters Spring and Dairy Creek. After 20 miles, you will come to a T-junction; turn left onto paved FR 28, go 2 miles, and then turn right onto dirt FR 047 to enter the camp on the left in 2.4 miles. FR 047 has some rough, rock-studded segments and washboard.

About the campground: This campground is loaded with rustic charm. It rests on the north shore of pretty Dairy Creek, with the campsites occupying a meadow flat dotted by aspen and ponderosa and lodgepole pine. It is a place where you can awaken to bird songs. Fishing, reading a book, or napping are popular activities (or inactivities). The campground is open from June to October.

154 Lee Thomas

Location: 36 miles southwest of Paisley.
Sites: 7 basic sites; no hookups.
Maximum length: 20 feet.
Facilities: Tables, grills, pit toilets, drinking water.
Fee: None.
Management: Forest Service.
Contact: 541-943-3114.
Finding the campground: From Oregon 31 at Paisley, turn west onto Mill Street, which becomes Forest Road 33. After 20 miles, you will come to a T-junction; turn right onto paved FR 28, go about 11 miles, and turn left onto FR 3411 for Lee Thomas and Sandhill Crossing Campgrounds. Go 5 miles more to this campground on the left.

About the campground: This campground unites a lodgepole-pine stand, a marmot-inhabited rock outcrop, wildflower meadows dotted by willow clumps, and the lovely Sprague Wild and Scenic River. A pole fence encircles the camp, with an egress to the river for fishing or just looking. The Lee Thomas Trailhead is 1 mile east of the camp; from here, the Deadhorse Rim Trail travels 6 miles to Deadhorse Lake, with Campbell Lake a possible destination beyond that. The campground is open from June to October.

155 Marsters Spring

Location: 7 miles southwest of Paisley.
Sites: 11 basic sites; no hookups.
Maximum length: 30 feet.
Facilities: Tables, grills, vault toilets, drinking water.
Fee: None.
Management: Forest Service.
Contact: 541-943-3114.
Finding the campground: From Oregon 31 at Paisley, turn west onto Mill Street, which becomes Forest Road 33, following the signs to Marsters Spring and Dairy Creek. After 7 miles, turn left to enter the camp.

About the campground: This campground fronts the picturesque Chewaucan River, presently being studied for wild and scenic river classification. The relaxing camp is sheltered by a mixed woods of pine, juniper, cottonwood, willow, and alder, with some sites directly overlooking the swift river. An arid hill rises across from the camp. Chewaucan Crossing Trailhead is 1 mile upstream on FR 33 and offers access to the Fremont National Recreation Trail, a long-distance trail that is still growing. Fishing is also popular. The campground is open from May to October.

156 Sandhill Crossing

Location: About 38 miles southwest of Paisley.
Sites: 5 basic sites; no hookups.
Maximum length: 30 feet.
Facilities: Tables, grills, pit toilets, drinking water.
Fee: None.
Management: Forest Service.
Contact: 541-943-3114.
Finding the campground: From Oregon 31 at Paisley, turn west onto Mill Street, which becomes Forest Road 33. After 20 miles, you will come to a T-junction; turn right onto paved FR 28, go about 11 miles, and turn left onto FR 3411 for Lee Thomas and Sandhill Crossing Campgrounds. Go 7.3 miles more to this campground on the left.

About the campground: On a lodgepole-pine bench, this campground overlooks the postcard-pretty Sprague Wild and Scenic River, with wildflower-dotted meadow banks. Indian paintbrush, shooting star, and buttercup are among nature's palette. Small gravel bars and deep pools are part of the meandering river's character; fishing provides a challenge. Mosquitoes are the lone detractor; come prepared. The campground is open from June to October.

LAKEVIEW AREA

		Hookup sites	Total sites	Max. RV length	Hookups	Toilets	Showers	Drinking water	Dump station	Recreation	Fee	Can reserve
157	Cottonwood Meadow		21	22		NF		•		HFBL		
158	Deep Creek Forest Camp		4	16		NF				F		
159	Dismal Creek Forest Camp		3	16		NF				F		
160	Dog Lake		7	20		NF		•		FBL		
161	Drews Creek		5	25		NF		•		F		
162	Goose Lake State Recreation Area	48	48	50	WE	F	•	•	•	HFB	$$	
163	Hart Mountain Nat'l Antelope Refuge		12	T		NF				H		
164	Lake County F.G. and Rodeo Facility	32	32	40	WE	F	•	•	•		$	
165	Lofton Reservoir		26	30		NF		•		FBL		
166	Mud Creek Forest Camp		7	30		NF						
167	Willow Creek Forest Camp		8	30		NF				F		

Hookups: W = Water E = Electric S = Sewer **Total sites:** T = Tent-only campground **Maximum trailer/RV length** given in feet.
Toilets: F = Flush NF = No Flush **Recreation:** H = Hiking S = Swimming F = Fishing B = Boating L = Boat Launch
O = Off-Highway Driving R = Horseback Riding C = Cycling
Fee: $ = $1-9 $$ = $10-19 $$$ = $20-29 $$$$ = $30-39. If no entry under **Fee**, camping is free.

157 Cottonwood Meadow

Location: About 30 miles northwest of Lakeview.
Sites: 21 basic sites; no hookups.
Maximum length: 22 feet.
Facilities: Tables, grills, vault toilets, drinking water, boat launch (boating: human-powered or electric motors only), horse facilities.
Fee: None.
Management: Forest Service.
Contact: 541-947-3334.
Finding the campground: From Oregon 140, 20 miles east of Bly, 23 miles west of Lakeview, turn north onto Forest Road 3870 at the sign for Cottonwood Meadow Lake and go 5.7 miles. Turn left onto FR 024 to enter the camp in about 1 mile.

About the campground: At this pleasant campground, the sites line Cougar Creek or rim Cottonwood Meadow Lake. The lake generally has good fishing and is open to rafts, canoes, and small boats. The lake basin features wildflower meadows, scenic stands of ponderosa pine, groves of aspen, and views of Cougar and Grizzly Peaks. Trails explore the greater lake area and climb to the top of Cougar Peak. The campground is open from June to mid-October.

158 Deep Creek Forest Camp

Location: About 28 miles southeast of Lakeview.
Sites: 4 basic sites; no hookups.
Maximum length: 16 feet.
Facilities: Tables, grills, pit toilets. No drinking water.
Fee: None.
Management: Forest Service.
Contact: 541-947-3334.
Finding the campground: From Lakeview, go north on U.S. Highway 395/ Oregon 140 East for 4.7 miles and turn right to remain on OR 140E. Continue 7.2 miles, turn right onto Forest Road 3915 (South Warren Road), which begins paved, then becomes gravel. Go 10.2 miles to a Y-junction and bear left to remain on FR 3915 for another 5 miles. Bear right onto FR 4015, continue 0.7 mile, and then turn right onto FR 011 for the camp.

About the campground: This intimate little campground faces out at Deep Creek and occupies a pine-meadow habitat, with some stout ponderosa pines. Deep Creek is broad, deep, and braided, with cottonwoods and aspens shading its shore. Because site parking is along the road shoulder, this camp is better suited for tents. Campers can try their hands at fishing, but mostly the camp offers quiet leisure. The campground is open from June to mid-October.

159 Dismal Creek Forest Camp

Location: About 28 miles southeast of Lakeview.
Sites: 3 basic sites; no hookups.
Maximum length: 16 feet.
Facilities: Tables, grills, pit toilets. No drinking water.
Fee: None.
Management: Forest Service.
Contact: 541-947-3334.
Finding the campground: From Lakeview, go north on U.S. Highway 395/ Oregon 140 East for 4.7 miles and turn right to remain on OR 140E. Continue 7.2 miles, turn right onto Forest Road 3915 (South Warren Road), which begins paved, then becomes gravel, and go 10.2 miles to a Y-junction. Bear left, remaining on FR 3915 another 5 miles. Go left on FR 3915 to reach this camp on the left in 1.1 miles.

About the campground: This camp is situated in an open stand of ponderosa pines above Deep Creek and along the stair-stepped waters of Dismal Creek. With few neighbors in camp, the spot promises quiet, chances for wildlife sightings, and an occasion to fish. Balsamroot adorns the sage-grass floor. The campground is open from June to mid-October.

160 Dog Lake

Location: About 27 miles southwest of Lakeview.
Sites: 7 basic sites; no hookups.
Maximum length: 20 feet.
Facilities: Tables, grills, pit toilets, drinking water, boat launch (boating: 5 miles per hour).
Fee: None.
Management: Forest Service.
Contact: 541-947-3334.
Finding the campground: From U.S. Highway 395 in Lakeview, go west on Oregon 140 for 7.3 miles and turn left (south) onto County Road 1-13 for Dog Lake. Go about 4 miles and turn right onto CR 1-11D, which becomes Forest Road 4017. Stay on it for about 16 miles to reach the main campground on the right; the day-use area, Dog Lake, and a gravel road to additional sites are all on the left.

About the campground: Dog Lake, the central draw to the area, is an attractive, artificial lake. It claims a pretty forested basin and displays areas of rush, cattail, and pond lily along its shallows. White pelicans, ducks, geese, killdeer, and yellow-headed and red-winged blackbirds favor this lake, as do campers, boaters, and anglers. The main part of the campground sits on a pine-forested knoll above the lake and FR 4017. It is a typical forest camp, with dirt parking; a path links it to the boat launch area. Water is available on the knoll and at the day-use area, but not at the second camp area, which is 0.2 mile from the day-use area via a gravel road. This camp, too, rests above shore. Bass and trout are the catches of the day. The campground is open from June to mid-October.

161 Drews Creek

Location: About 17 miles southwest of Lakeview.
Sites: 5 basic sites; no hookups.
Maximum length: 25 feet.
Facilities: Tables, grills, vault toilets, drinking water, horseshoe pits.
Fee: None.
Management: Forest Service.
Contact: 541-947-3334.
Finding the campground: From U.S. Highway 395 in Lakeview, go west on Oregon 140 for 7.3 miles and turn left (south) onto County Road 1-13 for Dog Lake. Go about 4 miles and turn right onto CR 1-11D, which becomes Forest Road 4017. Stay on it for 6 miles to reach this campground on the left, crossing over a bridge.

About the campground: This camp is tucked at the foot of a low hill in a ponderosa-pine setting and serves as a popular group-camp facility. It has a central area of long tables and community parking, with just a pair of individual site turnouts. Pole fencing isolates the camp from Drews Creek, which flows slow, wide, and murky at this point. For fishing, the camp is 2 miles from Drews Reservoir. The campground is open from June to mid-October.

162 Goose Lake State Recreation Area

Location: About 16 miles south of Lakeview.
Sites: 48 hookup sites; water and electric hookups.
Maximum length: 50 feet.
Facilities: Tables, grills, flush toilets, drinking water, showers, dump station, telephone, horseshoe pits (at day use), nearby boat launch.
Fee: $$.
Management: Oregon State Parks and Recreation Department.
Contact: 541-947-3111.
Finding the campground: From the junction of U.S. Highway 395 and Oregon 140 West in Lakeview, go south on US 395 for 14.7 miles and turn right at the sign for Goose Lake State Recreation Area, just as California welcomes you. Go 1.1 miles and turn right for the campground; straight leads to the day-use area.

About the campground: On the Oregon-California border, Goose Lake is an enormous Great Basin lake spanning between distant low ridges; its level fluctuates year to year. The campground is slightly removed from the lake, occupying a lawn and shade-tree flat, with paved parking. At the outskirts of the camp stretch fields and willows, with mowed passageways through them. Giant lupine and wild rose color the corridors; songbirds flourish. This recreation area is a favorite with birders, with quail right in camp, western tanagers donning the tree branches, and migrant and resident waterfowl. The lake welcomes fishing and boating, but access is away from the camp. The campground is open from mid-April to late October.

163 Hart Mountain National Antelope Refuge

Location: About 68 miles northeast of Lakeview.
Sites: 12 tent sites; no hookups.
Facilities: Pit toilets, hot springs "bathhouse." No drinking water.
Fee: None.
Management: Hart Mountain National Antelope Refuge.
Contact: 541-947-3315.
Finding the campground: From the town of Plush (40 miles northeast of Lakeview), drive 0.9 mile north and turn east at the sign for Hart Mountain and Frenchglen. Go 23 miles to the headquarters or 27 miles to the camp and hot springs, bearing right at the junction past the headquarters. The route is paved and gravel to the refuge, but the rough road into the camp is not recommended for trailers or RVs.

About the campground: The route to the refuge is part of the Lakeview to Steens National Back Country Byway. The refuge road system then continues the discovery, serving up wildlife sightings and stunning dry landscapes. The isolated camp consists of a casual cluster of primitive sites radiating out from an open-air, concrete cell housing the refuge hot springs, a pleasant, 5-foot-deep steamy pool. The camp claims an aspen-shaded grassy flat between Rock and Bond Creeks; scenic hillsides of sage, juniper, and mountain mahogany frame the setting. Near the headquarters, you will find a small museum and nature garden. Antelope are the primary attraction. The campground is maintained from mid-May through October.

164 Lake County Fairgrounds and Rodeo Facility

Location: In Lakeview.
Sites: 32 hookup sites, with dry camping and tent camping available; water and electric hookups.
Maximum length: 40 feet.
Facilities: Flush toilets, drinking water, showers, dump station, telephone, food concessions when open.
Fee: $.
Management: Lake County.
Contact: 541-947-2925.
Finding the campground: The fairgrounds is north off Oregon 140 (at 1900 North 4th Street) in Lakeview, with the RV camp left off the West Gate Entrance.

About the campground: This is another serviceable fairgrounds RV camp, primarily for fair-goers and participants, but it is also available to area travelers. It is a shadeless, gravel parking area, with hookup posts. For individuals looking to dry camp or tent camp, ask at the office about suitable areas.

165 Lofton Reservoir

Location: About 38 miles northwest of Lakeview.
Sites: 26 basic sites; no hookups.
Maximum length: 30 feet.
Facilities: Tables, grills, pit toilets, drinking water, boat launch, accessible fishing pier for individuals with disabilities.
Fee: None.
Management: Forest Service.
Contact: 541-353-2427.
Finding the campground: From Oregon 140, 13 miles east of Bly and 30 miles west of Lakeview, turn south onto paved Forest Road 3715 for the reservoir. Go 7.2 miles and turn left onto FR 013 to reach the camp in another 1.2 miles.

About the campground: In a location that has been largely cut over, this family campground is secluded in a full forest of ponderosa pine and white fir along the shore of Lofton Reservoir, a holding lake for irrigation, open to recreation. The lake is at its prettiest when full. Electric motors are allowed on this lake, which has a boating speed of 5 miles per hour. Fishing is generally good. The campground is open from May through October.

166 Mud Creek Forest Camp

Location: About 20 miles northeast of Lakeview.
Sites: 7 basic sites; no hookups.
Maximum length: 30 feet.
Facilities: Tables, grills, pit toilets. No drinking water.
Fee: None.
Management: Forest Service.
Contact: 541-947-3334.
Finding the campground: From Lakeview, go north on U.S. Highway 395/ Oregon 140 East for 4.7 miles and turn right to remain on OR 140E. Continue 8.5 miles, turn left onto Forest Road 3615 (North Warren Road), and go 7 miles more to enter this camp on the right.

About the campground: At the edge of a sage prairie and along the wet meadow threaded by tiny Mud Creek sits this quiet camp in a forest of lodgepole pine and white fir. Mud Creek is a meandering black ribbon parting meadows. Privately held Bull Prairie is on the opposite side of FR 3615; in spring, the camas blooms adorn it with seas of purple. Area trails can be reached 2.2 miles south of the camp, and Drake Peak Lookout might suggest a drive. Fishing and hunting are other area pursuits. Come ready for mosquitoes in early summer. The campground is open from June to mid-October.

167 Willow Creek Forest Camp

Location: About 23 miles southeast of Lakeview.
Sites: 8 basic sites; no hookups.
Maximum length: 30 feet.
Facilities: Tables, grills, pit toilets. No drinking water.
Fee: None.
Management: Forest Service.
Contact: 541-947-3334.
Finding the campground: From Lakeview, go north on U.S. Highway 395/ Oregon 140 East for 4.7 miles and turn right to remain on OR 140E. Continue 7.2 miles, turn right onto Forest Road 3915 (South Warren Road), which begins paved, then becomes gravel, and go 10.2 miles to a Y-junction. Bear right onto FR 4011, go 0.7 mile, and turn right onto FR 011 followed by a right onto FR 012 to enter the camp in 0.3 mile.

About the campground: A rail fence separates this campground from the meadow of Willow Creek. The sites are dispersed throughout a mixed woods of ponderosa pine and aspen; arnica sometimes lends a cheery yellow glow to the forest floor. Signs of beaver are evident throughout the meadow. Fishing is the lone activity of this camp. The campground is open from June to mid-October.

Campground Index

About the Authors

Over the past 18 years, these veterans of the outdoors, Rhonda (a writer) and George (a photographer), have collaborated on almost a dozen guidebooks and have sold hundreds of articles on topics of nature, travel, and outdoor recreation. Rhonda was born and raised in Montana and earned her degree in English there. George hails from Connecticut and studied geology at Arizona State University. It was while working for an oil company in California that this duo came together. Their passion for the outdoors is apparent in their writing and photographs; they speak from firsthand knowledge of the campgrounds and trails.

Other FalconGuides by the Ostertags include *Scenic Driving Pennsylvania, Hiking Pennsylvania, Hiking Southern New England,* and *Hiking New York.*